The Long Rifle

Also by Win Blevins

Fitz

Rendezvous: Volume One

Rendezvous: Volume Two

Rendezvous: Volume Three

Rivers of the West

The Yellowstone

The High Missouri

The Snake River

The Powder River

Classics of the Fur Trade

The River of the West, The Mountain Years: The Adventures of Joe Meek Part One

The River of the West, The Oregon Years: The Adventures of Joe Meek Part Two

The Long Rifle
Classics of the Fur Trade
Book 3

Win Blevins

The Long Rifle
Paperback Edition
Copyright © 2024 (As Revised) Win Blevins

Wolfpack Publishing
1707 E. Diana Street
Tampa, FL 33610

wolfpackpublishing.com

All rights reserved. No part of this book may be reproduced by any means without the prior written consent of the publisher, other than brief quotes for reviews.

Paperback ISBN 978-1-63977-670-2
eBook ISBN 978-1-63977-669-6

Author's Note

I desire to express my indebtedness to Capt. John Dillin, who will recognize herein material derived from his admirable book, The Kentucky Rifle, and who, I hope, will forgive a slight wrench in chronology.

Introduction

Listen to the old, old song this novel sings.

Fleeing his oppressive stepfather, young Andy Burnett heads for the wild, untrammeled Rocky Mountains, where adventure and *Injuns* await. He walks as heir to the men who have made such journeys before him. His shoulder bears the long rifle of Daniel Boone, the very one carried by the great hunter on his first trip to Kentucky.

Listen, our author, Stewart Edward White, beats the drums of a great American myth.

Despite the pull of family, Andy must follow his destiny. He finds partners, he ventures forth, and he begins to learn. And Andy learns well, for in him runs the blood of frontiersmen.

Listen, this is our immemorial American story.

Andy goes through the rituals—his first buffalo hunt, his first experience with love, his hair-breadth Indian fight, his tests of character. He learns what it means to be a partner. He is intoxicated by seeing new country. He has shining times and starving times and loves them all.

Imperceptibly, Andy and the reader come to realize that the lad has become a man. And then, much too soon, he feels it all slipping away, the grand adventure coming to its inevitable end.

Thus, *The Long Rifle*. It is less a novel than a sacrament. It is a campfire tale as old as the Neanderthals. It reminds us of who we are, as campfire tales always do. It affirms a way of growing and living repeated through the experiences of generations of Americans and celebrated countless times on page and screen. If this is not *the* American experience, it certainly feels like it.

The book has power. Millions of readers have confirmed this over the years.

Surely criticism has nothing to say about such a tale. A storyteller does not write it so much as launch onto its primal energies and roar downstream with the current.

Yes, it is old-fashioned. It is romantic, heroic, sentimental. It is touched with magnificence. It is imbued with the innocence and optimism that young men about to venture into unknown worlds want to believe in. It is what the storytelling sacrament should be.

And it has a marvelous spirit we've nearly forgotten. It is filled with wonder at creation—fresh and unspoiled—and the crazy joy of going somewhere just to go and see it, to feel the earth and drink its water. Our forefathers felt this urge and were privileged to act on it.

Andy's partner Kelly expresses that spirit perfectly. When Andy yearns to go farther west, Kelly upbraids him.

"Will there be more beaver?"

"No," Andy admits.

"Could we make more money?"

"No."

"Would we be better off?"

"No."

"Mightn't the Indians be dangerous?"

"Yes."

"Then why go?"

"I reckon I'd just like to go see."

And Kelly surprises Andy by saying, "So would I."

Explains the older trapper explains, "There is no sane reason for doing so, but you and I are the same kind of damn fool."

What a wonderful moment of illumination.

The book is now a child out of time. In fact, it was a child out of time when published in 1932. The nation suffered that year not only from post-war cynicism and malaise, but from the Great Depression. The writers in ascendancy were such over-turners of traditions as Ernest Hemingway and William Faulkner. In 1929, each made a big mark, Hemingway with *A Farewell to Arms* and Faulkner with *The Sound and the Fury*. The country's most honored novelist, Sinclair Lewis, had just won the Nobel Prize for Literature for his gleeful satirization of American life.

Perhaps White's publisher, Doubleday Doran, feared for this literary remnant of a more optimistic time.

No need. Americans always love certain sorts of affirmation, and the public took *The Long Rifle* to its heart. The author quickly followed that novel with another Andy Burnett tale, *Ranchero*, published in 1933, then another sequel, *Folded Hills*, in 1934, and finally, *Stampede* in 1942. The entire tetralogy was published by Doubleday as *The Saga of Andy Burnett* in 1947.

When Stewart Edward White wrote *The Long Rifle*, he was nearly sixty years old and well-established. Thirty years earlier he had found an enthusiastic audience with *The Blazed Trail*, a novel based on his own experiences as a lumberjack. His time spent cowboying had given birth to several ranch novels, a move from his Michigan birthplace to California spawned several historical novels about the Golden State. He also published books about the outdoors and Western history and had produced a stack of volumes based on his extensive travels in Africa and Alaska. In 1932, his books about psychic phenomena were mostly still ahead of him.

White was an active writer—his career comprised nearly sixty books. He was also an active man, an avid outdoorsman, and a friend of Teddy Roosevelt. White believed that outdoor living, strenuous effort, and hardship formed character. Though born to an affluent family, when a still young White worked as a lumberjack in the north woods and as a cowboy on Arizona ranches. All his life, he went traveling and adventuring, and he made this life the material for his writings.

Perhaps the impetus for *The Long Rifle* came from White's biographical novel, *Daniel Boone: Wilderness Scout*, published ten years earlier. White admired this celebrated pioneer. Boone is the central character in the prologue of *The Long Rifle*—the mysterious stranger who wins a shooting competition with a new kind of gun. Not until page forty-seven does the hero of the newer book, Andy Burnett, make his first appearance. In another age, such a leisurely pace was welcome.

Andy is a hero, a sort of fellow now absent from most novels and movies. He is bright enough to catch on quickly but unwilling to get mired in deep thought. He is willing to work hard, is a fine hunter, and has a yen for action. He loves the West—its grassy plains, its high mountains, its trappers' holes with quicksilver streams, its abundant wildlife. Sometimes, he seems to be in mystical accord with the grandeur of it all.

The qualities that set Andy Burnett apart from his fellow trappers are decency, sympathy for others, and loyalty. Andy becomes part and parcel of his partners—he's the sort of fellow you'd want to ride the river with. Unique among White people in the book, he is also deeply sympathetic to the Indians. Though the Blackfeet are hated equally by other Indians and all whites, Andy makes a blood brother among them, and treats the Blackfeet like his own family. His love for his red comrades underlies the novel's tragedy.

Andy Burnett is not complicated, hard to fathom, or difficult to identify with. He is a hero, plain and simple. He is what Gary Cooper was in many Westerns, the common man ennobled. In this kind of story, that is enough. Plenty.

Some readers will quibble. Yes, the language is ornate. It is also a marvelous artifact of a bygone style. Yes, White gets a good many historical details about the Rocky Mountain fur trade muddled. But he wrote fiction, not history, and at that time, less was known about those grand days. Yes, it sings with a certain boyish naivete. Ain't that fine?

When *The Long Rifle* was written, novels about mountain men were a comparative novelty. The knight errant of the West in books and movies was the cowboy, a different breed of cat entirely. The fictional cowboy is generally reticent and self-effacing, the mountain man wild and exuberant. The cowboy is modest, the mountain man full of brag. The cowboy makes the West safe for women, children, and civilization, while the mountain man lives in an untamed land and exults in its wildness. In brief, the cowboy is a figure from realism, the mountain man from romance.

I love the mountain man. In one of the most delicious scenes of all trapper tales, Vardis Fisher's Sam in *Mountain Man* rides down a ridge in a thunderstorm, bellowing Beethoven back at the gods. No cowboy ever did that—at least, not in a book.

In the decades since *The Long Rifle* was born, the mountain man novel has become a very distinguished subgenre of the Western. Its more notable practitioners have included—in roughly chronological order—Harvey Fergusson, Forrester Blake, A.B. Guthrie, Jr., Vardis Fisher, Frederick Manfred, and Don Berry. My favorites are Guthrie's *The Big Sky*, Fisher's *Mountain Man*, Manfred's *Lord Grizzly*, and Berry's *Trask* and *Moontrap*.

Add *The Long Rifle* to that.

On this novel rests the reputation of its creator. Some critics would add another of the Burnett stories, *Folded Hills*, and one of the Alaska novels, *Wild Geese Calling*.

It is enough.

The Long Rifle

Prologue
The Grooved Barrel

In our country, two hundred years ago, shooting was the national pastime, and people shot guns as today they shoot golf. Popping at an Indian or a turkey or deer was part of the daily occupation of those who lived on the frontier and in the backwoods, but these men had no monopoly on either the interest or the skill. They might be considered the *pros,* but the cities and civilized seaboards were full of amateurs who would never have occasion either to save their scalps or to fend off starvation. And they were just as zealous afield, and just as partisan in the matter of equipment, and just as jealous of their marksmanship, and just as studious of technique, and just as persistent in practice as any modern divot digger you ever saw. No village so small that it had not its measured range and no crossroads tavern could be successful unless it offered facilities for tests of marksmanship. For rarely did any gathering of men—convivial, business, political, even religious—disperse without a shooting match. And at stated intervals, and at stated places, were what might be called the big open tournaments where men collected for the express purpose. It was here that reputations were made, so that the time had its Bobby Jones or its Walter Hagen, with a host of skilled aspirants only a stroke or so behind. Or perhaps the parallel of state or district champions would be more exact. Travel in those days was so difficult that it was impossible to hold a National Open. But each locality had one or more local champions, the names of whom would be mentioned wherever in the colonies men talked of marksmanship.

It was first blackbird time, when the snow water was not all drained away but when the grass beneath the surface of its little pools waved green. A young man was journeying steadily afoot alongside the deep wheel ruts of a crude country road. It was a mere track, winding across the country's face, turning to avoid high stark stumps, twisting away from a bog hole of too great steepness of hills, innocent of flanking fence or ditch. For a mile, sometimes, it ran in the dim coolness of the old forest, where red tanagers flamed in green shadows, and the wild pigeons beat like distant surf. For another mile, perhaps, it threaded a marsh where poles had been laid in corduroy and soft-winged bitterns slanted aloft in erratic flight and trim, small peoples swayed on limber reed ends with chucklings. But soon, it shook free from these petty wildnesses, again to emerge into cleared, stumpy uplands and wide fields, fenced-in rail, and Pennsylvania farmhouses of a civilization by now over a hundred years old.

The youth was a tall young man, standing well over six feet, lean with the slenderness of whalebone, his face golden brown with sun, his somewhat aquiline features cast in that brooding yet watchful repose characteristic of the backwoodsman and the Indian. His blue-gray eyes too would, to the competent observer, have identified him with the wilderness, for while their quality was mild, peaceable, and serene, they were never still, turning from right to left and from left to right again, ceaselessly, in a tireless vigilance so habitual that it had become subliminal. The traveler knew he had nothing to apprehend in this peaceful countryside. Indeed his thoughts were busied far from the actual scene. Nevertheless no smallest stir of leaf or feather escaped the mechanics of his attention, which held its report of those matters only just below the surface of his consciousness. His basic sense of security was further evidenced by the fact that he bore his rifle carelessly across his shoulder and had attached to it for the convenience of carriage against his back a leather portmanteau. He was dressed in plain garments of homespun and wore on his head the stiff felt hat of the period.

Though the sun was already past midafternoon, and he had been afoot since its rising, he swung unweariedly along in the bent-kneed woodsman's slouch, which is apparently so deliberate but in reality is so swift that one unaccustomed can with difficulty keep pace, and that for a short distance only. No inequality of footing or steepness of hill broke the rhythm, nor did he pause for breath or contemplation until the road broke over a crest to disclose below him a scattering settlement among noble trees in the bend of a great river. Here, he stopped for a moment, surveying the scene gravely, then plunged down the slope to the village street.

The place was of the ordinary type and kind—many frame, and a few brick homes, wide scattered at first, clustering more thickly as one approached the main street where stood the hotel, or tavern, two or three shops, and a court or meeting house. Old forest trees and planted elms, new spangled with spring overspread the roadways and later would almost completely submerge the roofs of the town. To one side swept the bend in the river, and here along a canal were stone and frame buildings with sputtering mill wheels. At the time of week and the time of day, one would expect to find such a place moving in only a feeble current of external life, perhaps a horse or so dozing along the hitching rails, possibly a loafer or two chair-tilted before the tavern, or mayhap a housewife picking her way on wooden clogs through the soft earth toward the one sidewalk of the shops. Such a normal condition of somnolence was evidently anticipated by our young traveler, for he paused in grave and puzzled observation of what he saw.

The street was aswarm with men of all ages and conditions in life. They sauntered back and forth, they stood in talkative groups beneath the elms, they sat in rows on the edge of the high sidewalk. But principally they milled in and out of the wide hospitable doors of the tavern, whence arose such a clatter mingled of talk, argument, song, shouts, laughter, and the clinking undertone of mugs, glasses, and dishes slammed about, that the combined noise seemed to burst forth like a palpable flood gone aleak. No women were to be seen, but numerous small boys and dogs were engaged in attaching themselves to the situation with as convincing an air as they could manage.

Our traveler was obviously puzzled and interested. His long free stride slowed to a saunter, and his eyes, heretofore roving in the mechanics of an automatic vigilance, now brimmed with the keenest of intelligent observation. He moved forward with every sense awake to catch the smallest indicatives that would synthesize into an estimate of the situation, precisely as it might be imagined he would move in the shadows of an unknown forest. Indeed, he made a slight instinctive shrug as though to bring forward his rifle to his hand. It was with him an integral part of alertness, but he caught back the movement with a flicker of a smile at the corners of his grave lips. It would have been a simple matter to resolve his curiosity by an appeal for information to the nearest group, but such a procedure would have written him down as no woodsman, for it is a curious fact that those who live by observation rarely ask.

Moving thus, the young man gradually drew nearer the focus of the tavern. There, men jostled in a throng, and the opened doors crowded and eddied as those who went in made their way with difficulty against those who came out. Everybody talked or shouted or sang, for obviously the spirit was of a holiday. Many were more or less drunk. Across the bobbing heads one might glimpse in the dim interior the red round faces of waiters moving here and there, clusters of tankards held aloft. A swirl of many emotions caught at the poise of stabilities, swept men loose from grave accustomedness into the exhilaration of temporary irresponsibility. A certain recklessness was in the air, a loosening inconstancy into which men plunged gratefully from the aridity of their daily lives. Though his outward appearance differed in no marked degree from the many who composed the throng, the gravity of the stranger's unbroken aloofness seemed to set him apart, an individual from the herd, and this very separateness drew to him men's notice as though he had carried some blazon of distinction. Heads turned, men exchanged inquiries, and some few of the drunker or more reckless even threw in his direction good-naturedly jeering remarks. He seemed quite unaware.

Before the tavern veranda, he came to a halt, his attention at last seizing upon a definite point of considered examination. This was a long poster of coarse paper that had been tacked into the bark of an elm by means of sharpened wooden pegs. Before it, the young man took his stand, unslinging his rifle from his back, resting its butt against the ground before him, clasping his palms across its muzzle, settling himself easily and gracefully to the interpretation of the message. To the task, he gave all his serene concentration, his lips moving slowly, spelling out the words. So evidently unaccustomed and difficult was this task, that the men nearest hushed their noise to watch him in amusement. One young chap in the broadcloth of the cities, a youth with a weak, reckless face, who had evidently been drinking heavily, lurched alongside.

"Want me to read it for you?" he asked, his derision thinly veiled by mock politeness.

The stranger turned his eyes from the printed words to contemplate his interlocutor. For perhaps ten seconds he held silence.

"No, suh," he then replied and returned tranquilly to his perusal. That was all, but the other stuttered and fell back, and a low chuckle of appreciation rippled among the bystanders.

The proclamation announced:

God save the King! Hunters and others look this way. A great shooting match will take place on April thirtieth at the place by the Big Bend. The first prize will be a great fat ox and the second a snap bounce gun with a long barl. To the maker of the winning piece, the Gunsmith's Medal. Distance 15 rods. A charge of four shillings for each man. Only one shot for each four shillings. There will be more prizes for lesser amounts. Lead, powder and flints to be sold. Plenty to eat and drink for all that come. Bear and wolf traps to be sold. Tell any man to come to the match. God save the King!

Having finished his painful deciphering of this document, the young man swung his rifle into the crook of his arm, and had turned to enter the tavern, when his steps were again arrested. A little girl of eight or nine years was threading her way sedately between the lounging groups on the sidewalk. She was a personable little girl, but her mere prettiness of features would probably not have sufficed to rivet the stranger's attention. It was her getup, which was in the latest and daintiest style of the cities. It is to be conceived that our young backwoodsman, if such he were, had never seen anything quite like it before. His eyes lighted with an intense interest, and the contained gravity of his face was broken.

The child was accompanied by a medium-sized woolly dog of a species also strange to our young man's knowledge. She was quite composed, a dainty, incongruous, unbelievable creature from a storybook. So wholly did this apparition lie outside his experience that for the first time, he abandoned his self-containment, turning to the man next to him for enlightenment.

"Some rich man's darter, must be," he surmised.

"You'd think so, wouldn't you?" said the other with a short laugh. "Well, she ain't. She's the granddaughter of old man Farrell—the gunsmith. But he's crazy anyhow."

"He must be right fond of that little gal," surmised the stranger, surveying her keenly. "Granddarter, you say? Just her and the old man, I reckon."

"How'd you guess that?" asked the other.

"He must be right lonesome," continued the younger man, pursuing his train of thought unheeding. Then, having come to his conclusion as to this unfamiliar phenomenon, he almost visibly abandoned it. "I am obleeged to you, suh," said he, and again lifted his rifle and portmanteau. But the other man did not so readily relinquish this opening for his own curiosity.

"You in town for the shootin' match?" he inquired as a preliminary to an inquisition.

"No, suh," replied the young man politely, but with finality. "Just travelin' through."

From across the earth street, a large mongrel launched itself like a thunderbolt straight for the woolly dog. The latter, bowled over by the suddenness and weight of the onslaught, shrieked aloud in terror, writhing and snapping in the grip of its more powerful antagonist. The air was vociferous with growls, yelps, and snarls.

"Dog fight! Dog fight!" yelled those nearest.

The idlers surged forward joyously, forming a compact, eager group around the center of disturbance, those on the outside crowding and shoving for a better view. The little girl, jostled unceremoniously aside, beat and pulled at the braced legs, frantic but quite unnoticed. She was beside herself, all her pretty poise shattered by the urgency of the crisis. The world had become a world of inhuman and indifferent backs. Casting about her distractedly, she ran in appeal to the one face turned in her direction.

"He'll be killed!" she cried. "It's that old Tiger! He's always tried to kill him! Oh! Oh!"

The young man contemplated her gravely for a moment, then, with an air of having come to a deliberate decision, began to shove his way to the center of the close-packed ring. So sudden and so determined was his movement that he met no serious opposition. Some of those he thrust aside flared angrily, and would have laid hands upon him, but so quickly had he moved that he was beyond their reach. Before anybody had grasped clearly what he was about he had snatched the woolly dog aloft and had delivered a very convincing kick into the short ribs of its assailant.

"You, Tiger! Down!" he further admonished that canine. His low, soft voice snapped like a whip. In its tone was that entire expectation of obedience which alone penetrates effectively to a dog's consciousness. Tiger hesitated and licked his lips, but he obeyed.

At once, the air was rent by cries of angry expostulation.

"Hey you! What you think you're doin'!"

"Who the hell you think you are?"

Men, red-faced, crowded belligerently forward. Fists were clenched, hands were raised. Had the young man stirred by a palm's breadth it is probable the mob would have fallen upon him bodily. He did not move. Holding the cowed and whimpering woolly dog in his arms, he waited. His blue eyes were calm, and a little remote, as though, pending the moment, he had withdrawn to secret, inner, and distant preoccupations of his own.

"Folks," said he pleasantly at last. He did not raise his voice, and instinctively, the mob hushed to quiet that it might hear. "I like a good dawg fight same as anybody. But this here ain't no dawg fight. It's a killin'. Besides, this here thing ain't rightly a dog, according to my raisin', and besides that, it belongs to the lady yander."

He tossed his head ever so slightly from the abject woolly dog toward the gulping small girl. Several responded, with a faint laugh, to the grave and sardonic gleam in his eye. But one burly and red-faced man was unreconciled and belligerent.

"By God!" cried this one. "Who are you to come pushin' yourself in where you ain't wanted? For a ha'penny I'd—"

The young man turned his head deliberately.

"Dawg fights most gen'lly turns into man fights," he remarked. "Don't seem no sense to it, but that's the way it is. I ain't aimin' for no trouble. I'm just a-travelin' through."

"Afraid be ye!" sneered the red-faced man. "Well, I'll—"

"No, I'm not afeard," interrupted the stranger placidly. "I'll fight ye, if so be ye're set upon it. But yere ain't no time nor place. For one thing, I'm aimin' to take this young-un and her"—he glanced down, a gleam of humor crossing the bleak gravity of his face—"and her dawg," he drawled, "back home where she ought to be."

"Runnin' away," sneered the red-faced man.

"I ain't leavin'," stated the young man. He surveyed slowly, one by one, the faces of the crowd. "I reckon that's all," said he. "I'll be back yere afore sundown, and then you can suit yoreself." He turned away with a decision that parted the ring before him, picked up his rifle and leather portmanteau which he slung again across his shoulder.

"Come on, sister," said he.

She raised her tear-stained face to his confidingly and took his hand. They moved away, and the woolly dog snuggled in the hollow of his left arm. He shortened his long woodsman strides, while she skipped valiantly to keep pace.

———

But they had not proceeded far in the direction the young lady rather vaguely indicated before they were met by her grandfather, out in an anxious search for her. When he had learned, partly from the child, partly from the young stranger, an inkling of what had happened, he expressed his relief. The expedition had been her own fancy.

"She would be better housed just now," submitted the young man. "Nobody rightly would mean to harm her, but men git rough in drink."

"She got away," agreed the gunsmith, "and I am obliged to you for your trouble. You're in town for the shooting, I suppose," he said, glancing with professional interest at the stranger's weapon.

"No, suh," the young man denied, "just travelin' through. I am from South Branch since sunup and knew naught of the shooting."

"Where are you stopping for the night?"

"Nowhere as yit. I aim to stop at the tavern."

"But man alive, you'll find no place there!" cried the old man. "Every nook and cranny is filled long since." He stopped abruptly and considered for a moment. "You must stay at my house," he decided. "Nay, I insist."

But his urgency was unnecessary. The young man accepted the proffer as simply as it might have been conceived. He would have accepted the good cheer of a dry cave in the wilderness. He deposited the woolly dog on the ground.

"Which way, suh?" he inquired.

The four proceeded down the earth road toward the canal. The little girl prattled eagerly at her grandfather about the horrid Tiger and his attempt at canicide. The stranger moved in his serene silence. Shortly, they arrived at a rambling sort of structure, or series of structures attached one to the other. A small mill wheel indicated that the greater group of these were used as a manufacturing plant. The old man unlocked the door of a smaller wing and led the way to a cool interior of plain old polished wood, diamond-shaped panes, a dark table, a great fireplace, two benches, and a number of easy chairs. Ornament, there was none, unless a score or more of guns slung on pegs about the walls might be so considered.

"Sit, lad, sit!" urged the old man, thrusting forward one of the chairs. "South Branch is distant, and even young limbs must weary."

"I am obleeged to you, suh," acknowledged the youth. He deposited his rifle and portmanteau in a corner, removed his hat, and perched himself upright and a little gingerly on the edge of one of the great chairs, his eye roving in deliberate scrutiny of his surroundings.

The old man hung his own three-cornered headpiece in the corner, disclosing the fact that he wore no wig. He was a small, compact old gentleman with a stiff, upright brush of brown hair on a bullet head, and he moved with the swift darting certainly of a bird. His speech, too, was swift and darting and as voluble as that of his visitor was spare.

"My people are all abroad," he observed. "There is no keeping them at their tasks, so perforce and with good grace, I declared holiday. You must take cold cheer."

He darted here and there, in and out a door on the right side of the fireplace, opening and shutting a cupboard on the left, clattering tankards and trenchers, with a continued buzz of movement like the sustained high hum of a bee. Behind it, as a bridge across to the hushed and aloof serenity of the room, a serenity into which the stranger had slipped as naturally as into a grateful and familiar element, beat the measured slow *tick-tock, tick-tock* of a tall clock in the corner.

"There!" cried the old man at last. "Draw up, young man! 'Tis but cold fare but will suffice. I'll warrant ye've done worse in your time! A venison pasty, good bread of rye, honest ale, home-brewed, and none of your raw spirits. That is the drink of fools."

"I am obleeged to you, suh," said the young man, and unfolded his long frame from the great chair and took his place at the table.

"I have naught by which to name you," Farrell reminded his guest as they sat. "Don, eh? A good Scotch name, I warrant. Nay, fall to, lad, and use your mouth for more grateful work than talking."

They ate—the stranger for most part in the calm silence that held no hint of awkwardness, the old man chattering as suggestively near to questioning as his notion of politeness permitted. The little girl, who had at first curled herself into another of the great chairs, at length slipped to the floor and sidled over to take her stand against the young man's shoulder.

"I hope you hurt that old Tiger—when you kicked him," said she.

"Leave her stay," the stranger interfered to her grandfather's admonition. "I like young-uns. There's been a plenty of 'em in my raisin'." A slow grave smile sketched his lips, and he reached a strong finger to touch her ringleted head. "But we ain't got no little ladies like this un," he added. Beyond that, he volunteered nothing about himself.

They finished the meal. The old man produced clay pipes and tobacco. But before joining his host in the great chairs before the fireplace the guest stretched his long legs, wandering about the room, examining attentively the weapons on the walls.

The old man watched him a moment, then arose to join him.

"You are interested in guns?" he asked.

"Yes, suh," acknowledged the other. "You see"—his manner almost implied an apology for intruding even so much of his personal intimacies—"we livin' on the border use 'em a lot, what with shootin' game and takin' keer of ourselves like, when it comes to Injins and such."

"You have fought Indians?" pounced the old man.

But the younger withdrew into vagueness.

"Injins is not bad folks in some ways," he submitted. "I got good friends among the Injins. But a man must take keer of himself."

"These guns are a sort of historical collection," explained the gunmaker after a moment's bright-eyed contemplation of his visitor. "I have tried to show how they have developed. See, here is an old matchlock, and here, a wheel lock. And this is a sample of the very first rifle with a straight-cut groove without a twist. And here is a bell muzzle that shot slugs, or even stones."

"They surely are a clumsy-lookin' contraption," marveled the young man. "A man wonders how they ever hit anything."

"They didn't—much."

"Man has a hard enough time gettin' along nowadays, what with shots that go wild even with good holdin'." The visitor turned finally to the chairs and the pipes. "But it's surely interestin' to me, suh, and I am obleeged to you."

He lit his pipe thoughtfully, and somehow it became evident that he was slowly coming to a decision.

"I'm figurin' on something', suh," he said at last. "You're the first man I ever saw that made guns. I wouldn't wish to ask too much of you, suh, but—"

"What is it, lad?" urged the old man.

"I fit ain't no secret, suh, how kin you make a true bar'l? Many a time I've figgered on it—if it ain't no secret."

"Come with me, lad," he cried, eager with the master's enthusiasm over his craft. He remembered the little girl.

"Time for your posset, child, and then to bed. She is already a good housewife"—he turned proudly to his visitor—"and shall manage her own supper—and mine and yours for the matter of that—as well as any woman grown. Make your curtsy to Don here, and kiss your old gran'ther, and run along."

He unlocked a door, and the two entered the long, low workshop, now deserted for the holiday. Through the clutter of tools and half-finished pieces, he led the way to a rack on which were stacked broad flat bars of iron.

"Here are your barrels," said he.

The young man knit his brows.

"You can't bore no hole in such," he objected.

The old man smiled.

"Certainly not," he agreed. "Here"—he exhibited a long, slender rod—"that's what we call the core rod. First we heat the flat bar to welding heat, then we fold it around the core rod, and weld it together, then we draw out the core rod. There's your barrel with the hole in it. It is rough, of course," he added.

"How come the core rod don't stick?"

"We weld only a few inches at a heat, withdrawing the rod each time, but even then, on occasion it will not come away." The old man sighed. Then, we must cut it out with a cold chisel or throw it away. Next, of course, we smooth the new barrel as much as possible. Have to do that with a hammer for the outside and a hand reamer for the inside, like a carpenter bores in wood."

"Cain't you use a lathe?" asked the young man keenly.

"Doesn't run steady enough."

"Can you get her straight that way by eye?"

"Pretty good. But look here." The gunsmith picked up a half-finished barrel from the bench and took down a long hickory bow from a nail on the wall. It was precisely like a bow used as a weapon, except that it was lighter, and its cord was but a fine silk thread. Farrell loosed one end of the thread, dropped it carefully through the barrel, and again attached it to the bow. He held the barrel to the light. "Look through it," he commanded. "Look at the shadow of the thread, and you can see where it does not touch. That means a crooked place. We've got to straighten that out by tapping with a light hammer."

The young man turned his face slowly in admiration of this ingenuity.

"Always begin straightening in the middle of the barrel," chortled the old man, delighted. "Chase the rascals out at the ends!" he cried.

The stranger shook his head.

"I'd sure hate to try to do it, suh," he submitted.

"It's as easy for me to take a kink out of a barrel as it is for you to make shavings off a pine stick with a sharp knife!" the gunsmith boasted.

His visitor turned the barrel slowly over and over, examining mentally the problem rather than physically the thing he held in his hand.

"Yes, suh," he said at last.

"Here," said Farrell, leading the way to a long, low bench, "is the most important part of all. Here's where we cut the grooves for the rifling."

"I do admire to see that!" cried the young man with an approach to eagerness.

He saw a long cherrywood cylinder of four or five inches in diameter in the surface of which had been cut four deep grooves that ran in a long spiral about the cylinder. They resembled the grooves in a rifle barrel, except that in this case, of course, they were on the outside. The cylinder was suspended in a framework. Midway in the framework had been fixed rigidly and immovably four projecting nubs that fitted into and engaged the four grooves. So, if one were to push the cylinder forward on its carriage past the nubs, it must revolve at the rate and the pitch determined by the grooves in it.

"And that," explained Farrell, "is exactly the rate and pitch of the rifling we want in our barrel. All we've got to do is clamp our barrel in an exact line, hitch our groove cutting tool rigidly on the end of the wooden cylinder, and it is *bound* to cut grooves exactly the same as those in the cylinder. See?"

His visitor shoved the simple contrivance back and forth a number of times, noting the slow turn along the rifled guiding groove.

"Well," he sighed at last, "that is ce'tainly a smart trick. I'll remember that. How long mought it take you, now, to rifle a bar'l?"

"Takes about a hundred cuts to cut a groove—about two hours," replied Farrell. "Then she needs polishing and smoothing. We use lead plugs for that mostly."

They proceeded slowly. Excited by his guest's intelligent appreciation, the old gunmaker expanded. He showed how the new barrels were plugged at one end of the tube, and how they were then browned by a mixture of aqua fortis, blue vitriol, tincture of iron, and water. In sketchy pantomime, the old man demonstrated how the locks were constructed and applied. At the woodworking bench, he paused for but a moment.

"Curly maple, that's the wood," he stated dogmatically, "and you want to work her by hand. And stain her by hand with good honest soot and oil. Then you've got a job."

They returned to the living room. The young man picked up his own rifle, which he examined gravely in the light of new knowledge. Farrell stood at his elbow.

"I see you have one of Martin Meylan's," he observed. "Like it?"

"She holds her own," replied the young man, noncommittally.

"What you done to the trigger guard?"

The stranger smiled his slow smile in modest deprecation.

"I expect I'm wrong, suh," said he. "I expect they's a right good reason why all the gunsmiths do thisaway and not that away, and I expect they must be right. But just for me, suh—in my own use, this trigger guard suits me better."

"Made it yourself, eh?"

"Yes, suh. Taint much of a trigger guard f'r looks, but it suits me better."

"Humph!" grunted the gunmaker, setting the weapon into the corner again, and leading the way to the pipes and chairs.

"I mean no offense, suh," said the visitor. "It's just my own idee for myself."

"Offense!" snorted the old man. "But you're right, lad! Do you know why every gunmaker in the colonies puts that foolish, cumbersome, fragile trigger guard on every gun he turns out? Simply because that is the kind they put on guns in Europe! No other reason! God knows why they wanted that kind there—thought 'em pretty, I suppose. Same way with a lot of other things. Gunmakers are pigheaded fools. They listen to no reason, but sit puffed in the arrogance of their self-conceit like toads, crying down those who—"

He had arisen and was waving about his long pipe, but catching the expression of honest bewilderment on his guest's face, he broke off in a calm as startling as his excitement, and sat down again abruptly.

"Tell me, lad," said he persuasively. "You spoke but now with a lukewarm indifference of the quality of your piece. What is its fault? And why procure ye none more to your fancy, since, as you say, your life may depend on it? Is the barrel not true, then? Perhaps we might remedy that."

"You mistake me, suh," the young man assured him earnestly. "The barl is true and finely made."

"It should be. Meylan is a gunsmith of reputation."

"I would not have you think otherwise. I but spoke aloud an idle thought. I know naught of these things and would not set my poor notions against the experience of my worshipful masters."

"Worshipful fiddlesticks!" exploded the old man. "Did I not tell ye, lad, that gunmakers are pigheaded fools, copying slavishly what is patterned for them in Europe and listening to no reason, but sunning themselves in arrogance? Come, lad! Your ideas?"

"They are without doubt impossible, suh, for I have no understanding of the craft."

"Perhaps, perhaps!" Farrell waved this aside. "But let us pretend there is no impossible. I would know your ideas, lad! Speak them freely."

"Well, suh, I would have a piece that used not so much good powder and lead, for powder and lead are hard to come at in the wilderness, and it has seemed to me that a well-placed ball will do its work—"

"Even a smaller ball," supplied the gunsmith. "There is naught of impossibility there, only common sense. Do you know the reason—the only reason—why all men contrive to use these great slugs? Because, in Europe, they know little of well-placed balls, and care less, because their only idea is to hit a regiment of men. And then?"

"Well, suh, a longer bar'l would suit me better, and I think most men who range the forests."

"Why?" snapped the old man.

"For better sighting. The woods are dark, and if a man would hold true in twilight, he must have his front sight far from his eye."

"That is true, too. And there is naught impossible there—save that gunmakers are a pigheaded lot. And then?"

For the first time, the young man chuckled aloud.

"Yere is where we touch the impossible, suh, for as long as I'm a-dreaming, I will tell the whole. I would have a piece that would place the ball truer to where I hold, so that when I drawed my bead and pressed my trigger true, I would find my ball where my eye had rested."

"And you do not? You think you can hold truer than your ball can speed?"

"So can any good man," submitted the youth modestly, but with entire confidence. "For be yore bar'l never so truly made, and load yore piece never so carefully with the best of French powder and priming of the finest grain, cast you yore balls never so cunningly, nevertheless it may so hap that it strays, and no man can tell when this will befall."

"Why is this, in your opinion?"

"Nay, that I cannot guess," replied the young man good-humoredly. "It is, I must suppose, in the natur' of things and we must bear with it."

The old man hesitated, weighing a decision.

"Nevertheless, even that might be compassed, in my belief," he said at last.

"Anon?" queried the other.

The old man leaned forward excitedly.

"Can you guard a secret?" he demanded.

"Yes, suh," said the young man gravely.

The gunsmith arose and left the room, to return after a moment bearing a rifle. This he withheld for a moment. Then, as though finally making up his mind, he passed it into his visitor's hands and stood back in silence. It was a graceful weapon, strong without clumsiness, its octagon barrel nearly three feet and a half long, but so light that it would probably not have tipped the beam at over eight or nine pounds. Its stock of polished curly maple extended its full length and was gracefully carved. Its trigger guard was small and compact. Beneath the barrel rings of brass held a long hickory ramrod. In the side of the buttstock opened a brass-covered trap. The lock was small, compact, about half the size of that on the usual arm of the day, and the clean, small flint was held in leathered jaws.

"There's your long barrel, and your spread of sights"—the old man could not keep silence long—"and your small strong trigger guard. There's your smaller bore. The balls run fifty-two to the pound instead of a score or less—you can carry three times the ammunition. The lock is as swift in action as a flash of light. See how smoothly the flint meets the frizzen! Throw it to your face, man! Held you ever so sweet a balance, or one that steadied itself so in the hand?"

The young man obeyed, and the extended muzzle of the long weapon came to the immobility of a rock.

"What say you?" urged the gunmaker, surveying his visitor's stance and handling with approval, but shifting from one foot to the other with an impatience ludicrously like that of a small boy.

"It is a sweet piece," sighed the visitor, lowering it at last. "A sweet piece, such as I never thought to hold atween my hands." He examined its details keenly. "I think, suh, if you don't mind my sayin' it, that you will have to make you another loadin' rod of iron."

"Hickory makes quieter loading."

"I know. But forcin' the ball down the bar'l is rough work, and a broken rod—"

The old man, for the moment, did not meet this issue.

"Is it not such a piece as you have dreamed?" he insisted. "Such as you described to me, but now?"

The youth smiled a slow gleam of humor.

"All but one thing," he reminded.

It was Farrell's turn to look at his inquiry.

"These things you have yere," explained the woodsman, "and I do not deny they are a great leap ahead—all these things are but aids to a man's holdin'! But they do not place the ball."

"Aha, lad!" The old gunmaker burst forth in a triumph for which it was now evident he had waited not too patiently. "That too I have compassed." He placed his finger alongside his nose with a comical air of cunning.

"Tell me, lad, what causes the ball to stray, when, as you say, the holding is good?"

"Nay, suh," replied the other. "How could I tell you that? It is, as I have said, in the natur' of things."

"Then I will e'en tell *you!* The first of these causes is a fouled and thereby roughened barrel."

The young man nodded acquiescence.

"That is true, in my own knowledge," he admitted, "so that, when time serves, I wipe out my piece very carefully after each shot."

"You can clean away thus the hard ash of burned powder," Farrell told him, "but you cannot thus remove the lead that is stripped from the ball flake by flake until the smoothness of the barrel is gone. The second reason is married with the third, and both have as parent, the fit of the ball in the barrel. For if it sets not snugly in the grooves, the force of the powder in great part leaps past it and is lost, and if it does fit snugly then it must be hammered home by force, and is thereby upset and malformed, no matter how shrewdly and gingerly one handles his rod. And a malformed bullet cannot fly straight."

"That is very interesting to me, suh," said the young man, "and part of it I had suspected, but not all. But can see no cure."

"Here," proffered Farrell, "are the balls for this rifle."

The visitor took one of them in his fingers and examined it without comment.

"You see no difference from any ordinary bullet, save for the size. You are right. There is no difference. But look!" He dropped the butt of the rifle to the floor and inserted one of the bullets into its muzzle. In ordinary loading, it was customary to drive the ball several inches into the barrel by means of a short metal rod and a small hammer called a *starter*, after which it was forced home with the ramrod. In this instance, when the old man relinquished it, the ball dropped down the barrel freely, and as he reversed the muzzle, it rolled slowly out again into his palm. He made no explanation but looked expectantly toward his visitor. The latter knit his brows, knowing some comment was awaited.

"If you aim to hold it in with wadding atop," he submitted at last, "I have tried that, and it flies wild as a hawk."

"Every child knows that—has tried that!"

"Yes, suh," agreed the stranger, "but it was all I could think of."

"Now I am going to show you something. And this is what you must keep secret. You must not tell a soul of what you are to see. Remember!"

"I have passed you my word, suh," stated the young man with a quiet dignity.

The old gunmaker paused in his tremendous inner excitement long enough to pat the other hastily on the shoulder.

"No offense, my lad. I trust ye," said he. "Now see." He opened the brass trap in the side of the stock and from it took a piece of greased linen cloth cut in a round a little less in size than a half-dollar. This he stretched across the muzzle of the gun, covering with it the hole of the bore. Next, he laid the bullet atop and pressed it into the aperture with his thumb.

"We are supposing we have charged the piece with powder," he explained. "Here," he forced the ramrod into the visitor's hands. "Push her home, lad!"

The young man, with the grace of long accustomedness, swung the butt of the weapon to the left and in front, and at the same time, inserted the tip of the ramrod into the bore and applied strongly the thrust of his right arm. An expression of surprise crossed his face.

"She slides slick and smooth as a greased shoat through a cornfield!" he marveled.

"And she stays there," supplemented the old man, snatching the rifle, turning it upside down, and striking the butt sharply by way of demonstration. "Is not that quicker than the old way? And quieter? And need ye fear now that the hickory rod will break? And mark you, each new loading wipes away the burned powder of the last shot, so that the barrel is ever clean. And the ball is left true and round as it came from the mold. And no lead strips from it to the barrel. And the linen patch, filling well all space within, let's not the force of the powder by. So there are your reasons for wild flight all answered!"

But the visitor was not wholly satisfied.

"And the ball still takes the twist of the grooves when the naked lead touches them not?" he commented doubtfully. "How can that be?"

The old man paused in his task, which was of abstracting the bullet by means of a screwworm which he had attached to the end of the rod.

"Nay, lad, that I cannot tell you. I have thought much on it. It must be, as you say, in the nature of things. But it does."

The youth pondered in his slow and deliberate fashion.

"And the ball flies true?" he asked at length. "I do not doubt you, suh," he hastened to add, "but I mind me my father's sayin', for when one showed him a piece and boasted of the hang of its stock and the prettiness of its carvings and the smooth dark brown of its bar'l, and the cunning of its make, he always said, 'Yes, she's purty, but she ain't worth a damn unless she shoots straight. Let's try her.' No offense, suh, but have you tried her?"

"I've shot her," replied the gunsmith briefly. He broke off, but was compelled to answer the other's waiting. "I can make a gun," he continued in a gruff tone, "but I cannot hold one true. A slight palsy—a shaking of the hand. But"—his voice rose to a vehemence almost of hysteria—"I'll stake my life that I am right, sneer and laugh these other pigheaded fools as they may! They know naught but what their fathers have told them, and their conceit is such. But they will sing a different tune. Fools! pigheaded fools!" He fumed, walking up and down with quick, uneven steps. Abruptly, he came to a halt before his visitor. "Would you credit it," he resumed in a quieter and more reasonable voice, "when, as a brother craftsman, I sought to share the workings of my mind, when I strove to discuss reasonably the things we have discussed so reasonably here—and you are an intelligent lad, Don, with more sense in your noodle than all of them together—when I would have spoken of the need for a rifle fitted to American rather than European hands, I was set aside as one sets aside a presumptuous urchin and rebuked for conceiting myself wiser than the masters!" He snorted, and again changed his mood.

"But tomorrow!" He chuckled, and again laid his finger alongside his nose. "You must linger tomorrow, lad, you are welcome here. Tomorrow you shall see."

"You will shoot the piece in tomorrow's match?"

"Not I. But I forget you are a stranger here, and perchance know not the significance of tomorrow. Know then that this is no ordinary shooting, but is an event to which once each year, all gunmakers bring their best and truest pieces to the trial, so that he whose rifle carries away the palm is winner of the golden medal of the craft, so that all men come to him, and his business gains great increase and himself reputation."

"But, suh," suggested the young man diffidently, "you yourself but now said—"

"That I cannot hold true," agreed the other. "But it is an article of the contest that the maker of the piece may engage another to stand for him, and for that reason, it is customary in the craft to bespeak skilled men to shoot for them at the butts. Few gunmakers test their own rifles. And I"—he chuckled again and rubbed his hands together—"I have been beforehand and have compacted with John Gladden of whom even in the borders you may have heard."

"His name has reached my ears," acknowledged the young man. "I should greatly admire, suh, to see so notable a marksman perform."

"You shall!" cried the gunmaker. "You shall! Tomorrow! And with the best shooter and the best rifle in the colonies, it shall go hard if I do not thrust their sneers adown their very throats! And I'll tell you this..."

The tall clock in the corner clucked in its throat, hesitated, then struck solemnly. The young man glanced up, startled at the level shafts of light.

"Yore pardon, suh, for interruptin' you," he cried. "But I must be excused. I have made a promise which I am tardy in fulfilling. It will not take me long, and I beg you to be patient, for I will hear more of these things on my return."

So saying, he snatched up his hat and hastened from the room.

Nor had he time to spare, for the last rays of the sun were lifting from atop the elm trees when he had regained the tavern square. His antagonist, slightly drunk, was parading to and fro at the appointed spot. He had evidently worked himself into a high state of braggadocio and belligerency, and ever and anon, he would stop short, flap his elbows, and crow lustily like a cock. Many men surrounded him in a loose group, cheering him on, half laughing, half in earnest. Someone caught sight of the young man approaching and raised a shout, hastily opening a passage. The red-faced man stopped short and peered evilly from beneath bushy brows.

"So you've come to take your licking after all, eh!" he growled.

"If so be you're of the same mind, which still seems to me a foolishness to fight like dawgs just because dawgs be a-fighting," replied the youth. "Is it not more befitting sensible men to share a tankard of mine host's good ale—"

The older man leaned forward and brought the flat of his palm smartly against the stranger's face.

"Now will ye fight!" he snarled. "Or are ye still too skeered?"

The young man's steadiness did not waver, nor did he show other sign than a slow darkening of the cheeks.

"That was not needful, suh," said he mildly. "Nor am I askeered."

Without further parley, the red-faced man lowered his head and made a bull-like rush. The stranger slipped lightly aside in avoidance, at the same time glancing about in surprise.

A tall, heavy-set man in a bottle-green topcoat with many small capes stepped forward authoritatively.

"What mean ye!" he cried in resonant tones. "Is this mannerly? Fair play and a proper ring, say I, and hurrah for the best man!"

His interference met with approval.

"Good for you, Squire!"

"Fair play!"

"Well back ye in that!" came to him from many voices.

At this moment, also the tavern's landlord bustled forth, appealing for no brawls before his door.

"The stable yard, gentlemen!" he cried. "It is at hand, and much more seemly!"

"The stable yard it is," agreed the squire. "Come ye." He seized the combatants each by an elbow and marched them away like children, followed by the streaming and excited rabble.

"I thank you, suh," said the young man. "Methought for a moment that I saw the ruin of my only coat."

Arrived at the stable yard the squire, still holding his charges by the elbow, looked about him high-headed, and rapidly named a dozen to form the ring. Back of these appointed provosts, the crowd gathered dense, and men clambered rapidly atop wagons and walls, and even swarmed to the stable roof for a better view. When the stir had died, the squire released his charges, shoving each to an opposite side.

"Strip," he commanded them. It was evident that the squire was enjoying himself hugely.

The challenger, who was aflame with eagerness—and whiskey—tore his shirt from his back and handed it at random among the spectators, disclosing himself as a heavy gorilla of a man, bull-necked, barrel-chested, thick-armed, with heavy, strong muscle bands. The stranger methodically folded his coat and removed and folded his shirt, which he placed atop it. Holding the bundle in his arms, he looked from face to face of those about him. He stepped to confront a placid, kindly-faced man of middle age.

"Could I ask you to mind these for me, suh?" he asked courteously.

"Gladly," assented the burgher. He leaned to speak in a lower voice. "Beware of him, lad," he advised earnestly. "He is an ugly fighter, and he will kill you if he can. I am sorry this must be," he added.

"Thank you, suh, I can but do my best," rejoined the youth, and turned to the center of the ring.

His torso, now stripped of its garments, was seen to be molded in lines of a smooth slenderness that, at first glance, contrasted ill with the heavy power of his antagonist. Nevertheless, a connoisseur in bodies would have found somewhat to admire in the contrast of the broad spare shoulders and the narrow compact hips and would have appreciated the whipcord quality of the long muscles and the ripple of their perfect condition beneath the skin. But its force would seem the force more of long endurance than the power necessary to contend successfully with the crushing oaken strength of the man over against him. Here and there in the crowd, a few murmured in pitying deprecation of the inequality of the contest, but their protests were drowned in the general eagerness of excitement. Men shouted offers to wager, but the offers were all on one side and no takers, for none accorded the younger man a chance against a known and reputed rough-and-tumble fighter. Only after the clamor had died somewhat through lack of fuel did the squire's loud voice speak on the other side.

"Damme," he bellowed at one of the most vociferous, who now offered four to one. "Taken for a pound." But he added, "I'll not begrudge a pound for the sake of sport." He addressed the antagonists, "Now hark ye, this is all my say, if one or the other cries enough, at that moment ye cease, and if any offers blow or grip thereafter he reckons with me. Now fight it out."

He stepped back.

The big man slouched toward the youth, lowered his head, and rushed like a bull. The latter again slipped easily to one side, evading the outstretched hands. Thrice, this was repeated.

"Stand and fight, you poltroon!" snarled the red-faced man.

The younger made no reply, watching his antagonist warily. Twice more, the same maneuver with the same result, except that once the stranger laid a hand on the other's shoulder as he passed but snatched it away instantly when faced by a sudden turn in his direction. The crowd began to shout impatiently, for it was evident that if he so chose, the visitor's superior agility could prolong indefinitely this avoidance, and they wanted a fight, not a foot race. So clamorous became their demands that the squire at length raised his bull voice.

"Fair play!" he cried. "Give the lad a chance!"

At length, the challenger wearied of futile rushing that grasped nothing, and came to a stand in the center, sneeringly awaiting a move by the other. The latter, stooping, his arms hanging, began then slowly to circle just out of reach. It was notable that neither man had offered as yet to strike the other with his fists. Blows in the fights of those days were a secondary offense, delivered to batter into submission only after an advantage had been gained. Twice, the young man darted in, attempting some wrestler's hold, twice he failed, and wrenched himself away from the other man's countering grip.

The squire watched, his head on one side.

"Methinks if Jack once grasps him firmly, my pound is done," he observed to the man next to him. "Aha!" he shouted.

The stranger's third attempt seemed to have proved disastrous to him. His bear-like antagonist had caught him in a grip that could not be shaken off. For nearly half a minute, they strained. Then, the older man's superior strength began to tell. Beneath his smooth skin the youth's muscles strained as though they would burst, but slowly, inch by inch, he was bent back until he was securely held. And then powerfully and irresistibly the man called Jack half freed one massive arm, and his hand, inch by inch, overpowering the young man's opposition, crept upward.

A lightning-desperate upheaval, and the lad had twisted free and sprung apart. He was panting slightly, and for the first time, his face was aflame.

"He tried to gouge me!" he cried to the squire. "Is that what you call fair play!"

"And why not?" rejoined the squire coldly. "Stand and fight, or, if you will, cry quits."

The young man looked about the crowd in amazed appeal from the decision but was answered by derisive laughter. Its blood was up, and it wanted blood. Still incredulous, he looked at his antagonist. The latter grinned at him evilly.

"I'll do worse to ye than that, my cockerel," he growled.

"And is that your habit!" cried the stranger indignantly. "It is not so on the borders when men settle honest differences."

"Stand and fight—or cry quits," repeated the squire imperturbably.

No man was able afterward to describe clearly what next happened, though many words were wasted in the matter. They saw the young man stoop, they saw him dart in with the speed and swiftness of a snake striking, they were confusedly aware of a tangle and swirl, and even above the turmoil of excitement, they distinctly heard a clear sharp snap like the cracking of a dead limb. Then the young man leaped back clear, leaving his antagonist standing, an expression of bewilderment on his face, gazing stupidly at his left arm which he held in his right hand.

"Well, suh!" the visitor challenged in a ringing voice. His head was high, and his nostrils expanded.

A dead silence fell that endured for perhaps ten seconds.

"Will you go on?" inquired the squire, in a voice calm only above a compressed excitement.

"Go on!" repeated Jack furiously. "How can I go on? He has broken my arm!"

The stupefaction broke. The ring was instantly overwhelmed by the surge of men, shouting, whooping. They crowded around the stranger, pounding him on the back, shrieking in his face, commending him, congratulating him, all on his side, fickle as crowds always are. He thrust them aside scornfully, elbowing his way to the burgher in whose charge he had given his garments, which he reclaimed with a brief word of thanks, and proceeded to assume. The squire was at his side, red-faced and bellowing.

"Greatest thing I ever saw, lad!" he shouted. "You've won me four pounds! Damme you must drink with me! Come, I will not take nay."

The young man shook his head.

"You must excuse me, suh," he said firmly. "I must be on my way. I thank you, suh, for yo' kindness."

"But how did you do it? That you must tell me," persisted the big man. "Saw I never the like before."

"It was a trick," replied the stranger briefly. "A trick known to the Injins. They use it only when hard-pressed in battle," he added.

He turned away, and with an air of decision that none ventured to cross, threaded the gaping crowd and disappeared.

When he reentered the low, dark room, the great clock in the corner was tolling the last note of another hour. The old gunmaker dozing by the fire awakened with a start. The young man slipped into a chair.

"Now, suh, if you don't mind, I've been figgerin'," said he, "on what you been tellin' me. And I'd like to talk some more about these ideas of yours. You don't know how interestin' they are to me, suh."

"Surely, lad, surely," agreed the old man. He glanced incredulously at the tall clock, now dim in the twilight. "You have been long," he commented.

"Yes, suh," agreed his visitor apologetically. "But I would have returned much sooner had I known the customs of yo' people yereabouts."

All late afternoon and early evening, the contestants and spectators continued to pour into town. A few came in wagons, fewer still afoot, and the great majority on horseback. The inn was full to overflowing, men bought high the privilege of making down their beds on the floor of the less frequented public apartments. Every private house willing to do so accommodated its visitors. At the Big Bend the flicker of fires reflected downward from the great river trees, and it seemed that those campers were perhaps the most in comfort of any, for what with the revelers spilling noisily from the tavern bar, the songs and disputations of others determined to make the most of the rare holiday, only those of strong nerves and placid powers of withdrawal could obtain more than fitful rest in the village. And as the last of the night owls went to roost, and the wearied turned on their pallets with a sigh of anticipation of deferred rest, the small hours became murmurous with the activities of those who must make preparations for the coming day's activities. Then it was made known to the campers at the Bend that it would have been well to have retired earlier, for they were fairly upon the scene of the day's sport, and men with lanthorns moved busily and shouted to one another as they made last preparation for the entertainment of the crowd, which must here, upon the very spot, be supplied with food and drink if mine host of the tavern were most to profit.

To this end, long tables had been setup within bowers thatched with straw, and now men hurried about carrying or rolling or trundling provision of spirits and beer and ale, and others tended fires blazing beneath great iron pots from which steamed a most seductive savory of venison and beef stews. There was little more sleep for the campers, but plenty of grumbling, until the aroma of the cooking was too much for their sharpened appetites, and they arose and kicked together the embers of their own dying fires and shivered slightly in the chill of dawn, and ate and were comforted, and so, gradually, slipped into the eager vibrant excitement of the day, and fell to discussing the leading contestants and raising their voices in dispute and laying wagers on the men of their choice. Nor was the element of personal emulation crowded aside by the presence of champions, for in the course of the day was room for many minor sweepstake events open to all, not to speak of a number of lesser rivalries privately arranged. And those of more modest skill staked happily their hopes on chance, for a ball flying wild from the muzzle not too rarely compensated for an ill aim, besides which, in certain types of matches, a tyro with good luck might very well outdo an expert with bad. There would be plenty of powder burned this day!

Those in the village stirred more sluggishly, groaning and stopping their ears as the clatter of newcomers half aroused them, slipping back less and less successfully to unconsciousness, until at last, with a curse, they kicked aside their blankets and quilts. But their ill nature did not outlast the moment. For some, a morning draught, for some, a plunge of the head into cold water, for some, through opened casement, a breath of coming morning, composed of coolness and a streak of rose in the eastern sky and the soft mourning of doves in the trees, sufficed to bring them full into the eagerness of anticipation. The monotonous year filed before these pioneer people in a slow procession of gray days. Spangle days were rare, and they savored them with an expectancy and thrill, known nowadays only to children, not to be dimmed by smaller things. By the time the morning light was full, all men were again afoot, save a few whose potations of the night before had been somewhat too deep.

One dwelling house in the village was, however, exempt from this premature arousement. Protected by the soft, rushing silence of running water, no noise could reach it to trouble its repose. The mill race took all the world of sound for its own and translated it into a lulling and grateful peace. Those within its insulation slept tranquilly, undisturbed.

Nevertheless, robin-song found its inmates afoot, the young man at the call of long habit, the elder prowling about in foretaste of what he believed was to be his long-awaited triumph. They met in the oaken room below stairs, where they ate together at the board table, served by a grumpy and elderly woman who the day before had not been in evidence.

"Now, Don lad," advised the old gunmaker when they had finished, "I advise ye to take ye down to the Big Bend where, I doubt not, you will find much to see and to amuse yourself withal. The big shooting is not until afternoon, but there will be the smaller matches and many other doings worth your while to see."

"I will e'en do that, suh," agreed Don, "but come ye not also?"

"Nay, lad," replied the old man cunningly. "I have seen many such, and it is not my purpose to disclose for the common questioning my new production. I will be there when the hour strikes, but not before. And besides, I await John Gladden, who comes before the time to make trial of the new rifle and to fit his holding to its sighting."

"In that case, suh, I will follow your advice," said the young man, plucking his felt hat from the peg. "When the young-un awakens, give her my greeting."

"But Don!" Farrell halted him at the door. "Are you not taking your own piece with you?"

"For why?" The visitor smiled quaintly. "Do you expect an attack of the savages?"

"But will ye not enter in the shooting?" expostulated the gunmaker. "Not the great match, but there will be many others—block shoots and peg shoots and turkey shoots wherein many will take part."

Don shook his head.

"Perchance, if your piece is not quite true, another could be found for you in my shops," suggested Farrell. "Gladly may you have the loan of such."

"My piece is as true as any," the young man assured him. He hesitated, then went on steadily, "I had not thought to mention it, suh, but the truth is I am travelin' through on a visit, and must return, and my pockets are not so lined with shillings that I may spend them on aught else but the journey."

"Let me—"

"No, suh," Don interrupted firmly, "but I am obleeged to you, suh."

He turned toward the door. At the stairway's foot stood the little girl, barefooted, in her night shift, her ringleted hair towsled about her head.

"If you see that old Tiger, you *kill* him!" cried she.

For the first time the grave young stranger laughed aloud.

"If I see that old Tigah, honey," he replied, "I'll be shore to info'm him *just* what you told me."

By the time he had reached the Big Bend the day's activities were well under way. Don sauntered here and there, surveying them gravely. Mostly, he passed unnoticed, though here and there he was proffered a greeting from some spectator of yesterday's fight, and twice, he was invited boisterously to come up to the tables and take a drink as a stout lad! But he responded so gravely to the salutations and refused the invitations so firmly that they turned away from him without further thought.

The river grove and the meadow immediately adjacent were thronged. Many jostled about the tables in the bowers, breaking their morning's fast or fortifying themselves with ale or spirits. Smaller and shifting groups hovered about certain peddlers who had laid out their wares. Others clustered, talking politics or crops or religion, as was to be expected. Only a comparatively few partisans or acquaintances had as yet gravitated to where the rifles were already whanging away, and where hung the thin, acrid fog of powder. It was to this point, however, that Don at once betook himself. He arrived just as one match had come to an end, and the preparations for another were about to begin.

On a stool behind a table sat the man Don had yesterday heard called the squire. The day was yet young and cool, and he wore still his green greatcoat with the many capes. Below the table stood a large basket filled with pine blocks split to about six inches square, and the surfaces blackened by charring. These the squire was engaged in passing out to would-be contestants in the next event, selling them at the rate of sixpence apiece. As but one shot could be fired at each block, some were buying three, four, or as many as five. Others, either because of the slenderness of their purses or confidence in their luck or ability, contented themselves with but one. Each, on receiving his targets, drew apart to mark them. This was done either by scribing deep crosslines with a knife, or by tacking on a bit of paper or tin. The marks on the crosslines rarely centered the block of wood, for while the prize money would go to the man whose ball struck nearest the exact middle, each placed his point of aim at the spot where experience had taught him the sight should be held to compensate for the error of his gun.

The range for this match was one hundred yards, and each assumed what position and took what time he pleased. If a man missed clean, he cursed vividly or withdrew in sullen silence, leaving the untouched target to be retrieved by an attendant Negro, for sale and use again. If, under the bullet's impact, the block spun from its position, he whooped and ran forward to reclaim it himself, and was on his return immediately surrounded, all eager to examine how near to center the ball had struck. When the last block had taken its chance, the best were submitted to the squire's measurement, which determined the winner. The latter was immediately presented with the cash prize, which was a goodly percentage of the sum resulting from the entrance fees, the remainder constituting a *Kitty* that went to the promotion fund of the enterprise. In this match, nearly half the targets were hit, and the winning bullet was officially declared to have entered within two inches of center.

"What think ye of that?" exulted a spectator at Don's elbow. "Is not that a good shooting?"

"Why, I think it very good," agreed the young man, "and these men can stand with the best in any company."

He turned away to where, from the right, came the sounds of occasional desultory firing. Here, he found men engaged in shooting at a turkey loosely tethered at a full two hundred yards. The entrance fee was also but a sixpence, and he who hit the turkey would take it away for his dinner, but the fact that the bird could continually move about within a short radius, combined with the additional fact that the range was beyond what approximate exactness the rifles of the day possessed, made of the investment no undue risk to the management.

That both contestants and bystanders realized fully the large part played by chance was fully evidenced by the atmosphere of hilarity. Men shouted facetious comments and advice, dissolved in yells of laughter as a sudden movement on the part of the distracted turkey avoided a lucky bullet. The rivals muttered curses or voiced humorous chagrin according to their various temperaments. One elderly man held his rifle at aim for a full two minutes, following with his sights in vain the erratic motions of the bird—at last lowering his arm tired with its long exertion.

"Consarn the pesky critter!" he shouted in exasperation. "Hold still, if you want to be killed!"

At last, in desperation, he loosed off anyhow, and a puff of dust far to the right elicited only a startled squawk.

The mark was attained after a deal of banging by a smooth-faced boy who raced excitedly to retrieve his prey, only to be greeted by a great shout of laughter as he returned with it.

"Hope you like dark meat!"

"Never mind, bub, turkey hash is fine!"

The heavy bullet had smashed its way squarely through the middle of the breast.

Don shook his head.

"That's a waste of good eatin'," he remarked to one near him. "Whar I come from we just let the head stick out, and shoot at it—at a hundred ya'ds," he added.

Another small and amused group attracted him further. Here he found two men with rifles, seated on the ground. One, his piece held in a knee and elbow rest, was painfully and patiently squinting at a cockerel tethered a scant fifty yards distant. The other, his rifle laid alongside him on the ground, smoked a pipe and watched. The rooster was a noble and iridescent specimen of his kind, a beautiful creature except for one blemish. What should have been an abundant and sweeping tail consisted of four scattered feathers only.

For some time, the young visitor watched. Still, the rifleman held his fire. Don was puzzled.

"Why delays he, suh," he asked a bystander at last.

"Shorely it is no great feat to kill the fowl at that range."

His interlocutor, a middle-aged man of evidently the better class, chuckled.

"That is the last thing he wants to do," he replied in a low and guarded voice.

"I do not understand, suh," submitted Don.

"Why," explained the other, "I see you are a stranger here. Know, then, that this is a private match between two very noted marksmen who are such rivals that I think they would very gladly use one another as targets in a duel. E'en last night at the tavern, and they in their cups, I think it might have come to blows, but the squire, who is a rare wag at times, and hath ideas one would never suspect in so thick a noodle, bethought him of this. The terms are that each man, in turn, plucks with his bullet from the tail of that cockerel a feather. The one who shoots away the last feather wins the contest and the wager they have made. But he who by mischance slays the chicken not only loses the match but must double the bet."

The young man chuckled in his throat.

"Already," continued the gentleman, "they have sat there three hours. Each has fired twice, and the cockerel still unscathed. They are like to be there all day. What think you of that?"

"Why," rejoined the stranger, "I think it right good shootin'—and right good luck, suh, also."

The colloquy was interrupted by the resounding boom of the heavy rifle. The chicken squawked and leaped convulsively to the end of its tether. A tail feather whirled aloft and floated gently to the earth. The marksman laid aside his piece with the deep sigh of relief from long tension.

"Yore turn," he informed his rival curtly.

Beneath an arbor, and in charge of a young chap of about Don's age, was located the official sales place for ammunition. Here were canisters of the best French powder, both of the very fine grain for priming the pan, and of the coarser grain for the charge in the barrel, and clear, beautifully shaped English flints, each guaranteed to be good for fifty shots, and frizzen pricks, plain or ornamental, and bars of lead, and twists of unspun flax for swabbing the bore. Besides these essentials were exhibits of other things, brought either for sale or as samples by which to order. Of the former were hand-forged traps, moccasins and shot pouches sewn and decorated by the women, tomahawks fashioned by blacksmiths, knives of various shapes and hardness of blade, and powder horns scraped so thin that the grains of powder could be seen through their sides. This bazaar was a sort of company affair, and the young man in charge was paid by fees from whoever had matters to advertise or things to sell. Thus he was prepared to take orders for the products of any one of the half-dozen or so gunmakers of the neighborhood, or to accept for reboring worn-down or rusted barrels, and either to ream out the old bullet mold to fit the new size or to supply a new mold. Between other activities, he demonstrated over and over a new invention for the kindling of fire. This was in appearance a sort of pistol, with a very small stock, a full-sized flintlock, and a barrel not over an inch long, but with a huge bore fully as wide. The young man stuffed into this barrel a tight wad of unspun flax, poured a little gunpowder into the pan, and pulled the trigger. From the muzzle, he pulled the smoldering flax and blew it to a glow. He extolled this simple contraption highly as an immense improvement over the ordinary flint and steel, but he sold few. The thing was expensive, and citizens settled in houses rarely required to make new fire, for they took good care to bank their coals. As for the backwoods farmers, they plugged the touch hole of their rifles, placed the flax in the pans, and got the same result. If the plug did not fit tightly enough, the maneuver might result not only in the desired fire, but also in a badly frightened family and a bullet among the pewter, but it worked.

Since it was by now approaching noon, Don next took his way to the refreshment bower, where, after careful inquiry of prices, he purchased a half-loaf of bread, a slice of cold venison, and a chunk of cheese. With these, he retired to sit with his back against a post, unsheathed his knife, and set to with a hearty appetite. For several minutes, so busy was he with his meal, he did not overhear the conversation near him. Then, he could not but become aware that the four very solid men who sat at the table above him were members of the same craft as his host. He could not see their faces, but the wide, broad-clothed backs presented to him were the very sign of pompous dignity. Their talk was technical and therefore interesting to the young man, and he did not scruple to listen, though rather idly, and off the surface of his attention. It had to do with the softness and the toughness of various charcoal irons as materials for barrels, and the relative merits of sugar or red maple wood for stocks, and the pros and cons as to whether it paid better to import Belgian-made locks entire—which they acknowledged to be excellent—or to make them at home, in which case a man knew what he had, and a rather sneering unanimity of opinion as to some visionary who had ideas as to the value of gain twist, which evidently had been suggested to him by specimens of early arquebuses.

"There is always a fool or so thinks he can improve upon the ripe wisdom of the craft," remarked the broadest back contemptuously. "I have seen in my time a score such who would overturn the world."

"And speaking of such, I see not Master Farrell's sour face today," observed another.

"I deem his absence no loss to the company," pronounced broad-back. "I doubt not he mourns in private his champion's fall."

"How is that? What mean ye?" queried a third.

"Have ye not heard? Nay, but that is the choicest morsel of all."

"I arrived but an hour since," explained the other.

"Why," began broad-back in the unctuous tones of one about to retail a cozy bit of gossip, "Master Farrell, I would have you know, had retained John Gladden to shoot for him in the great match."

"Nay," rejoined the other with asperity, "that I know but too well, for I had thought to engage him for myself."

"Good fortune, then, attended you," said broad-back, and he paused, relishing the question.

"Good fortune? How now?"

"Why, that this John Gladden will not hold a piece today, nor yet for many days to come, and the reason is simple—that he cannot, on account that his arm is broken in two places."

Don jerked back his head, his whole attention caught. Broad-back chuckled.

"See ye not our good man Farrell—" he was going on, when he felt his shoulder seized, and turning in outraged dignity at the unmannerly assault, met two blazing blue eyes within a foot of his own.

"Broken, you say? How happed that?" cried their owner.

"How now, sirrah—" But broad-back broke off his indignation with a stare of recognition. "Meseems you should know that." He chuckled. "For, if my eyes deceive me not, you are he who—"

But the young man was gone.

With swift strides he threaded his way through the crowd, shook himself free from the throng, and breaking into a long and easy lope, hastened toward the village street. But before he had gained to the first of the houses, he recognized to his left a small figure hurrying in the opposite direction, and so changed his course to encounter it.

"Have ye seen or heard aught of John Gladden?" called his host agitatedly as he neared, "for he hath not—"

"Master Farrell," the young man cut him short, "I think I have unwittingly done to you the greatest disservice man has ever done another."

So manifest was his distress that the gunmaker's own anxiety was set aside.

"Why, how can that be, lad?" he asked.

Almost breathlessly, Don told of the incident of the two dogs and the little girl, and of how he had been forced against his will to take up the foolish quarrel, and of the fight in the stable yard on account of it, and of how it fared. The old man listened attentively.

"But that was well done," he commented, "and I am much beholden to you."

"But that is not all, suh," insisted the young man. "So we fought, and I do not know how it would have gone with me, for he was very strong. At last, he caught me in his grip, and then-then, suh, he sought to gouge my eyes! I had not thought men in fair fight would strive to maim, but he whom they called the squire would have it so, and those standing about called it fair play. It is not thus with us on the border, suh, for when men settle disputes, they wrestle fairly and fight as white men fight, not as savages do. So then I knew this was war."

"Yes, lad, and then?"

"Then, suh, I fit as a man fights in war, when his piece is empty, and he cannot come at his tomahawk or his knife. I used a trick long known to the Injins, and which I learned from them. By it, I broke his arm, and so the fight ended."

"But, lad, that was well done," the old man repeated, "and you can take no blame to yourself for that."

"Nay, suh, I knew it not. I have but just now learned—" He hesitated, in obvious distress.

"What, lad?" the gun maker had not yet guessed.

"The man was John Gladden."

A long silence fell while Farrell digested this information.

"Meseems I would gladly have lost an eye had not this happed—" the young man faltered, but Farrell stopped him with a peremptory gesture.

"Nay," he commanded. "You could do no different. I do not blame you. Nay, it was well done."

He drooped visibly nevertheless, remained for some moments in thought, bowed his head, then straightened with an assumed cheerfulness.

"We must accept what fortune brings," said he.

"Is it too late, suh, to seek out another—" began the young man anxiously.

The gunmaker cut him short with a decisive shake of the head.

"The Match is even now about to be called," said he, and every marksman worth the name is long since bespoke. Nor would I place the piece in the hands of any less."

They stood there facing one another, the younger man almost wringing his hands in distress, the older contemplating the ground in a brown study. Suddenly, he straightened.

"I have it!" he cried. "You shall take his place!"

"I, suh," stammered the stranger, taken aback.

"Even you," stated the old man with decision. "You can do no less."

"But, suh," expostulated Don, "I am not fitten to stand with these men. I would not do ye a further disservice. I am not practiced in these affairs. I care not for myself, but the new piece, suh—"

"Enough!" the old man cut him short with authority. "If I am willing, how should you draw back?"

"But you know not that my aim is true."

"I watched you last even as you handled the piece to your cheek. I marked you well, and I will stake my chances on your skill. Come, I ask it. You can do no less."

"If you are set upon it, I can but make the trial," agreed the young man, hesitating and troubled.

"I am set upon it."

"I can but do my best," then said he.

The volatile old man, his spirits popping up like a balloon, leaped into the air and cracked his heels together twice.

"That's my lad!" he cried heartily. "And now we must haste, for an we be not there to answer when the match is called, we shall lose our place."

He trotted back in the direction of his house, his very gait bouncing into a confidence evidently not shared by the troubled youth following at his heels. At the house Farrell carefully wrapped the new rifle in a blanket.

"They shall see no sight of it afore the time," he babbled, thrusting the muffled piece into the lad's hands. "And now let us see. Here is the great powder horn, and the smaller with priming, and here is the stock of balls, and not one flawed one among them, and spare flints, yes, and a stout frizzen prick, and patches and grease in the butt—all is here, let us hasten back."

"But, suh," expostulated Don, "have I no chance to fire the piece first that I may test my holding?"

"No time now, no time," returned the old man testily. "Come, hasten, or even yet, we may be too late!"

"That is a hard task you place on me, suh," observed the stranger, but more in comment than complaint.

"Hold a fine sight," panted the gunmaker as he trotted along. "Hold fine, and dead center. Allow for no error, merely hold true."

The young man sighed resignedly.

"And the trigger pull, suh?" he suggested. "I have not even the feel of that."

"You will find it smooth as a hound's tooth," rejoined the other, "so that a baby's touch would suffice to trip the hammer. There is but one thing to watch. In your loading, see that you center the ball on the patch, for if it be to one side or the other by any great span, the ball will not fly quite so true."

At the Bend all firing had ceased. Even the two men still patiently engaged in plucking with their bullets, the cockerel's tail had been ordered to desist, and that demoralized fowl was enjoying a respite and the continued possession of two widely separated feathers. The concourse, which now numbered almost every available human being, was held back of a designated line by men whose official position was advertised by a white handkerchief bound about the left arm. The open space in front was occupied only by the table at which still sat the squire, flanked by two assistants. But even as Farrell and his guest—the former somewhat out of breath—reached the outskirts, one of the assistants arose and cried out a name in a great bull voice that could have been heard in the village street. A man, whom Don recognized as broad-back, pushed forward, at his elbow, a small, unobtrusive fellow chewing tobacco nonchalantly and carrying a rifle which, even from a distance, could plainly be distinguished as brand new and of fine workmanship. The two took their places to the left of the table.

"We are but just in time," observed Farrell, removing his hat, and mopping his brow. "They call the contestants. That is Master Detrick, the gunmaker from Lancaster, and the small man with him is Mark Dall who will fire for him."

But now the announcer was calling other names, and other men were coming forward in response. Unlike the more impromptu and lesser matches of the earlier part of the day, the entries for this Great Match had been all made and paid for and closed the day previous, and there remained now but the formality of reading the entrants from the list. So it went until fourteen men had taken their places, of whom five were gunmakers standing only in the role of sponsors, five their hired champions, and the other four free lancers competing on their own for their chance at the *great fat ox* and the snap haunce gun and the glory. Then, the announcer sat down.

"How now! How now!" cried Farrell, breaking through the cordon. "Find ye not my name on your list?"

The squire slowly turned his great bulk to survey the speaker.

"And is it you, Master Farrell!" he exclaimed in surprise. He turned his eyes toward Detrick. "But of a certain, it is here, and you are welcome."

"Then why was I not called?" indignantly demanded the gunmaker.

"We were informed," said the squire slowly, "that you had withdrawn." He continued to stare at Detrick, until the latter stirred uneasily and muttered, "It is known to all that John Gladden lies abed and—"

"You take much upon yourself, sir!" interrupted Farrell, hotly.

"Peace, gentlemen!" commanded the squire with authority. "Your name is here, Master Farrell. You will yourself shoot your match?"

"Nay, I have a man for that."

"His name?"

"Don—nay, I know not the rest. Where is the pesky lad?" Farrell searched vainly with his eyes in the shifting crowd.

"Put him down as Master Don," the squire told the recorder. "Time passes. Your man fires last," he instructed Farrell. "See that he is here."

The first test was at one hundred yards. The targets were the six-inch wooden blocks already described. The number of shots, five. Each man was to fire once in rotation until the tally was complete.

Detrick's champion was called upon. The little man, still chewing his tobacco, stepped calmly forward. His piece was already charged, so all he had to do by way of preparation was to shake the priming powder into the pan. Any position was allowed, so Dall disposed himself deliberately with muzzle and elbow rest, aimed carefully for what seemed a very long time, and fired. His block spun backward as the heavy bullet smashed into it. Dall arose deliberately and withdrew to the background, where he at once set about an elaborate cleaning of his piece. One by one, the other contestants took their turn. The majority followed his example in selecting the muzzle and elbow rest as the most certain, though one man lay prone, and one other sat, his elbows clamped between his knees. Of the nine, seven registered hits, and a murmur of admiration swept the spectators, for this was marvelous percentage. The location of the hits would not be determined until later, where delay enhanced the dramatic suspense.

"Master Don, firing for Master Farrell," called the announcer.

Farrell slapped the young man on the back and pushed him forward.

"God be with ye, lad," he muttered.

He was shifting from one foot to the other nervously, and he was breathing sharply, but Don seemed unconcerned. He walked forward to the mark carrying the long rifle at trail, woodsman fashion. A wave of excited comment rose. Men's interest was caught by the strange appearance of the new weapon.

"Look at the length of that bar'l," they murmured to one another. "What think you is in the hinged boxes in the butt?"

"Flints," suggested another.

Farrell suppressed a cry of anguish, for Don, instead of disposing himself in any one of the several positions that afforded a steadying rest, had squared to his shot, standing upright on his two feet. And barely, it seemed, had the muzzle reached the level when, without perceptible pause for aim, as it seemed, the piece was discharged.

The excited babel was now full-voiced, for there was much to say.

"Don't you suppose the damn fool knows he don't have to shoot offhand?"

"He didn't hardly take no aim at all!"

"Must have a ha'r trigger and she went off on him accidental," surmised one sagely. And everybody commented on the salient phenomenon of the whole performance, the sharp whip-like crack of the discharge, in arresting contrast to the full roar of the other rifles. The fact that the block of wood had been struck was unremarked, unimportant, and dismissed as a lucky accident that could not recur in the same conditions.

"Lad! Lad!" agonized Farrell, as the young man returned to his side. "Be not so hasty and so rash! Get ye a steady rest and assure your aim better!"

Don dropped the butt of the long rifle to the ground and prepared to reload.

"Nay, suh," he returned tranquilly. "I have never la'rned these fancy tricks. I must e'en do as I may, and my schooling has been in the forests. An I dwell upon my aim or seek a spot whereon to rest my piece I am like to lose either my dinner or my scalp."

"Think you you can hit the mark again?" asked Farrell anxiously.

"That we shall see in good time," replied Don. "But this I will say." His grave face lighted for an instant with a rare enthusiasm. "Never have I held a piece so sweet to the hand, never have I pulled trigger so smooth to the touch, never have I looked across sights so clear to the eye. And if the ball speeds as true as the rifle holds, why, then, suh, without wishin' to boast, I may say that I will knock over those bits of wood as long as men will cut 'em fo' me!"

Suddenly, he lapsed into an embarrassed silence.

"I babble overmuch," he muttered, and went on loading.

The second round proceeded with no more than the usual cries of encouragement and comment. But when the young stranger again methodically took his place, and with the same absence of delay, proceeded to spin his second block of wood from its resting place, the noise rose to a pandemonium, and the guards found difficulty in holding back the surge of the crowd.

Farrell was hopping about with joy, and the young man himself showed symptoms of excitement. But it was the excitement of a growing interest and enthusiasm, not of nervousness, against which now his patron was frantically urging him to beware. At last, Don stopped him with a good-humored laugh.

"I will do my possible, suh," he reassured the old man. "And I think you need not be afeard, for yore billets carry neither arrows nor fusees, nor are they like to run away."

The five rounds finished at last and in an excitement that constantly grew, for never had the like been seen before. Men told one another that they were present at the greatest shooting match ever known. All records had gone by the board. For of the fifty shots delivered, thirty-seven had found the mark, which in itself was enough to make history. And of the thirty-seven hits, five must be accredited to the young stranger! He had not once missed!

This alone was sufficient to set men's tongues clacking with amazement. But still remained the decision, for the award must go to him whose ball had struck closest to dead center, and all awaited the announcement from the table on which the attendant Negro had piled the basketful of billets he had gathered up. Each had been marked with the name of its owner, of course, and the squire and his assistants sorted them out and laid them aside for examination, and the contestants and their sponsors gathered close about, awaiting his verdict. At last, the squire looked up, and his broad face was amazed.

"Gentlemen," said he, holding up one of the blocks, and it could be seen that the ball had cut almost into the cross itself. "Here is the winning shot, and a good one it is. But, gentlemen, here are the others that come nearest." He exhibited one after the other four other targets, and of them all, the farthest ball had centered not over three inches from perfection. "That is good shooting, each one of these is worthy of a prize, for never in the long years of my life have I seen the like!" He slowly arose to his full height, and his rubicund face was overspread with an emotion that was close to awe. "And this I must tell you, that these balls, one and all, were delivered by the same hand!" His face broke into a broad grin as he turned to Farrell. "Methinks," said he, "fate did you a shrewd good turn that this young man stood for you in the stead of Gladden. As for you, my lad, you shoot as well as you fight—or you fight as well as you shoot, I know not how to say it."

"It is the rifle," stated Don modestly. "Never was a piece made that shot so true."

"A man cannot win at cards without an ace," agreed the squire. "And of the rifle, more anon, for I confess myself curious to examine it. Natheless, the holding was better than I have seen. But to your places, gentlemen. It waxeth toward evening, and we must finish. Announcer, call the list for the peg shot."

Fortunately for our belief in this chronicle, records, both ancient and modern, are here to sustain us. Otherwise we could not be blamed for dismissing the whole story with a shrug. So convinced—and justly so—have we become of the superiority of our modern high-velocity rifles, that we have ended by unduly depreciating the old-fashioned arms, but especially the flintlocks dealt with in this our tale. Our impression of them is that they were slow to load, clumsy to handle, dilatory in fire, and of only approximate accuracy. Or if we admit accuracy at all, it is only within the limits of a very short *squirrel range*. As a matter of fact, we are in general, very skeptical of even that much, suffering, I suppose, from a reaction against Fenimore Cooper's impossible absurdities.

But in sober earnest, these impressions are libels upon an excellent weapon, and many of them, as accusations against its efficiency, must fall to the ground. That the old long rifles were not clumsy, a moment's handling will convince any experienced rifleman, if he can get hold of a good specimen. That the flintlock, when properly constructed, in good condition, and with the best flint suitably edged and sharpened, is, so far as the marksman can tell, as fast as a percussion lock is surprising but true.

With regard to the interval between the flash pan and the explosion, writes Captain Dillin, *actual tests under the most exacting conditions have proved that it is so trifling as to be negligible, that there is no time to flinch and therefore no bad deliveries.* He describes then the proper loading and priming and goes on. *Hangfires and misfires are* unknown *under these conditions and having had a wide experience with both flintlock and percussion, the author hesitates to give the claim of superiority to the latter system. And fortunately for our curiosity as respects the remaining point—accuracy—we need here depend on no mere legends. In ancient bullet pouches have been found many targets, tucked away there by their owners, probably after a successful shooting match. And in our own times a few perfect specimens of these old rifles have been tested by our modern experts. I have seen a few of the former, and the results of a number of the latter tests are before me as I write. At one hundred yards from the muzzle, and of course, from a dead rest, three successive shots were so closely grouped that a five-cent piece was large enough to touch all three, three more from the same rifle named*—Old Killdeer, *by the way—repeated this, and two other groups of three each could be covered by a silver half-dollar and a dollar respectively. Another arm of similar type made five straight bull's-eyes at the same range, placed six bullets in succession inside a dollar at fifty yards, and of five bullets at twenty-five yards, four cut into the same hole and the fifth was but three-sixteenths of an inch outside.* Captain Dillin quotes from an assistant to one of the old rifle makers, who said, "No gun ever suited him unless it was capable of driving a tack three times out of five at fifty yards."

While one hundred yards might be adopted arbitrarily as about the limit of this delicate accuracy, that by no means marked the effective limit of the gun, especially in war. Old Killdeer, *at two hundred yards, placed five balls which could be included in a rectangle five by seven and a half inches, which is a good grouping for any modern arm, except such precisionists as the high-velocity type. Careful tests at the standard silhouette man target gave ten straight hits at two hundred, and five out of ten at three hundred.* "And," reports the man who made the tests, "the penetration from any of these rifles at three hundred yards, and even beyond that distance, was sufficient to kill, or put out of action, anyone hit."

So we see that the commanding advantage of such weapons as the modern Springfield, as practical arms within the limits desired by the old-timers, lies largely in their speed, and that we cannot dismiss as apocryphal the tales of accuracy that have come down to us from old times.

The squire's command to proceed with the next stage of the Great Match was delayed in obedience to a storm of vigorous protest on the part of Detrick, backed by his fellow craftsmen, who demanded that this newfangled contraption be excluded from competition. The basis of the protest seemed to be a vague *unfairness*. But the squire, grinning in relish over the situation, brushed this aside.

"Nay, my masters," he observed, with fundamental common sense, "I see naught of unfairness here. This is a contest of rifles, and while this new piece of Master Farrell's is of unusual appearance, and most certainly of unusual performance—and I confess myself curious to examine it further—it is most indubitably a rifle. Continue."

In the course of the subsequent proceedings the crowd fell from its vociferous excitement to a low buzz of attention that, strangely enough, seemed to have in its elements a strong compound of something curiously like awe. Or perhaps not so strangely. Possibly, they felt across the occasion the shadow of greatness, realizing dimly in the instinctive parts of themselves that they assisted at one of those significant events that turn the currents of history. As why not? For in the chronicles of their country, the patched ball and the grooved barrel were to play a great part, and the sharp crack of the American rifle was destined to call them into far places.

The matches that succeeded were in no true sense contests, and need not here be described in what would prove wearisome detail. In the peg match, each man fired five shots at seventy-five yards. Pegs were inserted in the bullet holes, and around the outside, a string was stretched. He who had the shortest string was pronounced the winner. Of the others, the man Dall turned in one of nine and five-eighths inches, which was commented upon as close to a record, but Don's measured but a scant five, and one shot a trifle out. And even in the loading contest, which was a matter of speed and personal dexterity, the patched ball so advantaged Farrell's arm that Don reported ready in the astounding time of twenty seconds, which far outdid his nearest competitor.

It was a clean sweep, and nobody awaited the squire's formal announcement of the winner. The instant the Match had closed, the crowd swarmed about Farrell, eager to examine the new weapon, to hear the principles of its miraculous precision. The marksman, Dall, was the first to get his hands upon it, turning it over and over, his shrewd expert's eye noting its features, his ear cocked to Farrell's explanations.

"You must e'en make me one of these, Master Farrell," said he at the last. "I bespeak one now."

"And I!" "And I!" interposed several others.

It was the little gunmaker's great moment. He was the center of all attention, speaking his piece over and over again to changing audiences who listened to him with the keen and intelligent attention that men would now bestow on the impossible him who might suddenly bring forth a club that could never fail of a three-hundred-yard drive. Detrick and his fellow artisans stood apart in a disgruntlement that tried unsuccessfully for an air of disdain. Don, also apart, received likewise his share, though lesser, of the attention. Men's eagerest interest centered for the moment—and practically so—more on the possibilities of the new weapon for themselves than on the feats they had witnessed. A few praised his marksmanship, but most pressed him for his impressions of the rifle, its trigger pull, its sights, its powder charge and the weight of the ball, and the secrets of its loading. The young man replied as best he could, but always in modest repudiation of his own part.

"Nay, sirs," he insisted, "ye must award the day to Master Farrell, not to me. For these others be noted marksmen, as you well know, and with this same rifle, any one of them, or indeed any other man who is skilled to hold a piece, could have done as well, or better."

But at last, the concourse began to thin. The sun was low, and the air was cooling. Long flights of crows crossed the redness of the skies. Negroes and other servants were collecting together the various gear that had been used for different purposes and were piling it in a wagon. Lines of men streamed across the fields toward the tavern's cheer. Here and there in the village shone lights in windows.

Farrell, freed at last, joined his guest, and the two turned toward home. The little gunmaker was still so excited that he fairly babbled. The young man strode silently at his side, listening.

"Did ye note their glum faces, lad!" cried Farrell. "And did ye see how their own very champions left them apart to come to me! And did you remark how each of them jumped to possess one of my rifles? Nay, and gave order for them on the spot! I must hasten to write down their names, so that I shall not disappoint them! And"—the old man chuckled triumphantly—"the matter that warms my heart the most is that now, will they, nill they, these stiff-necked obstinate fools must themselves make arms of my pattern—unless they would sell only to farmers and the like! That will grind their haughty souls. For, lad, you shall see, all the world shall now use the long-grooved barrel and the patched ball, for the old style is past and gone, and ye shall soon see them only on the walls to be viewed by the curious, as one looks upon the arquebuses of ancient days!"

Which was, in the main, an excellent bit of soothsaying, though Master Farrell overlooked the asinine conservatism of government officialdom, or his prophetic eye would have seen the troops of otherwise progressive nations banging away with smooth-bore slugs a hundred years after.

But soon, he turned his paean of exultation.

"And you, lad!" he cried. "You were magnificent! Never have I seen any man who held so, and I have seen many of the best. You beat all records, as well I know, for I know them all."

"Nay, suh," repeated Don. "Any man who could hold a bar'l could have done the like. If so happed I beat records, as you say, it was because never on range before was fired a bar'l that shot so true."

"That is so. Natheless I do maintain, and always shall, that none could have done as well. Some might have done its equal from a rest, but none in my knowledge could have done so offhand."

The youth flushed with a pleasure he could not conceal.

"I am obleeged to you fo' your good opinion, suh," said he steadily. "And I am rejoiced if you deem I have been of service to you."

"Richly do you deserve the prize!" cried Farrell.

"Anon?" queried Don.

"The prize, lad," repeated the gunmaker. "Did you not realize it is yours?"

"Nay, suh. I but stood in your stead."

"Mine is the gold medal of the craft. Nay, do not protest. It goes to you according to established rule."

The young man stopped in his tracks.

"And what, suh," he inquired with quiet humor, "should I do with a *great fat ox*? Drive it afore me on my journey?"

Farrell laughed appreciatively.

"I doubt not the matter may be compounded for a sum," said he. "I will charge myself with that. And I shall insist you take the further sum I would have paid John Gladden. That is but just."

"Why, suh," said Don, "I will not gainsay you, but this is a welcome surprise, for the thought had not occurred to me, and I admit my purse is but slender."

"It is naught, naught!" cried Farrell. "And were it thrice as much I should still be in your debt, for were it not for this happy chance I would even yet be suffering scorn, and now I shall prosper greatly, for all men will desire a rifle of Farrell's make, and—"

He, in his turn, stopped short in the illumination of a sudden idea. He thrust the rifle, which he had been carrying, into the young man's hands.

"This is yours!" said he.

"Mine?" repeated Don, incredulously.

"Who's the better, right? Nay, protest not, I shall not listen."

A slow flush overspread the youth's face, then drained away, leaving it almost pale.

"Gainsay me not!" commanded the gunmaker peremptorily. "I shall make scores, nay hundreds more, and all because of you."

"I cannot refuse you, suh," replied the young man in a low voice, "for I will confess that ever since I first pulled trigger at the shooting, my heart has been eaten with the desire for one such. But I know not how to tell you—"

"No need, lad, no need!" Farrell interrupted, his face glowing with pleasure. "And with it shall go molds for balls, and a horn thin as paper and—"

"Nay, suh, you overwhelm me!" expostulated Don. His head was up, and his eyes were far away. "I shall try to do it honor, suh," said he slowly, "and I can see it is to stand me in good stead, for I shall take it with me over the mountains to the west, where even now I am preparing to go."

"Over the mountains?"

"Into the land known as Kentucky, suh, where, save for John Finley, no man has trod."

"And the work of my hands shall be carried into new and strange lands!" exulted the gunmaker. "And what could better befall, for itself is new and strange! And so shall I share in a great undertaking! And," he cried, inspired, "so shall we name it, so that men forever shall speak of the Kentucky Rifle!" He reached his hand and took the weapon from the young man's grasp. "See, right here, I shall set it down, in fair engraved letters, your name and mine together. That I shall do before you depart. But I know you only as Don. What is your surname?"

The young man looked a little embarrassed.

"No, suh, my name is not Don," he confessed. "You misheard me, and I did not trouble to set you right."

"Not Don? What is it then?" rejoined the other.

"Dan, suh," said the young man. "Dan'l Boone."

Part One
The Long Rifle

Chapter 1
The Grandmother

On a rock by a roadside sat Andrew Burnett. The season was early spring, a time when the snow water is but just draining away, the red-winged blackbirds are newly arrived in melody, and the wide-washed sky is ahum with the vigor of fresh joy in the world. Nevertheless the lad's expression was somber, his eyes smoldered with a sullen resentment well emphasized by his straight black eyebrows that almost met over the bridge of his nose. He was thinking what a hard time he was having in life, and how downtrodden he was, and what—in the somewhat hazy future—he was going to do about it. This was not an unusual state of mind for his age, which was nineteen.

He was entirely absorbed. He did not hear the liquid-voiced blackbirds and meadowlarks. He did not see the red squirrel that chirked and jerked toward him along the rails of the zigzag *snake* fence. He was even wholly unaware of a horseman galloping recklessly through the puddles, until a shower of mud brought him to his feet. He flared into furious resentment, unreasonable, for it was self-evident the horseman was innocent of intention, but natural as the leap of his discontent toward an outlet.

"Look what you're doing, you dirty whelp!" he shouted.

The horse was thrown on its haunches, then turned, walked slowly back, and was brought to a stand. The rider leaned forward in his saddle.

"What did you say?" he challenged softly.

His appearance further inflamed the other's anger. His clothing was of fine quality and in the height of prevailing fashion, his mount was self-evidently an animal of blood, the very expression of his finely featured, faintly disdainful face, the lift of his long, white hands raised the bristles on the country boy's contempt for the city macaroni. The fact that the stranger was also a lad, apparently not far from his own age, helped not at all.

Andrew repeated his sentiment.

"You tom fool, how could I see you, sitting there like a bump on a log!" retorted the horseman.

This was not unreasonable, but Andrew was in no mood for reason. He expanded his original idea. The city boy leaped nimbly from his horse. They fought wholeheartedly. Andrew was obviously the stronger, but the stranger's quickness and certainty of movement equalized matters. They inflicted some damage on one another, thrashing about considerably, and finally locked and went to earth. The horse trotted away, his reins dangling. The combatants struggled a moment or so without perceptible advantage to either, rolled down the low bank, and plumped into a puddle. The icy shock of the water tore them apart. They arose dripping. Andrew, his dogged, slow spirit catching its fuel fully, was in a dash to resume. But the other was laughing.

"We're a sweet pair!" he cried. "Now, why in tarnation were we both so cross? I'm not usually a crotchety person. Are you?"

Andrew stopped, his mouth falling open. This was too abrupt for one of his dispositions.

"Or *are* you?" inquired the other. "I don't believe it. 'Tain't reasonable. I didn't see you, you know. And why should I go off at half cock? That ain't reasonable either. Of course you were startled. Don't blame you."

"I take back the *dirty whelp*," conceded Andrew gruffly.

"Never mind about the *dirty*," amended the other. He glanced down humorously at his dripping finery, "And I take back—"

"Never mind the *tom fool*," interposed Andrew. "Reckon we're a pair of them."

"So that's all right. My name is Russell Braidwood. I live in Philadelphia."

"Mine is Andy Burnett. I live at the farm yonder, up the lane."

"Well, what made you so cross?" inquired Russell.

"I'm sick of the farm," replied Andy, falling somber again.

"The same with me."

"What?"

"I'm sick of Philadelphia."

They sat together on the rock. The warm spring sun steamed from their drenched garments. Overfield, the blackbirds and the meadowlarks distilled its brightness into song. A first bobolink overflowed its rapture. Drop after rapid drop, small water tinklings drained away the last of winter from the world. The red squirrel curved the sweep of his tail over his back and clasped his little hands to his head in an ecstatic worship of the fresh flood of life in the springtime. Of these things, the two lads, absorbed in one another, had no consciousness, but now, in the new expansiveness of feeling, they flooded in.

Why was Andy sick of the farm? Well, there was his stepfather, who was harsh and stern in religion, rigid in discipline, and strong for the duty youth owed to those who had brought it into the world.

"Only he did not bring me into the world," interpolated Andy.

"Your mother?" asked Russell.

"My mother is dead," replied Andy briefly.

But that might be borne, and the hard, iron, grinding, endless work, and the lack of all amusement so necessary to youth. It was the future, the dull gray appalling future. The same thing over and over. And for what? A living hardly wrung. And at the end of life, the acres still demanding, still grudging, and the bent, back of age, and possibly resignation. Like iron walls pressing in closer and closer.

Why not break away from it?

"There's my grandmother. You do not know my grandmother. I can't desert her. And anyway, I'm not of age. He wouldn't let me go. I'm too valuable to him," said Andy bitterly. "The only reason I'm here now is because he's gone to town for the day. You don't know him, either."

It was all very black. To youth, two years until the coming of age was forever. To youth, the inevitable passing away of age does not occur.

But Russell? How could he be sick of Philadelphia? A great city—leisure, amusement, money in his pocket, fine clothes, a horse to ride, position, family, and the silver spoon in the mouth? This was difficult to understand.

Russell's bright face darkened. He brushed these things aside. How did they count when one is in prison? In prison to position. Doing the same things over and over. One sickens of them, no matter how they glitter. In prison all one's life, sitting inside a cage while the world flashes by outside.

"They are set on my going into the Business, won't hear of anything else!" he cried bitterly, "Great-grandfather started the bank, and the family have carried it on ever since. Sitting in an office at a desk. Just the same as being locked in by a jailer. God, I hate it! Next year, that's when my term begins!"

"Why don't you just break away?" Andy repeated the question that had been asked himself.

"I can't. There's the family. You don't know the family."

They contemplated their hopelessness, and the world deepened to deep gloom in which the blackbirds, and the meadowlarks, and the single bobolink, and the sunshine and the little water tinklings were not. As for the red squirrel, he had gone away.

"Hullo," cried Russell, making a belated discovery. "My horse is gone!"

"Oh, that's all right," Andy reassured him. "This is our lane to the barn. We'll find him at the gates. Come on up to the house and we'll catch him."

They trudged to the end of the lane, found the horse against the gates, and led him through.

"You must come in to see my grandmother," urged Andy.

"I can't, I'm too filthy," objected Russell, then, seeing some urgency on the part of his new friend, he agreed. "All right. If she can stand it, I can."

They left the horse tied to a rail. The farmhouse was of the prosperous order, square, unornamented, relieved from being a box by six white columns that upheld a veranda roof above the second story. Its paint was old, but the structure was in repair. About it were remnants of what must have been a cherished garden, but these remnants were well attended. The picket fence was upright and intact. Before the front door stood two great locust trees. Behind the back door was an apple orchard and the long-armed sweep of a well. Russell's vivid imagination, darting in the speculation it loved, brought him its findings efficiency—tidy, careful efficiency—no thought of the ornamentation of life, only in the garden an awkward fumbling effort to preserve the memory, as it were, of a beauty whose full body had followed its vanished creator. He stopped appreciatively at a lilac bush, touching with a sensitive finger its new buds.

"I like the soft feel," he explained.

"It used to be a nice garden—when my mother was alive," said Andy. "Most of the flowers are gone now. I work on it a little when I get time, but I can't do much. Grandmother likes it."

Russell raised his eyes and became aware of a little old lady in a rocking chair behind a front window. He swept his hat from his head in the approved flourish of the period. A moment later, he stood before her, bowing again, and conscious of an amused scrutiny under which, in spite of himself, he felt his color rising. Though possessed of charmingly open qualities, and though nothing of a snob, Russell was nevertheless an aristocrat both by breeding and by the training of his day, which emphasized social differences even more strongly than is at present the case. That he should not find himself perfectly at ease in superiority before any old countrywoman was, in the harmless arrogance of his young conception, beyond his thought.

She was a little old lady, sitting in a Boston rocker. She wore a cap, very neat, and a voluminous black dress of heavy silk, and cobwebby half mitts of silk lace, and a pair of black satin soft shoes side by side on a hassock. Her only ornament was a cameo broach at her throat. Her lap held knitting. On the floor at her side lay an ebony cane topped with ivory. The Boston rocker was uncushioned, and in it, she sat uncompromisingly upright as one who sits in state, though not with rigidity but rather with the repose of energy. As Russell, raising his head from his bow of introduction, looked upon her thin, wax-like veined hands, and the sad lines of past care in her tiny face, he thought to himself that he had never seen anyone so old, and a certain choke of pathos gripped his throat. As he met the snap and twinkle of her eyes, he thought he had never met anyone so unquenchably and agelessly young, so that pity became an affront, and any thought of pathos an impertinence. And as Russell, though sensitive to impression, was as yet too young for analysis, he ended by standing before her at ill-ease, like an awkward schoolboy, conscious and ashamed of his muddied garments and his general dishevelment.

But his ill-case soon melted. Neither by look nor manner, save for a momentary deep twinkle in her eyes, did the old lady seem aware of the strange disarray of the two. The twinkle was amused, but it vanished unseen. To his astonishment, when he paused to think of it, Russell shortly found himself seated at her elbow chatting eagerly and easily, as to an equal not only in convention but in years, laughing delightedly over her quick, pithy comments, sometimes caustic in content, but welling from the relish of a deep quiet humor that mellowed them to a shared understanding that had no sting. Russell was of the vivacious and romantic disposition that expands under warmth. The old lady, tapping her Boston rocker into brisk motion, listened and questioned, and Russell glowed and chattered and had a wonderful youthful time telling about himself, secure in the comfort of some deep inner instinct that assured him that he would not later come to, as was so often the case, to look upon himself in reaction as a talkative fool.

As he talked, he looked about him at the furnishings of the old room, and his eye fell upon a weapon on pegs over the fireplace. He checked what he was saying.

"What a beautiful piece!" he cried. "May I look at it? I love guns. All kinds of guns. They are a sort of passion with me."

"Bring it here, Andy," commanded the grandmother.

Russell handled the weapon reverently.

"Do you mind?" he begged and put it to his face in the attitude of aim.

"I see you are a marksman also," observed the old lady. "You and Andy should match skill."

"I should love to try it—the rifle, I mean. It is in beautiful condition. But it is very old, isn't it?"

"I'll back it against anything newer," interposed Andy gruffly.

Russell turned the weapon over, examining its details. He looked up suddenly, a slight awe in his eyes.

"This inscription," he stammered. "Is it—was it really?"

"Colonel Boone's rifle? Yes," the old lady answered. "He gave it to my husband just before he left Kentucky for the West."

"Did you know Daniel Boone, ma'am?"

"Certainly." She paused, then went on in response to Russell's unspoken pleading. "You see, as a girl, I rode over the Wilderness Road into Kentucky to join Colonel Boone's enterprise. I lived at Boonesborough until my husband died."

"Were you at the great fight at Boonesborough?" inquired Russell breathlessly.

The old lady let her knitting fall in her lap. She leaned against the back of her chair, and her eyes softened in reminiscence.

"Yes, though I saw little of it. We women were busy within, cooking, carrying water to the men, molding bullets, tending the wounded."

Under urging, she told more. Nine days of bitter siege, the garrison so small that it must stand to arms day and night, the men gaunt and haggard from the strain, showers of burning arrows, fire, no water to spare, the roof swept by a hail of bullets.

"The British had supplied them with ammunition," said she. "The men said they picked up a hundred and twenty-five pounds of flattened bullets after the siege, and that takes no count of those embedded in the logs."

The fort seemed doomed. Then, a young man sprang to the roof and worked fully exposed to extinguish the fire.

"The Lord sustained us," observed the old lady piously. "For in all that hail of bullets, he was not touched."

Shortly after this it became necessary for the women to take their places at the portholes to relieve the men for a brief rest. The limit of human endurance had been reached.

"So I fired with the rest. I cannot believe I did much damage, but I made a noise." She chuckled. "But it gave me opportunity to see Colonel Boone perform a noteworthy feat. One of the savages had a very good rifle, and he had climbed a high tree in which he was completely protected and from which he could overlook the compound within the fort. He hit one or two of our people before we suspected where he was, but especially he was killing our cattle, which were huddled in the center. When his position had been located, Colonel Boone, himself ascended into the tower. After a little, the man in the tree, preparing for another shot, showed just the top of his head. Colonel Boone fired instantly and killed him. It was a very long distance away."

"Was he—did he use this rifle?"

"Yes, that was his favorite rifle always, though he had several."

Russel gazed down at the weapon with awe.

"What is this other name—Farrell?" he inquired.

"He made the piece, I believe, though I am not certain. The Colonel was always particularly fond of it. He had some association with it, though I do not know what it was. That is why Mr. Burnett always took such pride in the fact that it was a gift to him, for at that time he did not know Colonel Boone so well as later."

"How did it happen?" urged Russell.

"Mr. Burnett was of the greatest assistance—so Colonel Boone always maintained—at the time Jemima Boone and three other girls were carried off by the savages," said the old lady, a trifle primly, as one reluctant to boast. But Russell, aflame with excitement, would have no reticence. He learned how the four girls had been seized suddenly and spirited away, how their absence was not discovered for some hours, how the settlement was aroused to pursuit. Most of the men, under Mr. Calloway, cut across country on horseback in the probable direction of flight. Boone, with eight picked men, took the difficult job of following directly, on foot. For thirty miles they puzzled out a trail blinded by every device of savage ingenuity, furthermore, they managed to do so rapidly enough to move faster than the Indians had done in their flight. At last the marauders, considering they had got clear away, abandoned attempts at concealment and took the direct course.

"Colonel Boone had himself been captive of the savages," explained Mrs. Burnett, "so he knew their devices."

He struck boldly across country and cut the trail again in ten miles. Shortly after, they caught sight of the Indians making camp.

"Mr. Burnett has often told me that now came the moments of greatest danger for the girls," said the old lady, "for it was certain that the first act of the savages, on being surprised, would be to murder them. Colonel Boone picked out four men. One of them was Mr. Burnett. He was always very proud of this, for he was very young. They crept up. They knew that the least false move, a snapped bit of wood, even the rustle of a leaf would be the signal for the crash of tomahawks on the four girls' skulls."

At last, Boone gave a signal. The four men fired and rushed forward instantly. The remainder of the party bounded down the hill, yelling as loudly as they could. The savages nearest the girls, who were huddled together *tattered, torn and despairing* at the foot of the tree, were killed at first fire. The others were, for a brief but sufficient instant, paralyzed by surprise. All but one. He leaped across the fire, his tomahawk upraised over the head of Jemima Boone. But before it could descend, its wielder collapsed, a knife in his throat.

"Mr. Burnett was always very skillful at throwing a knife," stated the old lady. "But Colonel Boone considered he had saved Jemima's life, as, indeed, he had, and a little later, when Mr. Burnett and I were married, the Colonel gave Mr. Burnett this rifle."

"I think this is the most wonderful thing I have ever heard!" cried Russell.

"Ours was the second wedding to take place in Kentucky. The first was of Sam Henderson and Betty Calloway, and within the year, Frances Calloway married John Holden, and Jemima Boone married Flanders Calloway. Sam, John, and Flanders were the other three men, besides Colonel Boone and Mr. Burnett, in the rescue party, and Betty and Frances were the other two girls captured along with Jemima."

She stopped with an air of finality.

"You didn't tell Russell who the fourth girl was, Grandmother," said Andy with a mischievous grin.

A faint color crept into the old lady's cheeks.

"You know perfectly well who it was, you rapscallion!" she replied sharply.

Russell stared up at her breathlessly in dawning comprehension.

"Not another word out of you!" the grandmother checked his eager questions. "It is too fine a day to sit within, listening to an old woman's chatter. I am tired. Take him away, Andy. Get along, both of you. Try your skill at the rifle. Show him how your grandfather taught you the knife should be thrown. Off with you, now!"

She would have no more of them, and fairly bundled them out of the room with the dynamics of her energy, though physically, she did not stir from her chair. Only at the door, she stopped them with a word.

"I like your young man, Andrew," she observed. "Tell him to come see me again. I have often heard Colonel Boone say that there is naught like a good, honest fight to begin friendship." She smiled faintly at their confusion and deliberately closed her eyes. They hesitated a moment and stole out.

On the veranda, Russell faced his new friend with glowing eyes.

"I think she is wonderful!" he cried.

Andy nodded slowly.

"You see what I meant," said he. His face had darkened again, and he had fallen once more into his somber mood. "Well, come on," he aroused himself.

He led the way around the house and through the orchard to the pasture on the other side.

"Here's where I shoot, generally," he observed. "He doesn't like me to. Says it's a waste of time and money. I guess it is, but I like it. It's the only thing I can do that I do like. He'd stop it if he could. But grandmother won't let him. She gives me the powder and ball, too. She doesn't often get her back up about things, but when she does, she has her own way. He tries to take it out of me in other ways. Oh, well!"

He leaned the rifle against the fence and laid beside it a heavily laden belt, which also he had taken from the pegs on the wall.

Russell picked it up to examine it and its attachments.

"That was Grandfather's, too," explained Andy. "That was his shot pouch and powder horn. And this was his knife and his tomahawk." He took the hatchet from its sheath. "Come on, it's getting late. *He* will be back from town."

The pasture was still scattered with stumps of the old forest. On one of these, Andy, with the tomahawk, clipped a white blaze as a mark.

They shot, and turned about. Andy proved to possess almost a nail-driving accuracy. Russell was at first boyishly chagrined over being outdone at a sport in which he rather fancied himself. But the chagrin was soon lost in a generous admiration.

"Oh, I've had a lot of practice." Andy brushed aside his praises. "And I'm used to the gun."

"I'm more used to percussion locks," admitted Russell gratefully. "I always thought flintlocks couldn't be accurate, but you've shown me differently."

"Snap-haunces, Grandmother calls them."

"Well, this one certainly can shoot. And you certainly can shoot it!"

"So could you, if you got used to it."

"How about the knife throwing?"

"I'm not very good at that. But I know how it ought to be done."

He slipped the knife from its sheath, poised it in the flat of his hand, cast it with a long round sweep of the arm. The weapon turned once in its flight and stuck quivering in a near-by stump.

Russell tried to imitate the cast. The knife hit flatwise and bounded back. Two more trials were equally unsuccessful, one of them landing butt first, the other glancing off at an angle, carrying a sliver with it.

"Show me again," he urged.

Andrew repeated his feat several times to Russell's admiration.

"That's not very good," the country boy disclaimed the praise. "I ought to hit a pie plate every time at that distance."

"Well, I'd hate to have you throw it at me!"

"It's sort of fun. But what's the good?"

"It's sport. I'm going to get a knife and practice."

Andy unbent to explanation.

"I don't know as you can get one—a proper one," said he. "You see, these old woodsmen made their own knives. To throw right, they've got to have just the right balance, and a man's got to know the balance. You've got to know just how many times she is going to turn over. This one, with a full-arm throw, turns over twice in twenty feet. You've got to guess your distance and then give her a full-arm, or a half-arm, or whatever it is, so as to get her to land point first. Some men liked to have their knives turn every ten feet, others every eight or twelve, and they built them to do that."

"Why, all that is extraordinarily interesting," cried Russell. "I never heard of that before."

"My grandfather taught me." Andy's face softened. "He was a wonderful man, as wonderful as Grandmother. After Boone left Kentucky, he came here. But he never liked it, I think. Always he used to tell me that when I grew big enough he and I and Grandmother would go out there. Then, word came that Boone had died. He used to sit on the veranda and look over there." Andy waved his hand toward the reddening west. "He was very old. Oh, well!"

He gathered the equipment.

"I've got to see to the cows," he said shortly. "*He'll* be back soon. I'll catch it."

He had receded to a mood into which Russell could not follow. To Russell's lively comments on the afternoon's experience he returned short and distant answers. They returned to where the saddle horse stood hitched to the rail.

"I'll come again. May I?" begged the city boy, preparing to mount. "We'll have another shooting match. Perhaps I'll do better."

"I don't expect I'll have much time, what with the spring plowing." Then, rousing himself to a sense of his apparent ungraciousness, he said, "Of course I want to see you, Russell. But unless *he* goes to town, I'm at work from dawn to dark."

"Well, I'll try it anyway," returned the latter cheerfully. "And you take a day off sometime and come to see me in town. Promise!"

"I'd like to. I will if I can," promised Andy, but without an answering smile.

"Well, goodbye." Russell touched his horse with his heels. At the bend of the lane, he turned to wave a hand. But Andy was standing, a dark figure against the sunset, gazing into the west.

———

Days passed, but the friendship so auspiciously begun seemed to have stopped at that beginning. Andrew, as he had anticipated, never found the leisure to go to the city. The season was one of hard, close work on the farm and Birkholm, Andrew's stepfather, had no intention of hiring an ounce more than the necessary labor. But Russell did not repeat his visit, and the country boy, in consequence, nursed a dull ache of disappointment, which he carefully concealed. He had counted on it more than he would have acknowledged.

Thus, for close on two weeks. Then, late of an afternoon, the beautiful saddle horse came up the road, flew like a bird in a breath-taking leap over the fence, and with scarcely diminished speed, clumped through the fresh-plowed land to where Andrew was scattering the seed. Russell was breathless, and the words tumbled from him in excitement.

"I've won out!" he cried jubilantly. "Had the very devil of a row. They came near to cutting me off with a shilling once or twice, and I'd certainly have been on bread and water, if I'd been a little younger. Lord, what a rumpus! You'd think I'd stolen the mint. I'd have come out before, but I had to finish it. And now it's done. But I've got to leave this very night, for I'm to go out with Choteau, and he cannot delay—"

He broke off in a laugh at Andy's look of bewilderment.

"I'm not talking very clearly, am I? What I'm trying to say is that I have had a most fearful fight with the family, but I have won, and I don't have to go into the Business. It wasn't pleasant, I assure you. But we've finally compromised. Choteau happened to be here on some business with the firm, and it is agreed I go clerk with him for a year. So we start tomorrow. But I couldn't go without seeing you and telling you. Not after the other day. I wish you were going. Look here, why not? I'm sure I can fix it."

He leaned forward in the saddle, his mobile face aglow. The horse arched its neck against the bit, and blew softly through its nostrils, and pawed at the soft and yielding earth. Andrew, from his lower elevation, thought he had never seen a more vital and romantic a figure. But his feeling was, confusedly, rather of a bird poised gloriously for flight than of a boy on a horse. And a wave of desolation darkened him, for it seemed to him that the momentary gleam of a brightness in his life was being extinguished into darkness. Nevertheless, at the same instant, he steadied to acceptance, for that was an essence of his steadfast nature.

"Come on!" urged Russell, afire with the idea.

Andy shook his head.

"I'd like nothing better than to be with you—anywhere. Anywhere but here. But I can't. I'm not of age."

"Nonsense." Russell brushed this aside impatiently, then in reluctant recollection of the rigid laws of the time. "Anyway, nobody will know where you are."

"I've no money."

"I have plenty."

"There's Grandmother."

Russell was silenced for a moment by this. Before he could gather his wits, another voice broke in on them.

"Who are you?" it demanded roughly.

Both boys turned to face the speaker. John Birkholm stood surveying them. He carried his ox goad, and his harsh, fanatical face was dark with anger.

"What do you here, you bedizened popinjay, trespassing in my fields? Have you no sense in your head that you ride a horse on fresh-sowed lands?"

Russell flushed deeply and looked back at the soft earth gouged deep by the upfling of his mount's swift gallop, at the wide trampling of its pawing hoofs.

"I am sorry, sir. I did not think—"

But the older man would have none of it. He advanced a step.

"And what mean you holding my son in vain talk?" he demanded further, but still with repression. "Think you in your pampered idleness that there is no work to be done?"

Russell's head was up. He stared coolly at the angry man.

"I told you I am sorry, sir, for what damage I have done. If you will name it, I will make it good. As to the other, I but paused to say farewell to my friend."

"I heard ye," replied Birkholm grimly, "uttering the counsels of hell. 'Honor thy father and thy mother!'" His rage burst through its fragile governance. "Now get off my land!" he cried. "I'll hear no words from ye! Go the way you came, and do not show your face here again!"

Then, as Russell hesitated, half in bewilderment, half in affront, he brought the heavy ox goad with a sounding crack across the horse's rump.

The animal reared and leaped violently sideways, all but unsaddling its rider. By a desperate effort of magnificent horsemanship, Russell retained his seat, and by another, he prevented the plunging beast from bolting. His face was contorted. For an instant he seemed on the point of launching his mount in an attempt to ride the man down. The latter grasped the ox goad in both hands. For a moment, the two faced one another. Then Russell's expression changed to one of disdainful mockery. He bent low in his saddle and swept his hat from his head.

"I thank you, sir, for your most courteous entertainment," he said suavely.

With a turn of the wrist he whirled the horse in its tracks and gave it its head. Across the field they raced, the clods flying, over the fence they flew, and so away up the lane out of sight.

"You devil's whelp!" Birkholm shouted after him. "If I see you again, I'll have the law on you!"

For several seconds, he stared after the retreating figure, then turned savagely on Andrew.

"Now get back to work, you!" he began, and stopped.

Andy, his face white and set, his hands clenched at his side, was staring at him steadily. For near a full half-minute, he stood thus. Then, very deliberately, he undid from his shoulders the apron sack that contained the seed grain, and very deliberately and carefully, he laid it on the ground. Without a word, he turned away.

"What are you doing? Pick that up. Get on with your work!" commanded Birkholm.

Andy paid him no attention.

"Disobey me, will you!" roared the older man, beside himself. He raised the ox goad once more and brought its lash across the youth's shoulders. The latter spun around. From beneath the straight black line of his brows, his eyes blazed. After a moment, he again turned away. Birkholm watched him uncertainly, fingered the ox goad in nerveless hands, and at length, shrugged his shoulders, picked up the seed sack, and began to strap it on himself.

"I'll tend to you later, young man," he promised himself, but uneasily.

Andy went direct to the living room of the farmhouse, took down from its pegs the old Kentucky rifle, and went out. His grandmother was sitting, as usual, in her Boston rocker, but he did not look in her direction. Once outside, he loaded the weapon. Never had he done so more deliberately and carefully, filling exactly with the glittering French powder the conical measure that hung below the powder horn, centering precisely the linen patch beneath the ball, driving without undue pressure the missile delicately home, shaking with untrembling hand the fine grains of the priming powder into the pan. Then he closed down the frizzen and walked around the house, through the orchard to the edge of the field, where he disposed himself with deadly deliberation behind the fence, thrusting the muzzle of the rifle through the rails.

Birkholm had taken over the seeding. He was now at midfield. His shirt was open at the throat, caught by a button halfway down his chest. The front sight of the rifle came to rest on the point of the V thus formed, settled slowly into the notch of the rear sight. Andrew pressed the trigger. He was entirely cool, and wholly single-minded, without qualm or doubt. It was as though all the currents of life ran in the channel of this one inevitable action.

The rifle missed fire.

Contrary to what might be supposed by one unfamiliar with old-fashioned arms, this was a very unusual occurrence, if the weapon was well found with sharp flints and proper powder. It had never before happened to Andrew. The click of so sharp a break in a usual sequence seemed to shock him awake. He passed his hand across his eyes and stared at the rifle, at the slowly nearing figure of his stepfather. He shuddered, arose, and returned swiftly to the house.

His entrance to the front room encountered his grandmother's piercing black eyes upon him.

"Andrew, come here," she commanded. For a moment, she compelled his gaze with hers. "I heard no shot," then said she. He made no reply. "What happened?" she insisted.

"Miss fire," he muttered.

"How can that be?" she cried sharply, as though someone dear to her had been unjustly accused. "In distraction, you did not prime!" She seized the piece from his hand and raised the frizzen from the pan in examination. With astonishing strength in one apparently so frail, she flung the long weapon to the position of aim through the open window and pulled the trigger. The rifle roared in reverberation from the walls, and the powder smoke thickened the air of the room. For a moment, she sat tense and upright, then dropped the piece across her lap.

"It was the will of the Lord," then said she softly, and relaxed to her chair back with a sigh.

In the fields Birkholm raised his head at the sound of the shot.

"At it again!" he muttered vindictively, in his usual upsurge of resentment against the silly waste of time and money. He told himself that this time he would put his foot down once and for all, and he flung the seed viciously against the placid bosom of the earth.

Andrew stared at her incredulously.

"You knew," he stated dully. She gazed back at him unflinchingly, her eyes bright. "Why did you not stop me? I was as one bemused."

"It was in the hands of the Lord," she repeated piously, "as are all the great moments of life."

"You would have me kill a man!" he cried, arousing to a belated horror of what he might have done.

"Why not," returned the old woman stoutly, "if so, be it the time has come?"

"You would have me a murderer and say no word to stay me!"

"I know you, Andrew, through and through. I knew your father, and his father before him. They moved alone through the destinies appointed for them. That destiny is yours also. You will follow where it leads, for peace or war, for weal or woe. I would not have it otherwise. Never for a moment have I doubted it. But this I have known, your fate is not in these tame fields. They are not in your blood. It is out yonder"—she flung her hand toward the glowing west—"where a man's work awaits you, work bequeathed you by your breeding. I have sat here long in patience, but certain that your time would come. How, I could not know. Why should I presume to interfere when the moment arrives? Even if it cost a worthless life. Who am I to know the Lord's ways?"

Her small figure had straightened in her chair, and her eyes blazed. Through the blurring of her great years shone a fire. With a sudden movement, she held the long rifle to him.

"And this," she cried. "This that in the hands of Boone has spoken in the Dark and Bloody Ground! Do you suppose for a moment I have thought its voice was stilled? That its age was run, and that it must hang in place, an outworn relic on the walls of a Pennsylvania farm? No, my lad. It has but hung there in its fallow time, gathering the strength for its further destinies."

Mechanically Andrew took the piece from her, dropped its butt to the floor and crossed his forearms in an attitude of ease across the muzzle.

"Ah!" cried the old lady in triumph. "This have I seen, and now I see again. But beyond I see, not the tameness of walls, but the dusk of forests and the lurk of savage men and beasts—" She broke off suddenly and sank back as though weary.

"Tell me, Andrew," she commanded.

Andy told of the afternoon's episode. She listened, nodding understandingly from time to time.

"It is the moment," she broke in at last. "The hand of the Lord. You must go."

"Go?" repeated Andrew, at a loss.

"Go. Certainly."

"How? Where? He will not let me."

"Go anyway. Run away. Of course you can." She was impatient at his hesitation. "Don't tell me. I know the breed. I ought to. I've been one of them long enough. You must have money. Very well, I have saved for this. Nonsense, it's mine. I can do as I please. It is not his, it was your grandfather's. And this,"—her hand touched the rifle—"this too was your grandfather's. It is mine. I can give what is mine, I suppose?"

A dull spot of red glowed in Andy's cheeks. He straightened, and his hands gripped the rifle barrel until the knuckles showed white. Suddenly, a thought wrenched him.

"But you, Grandmother!" he cried brokenly. "How can I leave you?"

For an instant the old lady's face contorted, then stiffened again.

"Only for a while. Do you suppose I like this chair and this room? I, too, have waited. You will make a place for both of us—out there! When the time comes, I will join you."

"Yes!" cried Andy, taking fire, then a chill caution seized him again. "But he—what will he do? When he finds out, he'll—"

"I shall tell him at the proper time," stated the old lady with dignity. "I think you may trust me to give John Birkholm his comeuppance!"

"I believe I can!" cried Andrew delightedly.

The point decided, the old lady became all energy and animation. She took charge of every detail, overriding Andy's somewhat bewildered objections to making the proceedings so summary.

"No, now is the time," insisted his grandmother, "for if he misses you this evening, he will think you are sulking apart, so it will be well into tomorrow before he will understand that you are gone. By then, you must be well away. Do not travel by public conveyance, at least until you are beyond the gap, so that news of you may not be easily come at."

"I shall hide in the woods!" cried Andy.

But the old lady would have none of false romanticism.

"Time enough for that when there is need," she said. "He will make no great excursion," she gave her opinion, "save perhaps to send forth notice to law officers. He will not leave his work, and he will spend no money on a barren cause. I shall make him see that. No, lad, travel sensibly—but get beyond the reach of his grasp as soon as you may."

While thus they talked, she was busy gathering a small bundle of clothing, to which she added a package of food sufficient for the night and morning.

"You would best go as directly as you may to Missouri," she advised. "They say the land is fat, and there is room to breathe. Colonel Boone's last home was there. Get you a plantation, if it seems good to you—Lord, lad, you do not want that." She snatched away the low brogans Andy was about to include in the pack. "Remember, you must carry these things."

At the last, the bundle was formed, and they returned to the lower story, the grandmother's cane tap-tapping on the stairs. She disappeared for a moment in her own room, to return with a fat leathern wallet.

"Here is money," she said. "See that you bestow it in a safe place. Now you must hasten. The sun is low and you must be off before he returns from the fields." She picked up the long rifle from the corner in which it had been stood. A solemn hush abruptly terminated their bustling activities. They looked at each other. Andy's lower lip quivered in a sudden, overwhelming realization.

"Oh, Grandmother—" he began brokenly.

The old lady's softening eyes snapped back to birdlike brightness.

"Remember," she said briskly, "I have lived in a log hut in my time, and I can live in one again! Don't get any highfalutin ideas, young man. I expect you to send for me as soon as you get a good roof overhead. And take a good look around. They say it's all settled up near the river. Don't take up the first piece of bottom land you see. Go to the new country—like a Burnett. They'll try to scare you. They'll tell you there's no law, no comfort, no civilization. Make your own law. Comfort comes from within you, not outside. They'll tell you tales of Indians. Indians! Injuns, we called them! Pshaw, I've seen Indians aplenty!"

She looked down at the long rifle, then held it out to him in both hands. He took it. The moment swelled big with unspoken things.

"Kiss me—dear," she said at last.

He crushed her small form to him in a sudden agony.

But immediately she pushed him away.

"There!" she cried in her brisk, quick way. "There! Now you must go. Nay, it is hard, yes, I know—oh, how well I know! But it is only for a little time. Remember!"

"Yes, yes," muttered Andy, choking manfully against unmanly tears. "A little time. I'll be ready for you—"

She fairly pushed him from the door. He shouldered the rifle and the bundle, hesitated, turned and stumbled away.

"Andrew," she stopped him.

He turned.

"The piece has been fired. Mind you clean it well before you sleep."

He nodded and paused uncertainly.

"Go!" she commanded.

He bent his head and obeyed, nor did he again look back. She watched him from the doorway, her head held high.

In her eyes was the dazzle and glory of the westering sun. Thus, in the past, had she sent forth her men. She saw in the golden haze, not the tamed solid peace of the Pennsylvania farms, but the shadowy darkness of unknown forests, and against them, the trudging dogged figure of the boy, and the gleaming slant of the rifle barrel.

The figure turned the corner of the lane.

The old woman's straight back bent, her head drooped forward. Leaning heavily on her cane, she made her way to the Boston rocker. She sat down.

The air seemed to have turned cold, but she made no move to close the window. It did not matter. She was very small. Her veined hands lay inert in her lap. Her face looked shrunken. The snap and sparkle of her eyes had dulled. In her seemed but a feeble stir of life.

Her thoughts lay in a still pool, without motion. There was in them no bitterness, no keenness of sorrow, only a faint stirring of reflection. Her life was finished, its last destiny fulfilled. Now was done that for which her vitality had been sustained, that for which she had been preserved here until the appointed moment. For she knew now that she was very old. She heard John Birkholm's heavy tread outside, but the sound left her undisturbed. Nothing he could do or say could affect her. Even the thought of Andrew seemed withdrawn, far away, as remote as the thought of Boone and her husband and her son. She had no illusions, she knew she would never see Andrew again. All the outer world had become spectral. She had withdrawn from its reality, and now waited in patience at the portal of a new reality that was to be. Only one thing the eye of her spirit saw still solid, still valid in a world become shadowy—the long rifle. It was as though it were a symbol of the old purpose of her youth, and the youth of her men. It was as though the last remnants of her life force had revitalized it to its destiny. A great peace came over her.

"Thy will be done, O Lord!" she murmured.

Chapter 2
The Mountain Man

Andy traveled the back roads through the forests and by the little backwoods farms. He did so partly to avoid possible inquiry and pursuit, partly because he was only nineteen. With the long Kentucky rifle across his shoulder, his bundle at his back, the powder horn just nudging his elbow, the tomahawk and knife touching his hip, he felt somehow romantic as though he had set the clock back fifty years. The spring was swelling to maturity, and the tonic of her intoxication was strong. Andy stopped of nights at one or another of the rare farmhouses. He started out afoot betimes of each morning. On most days, he managed to hitch-hike a good proportion of the way on farm wagons or slower-moving ox carts. At noons, he stopped to eat his lunch, furnished him by his last night's hostess. Before resuming his journey after the meal, he drew the knife from its sheath at his belt and practiced throwing it at a selected mark on a tree. He cast it with a full round sweep of the arm. The long blade, turning slowly, nevertheless invariably struck point-in. Andrew did this practice studiously, pacing off odd distances, considering thoughtfully the result of each throw. The same care he bestowed on his rifle practice, for invariably, each day he fired five shots. Then, having cleaned the piece, he resumed his journey. All this he performed with an intense gravity of purpose, a gravity underscored, as it were, to the beholder, by the cast of his dark complexion and the straight, heavy line of his eyebrows. His earnestness managed to impart indeed quite an Indian-behind-every-tree illusion to the woods, an illusion only partly dissipated by the tootling of the stagecoach horn on the great highway a half-mile distant, or the peaceful blatting of the sheep in pasture just beyond the forest's screen. Certainly Andy himself, running away to the Wild West, entered wholeheartedly into his game.

Therefore it was that, turning at the sound of a chuckle behind him, he experienced no immediate shock of surprise at the figure he beheld. Only after a moment or so did he come to a realization of its extreme and theatrical incongruity in this peaceful and ordered land.

He saw a tall, slender, and wiry man of uncertain age. His face was clean-shaven, lean, leathery, and brown, and his deep-set eyes were blue and twinkling with humor. His head, innocent of hat, was bound about by a blue kerchief from beneath which escaped long hair. A plain cotton shirt was confined at the waist by a buckskin girdle from which depended a variety of little bags. Another belt, crossing his left shoulder supported, under his right arm, a powder horn and shot pouch. He wore no breeches. In their stead, his legs were covered by leggings cut away at the seat, so that as he moved, Andy saw the breechclout and the leathery, chapped, browned hard skin of the man's buttocks. The leggings themselves were tied at the knee, and were ornamented by many fringes, embroideries in beads, tufts of hair and feathers dyed in brilliant colors. His feet were encased in decorated moccasins. He carried across the crook of his left arm a rifle not unlike Andy's own, except that it was somewhat shorter and heavier.

Andrew stared at this strange figure, taking in these many details, his mind separating it slowly from the congruity of his play-acting, where it belonged, to the unbelievable actuality of the tamed countryside from which it should have vanished generations agone.

The man chuckled again, evidently relishing Andy's bewilderment.

"Look yore fill, lad, I'm used to it," said he. "Lord love you, an' you keep on far enough on the road you travel you'll see many a more of mountain men besides Joe Crane."

He seated himself on a fallen tree, laid aside his rifle, slipped from beneath his belt a pipe of stone with a long reed stem, which he proceeded leisurely to stuff with tobacco. His form was relaxed in every muscle, but his blue eyes were never still. Even as he drawled on, they flitted here and there about him. Not for an instant did they seem to rest, yet somehow Andy felt that their sharp scrutiny was seizing upon every item of his own appearance and equipment, and that behind them a shrewd brain was estimating him.

"Come, lad, sit down," advised the stranger, puffing forth a cloud of smoke. He reached out a long arm to pluck Andy's knife from the tree into which the last cast had buried its point.

"That is a proper blade." He balanced it appraisingly.

"And you cast it not badly. But you lose yore force."

He flickered his arm. The knife flashed through the air, to bury itself half-hilt deep in the soft pine.

"See!" commented the stranger. "'Tis a trick, I'll larn ye."

He reached for Andy's rifle, which he examined as critically.

"A proper piece, too," he said. "Properly made and kept. Though a leetle on the light side for buffalo. Still, it's said its say in its day, I'll warrant, and will say it again. Give me a good flint gun. Your percussion arms are all right"—he held up a didactic forefinger—"and you'll find a-many to urge you to a change. They'll tell you that in wet weather they are more sartin, and that the high wind of the prairies will blow away your flint gun's priming. That may be so for a *mangeur de lard* but not for one who looks to his priming as an old *hivernant* should. And mark you this, lad, with these newfangled cap guns, when you run out of caps, you're done. You ain't got no gun. She ain't even a good club. But with a flint gun, as long as they's rocks, you can chip you off a new flint. And thar you be!" he ended triumphantly. His scrutiny fell upon the patch box plate and its inscription. His eye narrowed, and he looked up suddenly at Andy, but he said nothing.

Andy's scattered wits focused at last.

"Who are you?" he blurted out. "What are you doing here?"

The stranger's face darkened momentarily, then cleared. He threw back his head and laughed.

"I nearly forgot," said he, "and came nigh to anger. You are a likely lad, but you have much to larn. When you come to the prairie do not ask a man his name or his business. That is not taken kindly.'

"I'm sorry," stammered Andy. "I meant no harm."

"No harm is done," conceded the stranger handsomely, "And mebbe you are not to blame. 'Tis a matter of upbringing mebbe. But look yere, I didn't ask yo' nothin' about yoreself, though you carry here Boone's rifle, as the mark on it states, and that is sure enough to make a man curious!" He glanced down at himself humorously. "I'd as soon tell you of myself, lad. I am from Washington, jist now, whar I've been to speak to the President of sartin things which have to do with the fur. It was decided that someone must speak. So I have been and now I return."

"You have been to Washington—you have seen Mr. Monroe..." Andy broke off, embarrassed that his bewilderment had carried him so far.

But the mountain man read him perfectly.

"In this guise?" He chuckled again. "Even so. I might well, thinks you, put on the foofaraw of proper dress, but thinks I. Joe Crane, never in all your life have you acted like anybody but yoreself. Do not make yoreself out a fool by trying to ape other folks now. Joe Crane, you have always been, and Joe Crane you still remain. Go ahead, Joe Crane!"

"I see," murmured Andy. "And was your—did you succeed in your mission, Mr. Crane?"

"I know now what I only suspicioned afore," replied the mountain man cryptically. "And now that you have shown me the way to the manners of this country, I'll make bold myself. How came ye by Dan'l Boone's rifle, and whither go ye with it?"

"It was my grandfather's, given him by Colonel Boone himself."

"Your name?" inquired Crane quickly.

"Andrew Burnett."

"Wagh! Then you're Gail Burnett's son—no, his grandson?"

"Yes. Did you know him?"

"I hear'n tell of him. Old Dan'l set store by him."

"You knew Boone?"

"Not to say I knew him. No. He was afore my time. But I met up with him one time on the Platte." Under Andy's breathless urging, he elaborated. It was at the time of Boone's great age, when he was living on the farm of Nathan, his son. He had heard trappers' tales of the salt mountains, lakes, and ponds, and he had made up his mind to see them. So, disregarding the family's protests, he set out.

"I was comin' into St. Loucy with my furs and possibles," said Crane, "and I run across him on the Platte. He had jist one Injun with him. He was a good Injun, an Osage. I talked with him. He told me he had orders to bring Dan'l back dead or alive before snowfall, and he was a-goin' to do it. The old Colonel was risin' on eighty-four years but he was as straight as an arrow. His eyes wasn't good. He had little pieces of white paper on his sights so he could see em, but his hand was as steady as mine is today, and he was eating his own meat. We come back together to Missouri. He shore hated to quit without seein' them salt lakes, but winter was comin' and his Injun headed him back. He allowed he'd make it next spring. We made heap many smokes together. He was worsen you for makin' me palaver. Nothin' must do but I had to tell him all about the mountains. Allowed mebbe he'd get him two—three Osages, and mebbe a white man or two and go see. So you're Gail Burnett's kin! Well, from what old Dan'l told me, you come of good stock."

The mountain man glanced at the position of the sun and arose from the log.

"You live yereabouts?" he asked Andy.

"No. I'm traveling, too." Andy hesitated. "I'm going west."

Crane dropped the butt of his rifle to earth with emphatic delight.

"Wagh!" he cried. "So that's the way yore stick floats! We will e'en travel together!"

For the first time in his life, Andrew slept out in a bivouac, for Crane declined flatly to stop at a farmhouse or an inn. All the days through, he strode behind the untiring figure of the mountain man, for he soon found by experiment that Crane was impatient of conversation while journeying and favored single file. Andy was willing to trail along behind. The strange, barbaric figure of the mountain man, his head turning constantly in a habit of watchfulness, was very satisfying to the romanticism of his years. And truth to tell, Andy found that after the first hour of the morning, he had scant breath where-with to talk if he would. The frontiersman did not appear to hurry, but the swing of his stride was such that Andy was well put to it to keep pace.

But in the evening when the campfire had been lighted and the simple evening meal disposed, Crane became as conversational as one could desire. Before Andy realized that he was being drawn out, he found himself confiding in his new acquaintance. The latter listened attentively, without other comment than the strange, throat-scraping *wagh!* That Andy should run away from a harsh and fanatical stepfather seemed to him a matter of course. That he should travel west only natural to a grandson of Gail Burnett. But that he should be going to Missouri with the idea of taking up a farm was too fantastic to rate consideration. Crane brushed that notion aside as though it were a mosquito.

"I don't deny you're green for the prairies," said he. "You can shoot, purty fair, and you can throw a knife a little. Beyond that you're mostly a total loss. You'd lose yore ha'r in two days. But yore likely in larnin'. You've the makin's in you. *Farm!* Wagh! That don't shine with me! Leave them things to farmers. They don't fit with Burnett."

Immediately after this talk, he took charge of Andy's schooling. He found the young man's ignorance appalling.

"Why, you ain't had any eddication at all!" he protested.

The curriculum was quite haphazard.

"If you see buffalo runnin' around in leetle, small groups," Crane would observe suddenly, "you'll know they's been chased by Injuns not long ago..."

"If you're looking for a way through strange mountains, remember to look for black rock, for when rocks is black, snow has not stuck—and this, where snow don't stick, a man can't climb..."

"In Injun country quakin' asp's yore best fire. It ain't got no smoke nor smell..."

"If you git caught in the fog in strange mountains, throw rocks ahead. If no sound comes back, set still..."

These and many other brief and pithy but unrelated bits of wisdom Crane threw back over his shoulder as he strode along. Later, perhaps at a resting period, perhaps at the evening fire, he would test Andy's memory, proposing imaginary emergencies to which the lad must state his remedy. And each evening, Crane catechized him strictly as to what he had observed along the road. Andy found that to notice a chipmunk trail counted more with the mountain man than any number of red-painted barns.

At every opportunity Crane drilled him in the handling of his weapons. Mere marksmanship with the rifle received little of his attention.

"You hold well enough," said he indifferently, "and you'll hold better. Burn powder, lad, that is all. But you must learn to load, for an empty piece helps no man but yore enemy."

It was not sufficient, it seemed, merely to understand the proper charging of the rifle. One must be able to accomplish that necessary act in all varieties of circumstances, lying down, in cramped space, even running at full speed, on horseback. Crane practiced him at estimating his powder charge poured direct from the horn. He showed him how a supply of bullets carried in the mouth could be flipped skillfully into the barrel by the tongue, and driven home by a smart smack of the butt of the weapon against a stone or a tree or even hard earth, or the pommel of the saddle if one were ahorseback.

"The spit'll hold her," explained Crane. "Don't need no patch for that." He removed from his mouth the long-stemmed stone pipe and pointed it didactically. "It's all right to measure yore powder to the last grain when you got time. But if you have to load quick, yore so close that you'll hit anyway. If yore fur away, you got time to load with a proper charge and a proper patch fur fine shootin'."

He made Andy perform the maneuver over and over. At first, Andy was clumsy. He was appalled at the amount of powder he spilled and wasted.

"Never mind spilled powder. Powder's cheaper'n ha'r," said Crane grimly.

He himself, in demonstration, spilled no powder. He was extraordinarily deft and could charge, prime, and discharge his rifle in an incredibly brief period, whether running, lying, or huddled behind shelter.

Likewise, he kept Andy almost tiresomely at his knifethrowing. In this, the boy made faster progress. He learned the knack that drove the point deep. And now he discovered that he should also be able to cast the weapon, not only straight ahead, but to right or left, and even over his shoulder, and that without turning his body. Crane possessed uncanny skill with his own knife. He insisted on Andy's practicing with that weapon also.

"She's a standard blade," Crane explained, "such as you will find in the sheath of every *hivernant*, and once you have the feel of one of them, you know them all."

The balance differed only slightly from that with which Andy was familiar, and his progress was so rapid that Crane expressed approval.

"That shines!" he cried, and patted Andy on the shoulder.

The schooling for the evening finished, the mountain man smoked and talked. Andy drank it in. The talk was of the sweep of plains, and the buffalo, and the rise of foothills, and the snowy peaks of great ranges, and the fall of beaver waters, and strange wild people, and hidden parks. And above all space and size and the fling of distances. Crane somehow made this country in which they journeyed seem very small and tame.

"Ain't hardly room to take exercise," said he contemptuously. He dismissed the surrounding forest with a lift of scorn. "Call them trees! Wagh! Why, out in the mountains, lad, there's trees so stout it would tire a rat to run clean around them!"

Thus, by slow stages, they gained to Pittsburg, which was at that time the point of embarkation for the West. It seemed to both the trapper and the country boy a busy and bewildering place. They made their way promptly to the river, stared at curiously, found by inquiry that a steamer was due to leave in two days, and betook themselves to camp in a hardwood grove outside the city. By now, Andy, with the quick adaptability of youth, believed himself to look upon houses with a scorn equal to Crane's own.

He had been accustomed to sleeping out, by a fire, and since he had had no blanket, he considered himself as a tough, hardy citizen, and was inclined to look down scornfully on such lads as passed. Indeed Andy may have strutted just a little, there is no question that he hung close to Crane and tried to look as though he had always belonged with the mountain man. Venturing, boylike, to hint at this enormous superiority over the commonplace slaves to comfort who stared at them, he was chastened by Joe's sardonic reminder that they had up to now enjoyed perfect picnic weather. He made Andy buy himself a blanket. The boy did so, rather under protest.

"But you have no blanket," he pointed out. He did not quite dare to claim, in so many words, an equal hardihood with his hero. Crane returned an evasive reply. "We better see about gittin' on this steamboat," he said, turning the subject.

The riverboat lay alongside a wharf. She was flat, broad, and built high in stories, with the pilot house grandly atop of all, and two tall slim smokestacks bound together with a crisscross of stays, and a diamond-shaped walking beam having a gilded Indian with drawn bow. Dozens of Negro laborers swarmed back and forth across her broad gangplanks carrying or pushing or rolling all sorts of freight. This was checked and disposed by clerks and mates, their sleeves rolled up, their shirts open, their caps thrust back, their voices hoarse, the sweat of honest exasperation on their brows. In contrast to the inferno of bustle and noise below, the upper deck dozed in a celestial calm. It was empty of life except for the figure of the captain, leaning, arms folded, over the rail. He looked cool and fresh and neat in his trim buttoned uniform, and he smoked a contemplative cheroot, and gazed down at the insane hurly-burly with the reposeful eye of complete detachment.

Joe Crane approached one of the busy checkers at the gangplank. The latter paid him no attention. After waiting uneasily for a few moments, the mountain man ventured to address him. Gone was his swaggering air of self-confidence. In this alien environment of bustle and noise, he was as ill-at-ease as a schoolboy.

"How much to St. Louey?" he asked in a small voice.

The checker did not even look up from his list.

"Sanborn!" he howled above the din. "Oh, you, Sanborn!"

At the summons, a small, pale, fishy-eyed man popped out from a cubby hole on the lower deck. He, too, was in his shirt sleeves and carried a list in his hands.

"Well?" he demanded impatiently.

The checker did not reply in words but jerked his head toward Crane and Andy. The mountain man repeated his question. The small man looked him over disparagingly.

"Hundred dollars, deck passage, find yourself," he vouchsafed at last.

"That the cheapest?" inquired Crane.

The purser half turned away.

"Fifty if you wood up," he flung scornfully over his shoulder, then vouchsafed to explain, "We'll take you for fifty dollars if you help carry wood aboard whenever we stop for fuel."

"I'm Joe Crane," said the mountain man, "I'm just back from—"

"I don't care who you are," interrupted the purser. "Do you want a ticket, or don't you?"

"Can't I work my passage?"

"We got plenty niggers already," sneered the little man.

Crane did not appear to resent this. He pondered helplessly.

"How much for a hundred and eighty pounds of freight?" he inquired at last.

"Eighteen dollars."

"That shines," replied Crane with a grin. "I'll go as freight."

The little man spun on his heel and stared malevolently at the mountain man, his eyes blazing.

"Say, you!" he snarled. "Do you think I've got nothing to do but listen to you trying to be funny? Get out of here before I have you thrown off the dock."

He turned away.

"Mr. Sanborn." The captain's cool remote voice from above arrested his steps.

"Sir?" the purser craned his neck upward.

"Book the gentleman."

"Sir?"

"I say book the gentleman. Take him as freight. And, Sanborn, stow him in the hold—under the flour barrels."

He had not raised his voice, but it had somehow carried above all the din of loading. Those within its immediate hearing burst into a roar of laughter. The Negro stevedores cackled, dropped their loads to double up in merriment unrebuked. They passed back the word to others who had not heard, and they, too, slapped one another in delayed appreciation. On his Olympian height, the captain smoked meditative, indifferent, remote, staring across the reposeful calm he alone inhabited. Joe Crane, followed by the bewildered Andy, fell back abashed behind the warehouse shelter. He looked at his young companion, humorously shamefaced.

"*Well!*" he said comically. "Here's damp powder and no fire to dry it!"

"Haven't you any money?" asked Andy.

"My possible sack is mighty nigh as clean as a hound's tooth."

"But," Andy was nonplussed. "How did you expect—how did you—"

"I didn't need none goin' east, so I spent what I had. But it seems like Joe Crane goin' to Washington to see the President and Joe Crane goin' home again is two different beaver," confessed that individual. "Looks to me like a man ought to be allowed to work his passage, anyway."

Andrew was fumbling with the cord about his neck.

"You got money?" cried Crane interestedly. He snatched the bills from Andy's hands, stared at them a moment, then leaped into the air and uttered a wild war whoop that brought several men running around the corner of the building to see what it was all about. He paid them no attention but marched swaggering across the decks and up the broad gangplank to the purser's office, thrusting aside without ceremony the laden stevedores, glaring down the first impulse of the officer who moved to stop him.

"Here, little man," he commanded, slapping down the roll of bills. "Two tickets to Saint Louey—and carry your own wood and be damned to you!"

Andy, trailing helplessly behind his triumphal progress, looked up to meet the captain's calmly amused eye.

Joe Crane and Andy lived during that voyage on the flat lower deck, next to the water. Their sleeping accommodations were where they chose to spread their blankets—for Joe now possessed such a luxury, thanks to his discovery of Andrew's affluence. At the sound of a gong they rushed into line to receive food dished out at a galley door. The rest of the time they could do what they pleased—on the lower deck. Above—the second story —it could hardly be called a deck—was reserved for slow-moving, low-voiced, well-dressed people. The men wore tall beaver hats and ruffled shirts and blue coats and light pantaloons, the women floated wide in crinolines. They leaned on the rail occasionally to look down with faint supercilious curiosity on the lower deck. And above them again were the pilot deck and the captain and the pilots and other ship's officers remote as gods.

With these inhabitants of the upper worlds, Andy was a little concerned. But the lower deck was occupied by as weird a hodgepodge as one could imagine—wood choppers, backwoods settlers, peddlers, raft men, boatmen, bullwhackers, a rough, tough lot. They nearly all chewed tobacco, they all swore, and most of them quarreled gustily over the slightest difference of opinion. Nobody interfered with them save when, on rare occasions, the customary turbulence threatened to develop into a riot. Then, from the engine room, emerged a colossal Swede armed with an iron bar who restored order in a most businesslike and impersonal fashion, and at once disappeared.

Joe Crane fitted at once into this motley disorder. He was, when he so chose, the center of a group. The rough men listened to his tall stories of the prairie and the mountains. They listened, though many of the hat-tilted tough boys, by their attitude of having paused in the group for but a moment, and by an expression of halfsneering amusement, tried to convey their general skepticism of Crane's validity. But it was to be noted that nobody opposed or quarreled with the mountain man. The latter thought nothing of them. He laughed at Andy's first awe of them as frontiersmen.

Some of the time, Andy listened or stood by watching the interminable card games on a spread blanket, but what he liked best of all was to huddle in a place he had discovered behind two bitts near the bow. He watched the river glide by.

Separated thus from the human microcosmos of the ship, Andy seemed to enter an aloof and hovering detachment. In afterlife, though his memory for the event was always remarkably clear and detailed, this interlude of voyage never defined itself as something in which he had actually taken part. It was like a dream, having neither the dimensions of space nor time. The water swished from the blunt bow, the walking beam swung up and down, up and down, its gilded Indian pointing his arrow now low, now high, as the banks glided by. Against this monochrome, things appeared as shadows on a screen and vanished again.

They stopped at Cincinnati and went on. The hills became lower, the houses and the settlements farther apart. Occasionally, they drew up at a wharf, and freight or passengers debarked or were taken on. More often, they merely shoved the blunt bow against the bank and held it there until necessary business was transacted. At such times, often, the gangplanks were thrown out, and long lines of passengers working out their part fare carried aboard the long sticks of cordwood from the piles maintained by the steamboat company's wood choppers. Now Ohio lay astarboard and Kentucky aport. They differed completely in character. On the Ohio side were cleared farms and farmhouses, neatly painted, and in the New England style, on the Kentucky side were ragged fields and the large log cabins of planters and the smaller log huts of the slaves. Between them and back of them gathered close the green forest down to the water's edge. Cool and dark and mysterious it lay, and Andy saw flashes of red as the tanagers and cardinals took wing. And the rolling clouds of wood smoke from the twin stacks broke against it and eddied between the trees.

They passed the rapids at Louisville on the flood, and stopped, and many of the ship's company ended their journey there, and most of the rest came back only at the urgent and repeated summons of the whistle, and some few were left behind, for the rougher element became unanimously drunk, and there was considerable quarrelsome disorder. Crane was drunk with the rest and came back alone in a very disdainful mood that even included Andy.

"If yore goin' to be a mountain man you got to learn to liquorize," was the grieved burden of his plaint.

A raftsman agreed with him profanely, adding embellishments. Crane instantly veered. Since when had a mere alligator horse acquired the right to criticize a friend of Joe Crane's? Joe offered to cut his liver out to see if it was white. Offer declined, but if Joe would lay aside his knife, the raftsman would...they drifted away, squabbling. Andy leaned his back against the bitts. All this seemed to pass him by, and he could not touch the waiting suspension of his westering spirit. The journey seemed to march by him as a pageant. The stream broadened, the bluffs fell away, the country spaced to broad undulations clothed always in the now almost unbroken forest. Next, the river was low, alluvial flats, with marshes and swamps and the wild cryings and uptiltings of innumerable waterfowl. The farms had been left behind. The wilderness was broken only by the rare huts of the wood choppers set on blocks or piles against high water, and the stacked cordwood. The bosom of the river was wide and glassy. One would have said it was as still as a lake were it not that here and there the slow, powerful turning of oily eddies, the veer of the ship against its rudder, the hastening of the shore, betrayed its strength. As afternoons drew to a close, the sun turned it to the red of dark wine and the air filled with gold, into which the steamer glided as into a mist.

And at night was the suspension of quiet. The blackness of the forest met the blackness of the river, and the dark blue spangled sky overhead, and the rare twinkle of lights ashore, repeated waveringly in the water, and the refraction against the stillness of the blatant lights and sounds of the steamer and the unintermittent pouring of bright sparks from the funnels that rushed up so powerfully as though with purpose, and eddied, and wavered uncertainly, and died against the evening as though rebuked.

At this time, the mountain man took to deserting his other companions to stand silent near Andy, his elbows leaning on the muzzle of his long rifle, his eyes, unblinking, staring straight ahead, his head raised, as though he snuffed for something in the breeze. He seemed at last caught in the younger man's hypnotic suspense of waiting. They exchanged no words.

The river widened. The banks fell away. To the right, a point defined itself, against which lay moored a strange structure. As the steamer swung in, it became clear that this was a huge flatboat, a hundred feet or more in length, supporting several log houses—a store, a saloon, a gambling house. Cairo, the delta of the Mississippi. Almost as far as the eye could see rolled the breadth of the Fathers of Waters, the farther shoreline dim and low in the distance.

"We're gittin' thar! Wagh!" cried Crane.

They plowed upstream against two hundred miles of heavy current. Crane, realizing that the journey was nearing its end, abandoned his careless companionships and gave his whole attention to Andy. He considered it nothing short of a crime that so likely a young man, the grandson of Gail Burnett, should become a farmer. He said so, very bluntly, and incidental to his protest sketched appealing glimpses of the wildlife beyond the Missouri and the Platte. Andrew's spirit yearned toward the adventure, but he continued to shake his head.

"I promised Grandmother," he persisted steadily, "that I'd send for her when I'd made a place for her to live. This money here"—he tapped his chest—"is hers. She gave it to me to pay the journey and buy land."

"You'll make more in a season with the free trappers than you'll make in ten years on a farm. And it's a man's life."

"I know," agreed Andy, sighing.

"There's a country nor'west," urged Crane. "It ain't never been trapped. It's Blackfoot country. Blackfeet is bad Injuns, but with a good man and a bright lad—like yourself...I know a park back in them mountains called the Tetons whar I g'arantee no Injuns will...why, lad, there's never a trap been set in' them waters. We'll have it all to ourselves. If we save our ha'r we'll come out to the rendezvous with a thousand plew! Think of that, lad! A thousand plew, or more! That'll buy ye a dozen farms—if you still want the things. Yo'll git Missus Burnett out jist as quick, and you'll have money to make her comfortable," said Crane cunningly.

"I can't! I can't!" cried Andy with a desperation that indicated his temptation. "I promised, and I took the money, and I've no right—besides," the words were dragged from his reluctance, "I'd be no good to you in that country. I'm such a greenhorn. I know nothing."

"Of course, if yore afeard..." said Crane deliberately.

Andy's head jerked up. A dull red suffused his face. His hand dropped to the pan of the weapon in his lap.

"I'm not afeard," he said quietly.

Crane looked at him and sighed.

"I know ye're not, lad. I take that back. Shore yore a greenhorn, but you got good makin's and you come of good stock. And you larn quick. Look a yere, lad." He thrust his hand forward earnestly. "We need ye. The big companies is comin' in. They're sendin' out their burgeways to build forts and liquorize the Injuns. The mountain men must make a stand or the beaver streams will be tromped and the Injuns hostile. The mountains won't be no place for a white man." He brooded. "What you think yore grandpop—and Dan'l Boone—would say if they knew that this"—he reached forward and laid his hand too on the long rifle—"was a-poppin' black squirrels in a Missouri bottom, and buffalo and Injuns and grizzly b'ar and antelope and sich just over the skyline?"

"I can't! I can't! I can't!" cried Andy. "And," he repeated bitterly, "I wish you'd let me be! I promised, I tell you! I don't see why you want me, anyway. I'd probably just do some fool thing."

"That's why I want you," replied Crane.

"What?"

"You stick," said Crane simply. "Well, if that's the way yore stick floats..." He spat disgustedly. "It's always a woman, young or old, it's always a woman spiles a good man."

"My grandmother—" Andy fired up at this.

"Shore! She's all right," Crane placated him. "I ain't sayin' a word agin her. But that's the way it works. The good ones is wuss'n the bad ones." He apparently gave it up. "I know. Nigh got me one time. Might have been on a farm myself if a good friend hadn't stepped in and saved my ha'r for me jist in the nick o' time. She was a good gal, too. Run plumb onto her in St. Louey when I come in with my fur, spring of 15. Hit me like a dose of alkali water. Felt queer all over like a buffalo shot in the lights. Had no taste for mush and molasses, no interest in hominy and johnnycakes. I didn't care whether my rifle had hind sights or not. Couldn't help myself no more than a man who's kicked a yeller-jacket log. If it hadn't a-been for that friend, I'd have been a gone beaver."

"What did he do?" asked Andy.

"He married her," said Crane.

Andy laughed. Crane grinned reluctantly.

"Don't suppose nobody'd marry yore grandmother," he admitted.

The steamboat curved grandly and ceremoniously to the docks at St. Louis. The ship's company had shaken off its monotony of routine and crowded the rails. Andy, clinging with difficulty in the jostling of the crowd to his place by the bitts, looked with all his eyes.

St. Louis of that day lay on a terrace below abrupt limestone bluffs, long since graded away, atop which defensive works stood like sentinels. A row of warehouses faced the docks, and behind them straggled streets parallel with the stream. The docks themselves were wide and long. At this moment, they were crowded with a mixed and miscellaneous throng. Andy filled his eyes with their picturesque incongruity. There were gentlemen in the height of fashion, French *engagés* dark and vivacious, rivermen in high leather boots, absorbed and businesslike clerks in sober garb, ragged stevedores, bullwhackers swaggering bare-chested and hat-tilted, and plainsmen leaning on their long rifles, eyeing the hubbub sober and aloof. And here and there, Andy's first Plains Indians, gaudy and painted. The din was tremendous. Men shouted, the paddle wheels beat and the safety valve took this occasion to cut loose with a devastating roar.

Joe Crane thrust himself through the crowding passengers to Andy's side. He had become abrupt, businesslike, remote.

"You can get track of me at the Rocky Mountain House, if you change your mind," said he briefly, and was gone. A moment later, Andy saw the mountain man gain the wharf by a flying leap, and indifferent to the protests and invectives hurled after him by the outraged crew, disappear in the throng.

A lump of hurt and resentment arose in Andy's throat at this abrupt and indifferent farewell. But now the gangplank was lowered, and he was swept away by the rush toward shore, carried helplessly forward, his arms jammed to his side, crowded and jostled. It was a human stampede, each regardless of anyone but himself. Buffeted, his nostrils filled with the reek, Andy was swept forth at last to the wharf. As soon as he could do so, he stepped aside, drawing a deep breath of relief, his hand seeking the little sack of money suspended about his neck beneath his shirt. The long breath strangled in his throat. The bag was gone.

The shock of the loss turned Andy physically sick for a moment. He groped for a pile head and supported himself against it. The noisy wharf had gone black in a reeling world. Gone! When? How?

Dimly, he became aware that somebody was speaking his name. With difficulty, he brought his mind to a focus. The captain of the steamboat stood before him. He was made to understand that the captain had a letter for him. How could a letter reach him in this crowd? More trouble, probably. He wanted to get away as quickly as possible. He took the letter mechanically.

"You sure this is mine?" he asked, wondering. "How did you know?"

The captain grinned in his beard.

"There are not many boys of just your description carrying one of those things." He indicated the long rifle. "The letter was sent to the company's office at Pittsburg, and as soon as you took passage with my ship, it was handed to me."

"Why did you not give it to me before, then?"

"Instructions. It was to be given only when you debarked." Nodding acknowledgment to Andy's thanks, he strolled away.

Andy stared at his grandmother's fine angular handwriting and thrust the letter unopened into his pocket. In this crash of all the plans they had made together, he could not bear to read it. He shouldered his entire earthly possessions and left the wharves.

For an hour or more, he walked about, dark in the misery of his loss. Up the Rue Royale—business places, board sidewalk, mud, back down the Rue de l'Eglise, ditto ditto without the sidewalk, double again, one block nearer the limestone bluffs, on the Rue de Granges to the French Quarter, derisively called Vide Poche. The Rue Royale was crowded, the others nearly empty. He was as though living a double exposure on a negative. His impressions were fragmentary, snatched in his brief emergences from his inner trouble. The mud, the number of creoles speaking French, an occasional strikingly picturesque figure of trapper, trader, or boatman, the wild rolling eyes of the otherwise stolid Indians, an overnote of truculent rowdyism, the prevalence of arms, and Negroes. He was only partially aware of them. He found himself gazing fixedly at things which he did not see until slowly they seeped down to his attention. Thus the feet of a barefoot Negro in profile, grotesque, and the gradual clarifying of the picture in Andy's attention until he realized that never before had he seen heels extending back so curiously in excrescence. And with this realization, a long rifle barrel thrust past Andy's shoulder, and a shattering discharge and cloud of powder smoke, and a wild yell from the Negro as he rolled about clasping his heel creased by the bullet. Shaken completely from the somnolence of his misery, Andy found himself in the center of a whooping, instantly gathered crowd. A tall, quiet man in black thrust through and laid his hand on the shoulder of the drunken trapper with the smoking rifle. The latter protested, aggrieved.

"God a'mighty, man," explained he, "I jist aimed to trim him up so he could wear a genteel boot!"

"Kyant do no shootin' in the streets," said the tall man firmly.

He shook the drunken man, faced him about, gave him a shove in the broad of the back. He staggered away. The crowd howled with laughter. Several clapped him on the shoulder, admiring his accuracy, inviting him to *liquorize*. They scattered slowly. Andy was alone again. Nobody paid any attention to the Negro, hippity-hopping away as fast as he could go.

But Andy was now shaken awake. The thing was done and over, and to be faced. Andy faced it squarely. The money entrusted to him to buy the farm was gone. He must get some more money. The only way he could think of to do that was to take up the mountain man's offer. What was it Crane had said? A thousand plew. What was a plew? He must find out. Having made this decision Andy instantly set about acting on it. Thus, already he displayed two of the qualities that later were often to stand him in stead. And having come to his resolution, Andy was ashamed to find, beneath the chagrin suitable to the occasion, a sudden leap of exultation. It was positively indecent. He sternly made it downcharge and turned his inner eye away from it. Nevertheless, it glowed away down inside, awaiting its chance to burst out. But he was going west! Couldn't take that away, whatever the austere reasons.

He inquired the way to the Rocky Mountain House and had turned in that direction when he remembered the letter in his pocket. He could read it now, albeit with still a bit of dread and shrinking. He drew one side for the purpose.

Dear Boy, it began. *You will wish the news of the farm, and the situation here, so I will say at once that your stepfather has instigated no pursuit, as I suspected, due to his great stinginess. Nor has he been disagreeable to myself, due I think, to his idea that I have money to dispose, not knowing that it is already disposed. So your mind may be easy on these accounts, and you may think of me as quite happy with my book and my memories and my thoughts of you, at last, doing what your blood calls you to do and which I had planned for you.*

You will be wondering why you get this letter only now and not at Pitt's town whither it was sent. I arranged that in order that you might not be tempted to turn back. By now, I think, you must know that you are not meant to be a farmer. I have known that for a long time. The knowledge of it has been the joy of my old age. I never intended you to make a place for me out there, but otherwise you might not have gone. I would be very unhappy watching you grubbing at a farm. I could never stand half that journey, now. But don't you worry about that. You'll write me of your great doings, and I'll be very happy here in my old rocking chair, for remember this, it is only through you that all that I have loved and cherish lives on. So do your part, boy, like a man. Make your mark on your time, like your grandfather before you. Let others make the farms—after you have found the country and made it safe for them. She signed her full name with the painstaking flourish of the period. But there was more. *I had not thought to touch upon it,* she had added, *but the thought must occur to you, and I would not have it weaken your resolution. We may not see one another again. I am eighty-seven years old, and I know too well the dangers of the life you must lead. But we shall not be snuffed out when our bodies go. Our sort goes marching on.*

The Rocky Mountain House proved to be a small two-storied rude structure on one of the streets back of the Rue des Granges. Nearly the whole lower story was taken up by a single large room, crowded with men. Some of them stood at a bar, a few occupied chairs, the most sat cross-legged on the floor. They were a wildly picturesque lot. Heads were covered with handkerchiefs, wide felt hats, caps of fur, bodies with cotton, with fringed and beaded buckskin yellow in newness with buckskin black and shiny from wear. Legs also with buckskin, or with stout stroud, feet with moccasins both plain and fancy. A few were dressed decently and quietly in the fashion of the cities. Smoke hazed the air.

Andy stood in the doorway, accustoming his eyes to the dimness. Nobody paid him the least attention.

He was thrust aside by a man entering. The newcomer strode to the center of the room. Over his shoulder he carried a buffalo robe which he spread tanned side up. At one end, he seated himself cross-legged, crashed down a hatful of silver dollars, and with a sweeping motion, spread a pack of cards.

"Yere's the deck and yere's the beaver!" he challenged. "Who dares set his hoss? Wagh!"

They gathered close, squatting cross-legged and on their heels. Only the man back of the bar remained standing, and two others near a farther door. Andy felt himself keenly scrutinized by them, and after a moment, he recognized one of them as Crane.

He picked his way across to them.

"Well, here I am!" he announced.

Neither man replied for a moment.

"I'm going with you, after all," Andy supplemented, "that is, if you still want me," he added, the chill of the possibility rendering his voice uncertain.

Crane glanced toward his companion.

The latter was a tall man and muscular, clad from head to foot in fresh buckskin. His hair hung to hide the broad of his shoulders, but he was clean-shaven. His eyes were hard and direct, puckered into cold scrutiny. The lines of his brown face were keen-cut and fine. His expression was of deep gravity. The general impression of the man was of power and alertness held in the reserve of repose.

"This is Jack Kelly, my pardner," said Crane, and to Kelly, "this is the lad I was tellin' you about. If he sez so," he told Andy.

Andy was conscious of the plainsman's slow appraisal, sweeping him from head to toe like a cold flame. Abruptly he spoke. His voice was low, and surprisingly, inflected with that peculiar quality we call cultivation.

"You've changed your mind—why?" he asked.

"I told you he was no farmer!" interpolated Crane confidently, "He—"

Kelly silenced him with a gesture.

"Why?" he repeated.

"Well, for one thing, somebody stole my money off me," admitted Andy, and laughed.

"The money your grandmother gave you to buy a home," Kelly said bitingly. Andy flushed, but his eyes did not waver. "So you've lost it, and now you're running away."

Andy's head jerked.

"I'm not running away!" he denied hotly.

The stranger's eyes bored into his.

"Money's not hard to get," he said, "nor farms, in this country. Suppose I put you in the way of one."

"The boy's no farmer!" cried Crane.

"Shut up, Joe. Well?" Kelly challenged Andy.

Andy hesitated, then thrust his letter into the plainsman's hands. The latter read it slowly and passed it to Crane. He in turn spelled it out, his lips moving.

"Wagh!" he said, amazed, when he had finished. "That old woman shines!" He turned on Kelly indignantly. "What I tell you?" he demanded. "Whar floats his stick?" He seized Andy by the shoulders. "We'll make a mountain man of you, never fear! And," he returned to Kelly, "you mark my words, hell shore make them *come*!" A sudden recollection caused the expression of his face to change ludicrously. He hesitated a moment in indecision, caught Kelly's eye fixed upon him, and grinned shamefacedly. He fumbled in one of the pouches suspended from his belt and thrust something into Andy's hand.

"Reckon I might as well give you this back," he mumbled. "You ain't no farmer," he alleged defensively. "I allus said so. But somebody had to keep you from bein' one. Wagh!"

Andy looked down at the stolen sack of money. For a brief instant, he felt himself as though lifted by the sweep of greater destinies than those within his command.

Chapter 3
The Statesman

For over a week Andy Burnett shared with his new companions a tiny room at the Rocky Mountain House pending departure for the west. He paid for it twenty-five cents a day, and twenty-five cents each for meals. The two mountain men seemed to be much occupied with mysterious business of their own, which they did not offer to share with Andy. They paid him but just attention enough to see that he was properly outfitted.

Left to his own devices, Andy wandered much about the town. He liked especially the river and wharves. The great fur traders—such as the Chouteaus and Sublettes—would have interested him more, but he had gathered that for the moment some friction existed between them and the mountain men, and with the instant and complete partisanship of youth, he would have none of them. From a distance, he viewed the bustling activities about the warehouses where they were preparing several of the compact and elaborately organized trading expeditions—with their *bourgeois* and their *partizans* and their camp keepers, andengagés—which so aroused the scorn of the fiercely individualistic mountain men. Andy heard much of it in the evenings at the Rocky Mountain House.

"Used to be a man could travel anywheres if he kep' his eyes shining," they grumbled. "Injins don't mind a white man or so actin' same as them. They sort of trade sociable-like what furs they got, and mebbe marry you a squaw or so to keep yore winter camp for ye. And you ketch what fur you kin, and trade a few where you kin, and bring 'em out in the spring. But when these companies git to sendin' out a whole train and scatterin' hired hunters and trappers all over the kentry, the Injins gets skeered they're bein' crowded out and the game killed or druv off. And I don't blame 'em. Consarn it, a few more and there won't be room for nobody, and they'll ketch all the fur, and nobody'll have nothin'."

"We ain't got a show with them," agreed another. "They got likker to trade, and an Injin'll trade his best pony for likker. 'Course they git all the fur. And the likker makes trouble, too," he stated virtuously. "You put likker in an Injin and you cain't tell what he'll do. He cain't carry it like a white man does. Likely as not to sculp you no reason at all."

"I suppose you never traded liquor to the Indians, Fitz." Kelly's low and cultivated voice betrayed his amusement.

"*No* sir!" Fitz denied the insinuation vigorously. "How's a man to carry enough to make it worthwhile?"

The discussions were interminable, but inconclusive. Andy listening, gained the impression of a vanishing golden age. There stole over him a momentary depression of having lived just too late, succeeded by a passionate resentment against remorseless modern efficiency. But Kelly laughed at him.

"There are two or three hills out there yet," said he.

The end of his wandering about usually found Andy perched on a bench at Jake Hawkens's gun shop. This was a thoroughly satisfying spot. Andy liked the smells of oils and metal and fresh wood. He never tired of watching the beautiful, accurate processes in the making of rifles. He treasured proudly for himself the tolerance of the brusque, bullet-headed little Pennsylvania gunsmith, for Hawkens, as a rule, would permit no loafers about the shop, and drove forth unceremoniously any who seemed inclined to linger. He had no conversation for anybody, but he made no objection to Andy's sitting quietly out of the way.

This, Andy well realized, was due in no manner to himself. Kelly had brought him in. The frontiersman had insisted, overriding Joe Crane's arguments and objections.

"You're an old fogy, Joe," said he. "You and your flint guns! Nobody but an Indian uses a flint gun nowadays. Nobody but an Indian and some old fool like you."

"If you give out of caps, what you got?" Joe proffered his usual argument. "Nothin' but a club, and not a good club at that. Now, if you run out of flints, you can chip you off another somewheres, and thar you be!"

"Yes, and if she rains and your priming powder gets wet, or if she blows hard and cleans your pan out for you, *thar you be* too," rejoined

Kelly contemptuously. "Suppose you use elementary common sense and take along enough caps to last you, and a hatful more."

In spite of Joe's grumbling, he escorted Andy and his rifle to the gunmaker's shop.

At first, Hawkens would not even look up from his rifling machine.

"I make rifles," said he shortly. "I don't tinker. I got no time to fool with making over every old blunderbuss. If I started that sort of thing, I wouldn't do anything else."

"That's all right, Jake," agreed Kelly amicably, "but I don't want to take this boy out to the mountains with nothing but a flint gun."

"Let him buy himself a proper one, then. I'm making them."

"Well, just take a look at this anyway, and tell me what you think."

The little gunmaker glanced briefly and grudgingly at the weapon in Andy's hands.

"I know those things," said he. "Too light, anyway. All right enough for when they come from. Now, what you want for the mountains—"

"Is a Hawkens rifle, I know," said Kelly. He took the piece from Andy and thrust it beneath Hawkens's nose. "Take a look at it Jake," he urged.

The gunmaker took it grudgingly and ran his eye expertly over its lines.

"It's a well-made piece," he admitted, "and well-kept." He turned it over. "Who made it?" He squinted painfully at the brass cover to the patch box, deciphering its inscription. Suddenly, he straightened his bent back and looked squarely at his visitors. "Do you know what you've got here?" he demanded with some excitement.

"It was my grandfather's rifle," Andy spoke up, "but before that it belonged to—"

"Dan'l Boone, yes, so I see. But this"—Hawkens tapped a blunt forefinger on the other name.

"I've always been told it is the name of the maker."

"Of course it is," said Hawkens impatiently. "But this I suppose you do not know, that it is said in our craft that Farrell was the first to invent the long barrel and the patched ball. It is possible that this might be the very piece." He examined it absorbedly. "He was a fine workman," said he.

Fumbling about amid the litter of his workbench he produced a magnifying glass through which he continued his examination, muttering to himself. Finally, he looked up.

"I'll tell you what I'll do," said he. "I'll give you one of my new rifles for this. Kelly'll tell you that a Hawkens is better fitted than any other for the plains."

"Every plainsman worth the name has a Hawkens—if he can get it," corroborated Kelly. "It's more than a fair trade."

"I-I know that," stammered Andy, "but if you don't mind—you see, this was my grandfather's rifle—in Kentucky—and—"

"You won't trade," supplied Hawkens. "I supposed not. But this piece ought not to risk loss. It ought to be kept as a historical piece. Well, if so be it you are firm, I'll alter it to a cap gun. I'll do it myself and proud to," he added.

That was why Andy was tolerated on Jake Hawkens's workbench.

The other items of his equipment were quickly acquired. Andy would have liked very much to flower forth in full buckskins. If left to his own devices, he would undoubtedly have appeared rigged out wilder than the wildest. In this, Joe Crane would have abetted him, not because of any remote suspicion of Andy's romanticism, but because of despised *foofaraw*. But Kelly would have none of it.

"You'll come to buckskins soon enough," said he, "but you're silly to get them here—or to wear them here. The clothes you've got on are good for a while."

He superintended the purchase of a sort of greatcoat made of green blanket material, and a hard white wool hat. The latter even Joe admired, so Andy bought him one also to replace the customary bandanna. Andy's rifle implements—the bullet mold, the worm, and the shot pouch and powder horn—he supplemented with a flint and steel and an awl.

Joe shook his head over the rigid severity.

"I don't hold with foofaraw," said he, "but a man's got to hev some pride in himself."

Joe's awl he had set in a deer-horn handle and had made for it a sheath of carved cherry wood.

"He's got to hev pouches for his belt," complained Joe. "How's he going to carry his possibles?"

"He can make 'em—when the time comes," said Kelly shortly. His sardonic eye swept the bedizened mountain man from head to toe. "Same as you, Joe."

The latter accepted this complacently, missing the irony. He looked with satisfaction at his buckskin leggings, adorned elaborately with fringes, embroidered with beads, aflutter with dyed feathers and tufts of hair.

"Nat'ally he ought to git him his own sculps," he admitted, fingering one of the latter.

"Good Lord, are those *scalps!*" cried Andy, staring with mingled horror and fascination.

"And I still got mine," said Crane, patting his own top knot.

In one matter only did Kelly yield. Or rather, on the contrary, he insisted. From a squaw he caused Andy to purchase several pairs of moccasins.

"Wear them," he advised. "You've got to get used to them, and you may as well begin now."

So Andy began then and was secretly a little proud of the look of his feet, though he discovered the earth a lot knobbier than he had thought it, and was inclined at first to step mincingly when he forgot for a moment that he was a hardy plainsman. Soon, however, his feet hardened, and he learned instinctively to feel the ground for a brief fraction of a second before throwing his weight down.

His proudest moment came when the three of them visited a blacksmith shop on the outskirts. The smith was a gigantic Negro, who at first denied that he had any traps to sell.

"All spok' fo', Mistah Kelly," said he respectfully.

But Kelly paid him no attention. From nails on the walls he lifted a number of beaver traps, testing them thoughtfully one after the other, and from the lot, selecting six that met his approval.

"Only decent traps made in St. Louis," he told Andy. "There you are. Give him ten dollars apiece. That'll be right."

The Negro accepted the situation with a grin.

"Such good traps," he agreed.

They next visited a large store filled with fascinating and alluring things among which Joe Crane prowled longingly, but which Kelly sternly ignored. He purchased a quantity of powder, lead, and percussion caps.

"Better git a plenty of them things," muttered Joe, unreconciled.

A small store of coffee, a pot, some vermilion in packets, several yards of scarlet and blue cloth completed the list.

"There, that'll do you," said Kelly. "Shut up, Joe. That's all he needs, and you know it."

On the way back to the hotel, carrying these purchases, the tall plainsman unbent to explanation.

"You'll want horses and saddles, of course," said he, "and such gear. But we'll get them at Franklin. There are always a lot of fools who get drunk on their way out and have to sell their outfits cheap." He glanced at Joe quizzically. The latter looked virtuous.

Andy, accompanied by Joe, carried these few belongings to the tiny room he shared with his companions.

Joe rushed to the mirror to get the effect of the white wool hat. Apparently, his full expectations were not quite realized, for he examined his reflection from several angles.

"Well," he said finally, "not so handsome as I might be—but *damn* genteel!"

Assisted and instructed by the mountain man, Andy made himself pouches of buckskin for his belt, and a sack of buffalo skin for his traps. The mountain man continued to spend much pains on what he called the boy's education. Andy heard much quaint lore, and he shot with his rifle, when Hawkens had completed his work on that weapon, and he began, at first awkwardly, to practice throwing his knife with his left hand. Crane was scandalized when he discovered the boy's skill was all right-handed.

Joe was even more scandalized over his accidental discovery that Andy knew little of horseback. With horses, he was familiar, and knew their wants and dispositions, for he had had much to do with them on the farm, but he had never been atop them save for a sober jog under harness to or from work. From that moment, strenuous times began for Andy. Joe managed to get the use of two animals, and nearly the whole of every afternoon Andy spent in—or near—the saddle. He soon learned to stick on well enough in straight ahead going, for he was young and active, and after a few muscle-racking days, he began to harden so that sitting down in comfort became an art regained. But his attempts to put into practice Joe's demonstrations of the higher proficiencies were merely interesting failures. He managed to cling in concealment behind one side or the other of his mount just as long as the animal moved no faster than a walk. A trot or gallop shook him off with a thump, like a ripe plum off a tree. He was black and blue and sore, but Joe kept him at it.

"One of the shorest ways to git rubbed out is to fall off yore hoss," said he. "The buffalo'll tromp you, and the Injins will lift yore ha'r. You got to larn to stick yore hoss no matter what. Like you growed to him. Like death to a dead nigger."

The mountain man was a mine of knowledge in this department, too. Andy was filled with a new respect for the breadth and depth of the man's attainments. He began to see that, in spite of his lack of formal schooling, Joe was an exceedingly well-educated man. He began to realize what Joe had meant when he had called Andy uneducated. It was all a matter of what one was to do in life.

"It's a sayin' that a man ain't a good rider until he's fell off nine times," said Joe. "Well, Andy, at that rate you shore ought to be a hell of a good rider!"

Nevertheless, Andy really did make rapid progress. He acquired the automatic feel of balance that goes with every movement of the animal, and that is the basis of horsemanship.

One of the things that interested him most was his practice with the short, heavy bow.

"Helps out the rifle sometimes. Comes handy," said the trapper. "Don't have to larn to shoot very straight with 'em, jist to shoot *hard* and fast. Cain't never tell. Better'n a gun to run buffalo with sometimes."

So Andy discharged arrows from his galloping horse as happily as a small boy. For a time, he saw little of Kelly. The tall plainsman was mysteriously absent most of the time.

———

Time passed. The clientele of the hotel was thinning. By twos and threes and in larger parties, the mountain men were drifting away. Some departed on the river steamboat that one day set out up the Missouri. Regular service was not to be established for several years yet. This was made a gala occasion. The decks were crowded with a miscellaneous throng. Everybody in town was at the waterside to see the start. One of the great companies was sending out a trading outfit, well equipped, well manned, and well organized. Besides the *bourgeois*—or *burgeway*—in charge of the business, and his lieutenant, the *little burgeway*—was the *partizan* who acted as field general, and a multitude of French and Creoles to keep camp and perform necessary labor. The hunters and trappers stood apart. Tons of freight were piled aboard after them, goods for trade when the fur country should be reached, all packages made into loads of equal weight for packing, and plainly marked—vermilion, beads, red cloth, blue cloth, powder and lead, flints, blankets, knives, hatchets, fusils—a sort of musket—tin and iron kettles, sugar, raisins, thread, finger rings, brass wire —all sorts of things. And dozens of short, flat wooden kegs curved to fit a mule's sides, which received especial care, and were placed under guard.

"Likker," explained Joe sourly. He looked on the whole expedition with a jaundiced eye, and glared at the little group of trappers and hunters with a hostility that was returned with interest.

"Hired flunkeys," he snorted disdainfully, "workin' for wages and takin' orders like a passel of sojers. Don't even get the valee of the furs they ketch. Jist wages! Sp'ilin' the kentry fur a white man!"

So, of course, Andy hated them too, though with a sneaking appreciation that they were a pretty competent-looking, hard-bitten lot at that.

The boat's paddle wheel churned the water. Everybody yelled. The whistle blew. There was a wild fusillade as the plainsmen discharged their rifles into the air.

"We oughta be aboard that boat ourselves," grumbled Crane. "I don't know what Kelly's a-thinkin' of or what he's a-waitin' fer."

Others of the guests of the Rocky Mountain House departed on horseback, still others on foot. Their places were partially filled by a different class of men from the river or the farms. Still the trio lingered, and still Kelly would give no word for departure. He came and went, ignoring Andy almost entirely, intent on mysterious affairs.

Andy and Joe sat chair-tilted on the veranda of the Rocky Mountain House. The evening meal was over, and the dusk had fallen. Kelly had been invisible since early morning, and Joe, as usual, was grumbling over the delay in starting.

"I cain't rightly understand what he's up to," he complained. "Everybody's gittin' the jump on us. But they's no use tryin' to do anything with him. He'll start when he gits a good ready. Well," the mountain man spat resignedly, "he's got his idees. And my stick floats with his. I've parderned with Kelly for nigh on four years now and I've larned to follow. When he gits his eye on a stream, it's gone beaver. For all his college eddication and his soft talk, he's the best man of the lot. He makes 'em *come*."

"Thanks, Joe," Kelly's sardonic voice startled them. "That's all right. Come with me, you two."

He led the way swiftly through the gathering dusk, down through the gaily noisy squalor of the Vide Poche, through the Rue de l'Eglise, to the more dignified quarter of town where stood the mansions of the St. Louis aristocracy. Turning in at one of these, he rang the bell. Preceding Andy and Joe Crane, he followed the Negro servant into a study where awaited them a tall, clean-shaven man of between thirty and forty, dressed carefully in the long coat and strapped pantaloons of the man of importance. A mane of hair tossed back from a high, narrow forehead, aquiline features, and haughty and piercing eyes, together with a backflung carriage of the head, but emphasized a peculiar vivid and burning dynamic force of personality that was almost arrogance.

At the introduction of his visitors, he arose from an armchair and laid aside a book.

"Ah, Kelly," he greeted the tall frontiersman, "I am glad to see you. And these, I suppose, are the men of whom you have spoken."

"My partners," replied Kelly. "Yes, sir. This is Joe Crane, a mountain man of old standing and long experience, none better in mountains or on the plains. And this is Andrew Burnett. His experience is as yet slight, but I have confidence in his ability. His name will be familiar, sir, when I mention Gail Burnett."

"The friend of Boone," agreed their host. "You are of distinguished blood, sir, and I am sure will do credit to your breeding. Be seated, gentlemen."

Kelly obeyed the invitation with easy unconsciousness. Joe perched himself awkwardly and warily on the edge of a chair. Andy, embarrassed and a little awed, he knew not why, took refuge in the background.

"I have brought them with me," said Kelly, "because they are my partners to whom I am pledged, and I can make no undertaking without them. I also wish you to see them for *yourself*. And as I told you, you'll have to make it clear what you want, or it's talk wasted. I know Crane."

"Quite right." Their host ran his hand through his upstanding hair and turned to Joe and Andrew. "Here is the situation," said he. "You probably know as much or more of it than I do, Crane, but I'll run it over for the benefit of this young man. The population of New Mexico, Spanish and Indian and mixed blood—largely mixed blood—import about everything they use. About all they make themselves is a little pottery, some kinds of blankets and leather, and such things. Everything else they use comes from Old Mexico. Not only is that a long carry, but the class of goods sent in is poor, the remains of old stock, often, sometimes damaged stuffs. And the charges are outrageously high. We could, here from St. Louis, send them better goods, at half the prices they are paying now, and still make a fine profit."

Joe Crane grinned.

"Try it," he advised, "and see what happens. I reckon you're a trader from the way you talk."

"This is Senator Benton, Joe, and I'd advise you to shut up and listen."

"Well, maybe the Senator's thinkin' of goin' into the trade," was Joe's stout comment, "and I'm tellin' him."

Benton's uplifted hand checked Kelly's rejoinder.

"I want to hear," said he. "Go on, Crane. What is your point?"

"My p'int is this," replied Joe, "that it's been tried, and it most ginerally never works. Take Dave Merriweather or Jules de Mern or Bob McKnight. They got *in* all right. Nothin' to stop a good man gittin' thar, though it's mean kentry to travel through. And when they got thar, what happened? Why, they got their trade taken away from them, and they landed in the calaboose. And they'll do it that way every time. As you say, Senator, it's a purty vallyable trade, and them Spanish governors is going to keep the pickin's, and those *hombres* ain't too partic'lar what they does to keep it, either."

"You have correctly stated the situation, as it has existed," Benton acknowledged. He hesitated and turned a doubtful eye in Kelly's direction. The latter nodded.

"You can talk freely, Senator," he said. "I'll answer for this young man, and Joe can keep his mouth shut, even when drunk," he added with a grin.

"The situation is going to change," Benton resumed. "This is confidential, but by secret dispatches, I learn that the tide of revolution is rising, and that General Iturbide is even now at the gates of Mexico City. If so, Spain's power in Mexico is at an end."

Joe Crane slapped his thigh.

"And out goes the hidalgos and in comes the greasers!" he cried delightedly. "They been hangin' around the feedin' pen with their tongues hangin' out. Now's their chance!"

"Which means a Mexican governor in place of a Spanish governor in New Mexico. And that offers an opening heretofore non-existent for the trade."

"I don't see that," objected Joe. "Senator, you don't sabe these people like I do. I've lived with 'em."

"That is why I asked Kelly to bring you here. What about it?"

"Wall," observed Joe dryly, "you line up a Spanish governor and a greaser governor 'longside each other, and shuffle 'em up a leetle, and you can't tell a one from t'other. They're both thisaway." The mountain man held up a receptive palm.

"I expect you are right," admitted Benton, and added slowly, "I hope so."

"Huh?" Joe was surprised.

"For this simple reason, a Spanish governor wanted a monopoly for Spanish goods—in which, as you suggest, he might be personally interested. A Mexican governor cares nothing whatever about Spanish goods. It might be better worth his while to make an arrangement with others. Ourselves, for instance."

He paused to let this soak in. Joe caught the point immediately.

"And somethin' *on the prairie* is what'll do the trick. I take it back, yo're right, Senator."

It was Benton's turn to look puzzled.

"*On the prairie* is plainsman's talk meaning a free gift, Senator," Kelly explained.

"Or a bribe," amended Joe bluntly.

"I think we understand. The point is, here is a chance to open a valuable trade, if we take advantage of it, a trade that will prove valuable not only to those who engage in it, but to our country. It is an opportunity of which we must take instant advantage. That is why I have asked you men to meet me here this evening."

"If yore tryin' to make a trader out of me, yore barkin' up the wrong tree," stated Joe positively. "A trapper I am, and a trapper I'll allus be. I ain't got no use fer tradin' or traders."

"I understand that," replied Benton. "I am not asking you to enter trade if you do not care to do so. But the trade can be established, it must be established. There are difficulties, immediate difficulties, to be overcome. One of them is the route."

"There's a plenty knows how to git thar," said Joe.

"Not many. And they are not available. And it is not sufficient merely to get there. We must find a wagon route. I understand you have made this journey."

"I have. And it's a tough one, what with bad kentry and bad Injins."

"Nevertheless, you could make it again. I would like to have you do so."

Joe Crane studied Benton keenly.

"I don't aim to dry-nuss no tradin' outfit," he stated. "I aim to trap the Blackfoot kentry, soon as I kin git thar."

Benton arose from his chair.

"I do not wish you to act as guide. Nor do I contemplate sending out a wagon train this year. What I want is a scouting trip—and a messenger. It will not interfere with your plans. You could, without too great a delay, go to the Blackfoot country by way of Santa Fe, could you not?"

Crane considered carefully.

"We might," he admitted with caution.

"I want only two things. To determine in detail the best route, and to convey secretly to the new governor certain ideas of my own."

Joe pondered further.

"How you goin' to know about it?" he inquired. "I don't reckon we aim to come back yere. Season's too late."

"I can fix that," spoke up Kelly. "Old Pedro Vial has made the trip in '92, and he is still alive. I can fix it with him to bring back our reports."

"The job will be worth a thousand dollars," added Benton.

Joe knit his brows. He glanced toward Kelly.

"How about it, Jack?" he asked doubtfully.

Kelly nodded.

"Well, all right," agreed the mountain man. A slow grin illuminated his face. "Santa Fe gals! I never thought to see them agin! And," he added, "I never thought to throw in with no traders, neither!"

"That being agreed, we will drink to success," said Senator Benton, and struck a bell.

The ceremony completed and all arose to go. Benton laid a hand on Andy's arm.

"If you've nothing better to do, I should much enjoy a chat with Gail Burnett's grandson."

The Senator lighted a long cheroot and relaxed into the depths of an easy chair. Benton was always possessed of an extraordinary personal charm, and he now took pains to exert it. He proved to know more of the Burnett family in the early history of Kentucky than did Andy himself.

"It seems eminently proper and fitting that you should be in your turn going into the West," observed the Senator, "as your grandfather went into the West of his day. And you are going with the two most competent men I know. You could have no better mentors. Some of these mountain men are a wild lot, and how they survive is a mystery. Most of that sort do not survive." He was talking on quietly to give the lad a chance for ease. "You'll be in a position to learn all there is to learn from Kelly and Crane. It's very exciting to look forward to, isn't it? Then what?"

"Sir?"

Benton considered and came to a decision.

"It's always a good idea to face facts," said he. "For Crane and Kelly and their like, it is all very well. But you are a young man. You are going to live to see this present life change to something else. It is inevitable. The day of the free trapper is drawing to a close." He smiled at the fall of Andy's countenance. "Oh, not today nor tomorrow nor the day after. You'll have your fling, my lad. But more and more will go into the mountains.

They are going now—as they went into Kentucky in your grandfather's day. It's only to be expected. A few cannot expect to monopolize the half of a continent. Where one man goes, ten will follow—eventually."

He knocked carefully the ashes from the end of his cheroot and resumed, "The one man does not like it, naturally. He wants to keep his old life. Joe Crane is just back from Washington on some wild errand against the organized trading companies." He looked across at Andy keenly. "That could not succeed, of course. I understand how he—and his kind—feel about it, and I can sympathize, but I can see the futility of it."

He surveyed, with a twinkle of kindly amusement, the increasing blankness of the boy's face.

"I would not have you think for a moment I am underrating your new Mends," he went on. "Nor am I trying to throw cold water on your great adventure, least of all am I trying to turn you from it. God forbid! You are, to my mind, privileged beyond most. The mountain men!" He turned to his desk and flipped open an atlas on which he laid the flat of his hand. "Ask them. They will tell you that all they want is the beaver. Most of them will die poor, leaving their bones to bleach on the plains and mountains, and no one to miss them and no one to mourn them and no one to remember them. They are gone as if they never were. In the eyes of the world, all they have managed to accomplish is to put silly beaver hats atop a lot of numbskull pates, and money in the pockets of merchants and saloon keepers."

His beautifully modulated orator's voice—it was the day of the orator—sunk at the last words. Andy twisted his hands nervously. His world of enthusiasm was flattened. He had to remember he was too old to cry.

Senator Benton removed the flat of his hand from the map.

"What does this say?" His long forefinger tapped it nervously. "*The Great American Desert, Unknown, Unexplored*. That is for the world. But the mountain men know better than that. And before the legend of that blank space is changed in the geographies of the future, there will not be a park in the Rockies, a stream in the hills, a patch in the *desert* that one of you has not ridden over, walked over, trapped over. You will know! You have been there! Those who come after will follow your trails! You will lead the *explorers* when they come. Nobody will know that, but it will be true. You seek the beaver streams, that is all you know. But more surely than most, you play your part in larger destinies.

"You are going with Kelly and Crane into the Blackfoot country. That is unknown, and I understand, dangerous. If you win though alive—as I am confident you will—you will be rich in beaver skins. But also this"—he tapped again the legend on the map—"will be by that much more untrue. Do you see now why I said you were highly privileged?"

"Yes, sir," said Andy. His head was up again.

Benton arose suddenly from his chair and began to pace back and forth the length of the room.

"We are born to a noble destiny. But we must work with destiny if we would have it come true. Nothing must be allowed to stand in our way. By every means, with all our heart and strength, we must play strange and alien peoples—"

He stopped suddenly in mid-stride and looked down almost quizzically at the lad before him.

"It is too big for one man. It is too big for me. But we can play our part, however blindly, can't we, Andy?"

"Yes, sir," said Andy again. He had risen and was facing the older man. For a moment, Benton looked at him searchingly.

"You are Gail Burnett's grandson," said the Senator at last. "I suppose that is why I am talking to you so. You must not let what I have said dishearten you. Go trap your beaver, and hunt your buffalo and deer, and learn to take care of yourself among the savages. It is the adventurous life that will appeal to your years and your blood. But when the time comes, remember!"

He poured two glasses and handed one to Andy.

"To the mountain men," he proposed, "and those who come after them! And to our country! One people, one flag, a mighty civilization that shall extend, that *must* extend, from sea to sea!"

Andy gulped at the unaccustomed wine.

"I remember once," said the Senator conversationally, "asking Colonel Boone to what he ascribed, having escaped so many dangers to have attained his great old age. He answered me, 'I was ordained by God to open the wilderness.' He meant it, and I believe it. Some of us are. And now, my boy, goodbye, and good luck to you. I shall hear of you."

"Yes, sir!" cried Andy. "You shall!"

Benton's eyes followed him musingly, and a little wistfully, as he left the room. Though still in the earliest years of his senatorship in the new state, already the ambition of his statesmanship was defining itself in his mind. The settled *facts*, so solid and real to his contemporaries, his eye alone saw to be illusory. With one gesture of prophecy, he brushed aside the impossibilities—the vastness of an unexplored continent, its apparently insurmountable obstacles of beast and savage and thirst and mountain and the unknown, the new occupation by the British in Oregon, the old established sovereignly of the Spanish in California and the whole southwest. In imagination, be stood on the shores of the Pacific, still looking westward. His fine eyes glowed, then darkened. The *facts* took on solidity and pressed him close. Spain and Britain and the Unknown towered formidably against his vision. What he had accomplished shrunk to nothing in face of what must be done. A few men interested in trade, the beginnings of a thrust toward the locked land, a feeble public interest in the fate of the Northwest—now that Astoria had fallen and it was almost too late. Weary years thrust between the vision and its accomplishment. For a moment, the Senator's high courage drooped. He could count his supporters on the fingers of his hand! He felt alone in a world of emptiness.

Then his head went up again. His eye turned to the door through which Andy had taken his departure. Alone? How could he have been so foolish! Back of him pressed the irresistible genius of a people. This boy who had just gone out, Benton saw him as a symbol—the youth of the land pressing forward, it knew not why, to the accomplishment of its appointed part, and after it, the people as a flood into channels prepared. Suddenly, the Senator experienced a tremendous uplift of vigor and hope. Succeed? Why, it was impossible that he should fail.

"It is manifest destiny!" he cried, for the first time using a phrase which was in later years to be at once his war cry, his excuse, and his justification.

Chapter 4
The Trader

For the third time the flat-bottomed Missouri River steamboat slid up on a sandbar, half turned in the current, splashed for a few moments like a whale, and gave it up. The motley crowd aboard cheered ironically and returned to its card games and its talk. Some of the crew baited lines and dangled their legs overside in hope of a river cat. The captain shrugged his shoulders, lighted a cheroot, and waited. He was somewhat of a philosopher, the captain, an educated man, given to airing his views in any company. Thus it was to Andy Burnett as the nearest at hand that be turned on this occasion.

"Of all variable things in creation," he remarked, "the most uncertain are the action of a jury, the state of a woman's mind, and the condition of the Missouri River."

He seemed entirely resigned and patient, as was not Andy, who burned with eagerness to enter on the great adventure of his first trip with the mountain men. But he had already learned that running aground was not serious, for the rapid current working, against the resistance of the hull soon carried away the light loose quicksand to set her free. And in this the Missouri differed from all other rivers.

Sure enough, inside an hour, helped by a judicious occasional stroke of the paddle, the steamer had extricated herself and was again plowing against the heavy yellow current. The following day interminability actually ended, and with the rest, Andy disembarked at the little settlement of Franklin.

It was not, in this year of the early twenties, much of a settlement, but it was the jumping-off place for the prairies and mountains, and therefore possessed of certain activities and industries. There was a saddler, and a provision merchant, and a gunsmith, and a number of saloons. These were housed in logs, and back of them straggled other log cabins used as dwellings. Franklin lay in a bend of the river, below rolling wooded hills. At this time men were beginning to see a brilliant future for it as the commerce of the prairies should increase, and certain primitive forerunners of the booster tribe were beginning speculation in town lots. Their reasoning was sound enough, but a few years later the Missouri completely justified the captain's statement by deciding to change her bed. In the process she removed Franklin. Thenceforward the new settlement of Independence, nearly two hundred miles farther upstream, more safely situated, grew to be the starting point for the westward caravans, even through the covered-wagon days.

At Franklin Andy's companions reclaimed from a man who made a business of horses the animals they had left in his care. Five of them were horses, the sixth was a big raw-boned mule. This proved to be Joe's especial pride. He bragged about it with a vehemence that suggested a defense complex against not infrequent ridicule.

"He ain't sich a lot to look at," he told Andy, "but I wouldn't trade him for an even dozen of them things." He jerked a scornful head toward Kelly's horse. "He'll climb whar a goat can't make it, and he'll git fat whar a horny toad'll starve, he'll smell out an Injin further than—"

"You can smell a drink, Joe," supplied Kelly with a grin.

"Yes." Joe accepted this as a sufficient compliment. "And what's more, when you *cache*, he won't nicker and holler and give you away like no fool hoss. And they ain't nobody goin' to steal him on me. He'll kick ary stranger so high the black birds'll build nests in his ha'r before he comes down."

"And," Kelly told the boy with mock enthusiasm, "you just ought to see him run buffalo! Steady as a church, and moves just about as fast."

"If I want to run buffalo, I'll git me a fool hoss," said Joe gruffly.

They bought three horses for Andy, consulting earnestly together after inspection of several hundred offered for their choice, and a stout second-hand saddle and bridle, and two pack saddles, and three rawhide ropes to be carried wound in a coil around the animals' necks. Then they moved, with all their few and simple belongings, to a little grove outside the settlement where already were encamped a dozen Western wayfarers.

Andy was surprised to recognize many of those who had left St. Louis on the preceding steamboat nearly a month before. His feelings was not shared by either of his companions. Indeed, they seemed to have expected something of the sort. Many of the tardy ones appeared to have postponed departure for the simple reason that they had paused to celebrate further their abandonment of what civilization they knew. The seductions of Franklin's simple but effective red-light district had been too much for them. Their takings of the season before had gone into the pockets of the saloon keepers. This temporary embarrassment of resources did not appear to bother them much, for Andy found that recuperation seemed to depend on the artless process of waiting for enough newcomers in sufficient funds to outfit everybody. It was a true communism. Those with something over and above the immediate need did not hesitate to produce for those gone broke. Thus the whole band slowly gathered strength as a unit. Since a man's rock-bottom necessities were few and simple, this could not take long. Three ponies, some jerked meat—which the surrounding country quickly supplied–a little coffee to start the journey, tobacco, lead and caps, a half-dozen traps, these were sufficient to set any good mountain man up in business again.

But the immediate cause of delay proved to be a more serious matter. It seemed that the trading outfit that had taken passage on the earlier steamboat also lingered, strangely and inexplicably, at Franklin, were, in fact, still camped the other side of town. It was equipped, organized, ready, but it did not move. By all plains common sense it should have been by now well beyond the Platte. The mountain men, through long training, were quick to react to the unusual. Accustomed to the instant arousing of suspicion and wariness by the smallest deviations from the normal, they were instantly alert.

"What these burgeways a-waitin' for?" they asked Kelly. "Whar floats thar stick? Looks to us like they're waitin' to trail after us and find out whar's our kentry. They been tryin' now for two-three year to git into our trade. What you think, Jack?"

"Quite likely," agreed Kelly. "They got any good men?"

"Sublette's with them."

"Well, they'll get in," Kelly pointed out, "eventually. How you going to stop them?"

"Wall," said the other stubbornly, "we ain't a-goin' to lead 'em in and have them squattin' under our noses stealin' our trade. Let 'em do their own findin'."

The matter was discussed at length about the campfires, heatedly, but it must be confessed rather aimlessly. The mountain men's only positive unanimity was an instinctive resentment. Reluctantly they were forced to admit that their clearer-sighted and cooler members, like Kelly, were right, that slow invasion of the mountains was ultimately inevitable. But they were firmly and irrationally resolved to resist the inevitable in every way they could. Especially were they united in resentment of this presumed effort to force them in spite of themselves to act as guides to the enemy! The first idea, which was acclaimed with delighted and mischievous chuckles, was to lead the trading outfit on a wild goose chase.

"We kin toll 'em up into the badlands, and scatter and leave 'em thar!" they cried.

This would be annoying, and highly satisfactory. But only an annoyance, only a temporary expedient. Scatter as they might, the mountain men must eventually round back to their trapping grounds.

"And don't believe for a moment they are not good enough to follow," said Kelly. He had been thinking and now came to a decision. "Look here," said he, "I have a plan." He looked about him at the dozen weatherbeaten faces turned expectantly toward him, eyeing them thoughtfully one after the other. He nodded briefly in satisfaction. Mountain men all, here present by test of survival. "We three—Joe, this lad, and myself—have an errand to do. We are headed for Taos and Santa Fe. After delivering a message we intend to go on north to the mountains. Suppose we throw in together and all go that way?" He looked again from one to the other of the faces, turned doubtful. "Let them follow us there if they want to. What between the Comanches and the *jornada* we can deal them plenty of grief. I don't think they'll try it. Even if they wanted to face the journey, they'd know what to expect at the other end. Traders don't get much of a welcome out there. By moving rapidly we can make it back to the mountains by the prime of the fur. With as strong a party we won't have any trouble getting through the Comanche country, and as for the *jornada*, Joe here has made it and knows the way."

Bill Williams spat into the fire.

"The Injins is all right," said he slowly, "and I ain't seen no kentry yet so tough I was askeered of it. But I don't aim to spend no time in a greaser calaboose."

The others nodded agreement.

Kelly hesitated, pondering.

"I'll talk turkey," he decided. "This errand of ours is a sort of government matter. The men who carry the message won't be bothered by the greasers. I'll guarantee that."

"Nobody can guarantee nothin' with greasers," insisted Bill Williams stubbornly.

"All right," said Kelly. "We're going, anyway. This is Senator Benton's business," he added.

The name evidently made an impression. They discussed the matter. Gradually, they yielded. It was agreed that they were taking a chance. But to these men, taking chances was habitual. Once decided, they veered as strongly from doubt to a growing relish of the idea.

"As far as Painted Rock," Kelly pointed out, "we'll be following the old trace to the Platte. There's where the way forks."

"And that's whar I'm a goin' to *cache* somewhar whar I kin ketch a sight of that burgeway's face when he finds we've done turned south!" cried Bill Williams. "Got some money, anybody? I got to git me some powder and lead."

The men arose from their places about the fire. Each went in a different direction, busy with various last-minute preparations for setting out. Abruptly, as though cut off with a knife, the waiting phase had ended. An hour ago it had seemed to Andy that he was doomed to linger forever but just within the edge of the West to which for so long his eyes had turned. Now, he was to start tomorrow. He, too, sought out and reviewed, for the hundredth time, the few simple items of his equipment. He took from beneath his blankets the long Kentucky rifle that had belonged to his grandfather, the friend of Boone. Though he had only that morning put it in order, he drew forth the ramrod and worm and oiled its bore again. As he laid it back under the blankets, he patted it softly. Kelly's voice above him caused him to blush with boyish embarrassment.

"You'll find plenty for it to do," said the older man. Kelly was not often expansive, but this evening he was filled with an elation that must find vent. "A good evening's work," he told Andy with satisfaction. "Nothing could have turned out better. I'd rather have that lot with me than the whole United States Army."

Once the horses were caught up it did not take long to make a start. Although each man by custom was provided with two pack horses, besides his riding animal, they were for the purpose of later transportation of the fur take, and now had small burdens of the simple trapper outfits. Ten minutes sufficed to saddle and pack.

But the driving in and catching up of the pastured horses was not so easy. They were fresh and *sassy*. Even the experienced, well-trained beasts proposed to have a little fun before submitting. Andy had an opportunity to appreciate the fierce and ungoverned temper of some of the men with whom he had thrown in.

One trapper, named Tilton, had listened to Joe Crane's vociferous partisanship and had bought himself a mule. On this morning he tried to lead it, as one would a horse, by a rope about its neck. The mule refused. The man insisted, leaning his whole weight on the rawhide rope. The mule choked, twisted its neck, braced its hooves, and backed slowly. Tilton commanded, jerked, and swore. The mule closed its eyes, partly from the choking, partly from sheer stubbornness. Joe Crane happened by.

"Throw you a hackamore around his nose," he advised. "Then he'll foller you like yore shadder. A mule won't lead by the neck."

Tilton, red-faced, perspiring, paid him no attention.

"Throw you a hackamore," repeated Joe. "You'll git nowhere thataway."

"Hush up!" bawled Tilton. "By God, this mule's goin' to lead like I want him to."

It was evident that the man was as obstinate as the mule, and that now Tilton would rather die than compromise on the hackamore. But it was not he who died. With a suddenness that left Andy gasping, he snatched a heavy buffalo pistol from his belt and shot the mule dead. Nobody commented, either then or later.

For ten days, the excursion was to Andy a continuous and delightful picnic. The route led through a beautiful rolling landscape, at first of preponderant hardwood forest, then of plains and woodland, and finally of open grasslands adorned with groves of timber, as though planted, like a park. The country was perfectly safe. Indeed, after the last of the scattered crude farms had been passed, they, for a long time, laid eyes on no human being. The trappers rode scattered, in small shifting groups, talking, singing, or lost in the profound, long patience of the wayfarer. The pack animals were driven forward in a loose group in charge of two men. Someone was always away on either flank attending to the commissary, and would rejoin the cavalcade at close of day, the strings of his saddle dangling with wild turkey, squirrels, coons, and prairie chickens, with sometimes a deer strapped on behind the cantle. Before the farmlands had been left behind, the contribution was quite likely to include a young pig or a half-dozen domestic chickens, with possibly an irate farmer not far astern to be overawed. Evenings about the campfire Andy lay on his back and watched the sparks against the blackness and listened to tall tales.

To the trappers this was evidently only a part of the journey to be left behind them, and they displayed little interest in their surroundings beyond that comprehensive awareness which is second nature to the plainsman. But it was an awareness that was set only for certain dangers, which as yet lacked. It was blind to everything else. But to Andy, breathing deep of the freshness of winds from wide spaces, the days were alive with perceptions so numerous as to jostle into merely a series of almost unrelated impressions which he had no spiritual leisure to sort out and make orderly. In the hardwoods, the great pileated woodpeckers, large as crows, thundered their long roll against the tree trunks, wild pigeons roared in flight like distant surf, and innumerable black and fox squirrels chirked and chattered and chased one another madly. Occasional deer, startled from their forms, bounded away loftily, flaunting their white flags, and the new leaves shone in their freshness like green flames, while in the colder shadows lingered the red clusters of the maple flowers and Indian-apple blossoms. In the grass openings, golden plover covered the ground for acres, prairie chickens arose with a whir, tiny sedge-rimmed ponds were ruffled dark blue by the singing wind, ducks rode bobbing like little ships, and patches of last year's grass were bent soggy brown, with the new grass green beneath. A bewildering variety of wildflowers were abloom or preparing quietly an unfoldment—wild verbena, indigo, larkspur, lupines, morning-glories, and in the bottomlands and ravines, wild roses and hazel clumps filled with tiny busy birds. The sky was, in general, clean, and swept and blue, and in it was space for the singing wind. It arched far above the lower air, with its dipping flights of blackbirds and it's sailing questing hawks, high, remote, empty save for its chosen, the huge sandhill cranes. Some were so high as to be beyond vision, but still out of apparent emptiness came their strange, harsh antiphonetic cries.

But occasionally, sometimes after noon, fleecy clouds would gather at the horizon. With incredible rapidity, they swelled and built up, until the heavens had blackened. The wind died. A dark silence fell upon the earth, broken only by small frightened scurryings. Then, with a sudden vicious roar, the heavens opened, and torrents of rain fell. Lightning flashed almost continuously, and the deepthroated roll of thunder took majestic possession of the silence. The horses turned their tails and hung their heads. The men humped their backs. Their sodden buckskins clung to their forms like paper. Andy had difficulty in imitating their stolid endurance, but protection there was none, shelter there was none, and it did no good to squirm or lament. Nevertheless, he had still far to go before attaining that peculiar command of mind which is able to detach its attention at will from what is happening to the body, a faculty possessed in greater or lesser degree by every outdoor man, and *in excelsis* by those few who undergo torture unmoved. He did, however, gain by this experience to the elementary philosophy that things pass, and nothing is more quickly forgotten than discomfort.

The extreme violence of the storm rarely outlasted the half-hour, after which the journey was resumed. It was not pleasant. The rain still fell. The shallow streams that so often crossed their way were suddenly and miraculously torrents. The horses slid and slipped, plunged, and sometimes fell. A palpable and depressing gloom filled all the air, as with an infusion. Then, low in the western horizon appeared a narrow fringe of yellow light, as though a curtain lifted. The aperture slowly widened. Sun rays, like bars of gold, shot through horizontally. Across the gray gloom of the east arched the brilliance of the rainbow. Abruptly, the rain ceased. From a dripping thicket, a song sparrow sang.

Immediately the rain had stopped, every man looked first of all to his rifle, wiping it off carefully—*before the rust sets*, as Joe explained—with the greased rag from the patch box, examining the lock to see if water had seeped through the lock cover, repriming, if the piece happened to be a flint gun. The remainder of the day's journey was likely to be cold and shivery, for a breeze followed the storm. The trappers gave no sign of discomfort. Andy had not yet attained that hardihood. But once the campfire had steamed him dry, he forgot it, and he listened with a deep instinctive response, which he could not have explained, to whippoorwills, the owls, and the chorus of frog voices from the new-made pools.

On the fourth morning, Kelly did not start out with the cavalcade. He packed his pack horses, turned them in with the bunch, then rode off at right angles. Nor did he rejoin them until late that afternoon. He nodded to the expectation on the other men's faces.

"They're coming," said he. "You were right, Bill. They're following. They're about twenty miles behind us, traveling easy."

From this news the trappers appeared to get considerable satisfaction. Two days later, one of those who had ridden wide to hunt had another report to make.

"Injin sign," said he briefly.

A thrill of excitement ran down Andy's backbone. The trappers, however, appeared indifferent. But that evening camp was made, not as had been the custom in a sheltered bottom, but in the open, atop a gentle rise. The animals were grazed until dark, then picketed close to where the men had made their beds. The fire was carefully extinguished. Otherwise, there were no precautions taken, and as every man calmly spread his blanket or robe and prepared to turn in, it became evident that no guard was to be placed. Andy could not comprehend this. He nobly restrained himself for some time, but at last could stand it no longer.

"Kansas tribe yereabouts," explained Joe. "No account. I ain't sayin' they might not lift yore ha'r if enough of them caught you out alone, and you not lookin'. They know better'n to bother with a dozen mountain men. Besides, with that old mule of mine, don't need no guard. He smells an Injin better'n a dog. Don't fret yore mind about these Kansas. Steal anything they can git their hands on, shore! Like nothin' better'n to git hold of our horses and leave us afoot. But tackle us!" He laughed shortly.

Nevertheless, for some hours Andy lay awake, and a half-dozen times in the night he stirred to uneasy consciousness. Once the snort of a horse brought him up sitting, his heart beating wildly. In the dim starlight he could make out Joe Crane leaning on his elbow. After a moment, the mountain man lay back again.

Late the following afternoon, a group of mounted men appeared silhouetted on the skyline of a rise, and sat their ponies motionless. After an interval, one detached himself and came skimming down the slope toward the trappers. Except for a brief appraising glance, the latter paid him no attention. With superb horsemanship, the newcomer swept in a half-circle and at one plunge brought his pony to a walk. Andy looked with all his eyes, for this was his first plains Indian in his natural environment.

He saw a good-looking savage in breechclout and leggings with a blanket flung over his left shoulder and tied under his right arm. His head was shaved except for a narrow roached strip from nape to brow, held upright like a cock's comb by a stiffening of vermilion. His eyelids, cheeks, ears, and forehead were heavily rouged. From his stretched ear lobes depended bone ornaments. On his chest he wore two medallions. Small hollow metal buttons strung around his neck and fringing his leggings gave forth a small musical tinkling. He carried a long flintlock musket bound about with brass. Altogether, he made a brave and satisfactory show and looked well the part of the prairie warrior. From one corner of his mouth projected a leafy twig.

"Sign of peace," Joe explained to Andy. "He's a Kansas, apin' a Pawnee

—his top knot I mean. Kansas just leave a sculp lock, or wear their ha'r long. This fellow thinks he's *some*."

The Kansas let his eyes roam deliberately from one to another of the members of the party. Andy, in his turn, met them with something of a shock, for they were strangely unlike any eyes he had ever seen. Flat and lusterless, they seemed to stop him at their outer surfaces. Apparently satisfied as to who was the leader, the Indian drew alongside Kelly, laid his musket across in front of him and began to talk in sign language. Joe, good-naturedly and a little contemptuously, translated for Andy's benefit.

"Says he's a heap big chief," said Joe. "Says he's a heap big friend of the white man. He's doin' a lot of tall braggin' now about what a hell of a feller he is and all that. Says they's Pawnees about. Says he's travelin' our way, him, and his outfit, and will perfect us. Braggin' again what great warriors they all is, and how many Pawnees they's sculped. Reg'lar terror of the plains, accordin' to him."

Andy watched the Indian's sweeping, graceful gestures. This was his first experience of the sign language. He had had no idea it could convey as much and as accurately as Joe's free translation seemed to indicate. He said so.

"Oh, you kin say anything you want to," said the latter. "It's a reg'lar language. I'll larn it to you."

Kelly appeared to pay no attention, he seemed not even to look at the other. But after a few moments, he leaned from his saddle to pluck from a bush a bit of green which he thrust in his hat band. One by one, the other trappers followed his example. Joe grumbled a bit at this.

"I'd like to tell him to go to hell," he told Andy disgustedly. "They'll just clutter us all up, and you want to watch your possibles or they'll turn up missing."

They rode on steadily, the trappers ignoring the Kansas chief as though he were not there. The latter seemed unembarrassed. From a fold in his blanket he produced a small mirror and seemed to derive much satisfaction in the contemplation of his image.

In the meantime, the small group on the skyline had been augmented until it had become a great and disorderly rabble, which streamed down the slope in a slow convergence toward the trappers until shortly they were paralleling the line of march some fifty yards away. There were several hundred of them in all. A few men, evidently the upper warriors, or sub-chiefs, rode in a small exclusive group a few paces in advance. Many of the women trudged along on foot. Ponies carried burdens piled high and haphazard, and atop them clung the smallest children. Naked boys with bows and arrows ran about shouting. Dogs, also with burdens, trotted along, and disheveled hags with sticks screamed at them and chased them about. Most of the tribe was poverty-stricken in the extreme, and seemed to have made no attempt at decency. Their robes or blankets were tattered, their hair long and matted. All were dirty. They marched without order, shifting and changing, clamoring. Each of the men carried a green twig in his mouth—the sign of peace.

Toward sunset, the trappers stopped in a creek bottom to make camp. The tribe scattered about, and the squaws began to catch the pack ponies.

But now Kelly asserted himself. Turning squarely in his saddle to face the chief, he made a dozen emphatic gestures. The Kansas watched him closely. When he had finished, the Indian uttered loud commands. The tribe regathered its scattered belongings and moved away down the stream bed a quarter mile, where Andy could see them moving about confusedly, making their preparations for the night. The trappers were left alone.

"Consarn it, Jack," grumbled Joe Crane. "Whyn't you send them on their way?"

"Rather have them near," replied Kelly briefly. "They won't try to steal much with all their women and children within easy reach, and I'd like to get the state of the country from them."

But already in twos and threes, the younger male members of the tribe were returning up the creek bottom, and soon, the trappers' camp was surrounded by them. Many merely squatted on their heels and stared. More walked solemnly here and there, eyeing sharply every last item of equipment. They were as annoying as gadflies. With tireless persistence, undeterred by rebuff, they begged for everything they saw. They asked for rum, tobacco, powder, lead, coffee, anything and everything. The trappers paid them no attention, they might have been thin air. Stolidly and methodically and in silence, the mountain men went about their business. Only, Andy noticed, each kept his rifle at hand. Once or twice, one or another of the bolder Indians, in the course of his urgent begging, laid hand on something he desired. Then the mountain man turned with a throaty and menacing growl, like a bulldog. Only once did action flash. Andy saw a hand and arm steal cautiously from the grass screen toward a buckskin bag lying on the ground. Before he could move or say anything, a knife flashed past him to bury itself hilt deep, accurately halfway between the bag and the reaching band, where it quivered as a warning.

"I'd like to have pinned the varmint's hand," muttered Joe Crane, striding forward to reclaim his weapon. He took off his hat, stared at the wilting green of the twig and sighed. The Indians within sight placed their hands over their mouths in token of wonder at the demonstration.

The trappers cooked and ate their meal, caught up the grazing horses and brought them in. Dusk was falling and the fires in the creek bottom gleamed the brighter. Now suddenly, the idle visitors melted away. From the direction of the Indian encampment Andy saw approaching a small group, blanketed and robed. At first, merely in dark silhouette, as they neared, Andy perceived them to be the same group of upper warriors that, during the march, had ridden apart. Before them, several paces in advance, strode the chief, holding at arm's length before him a pipe whose bowl was of red stone, and whose long wooden stem was carved and fluttering with feathers.

The tall trappers rose leisurely from their various occupations and sat down in a half-circle on one side the fire. Joe dropped to Andy's side.

"Well, lad," said he, "yere's more of yore eddication comin'. Goin' to have a medicine smoke jist like these was real Injins, 'stead of a thievin' dirty lot of beggars without a sculp to their belts, a lesson they slips up on a man drunk or asleep. But you'll larn somethin' at that, that'll come handy to you some day."

The warriors disposed themselves to complete the circle around the fire. In spite of Joe's contemptuous description, Andy could not subdue a thrill of excitement. The impassive shrouded figures, the painted faces, the shaved heads surmounted with the stiff roached mane of the scalp locks, the glittering eyes of beadlike surface lights, the forms of the spectators in the background half blending with the shadows of the darkening earth, the upleap of the flames, the slow-spreading evening of the skies were quite sufficient to kindle his imagination.

For a considerable interval, no one spoke or moved. Then Kelly took the calumet from the chief's hand, stuffed it full from the pouch at his belt and returned it. The Indian deftly flipped a coal from the fire into the bowl and puffed at the tobacco until it was well alight. In a low voice Joe explained to Andy. The Kansas pointed it stem-first toward the sky—that was for the Great Spirit, toward the earth, that was to avert demons, then horizontally in a complete circle to call upon the help of the beneficent elementals. Twice he puffed a cloud of smoke toward the heavens, twice toward the earth. Then he passed the pipe to the man at his right.

"Medicine smoke," whispered Joe. "Everybody's goin' to talk straight— mebbe. If he'd give it to the man on his left, that's jist a common smoke and everybody'd say jist what he thought he could make stick."

The ensuing council was carried on between Kelly and the Kansas, partly in the sign language, partly in a very crude English, and partly in what was probably an equally crude Indian dialect. No one else said anything, but all listened with the greatest attention, and all maintained the gravest decorum. Only after the visitors had stalked away into the darkness did Joe tell Andy what it was all about.

"Not much," he answered the boy's questions. "Pawnee young men are out lookin' for sculps. No buffalo this side Painted Rock. Don't know nothin' about the trace to Santa Fe—or don't want to. Lot of braggin' about him bein' heap big Injin, and how friendly he is."

For the first time Kelly that night set a horse guard. Some of the men objected.

"With all their squaws 'n possibles right yere to hand, they ain't goin' to try to run off no horses," Tilton repeated Kelly's own argument. "They couldn't move out quick enough."

"There may be some ambitious young men among 'em," said Kelly.

As the guard was to be more a discouraging show of vigilance than a serious matter, Andy was assigned to one of the watches. He enjoyed himself thoroughly, pacing slowly about the picketed horses, peering into the blackness, his rifle on the alert. The day had been hot, and so the night was soft. The prairie-warmed wind was breathing back toward coolness, bearing its perfume trove of wild rose and resinweed. The earth was low and black in obeisance to expanded skies. A deep and serene silence hovered but just above, upheld from alighting only by the small valiant night noises—rustlings of the breeze, the occasional soft snort of one of the dozing animals, the barking of the Indian dogs, the more distant answer of the coyotes, the persistent, emphatic, reiterated insistence of a little owl—ko-ko-ko-*oh!* ko-ko-ko-*oh!*—over and over again. At the end of two hours, he was relieved by Joe Crane, who laughed at him, much to his chagrin.

"All you git, walkin' around like that, is a good chance to ketch an arrow," said he. "And you can't see nothin' or hear nothin'. Next time you git down low, right next to the ground, so's you git things again the sky as much as you kin." He called Andy back for another bit of information. "And mostly keep yourself pinted to that Buggs mule of mine. He'll tell ye."

Next day, when the trappers moved out, the Indians remained in camp, much to Joe's satisfaction. The latter was now as full of admiration for Kelly's diplomacy as he had been full of grumbles the day before.

"Jack's a wolf," said he.

The tall mountain man had got rid of the savages by the simple expedient of dropping a hint as to the expedition following after. Nothing *on the prairie* in the way of gift was to be expected from the hard-bitten trappers, but a large and wealthy trading party offered better prospects. But Kelly had done even better. It seemed he had, the evening before, inquired repeatedly and with great particularity as to all sorts of details concerning the Taos Trail, the game, the water, the people. Joe had not been able to figure why he had done so.

"These Injins don't know nothin' about it," said he. "They know they'd git gobbled by the Comanches if they stuck a nose beyond Painted Rock. Jack knows that, too. I didn't git the cute of his notion at first."

Andy did not get the cute of the notion even now.

"Why," Joe explained, "don't you see? These Injins pass it all on to them fellers behind us, how we're interested in Taos. That'll give them something to think about! Wagh!"

On the tenth day, they arrived at a continuous strip of timber, a half-mile wide by several in length, of oak, ash, elm, and hickory. Here they lay over a day. The men spent the time in hunting. The grove sheltered wild turkey and deer, besides an abundance of smaller game. The vast plains, in contrast, were seemingly almost destitute of life, save for small bands of antelope gleaming white and tenuous in the heat shimmer. These interested Andy and aroused his sporting spirit, for he had never seen any before, but the trappers did not consider them worthwhile.

Joe showed Andy a circle in the grass, about forty or fifty feet in diameter, filled with sunflowers. It marked a spot where, sometime in the past, a small band of buffalo had stood compact, cows and calves in the center, the lowered shaggy fronts of the bulls facing out in all directions against the circling wolf packs.

"Used to be plenty buffalo yereabouts," said Joe. "Sometimes a few comes back, but mostly they's pulled out. Don't know why."

Joe never bothered to hunt the deer and small game on which, for the present, they were subsisting. He left that to Andy and the others. He looked with an indulgent eye on Andy's sportsman's enthusiasm. It was good enough practice for the lad.

"Buffalo's the only eatin'," he insisted. "You'll see!"

But today, he discouraged Andy's desire to go deer and turkey hunting with the rest.

"This is the last of the hickory," said he.

The two spent their time hunting straight and clean shoots and shaping them painstakingly into spare wiping rods for their rifles. Andy noted that the hunters returned early for the same purpose. Here, the trail forked. Here, the traveled trace struck north toward the Platte and the Rockies. Here, the little company would turn southwest toward the unknown.

Near the close of the afternoon, a dark speck topped the rise of land to the east and descended the slope. The trappers suspended their various occupations to watch it. The horses stopped grazing and picked up their ears. The speck defined itself at last as a lone horseman swinging along at an easy gallop.

"White man," said Joe after a little. "Way he rides," he explained to Andy, "and you'll never see an Injin all alone that way." They watched in silence the steady approach.

"It's Bill Sublette." One recognized the newcomer after a little. "Wagh!"

With one accord they seemed to fall back into a flint-like stolidity as into some fourth dimension of remoteness, from the shelter of which they watched warily.

The lone horseman brought his horse to a stand. Andy saw a lean, keen face, a lean, wiry form bending easily to the movement of the horse, a pair of piercing blue eyes. With a shock of surprise Andy recognized the fact that the stranger could not be very much older than himself.

"Howdy," the man greeted the silent, watchful trappers.

For an appreciable pause, no one spoke.

'Light and eat," then said Kelly briefly.

Sublette swung himself from his saddle, removed the gear from his horse, and slapped the animal on the rump. It was a magnificent beast, tall, well-boned, straight-backed. The eyes of the impassive men followed it with a flicker of admiration as it trotted off high-headed to join the herd grazing on the rich grass of the bottomland. The flicker died.

Sublette appeared unaware of the withdrawn, almost unfriendly attitude, or he chose to ignore it. At a considerable distance from the fire, he piled his saddle gear, unstrapped the robe from his saddle and spread it, laid beside it his long rifle, and made the other simple dispositions of the plainsman's bivouac. When this was accomplished, he strode back to the fire and squatted on his heels. He accepted in silence the roasted deer ribs and the tin cup of coffee which Kelly as silently offered him, and proceeded composedly to make his meal. No word was spoken. The trappers sat, withdrawn, watchful, noncommittal. Only their eyes moved.

The visitor finished his meal, wiped clean his knife, and produced a pipe. Kelly held toward him his tobacco pouch, which Sublette accepted. Kelly filled his own pipe. For a few moments, they smoked in silence.

"I am told you go to Taos," Sublette spoke suddenly. Kelly made no reply. "I cannot guess why you do this except you imagine I am following you and you wish to shake us off."

Two or three of the trappers glanced toward one another in amusement at the accuracy of this surmise. Kelly still said nothing.

"If that is the case," continued Sublette, "you are unnecessarily alarmed. We have no wish to crowd in on your trapping grounds."

This was too much for Tilton, the red-haired.

"Then why follow us!" he cried with indignation.

"To make money," replied Sublette. "If you will listen to me I will tell you how. But if you're going to fight me before I begin, as you have invariably done back in the settlements, it is useless."

"Say on, we're listening," said Kelly briefly.

"I don't aim to crowd into your country," said Sublette. "I aim to trade for fur. And the principal people I want to trade with is you. I aim to furnish you with everything you can get in St. Louis right on the ground, and will take your furs from you at St. Louis prices. That saves you nigh to two thousand miles of journey. There's sense in that, isn't there? Since Manuel Lisa quit, that's about the best you can do, isn't it? And I'll guarantee none of my people shall trap in the *pays d'en haut*—at least, as long as I get the fur from you."

"What you carryin' along sich a mob fer if you ain't a-goin' to trap the kentry?" demanded Tilton.

"I expect to do some trapping, but I'll keep them in the low country, and to run buffalo," promised Sublette. "They are working for me."

"It's taken me eight year to larn my district in the Rockies," spoke up Bill Williams, "and I don't *low*—" Kelly silenced him with a gesture.

"How do we know you'll keep your word?" he asked bluntly. "We've heard that sort of talk before."

"If I get the fur, why not?" asked in his turn Sublette, taking no offense. "If you find my men anywhere pushing back into the mountains, you'll probably know what to do."

Several of the trappers nodded grimly at this.

"You admitted you were following us," Kelly shot at him. "Why?"

"I did not admit that," countered Sublette. "I said you imagined I was following you. As a matter of fact, I was not. I admit it looks that way," he answered the unexpressed but evident skepticism. "But if you had delayed your departure another day, you would have found us ahead of you instead of behind."

"You expect me to believe that?" cried Tilton belligerently.

"I don't care whether you do or not," returned Sublette with a trace of impatience.

"But you would like us to," interposed Kelly quietly. "In that case I think you'll have to explain a little why you delayed at Franklin for nearly a month. That is not reasonable."

"Look here," said the trader impatiently, "if I wanted to follow anybody into the mountains, why should I wait for you? There've been a half-dozen parties gone already that I might have followed just as well. Use your common sense."

Kelly nodded.

"That's true. But there's still something that I think you'll have to explain."

For the first time, Sublette hesitated.

"I reckon I'd better lay my cards on the robe," he decided. "What I waited for was word from my partners. That is neither here nor there. But here is what I am going to tell you, whether we like it or not—the old days are at an end. Very soon, we are going to fight for our fur. For the past six months we in the trade have heard rumors of a new company opened in Boston and New York. Some say Astor's in it, and that it is really the American Fur Company. The plan is to do what I am doing. Transfer the trading to the plains. Well, I just got word that the rumor is true, and that they are going to start a Western branch. They've just forced a law through to close the government factories. That's a first step. That was what I was waiting to hear."

The mountaineers looked startled at this news.

"That is what is coming, and you cannot get away from it, and you cannot keep it out. In a few years you'll either be working for them or for us."

"The hell we will!" cried Bill Williams.

"I don't mean for wages. As to that, you'll suit yourselves. But you've got to sell your furs somewhere, and it'll be either them or us, whether you pack them to St. Louis or bring them in to the nearest post. That is the situation. Now I am trying to tell you it is better to trade with us. You know us. We are plainsmen, like yourselves, and we should stand together. We'll treat you fair, keep out of—at least until we're forced to it—your country, and take your fur. Do you expect they'll do that? If we do stand together, we shall make head, for between us we know the land, and they must find it out. If we don't stand together, we shall both be crowded out. Take your choice. We'll treat you fair. What do these fellows care about you?"

"Why didn't you give us all this palaver back in St. Louis?" demanded Kelly.

"There was nothing certain, then, and you wouldn't have believed us," said Sublette frankly. "I'm to look the ground over. Next year, we shall be established. General Ashley is our head," he added impressively. "Next year, if things go right, he will take the field in person."

This announcement had an effect. The trappers looked at one another. Ashley's was a name to conjure with.

"Look here, men," continued Sublette persuasively, these Easterners are going to make a big effort. If they succeed, they'll take over our country. But it will take time for them to get started. If we're to do anything, we must stick together. That's what I want to tell you, that and the fact that we are not trying to follow you. We know where we are going. We're going to trap the Missouri and the low country, we're going to see what we can do with the Crows, the Arapahoes, and the Snakes. In the spring you'll find us at Henry Fork, ready to take your furs. Now you can go to Taos if you want to, but if you think you're bothering us by doing so, you are badly mistaken. Think it over."

He knocked the ashes from his pipe, stretched his lean form, and strode away into the gathering darkness to his robe and saddle.

"What do you think, Jack?" The mountain men turned to Kelly. Their world was sadly shaken.

"I don't know," replied Kelly slowly. "If he's telling the truth—"

"Thar's one way to find out," spoke up Tilton roughly. "Wait and see. If he's squar', I'm with him. I don't aim to throw in with no Yankees."

"And I don't aim to throw in with no traders!" cried Joe Crane. "Traders is trouble, every time. We found that out with Lisa and Pitcher."

Kelly was thoughtful. He sighed.

"'The old order changeth, giving place to the new'," he quoted. "I reckon you'll have to throw in with traders, Joe, or go under. No question of that. Sublette is right on one thing, anyway, but the question is, which *do* we throw in with."

"Wall," drawled Fitz, who had heretofore contributed nothing to the discussion, "come to a ch'ice atween Yankees and Western men I know whar *my* stick floats!" His leathery face broke into a slow grin. "And I reckon I'd as lieve have my spring likker and possibles brung to me in the mountains as eat dust a thousand mile for them, and back again."

But in spite of a partial and tentative entertainment of the idea, it was decided to continue on to Taos, although there seemed now to be little sense in so long a detour if Sublette was to be believed at all. No one, however, suggested the abandonment of the enterprise, nor did Kelly's offer to share the thousand dollars paid by Benton for the service have much to do with it. They pretended to themselves and to one another that the money influenced them, and other excuses—Benton's business, perhaps Sublette was lying, rumored new trapping grounds north of Sangre de Cristo. But these things were not the deciding factor, which was quite simply the unquenchable spirit of adventure which had already made them what they were. A locked land from which so long Spanish jealousy had excluded them! Of them all, Joe Crane alone had ever been there, and he promptly to see the inside of the calaboose and to consider himself lucky to get out with only a warning. Taos! Santa Fe! They lay over the horizon, shimmering in the romance of the unknown. It would have taken more than a mere turning point in history to have deflected them now.

Chapter 5
The Buffalo

The little party of mountain men moved steadily toward the southwest. They were now four days out from Council Grove, where they had left the trace, known to all of them, that led toward the Rockies.

Those days had offered little but monotony. The grassland ran in long earth billows. The shallow troughs between their crests were wide. The cavalcade rode down the gentle slope, across the flat, up the other slope. From the hollow, the skyline was definite. Andy Burnett, in his inexperience, could not rid himself of the feeling that, once the crest was attained, he should be able to see abroad for miles. But when he had mounted the summit, he saw before him merely another billow of the earth.

There was no game outside a few bands of antelope, but smaller life was abundant. The brown grass of last year still stood, the green grass below it had not yet laid it low. Through it scurried rabbits and the littler rodents. Savannah sparrows and buntings swung from its blades, horned larks rose from its openings. Overhead sparrow hawks hung as though suspended, their wings vibrating, their sharp eyes cocked for a mouse or a bird. Curiously enough, in spite of the wide sweep of country, the scale of size was diminished. A coyote loping off looked as big as an elk, the cavalcade of horsemen were monstrous. This was due to the abundance of little things—the lack of tree or tiniest shrub, only the blades of grass.

These conditions, Andy found, made for modifications in life. There was now no fuel to be had, and little game. The company had to fall back largely on the meat it had dried—or *jerked*—before reaching Council

Grove. This, unleavened bread from the small store of flour, and coffee constituted the whole diet. The only possible fire was from the resinweed. It flared up hot, blazed for a few seconds and was gone. It was not good fuel, but by constant attention the men managed to make it do for their simple cooking. Campfires were, of course, entirely out of the question.

"Well git to the short grass purfy quick," said Joe Crane. "Then there'll be a plenty of buffalo chips. And buffalo, if the critters ain't all moved north. I don't know how they act down thisaway."

The men no longer rode in as careless a formation as before reaching Council Grove. They held together in a compact group, with the pack animals in the center. On approaching the crest of each of the earth billows, someone trotted ahead to examine the next trough. The day's march was ended in midafternoon, the horses grazed under the eye of a mounted herdsman. At dark, they were driven in and picketed close up to the camp. No guard was set for the first part of the night. Near one or two o'clock, however, Kelly aroused one of the sleepers who had been designated the night before. The man, instantly broad awake, shivering a little, arose in silence. Outside the horse herd, he lay flat—or merely sat down if the terrain was favorable—his rifle at hand.

"Not one chance in a thousand for Injins in this kentry," Joe told Andy. "Nothin' to bring 'em here. Only chance would be a party travelin' to git through, same as we are. But the pint is, they wouldn't any Injins be goin' through, 'lesson it was a war party on their way to raid the Kansas or Osages or mebbe to take a try at the Pawnees. And war parties is bad medicine, especially Comanche war parties. It's a slim chance, but when it comes to Injins you take *no* chances."

Andy, as usual when Joe became instructive, showed his interest. Joe, encouraged, went on.

"Then they's scouts. Injins is great hands to send out a scout or two just to look around. And they's always a young buck or two projectin' out on his own hook to pick up a sculp or so. You see, Andy, an Injin lad ain't got a show in the world till he can show one sculp. When they call him growed up, they give him a powwow and a medicine dance, and then he's supposed to go out with his gang and not come back till he's got him an enemy sculp. Then he's a warrior. If he comes back without one, he just ranks with squaws, and the gals won't have nothin' to do with him. He has to go to work, and the women can order him around. I've knowed 'em to be away nigh a year before they had any luck. When they been out that long—or a good sight less—they're gittin' kind of desp'rate. They ain't so partic'lar whether it's an enemy sculp or not. All ha'r looks alike. That's one reason it don't pay to git keerless. Now you take the Crows. Crows in gin'ral has always been friendly to us mountain men. If you ever meet up with a Crow village, ride right in and make yoreself to home. And if you meet up with a real Crow war party, ride right up to them. Probably they'll try to git you to j'ine them for a leetle sport with the Arapahoes or Snakes or mebbe the Blackfeet. Though they don't tackle the Blackfeet much. But I'd hate like p'is'n to meet up with any of the young 'uns headin' home without no sculp to show. Good idee to look 'em over afore you declar' yoreself. If they look young and hungry and you don't see no ha'r on their leggin's, you *cache*!"

Joe grinned at Andy's interest.

"Crows is good people, too," he added. "You got nice black ha'r, Andy. Don't be gettin' keerless."

"Wagh!" agreed Fitz, who was listening.

"That's why they's liable to be some strays, even in this grass kentry," Joe concluded his instruction. "'Course they won't bother us. An Injin's got sense, and twelve long rifles is too big odds. If we got keerless and scattered out, and lay around promiscuous, and left our horses stray, they might go back and tell the Old Man they's easy pickin's on the prairie."

"If I were an Indian I'd wait until we were all sound asleep, and then make a quick dash and kill the lot of us," suggested Andy, who had long been uneasy over the lack of precaution the first part of the night.

"If you was an Injin you'd act like an Injin," countered Joe good-naturedly. "An Injin never makes a move much afore daylight in the morning. That's one thing you can count on. There ain't many."

"Why is that?" asked Andy.

"Skeered," said Joe, "skeered of spirits. All the bad spirits prowl around night times. Shore they do! Don't the streams and waterfalls hush up at night? Don't the mountains throw big rocks all night?"

"Do they?" asked Andy.

"Shore they do! Snow quits melting. Water drops, and so the streams git small. Rocks that has been froze in gits loosened by the sun and takes a tumble when the ground freezes up again and gives 'em a push. You and I knows that. But we ain't Injins. Night's full of funny noises. All spirits. Why looka here, Andy, you take notice. You'll never see an Injin carryin' a grooved bar'l. What guns they got is all smooth bore. That's one reason you kin stand up and let an Injin shoot at you, barrin' accidents, till further orders. They won't tech a rifled gun. For why? Because the bullet whines. More spirits! Wall, I ain't a-goin' to tell them ary different! So don't worry about no Injins till long toward dawn. Then keep yore eyes shining."

Andy was learning fast. When his turn came to stand guard, he knew enough to keep low, to silhouette the earth's surface as much as he could, to lie quiet, and to listen.

Before the party had left the long-grass country he had one exciting experience. That day, they had come to the first sign of human activity. Left to his own inexperience Andy would never have recognized it as such. It manifested itself first merely as a thin pinkish milky haze filming the western horizon. He would probably not have noticed it at all, had it not been for his companions. From them he learned that the haze was smoke from a distant grass fire.

"Oh, it ain't going to bother us none," Joe told him. "The old grass is too old, and the new grass too green to burn fast. But it means somebody has sot her, and that means keep yore eyes shining."

They came up to the fire, which was eating its way very slowly forward in a long and irregular fringe of low flames, so low and narrow that an active man might easily leap across. Behind them, the country, but slightly blackened, showed green with the new grass. It was a lazy fire. Its only activity was supplied by a swarm of birds that darted back and forth through the smoke, and chattered shrilly, apparently excited almost to lunacy by the catastrophic possibilities. In reality, they were catching the insects driven up by the flames and stupefied with the smoke, and surely such abundance was enough to drive any hard-working bird into a frenzy.

The trappers camped that night to windward of the fire. As night came on, the fire seemed to gain in power, though this was probably an illusion strengthened by the dusk. The eastern sky was, for a time pink, with the reflected light after sunset. Then the moon rose, blood-red in the smoke.

That night Andy stood the before dawn watch. The fire fascinated him. In imagination, it was an army outpost of campfires, extending miles to beyond the horizon, a serpent winding its crooked way, a slow tide coming in on a broken beach. Occasionally, a clump of resinweed would catch and flare high, like a torch. As morning neared a breeze sprang up that quickly freshened to a wind. The flames rose like snakes rearing to look, bent, flattened by a gust, and reared again, throwing defiant sparks. From his place low to the ground, Andy watched them, fascinated. Between the fire and the camp stood tall resin weed in bunches four or five feet high, bending in the rising wind. If the wind should change...but then, Andy remembered, these morning winds never did change. It was a beautiful sight. Andy found his eyes straying back to it constantly, and it was only by an effort of the will that he turned them to the shadowed west whence, if anywhere, danger might be expected. For a long time he peered vigilantly, then permitted himself another look toward the fascination of the flames.

His heart leaped to his throat. Dark figures, dozens of them, were darting here and there, stooping low, surrounding the little camp, firing the resin weed—from a clump of it, the flames leaped upward with a roar.

"Indians! Indians!" cried Andy at the top of his lungs, and fired hastily at one of the crouching figures. As he flattened himself, reloading as Joe had taught him, he felt, rather than heard or saw, the sleeping men leap into action. In a moment, he was conscious of a touch on his leg, and the mountain man hitched himself alongside.

"What did you see, lad?" Joe's low voice came to his ear.

"See them?" the boy's voice shook with excitement in spite of himself. "There! There! They're setting fire to the resinweed!"

For a moment the trapper peered in the direction Andy indicated. Then, with a laugh, he got to his feet.

"Stand up, boy, and take a look!" he advised aloud.

Andy stood up. He looked and closed his eyes and looked again. The shadowy hurrying figures had vanished as though dismissed by magic. They had been an illusion evoked by his position so near the ground, the flames, hurried by the wind behind the swaying clumps, had conjured the appearance of crowds moving in the opposite direction. So vivid was the deception that Andy had to stoop again to convince himself. He accompanied Joe to the camp, burning with mortification.

The trappers, however, did not reproach him or laugh at him, for which he was absurdly grateful. Indeed, they made no reference to the matter, but seemed to take the dissipation of the alarm quite as a matter of course. Kelly remarked that it was near dawn anyway, and they might as well cook up. They kindled their brief small fire of resinweed and set over it the coffee pot. The business of getting underway proceeded in usual train. Andy obliterated himself. His face was still red with humiliation. Still no reference whatever was made to the affair. Only, when Andy had finished packing his pack animals and turned to mount his horse, he found neatly tied to his saddle horn a clump of resinweed.

"Didn't want you to go off leavin' yore first sculp," said Joe.

The trappers' leathern faces were grave. Andy caught no faintest twinkle in their eyes.

Abruptly, the character of the country changed. The high luxuriant grasses disappeared. Their place was taken by a short, curly growth so insignificant that after the lusher plains, the prairies seemed almost barren.

"Buffalo grass," Andy was told. "Wuth two fer one of common grass." Certainly the horses seemed to think so.

About this time, the fuel problem was solved by quantities of dry buffalo chips. Trough-like trails worn deep in the hard soil, round *wallows*, broad highways of trampled earth, the fairy rings of old herd formations further attested the beasts' abundance. But these were all old signs.

One night, Andy was awakened by a noise. It was not a loud noise, and was very distant. There were a thousand nearer and louder that had not disturbed him. But this was unusual. Andy had made this much progress toward plainscraft, that his senses discriminated, even subconsciously. He raised on his elbow, to find Joe also listening.

"Lobo wolf," whispered the trapper. The long, weird, mournful ululation again shivered across the moonlight. "Good sign fer game. Them varmints don't bother with prairie dogs and rats and sich, like the coyotes. Listen at him! In a minute he'll quit." Joe partly threw off his blanket and filled his pipe. "Funny thing about wolves," he went on in a low voice, once the tobacco was alight. None of the sleepers stirred. Joe's voice rang no bell of alarm in that part of their consciousness that guarded. Any one of them would have leaped to alertness at the smallest unwarranted rustling. "Coyotes howls all the time. Wolves mostly tune-up at midnight and at daybreak, and that's about all."

"I did not know they were such a silent beast," whispered Andy.

"Oh, they bark, sort of short and snarling, 'most any time. But they saves their howls. I like to hear him. Means meat. Buffalo, I hope. Perhaps only elk. Or mebbe he's just scouting. I hear only one. I'd rather hear Old Man Raven croak. He's the fellow don't git fur from supplies."

The howl of the wolf proved to be a reliable omen. The very next morning, Andy saw his first buffalo.

It was a lone bull. They came upon him at close range, and suddenly, over the top of a low rise. He was ancient and thin, and the fur on his hide was off in patches, but the hair of his head and shoulders was still long and shaggy. He stood alone at bay. A pack of gray wolves circled warily but just out of reach of his lunge, their eyes ablaze with the eagerness of the chase, trotting this way and that before the old warrior. The buffalo turned constantly. His enemies were trying to get to his rear, to hamstring him. Once down, he would be at their mercy. He was trying in vain to face them all. Every once in a while, one of the wolves darted in, snapped hastily at the old fellow's hindquarters, and darted out again as he whirled in that direction.

So occupied were all concerned that not one of them noticed the men and horses, even when by common impulse, they drew rein only ten or fifteen yards from the outside circumference of this strange battle. For some minutes, the trappers leaned on the pommels, watching. It was evident the issue could not be long in doubt. Already, the old buffalo was bleeding from a half-dozen shallow wounds where the sharp teeth of the wolves had snapped home. His sides heaved painfully. His tongue hung out, and a light foam blew away from his half-opened mouth. Each fresh attack he met more slowly, less certainly. The wolves were growing bolder, drawing closer their circle, darting in more frequently.

Kelly looked from one to the other of his companions.

"What say, boys? Shall we give them one?" he asked.

By way of assent, the men leisurely dismounted. The flint gunmen thumbed up the frizzens and shook in the priming powder.

"All ready?" said Kelly. "Let her go!"

A ragged volley rang out. A half-dozen of the marauders wilted or rolled over. One, caught at full speed by some sporting marksman, turned a complete somersault. The rest of the pack, surprised and bewildered, stopped short in full career, stared about them, and seemed only slowly to realize the situation, only slowly to replace the eagerness of the kill with their customary sense of self-preservation. A few loped away, a few trotted. One or two even hesitated, snarled, and bared their teeth. The trappers dropped the butts of their long rifles to earth, laughing in their silent fashion, immensely diverted.

Andy had welcomed Kelly's suggestion with a leap of joy. He had been the first afoot, the first to stand quaveringly eager for the word to fire. The wolf he had picked out as his mark had gone down satisfactorily. Now, while his companions stood in relish of the incident, he was hastily but methodically reloading. He was full of excitement and what might almost have been described as an indignant lust of battle. His sympathies had been strongly enlisted by the old buffalo's gallant stand. Nevertheless in spite of his eagerness he recharged the piece accurately, without mistake or false motion. The deer horn charger he filled to the exact brim. The powder went into the barrel without the loss of a grain. The ball was precisely centered on the patch. He drove it home with the deft neat thrust from the wrist that seated it exactly, but without undue pressure. He capped the rifle without a fumble. He was quite unconscious of the fact that the trappers were watching him attentively.

The remainder of the pack had come together and were loping away across the prairie. But they were not yet wholly reconciled to the turn of events. Every few yards one or the other of them stopped, turned, half reared to look back. As Andy finished loading, one of them did just this. Only its head and its forward-pricked ears were visible above the fringe of grass. Still heated with his partisanship of what had been a losing battle, Andy steadied the long rifle, and as the bead, nestling clearly in the notch of the rear sight, came to rest, be pulled trigger.

"Good shot!" cried Kelly.

"Wagh!" cried several voices.

Andy looked around, awakened from his absorption, a little confused to find himself the center of attention. Joe Crane was capering about delightedly.

"I told you!" he addressed them all in general. "He makes them *come!*" He seemed suddenly informed with a pride of proprietorship in the boy. "And did you see him load! Spilled nary a grain, and quicker'n ary rattlesnake coils. Forty rod, full, or I'm a horny toad. And I'll bet any of you a plew of beaver plumb atween the eyes!" He clapped Andy so heartily between the shoulder blades as almost to overset him, then across the prairie to the dead wolf.

"Ef you kin do it that away right along yo'll save yore ha'r yet, Andy," said Bill Williams.

Andy was embarrassed. He did not know where to turn. He tried to recover himself by setting about recharging charging his rifle.

Joe was back again waving the wolf scalp, daubed with gore.

"Plumb atween the eyes!" he cried triumphantly. He rushed up to Andy and with a bloody forefinger smeared the boy's forehead. "That'll make ye wise like a wolf, and they's no animal wiser." He tore from Andy's saddle the withered bunch of resinweed, which Andy had been too proud to remove, and in its place tied the wolf scalp. "Workin' up," said he with satisfaction. "You'll have real ha'r there yet!" He patted Andy again on the shoulder. "You make 'em *come!*" he repeated. A sudden thought checked him. "Has she got a name?" he inquired.

"What?" Andy found his voice, puzzled.

Joe laid his hand on the long rifle.

"The Boone gun," said Joe.

"I don't know. I suppose it must have. I never heard it."

"Well, she has now. Old Knock-'em-stiff, that's her!"

"Let's get on," said Kelly.

They mounted and turned away. The buffalo bull still stood in the middle of the trampled ground, his head low, his eyes fixed dully on the scattered bodies of his assailants. Andy looked back.

"What about him?" he asked.

"He's too old and stringy," returned Joe, misunderstanding the purport of the question. "Cast bull, druv out of the herd. Whar there's one there's others. We'll find fat cow shortly."

"But what will become of him? Will he get well?"

"Oh, the wolves'll git him tonight," replied the mountain man indifferently. "What you doin'?" he asked as Andy dismounted.

The boy did not reply. Slowly he walked back to where the buffalo stood, his front still lowered in defiance of imaginary enemies. For several seconds he stood contemplating the forlorn old creature. Then for the third time he raised the rifle, for the third time the silvered bead came steadily to rest on its mark. At the crack of the piece the old bull sank forward on his knees, slowly rolled to its side, stretched out as though to rest, with a tired sigh.

"Now whatever did you do that for, Andy!" Joe demanded in astonishment as the boy remounted.

Andy did not reply. Thus he killed his first buffalo. For the moment he felt that he never wanted to kill another.

This sentiment, naturally, faded when tested by the excitement of the game in numbers and abundance. Not long after the episode of the cast bull they saw a small band of twenty or thirty individuals in the middle distance, showing black and immense upon the short grass, and soon afterward others and others of similar groups, until the whole extent of the plain to the north was dotted with them here and there. Andy had never conceived of wild game in such numbers, but his companions made light of his amazement. According to them he had not even begun to see buffalo. These few and scattered individuals were negligible.

As time to camp drew near, one of the men loped on ahead. Shortly they heard the distant faint ping of his rifle, and turning in that direction, came upon him after a considerable ride seated on the carcass of a cow, smoking his pipe. He half apologized for taking them so far, the buffalo were scarce, and this was the first cow he could find near water.

Andy hovered about the butchering, fascinated by the deftness with which they went at it. It was so different from the dressing of tame meat. Four of them heaved the carcass on its belly, spreading the legs to hold it in that position. Then one slit the hide along the spine, and the skin was peeled away on either side, so that it lay flat on the prairie, a spread mat beneath the carcass, protecting the meat from contamination by the earth. They cut out the tongue, they peeled away the hump and back strap, which they piled on the skin. One of the men carefully filled his canteen with blood from the body cavity. Andy experienced a slight heave at the stomach. Others skinned back and chopped off the leg bones.

"Guess that's about all," said Bill Williams.

With a mighty heave the body was rolled aside. Bill Williams, with his tomahawk, opened the ribs and from within carefully extracted certain tidbits. The whole they wrapped in the hide, slapped it across a pack, and moved a few hundred yards to the water spoken of by the hunter. It was murky and fouled by the beasts, undrinkable except as boiled with coffee, and then with a strong menagerie flavor. Andy controlled his squeamishness with difficulty, but times were to come when he was to remember the tepid nauseous stuff with longing. But the abandonment of so much good meat bothered him.

"Oh, we got enough for everybody," Joe assured him. "Yore eyes is gittin' bigger'n yore belly."

He could not comprehend Andy's idea of waste. There would be plenty more tomorrow. Later, when it seemed they might be running out of the herd, would be time enough to begin to save meat. When finally he understood the boy's point of view, he was amazed.

"Why, they's plenty buffalo," said he. He laughed a little at Andy as having been brought up on a farm with a few cattle. "You ain't seen buffalo yit," he assured the lad. "These is nothing." He tried to give Andy an idea. Not hundreds, nor thousands, but millions, moving across the wide-flung country like locusts. The earth black with them from horizon to horizon.

"I've traveled six days through them, movin' steady," said Joe. "Solid pack. And then three days more of little bunches, like these yere, afore we got out onta clear plains agin. One time we couldn't move at all for three days. Too thick to break through. Had to roost top of a little rise. You'll see."

What did the few killed by man for his uses amount to? Nothing as compared to the stupendous natural waste incident to their mere numbers. Prairie fires in the dry of the year leaped on the fleeing herds like savage beasts and swept on, leaving the plains strewn with bodies, staggering with blind, singed victims. Stampedes trampled down the young and the weak by thousands. The ice of the rivers broke beneath their weight, and the swollen current of the spring thaws carried downstream, for days and days, a continuous line of the drowned.

"An old Nor'wester, name of MacDonnell, told me he counted atween seven and eight thousand drowned buffalo floatin' past his post, and then he got sick of countin' and quit," said Joe, "and of course that was just a few of the main herd that was out of luck."

And in addition, wolves and coyotes always hovering about the herds to snatch down a calf or a yearling or to pounce upon some old cast bull like the one of that morning, swarms of them. All of them made a living. In face of this orgy of nature's waste, what effect the few hundreds or the few thousands appropriated by man, white or red, for his own uses? Or even the additional few thousands sacrificed, perhaps, to his wantonness?

"Why, if we all had a ton of powder and lead apiece," concluded Joe, "and done nothin' but shoot buffalo from now till Christmas time, we wouldn't make a dent in the outlyin' fringe of one herd! The man who eats brisket when he can git hump is just a tarnation fool. Wagh!"

Andy turned in his saddle to look back. He was amazed. The carcass had almost disappeared. Only a partly dismembered framework remained, half visible through a black and flopping crowd of vultures. Other vultures soared and beat their wings just above. Still others, their wings held away from their bodies, sat upright on the ground, disgruntled or gorged. A dozen coyotes weaved restlessly back and forth. Joe too looked back, and laughed.

"Ain't much wasted thar!" said he.

They roasted the meat. Andy thought he had never tasted anything so delicious. Joe triumphed.

"What I tell you!" he cried. "That's *eatin'*!"

Andy sighed with repletion, eyed a choice bit uncertainly, and gave up the idea.

"Couldn't get down another mouthful," he confessed. "Lord, I'm full! Guess I'll turn in!"

"No you don't!" cried Joe. "That's jist the first course to sort of take off the edge."

One of the men put over a pot of water to heat. Others busied themselves in cracking the leg bones and deftly extracting the marrow, which they dropped into the pot. The man who had filled his canteen with blood produced it and stirred in its contents.

"Git yore cups," cried the one who was doing the cooking, after about five minutes. "Next course!"

Andy tasted the mess gingerly and with misgivings.

"Why, it's good!" he cried surprised. The marrow had melted. The whole had cooked into a rich, well-flavored soup.

The remark was greeted by a general laugh. Under the stimulus of feast after comparative famine the customary silent gravity had broken into a comfortable and expansive good-fellowship. Even the dour and saturnine countenance of Bill Williams bore the slightly fatuous satisfaction of a well-fed baby. They filled their pipes and smoked awhile. A comfortable drowsiness seemed to fall upon their spirits. The smoldering little fire died to acrid coals. About as Andy was sinking to a doze of repletion, Fitz roused himself.

"Come on, boys, time for dessert," said he.

They stirred lazily to action. One coaxed up the fire. By its feeble light others, volunteers, set about further preparations. On the clean inner surface of the buffalo's skin they proceeded carefully to chop a portion of the backstrap into a fine hash. As soon as a sufficient quantity of this had been prepared they stuffed it into cleaned intestines, stuck them on sticks, and roasted them over the coals.

"Thar!" said Joe, proffering one of these sausages to Andy. "Stick that in yore face, and tell me if you ever tasted any better in yore settlemints!"

"I can't!" protested Andy. "I'm full way up to here!"

"Wagh! Eat!" commanded the trapper. "If yore goin' to be a mountain man you got to larn to swell yore belly out like a dawg."

"I'll be as sick as a dog if I do," Andy remonstrated. "I'm full, I tell you!"

"Wild meat'll never make you sick," said Joe emphatically. "You can starve for a week and then eat till yore skin cracks and nary a bellyache in a ton of it. It's tame meat makes you sick. Yere, ketch a holt!"

To his surprise Andy found room for more. And it too was delicious. But he was benumbed by food, dizzy with repletion. He rolled into his blankets and fell instantly deep into torpor.

But his sleep was sound and dreamless. Morning seemed to come instantly. He arose in its freshness full of energy and life.

"What I tell you?" cried Joe. "That's the stuff'll put ha'r on yore chest! Wagh!"

As they rode forward that day the groups of buffalo gradually became more numerous, until one could look in no direction without a sight of dozens of little bands, each in charge of its vigorous and truculent bull. When toward close of afternoon Andy learned that more meat was to be required, he eagerly petitioned to be appointed the hunter. His sporting blood was hot with the sight of so much game. Receiving the desired permission he galloped ahead until he had placed a good interval between himself and his more slowly moving companions. Then he dismounted, tied his horse to an old skull, and set himself to a slow stalk of one of the little herds. He did so in approved fashion, with due concern for the light wind currents, and so, shortly, found himself lying flat in the short grass within a hundred yards of the animals. Some were lying down, some were afoot, grazing. One tremendous shaggy beast stood a few paces apart. He looked to be half again as big as any of the others.

His heart beating strongly from excitement, Andy thrust forward the long rifle, steadied its sights for a moment on the big beast's shoulder, and pulled trigger.

No result.

The buffalo did not budge a hair. Its companions continued to recline or to graze.

It did not seem possible to have missed completely at that distance, but there you were! Andy burned with mingled mortification and anger at himself. He reloaded in frantic haste, fearful that at any moment the buffalo would take alarm and depart. They did not. Again he took aim, more carefully this time. Again he fired. Again no apparent result.

After a moment the big buffalo seemed to awaken from his meditation. He curled his tail and began to walk slowly about. It began to look as though he had come to a reluctant conclusion that he was getting tired of being shot at, and was thinking of waking up his companions to a retreat. But as he turned Andy saw a thin froth of blood at his nostrils.

His heart leaped in a surge of new confidence as he drove the bullet down the barrel. Then he had not missed! He resolved that the next shot should finish the matter. By the time the reloading was finished, the buffalo was showing signs of weakness. He staggered slightly. Andy arose to his feet, walked forward as quietly as he could. All heads turned toward him, and every jaw stopped in mid-chew. For the space of time it took Andy to cover ten yards they stared incredulous. Then instantaneously they were all afoot and off in their strange, clumsy-looking but swift gallop. One moment they were immobile, the next they were in full career. Those lying down were no whit behind the others. They did not get up like a cow or a horse, but seemed fairly to spring afoot and off in one motion. Andy was completely surprised. He stared helplessly at the cloud of dust and the half-visible black forms weaving through it, unable to see anything clearly long enough to deliver a shot. The wounded buffalo had made off as spryly as the rest.

They ran for a quarter mile, then stopped, whirled, and looked back, stared for a moment, turned again and once more plunged into a gallop. In the course of their flight they had run near a number of other small herds. These had joined them. Still others, within easy distance to right or left, also set themselves in motion, paralleling the first. The movement spread, until in an incredibly brief span of time the whole plains were acrawl, and the dust clouds rose like smoke. Andy felt he had certainly started something!

Then his heart bounded with fresh hope. A single black speck had fallen behind its fleeing companions. It slowed to a walk. It lay down. The wounded bull! The animal was evidently dying. Its nose already rested on the earth. Andy hurried forward eagerly. But when he was still at some distance, his quarry rose to its feet, stood for a moment uncertainly, then appeared to gather strength and made off. Andy's shot, hastily delivered at the distant and moving target, seemed to take no effect.

But the beast did not go as far this time. It slowed to a painful, plodding walk, and at last lay down again.

Profiting by experience, Andy's second approach was more cautious. But there was no concealing cover, and the plain here was as flat as a board. Move as slowly as he might, he was still some hundred yards distant when again the buffalo rose to his feet. This time Andy took pains. He heard the bullet hit, and he was sure he had held steadily for the exact shot he had selected. But the shot had no other effect than to start the beast off more vigorously than ever.

Andy's blood was up. He set himself seriously to the task. In the next hour he got in four more shots, all at long range. He tried sneaking, he tried running as hard as he could, hoping to get into closer range. The last bullet did the trick—or the cumulative effect of them all. This time the buffalo did not rise again.

Andy reloaded and ran up. The beast was dead.

He came to himself. He stood alone, with his quarry, in the middle of an emptied plain. The sun had dipped almost to the horizon. Slowly his heart sank to dismay as he looked about him. He had not the remotest idea of the whereabouts of his horse, of the whereabouts of his companions, of the direction the chase had led him. Belatedly, he realized he should at least have noted its twists and turns, as the sun was plain enough in the sky. But he had not. Whether he was north, south, east, or west of his original position he had no means of knowing. Nor could he even remotely guess. He was lost, and lost aplenty, and be had not the least idea of what to do about it. He cursed himself heartily for all kinds of a fool. But that did no good. He sat down on the dead buffalo to think it over.

For a time he came near to panic. Only by a strong effort of what might be called subconscious common sense did he hold himself from rushing off regardless. However, he hung onto himself. Here at least was meat. He had his rifle, ammunition, flint and steel, a canteen of water. He would not starve immediately. What he could do ultimately he did not know. If he had had the faintest notion as to whether he was north or south of the line of march, he might, by angling in the proper direction, have cut it. But he had none.

By an effort of resolution he thrust aside all consideration of the appalling difficulties in the way of his mere survival. The thing to do was to attend to the immediate. He slit the skin above the buffalo hump, and rather bunglingly cut out a slab of meat. He twisted some grass into a tiny nest in the center of which he deposited a bit of burning punk ignited by the flint and steel. This he waved about in the air until it burst into flames. More grass, and little chips of fuel added gingerly—he had a tiny fire which he nursed with care. The sun had almost touched the horizon. Night hovered just beyond the rim of the world, ready to overflow, and with it a mighty and appalling spirit of loneliness. Against it and its engulfing terrors Andy had only the protection of his present tasks. He moved small beneath them, executing them slowly, spreading them thin, postponing the moment when he must front the gathering inimical forces. He did not dare look about him lest he meet their faces.

So he did not see Joe Crane, leading his abandoned saddle horse, nor suspect his presence until the mountain man spoke.

"Wall, bub," drawled Joe, "havin' a good time?"

Andy nearly leaped out of his skin. For a moment the reaction of mingled emotions overwhelmed him. He could not speak. Strangely enough this solution of his predicament had never occurred to him.

Crane leisurely dismounted, dropped the reins of his horse to the ground, and walked over to the buffalo. He poked the toe of his moccasin here and there in the shaggy fur.

"Put enough lead in him to sink a bull boat, didn't ye?" he commented casually. He continued his examination. A quizzical smile curled his grave lips. "You shore picked you a good old tough one," said he. "Wa'nt they no cows to be had?" He stooped to inspect Andy's butchering, and straightened his back with every appearance of indignation. "What do you mean by that!" he cried accusingly.

"What?" stammered Andy.

"Don't you know better than to cut good meat across the grain?" demanded Joe. "Whar you been brung up? My God, I never *see* sich ignorance!"

"I-I'm sorry, I didn't know," gulped Andy.

"Didn't know! Didn't know! I should say not!" grumbled Joe. "It's a crime to spile good meat that away! Not that it's good meat—a tough old bull like that!" He fussed about for a moment or so longer, muttering to himself. Then he sat down on the buffalo and filled his pipe, watching the disconsolate Andy the while from beneath his bushy brows. "If I didn't know you had the makin's in you, Andy, I'd think you was a plumb fool," said he after a moment. "Look at what you've gone and done! Fust off you leaves yore hoss whar ary redskin kin pick him up, and pick you up afterward. Then you picks you out the oldest and toughest bull in a herd of fat cows. Then you spatters him anywheres in his carcass regardless."

But Andy's reviving spirit interposed a mild objection to this.

"I hit him where I aimed," he muttered. "My rifle is too light." And indeed the bullet holes were well grouped behind the beast's shoulder.

"And whar did you aim?" Joe countered relentlessly. "Don't you know a buffalos heart lies low? Looka here." He reached out and moved the animal's foreleg back and forth, to expose a small bare spot just behind the shoulder. "Thar's yore mark. You kin see it when he steps. Yore rifle is heavy enough, thar's many a buffalo killed with balls lighter'n yours. Yore shootin' too high."

"I didn't know," protested Andy.

"They's a lot of things you don't know. And then you goes chasin' him all over the prairie."

"I didn't want him to get away."

"Then why didn't you let him lay? If'n you chase a wounded animal he'll run fer miles. If'n you let him be, he'll lie down and all you have to do is to wait. Then you gits so busy I'm right on top of you afore you knows I'm yere. Supposin' I'd a-been an Injin? And then you finishes off by cuttin' meat across the grain!" Joe seemed to think this the greatest crime of all. He surveyed Andy severely, then relented a little. "You did know enough to send up a smoke," he conceded, "to find you by."

But Andy could not claim even this small credit.

"I didn't think of that," he confessed. "I was just going to cook me some meat."

"Wall"—Joe spat at the guilty fire—"if'n you'd only fell down a prairie dog hole and broke yore leg, she'd have been complete!"

Andy was uncomfortably in the feeling of a small boy. He had to take thought to keep himself from shifting from one foot to the other. But as Joe continued placidly to smoke his pipe, and the sun continued to dip, he at last mustered up courage to ask a question.

"Oughtn't we to be getting back to find the others?" he suggested.

Joe grunted.

"They'll be along. No, you needn't bother to hunch up that fire. *They* got hoss tracks to follow."

Andy subsided.

A little later the trappers rode up. Each man dismounted and looked about him. Andy stood shrinkingly tense, awaiting comment on his performance. He knew that no detail escaped their slow, grave, expert scrutiny—the tough, stringy bull, the exposed position, the lack of water. But nobody said anything. They dismounted, unsaddled, and hobbled the horses for the too brief ranging that could be permitted them before dark and the restrictions of the picket rope. Andy experienced a gush of gratitude for this forbearance.

But, it seemed, all did not take the situation with equal philosophy. Tilton, the man who in a fit of rage had killed his mule at the start of the expedition, was in a bad temper over the affair. His black looks shortly found a voice. He grumbled to himself as he moved about. Finally he began to express himself audibly. Addressing nobody in particular he gave his unbiased opinions.

Miles off the route! No water! No meat fit to eat! No chance to graze the horses! That's what comes of taking a greenhorn along! Why he didn't even know enough to—

"You said enough, Red. You leave Andy be!" interposed Joe Crane steadily. "Mebbe he didn't know enough to—this-an'-that. But he does now. He larns, and that's more than I'll say for some."

"Meanin'?" demanded Tilton.

"You know the size of yore moccasins, and what fits yore feet." Joe sketched in the air the merest suggestion of the sign language symbol for mule.

Tilton uttered a strangled bellow of rage, snatched his knife from its sheath. Joe bared his own blade.

But before they could come together Kelly, who had been lying on his side at some little distance, with one motion, like released whalebone, leaped between them.

"None of that!" he commanded sharply, and then, as they continued to press forward, he placed the palms of his hands against their chests and hurled them violently apart. It was a remarkable exhibition of agility and strength, for the belligerents staggered back like children.

Tilton was now foaming with rage. Given a split second he would have turned his attack on Kelly, who was unarmed. But the latter allowed him no split second.

"Stand still!" He did not raise his voice, but the command cracked like a rifle. "If you want to fight, there is the open prairie. But understand this, if you leave this camp for any such purpose, you needn't come back. I'll have no quarreling. And if there's any fighting among ourselves while this outfit is together, I'll be doing some of it." He held them for an appreciable time by sheer force of dominance.

Joe thrust his knife into his belt and turned away. Tilton's lowered red head shook back and forth sullenly, but he, too, reluctantly sheathed his blade. He muttered something about the mountains, "—ain't through with me yet—"

"I don't care what you do when you get to the mountains." Kelly cut him short. "But as long as we're together I'll have no fighting among ourselves. We'll save that for the Comanches."

The other men made no comment. They had sat grave and impassive, aloof. No one could have guessed their opinions.

Nothing further was said. But the atmosphere was troubled. The psychic climate, so to speak, had changed.

Andy wrapped himself in his blanket. He was very low in his mind. In spite of his companions' forbearing tact, so little to be expected from such rough and direct characters, in spite of Joe's championship, it had been a miserable day. At any other time this first bivouac among the buffalo would have thrilled him to the core. Evidently the beasts had drifted back, or new bands had taken the places of those his awkwardness had driven away. The night was resonant. Bulls snorted, coyotes wailed like devils, wolves snarled and barked, ravens, not yet settled down for the night, screamed and croaked in a thousand voices. A surge of restless vitality arose from the darkened earth like an emanation. Calmness, the peace of night, had withdrawn to the remoteness of the stars, but it was not missed. The tumult of replacement excited like the beat of savage drums.

Andy, however, was encased in the complete insulation of his boyish chagrins. Over and over the events of the day thrust themselves upon him. He writhed beneath their recollection.

Alongside, Joe was disposing himself deliberately for the night. When he had settled down to his own satisfaction he turned his head in Andy's direction.

"Ain't nary wolf born wise," he observed. "Know a lot more'n you did this morning, don't ye, bub? That's somethin'. Funny thing is, Ben Tilton don't. Never will. That's about all the differ atween folks. Some larns, some don't."

Andy choked. He dared not trust his voice. He reached out his hand and timidly patted Joe's recumbent form.

"Wagh!" said the mountain man roughly. "Go to sleep and git ye a good rest. And don't never cut no more meat across the grain."

Chapter 6
The Señorita

Andy Burnett's impressions of the journey after leaving the buffalo country were like the troubled unrealities of one slightly in delirium. While involved in them, they are without beginning or end, one seems doomed to them indefinitely, and settles to a spirit almost of eternal acquiescence. Then, as it seems abruptly, he finds himself out on the other side, into solid life again, astonished that it is finished.

Thus Andy found it difficult to realize that he actually looked down into the valley of Santa Fe, for by this time the length of the journey and its hardships had thrust Santa Fe into the distance of legend. Yet there it was, and here he was, the same Andy. But he was not the same Andy. He knew more than when a month or more ago he had started from St. Louis. Experience, a quick adaptability, Joe Crane's careful elucidations had given him a fairly respectable knowledge of plainscraft. But over and beyond the mere skills and theories, the fiber of the lad had steadied. It would have been obvious to any thoughtful observer that this boy had become possessed of a maturity, not only beyond his years, but beyond that possible to most at any time of life. His eyes looked out gravely and steadily from a calmly sober confidence. And in this he had, in a ridiculously short time, entered into a genuine spiritual kinship with his companions. He was already in a fair way toward becoming a mountain man himself.

I think this chemical rearrangement of Andy's spiritual particles took place after they had crossed the ford of the Arkansas, for there began that portion of the journey referred to by the Spanish as *la jornada del muerto*, shortened to the *jornada* in common talk.

Nobody told Andy anything of what was in store, and he was at first too boyishly heedless and interested in the moment's excitements to think of inquiring as to what was ahead, but he could not avoid perception of something grave impending. Buffalo were killed beyond the present needs, their flesh made into jerky. The horses were shod with *moccasins* of the green hide. Spare water carriers were prepared of bladders.

"It's the water scrape," Joe answered briefly.

They passed, at several miles' distance, a singular landmark, a sandstone column, like a monument, alone on the prairie.

"Pawnee Rock," said Joe. "We're on the Trace."

Shortly they came to the Arkansas. To Andy it was a complete surprise, for its bed was below the level of the plains, which appeared unbroken until they had arrived fairly on the rim of the ledge. It was a noble river for width, with many islands green with groves of cottonwood, but it proved to be so shallow that it seemed one might splash across it anywhere. But Joe shook his head at the suggestion.

"Likely to swallow you down like nothin' at all," said he. "Quicksands."

For three days they followed the course of the stream. Then the opposite ledge broke into low sandhills.

These, it seemed, constituted another landmark. They forded here and set out to cross the Cimmaron desert.

Flat, simple, terrible. No landmarks, like a sea. Solemn and frightful. No animals, no insects, no breeze except sudden whirls of wind that lifted the light earth into tall columns moving in limitless space. A merciless sun waxing to the red glare of noon. Cactus. Sparse, rare curly grass in bunches, the only friendly manifestation of life. Deep ashy earth into which the horses sank to the fetlocks. It rose in choking clouds to powder them all with dust that turned them to a ghastly gray, through the mask of which their eyes peered red-rimmed. Dancing, shimmering heat that rose in palpable waves. The animals hung their heads and plodded doggedly a painful step at a time. The men rode silently, intently. It seemed as though they husbanded their fortitude, doling it out sparingly against the future need. The desert sucked them in until they moved completely lost in its enchantments. The hours and the miles expanded to a new dimension measured by new standards, while with each minute, each foot forward, the busy spirit of the desolation wove thicker and thicker about them the web of illusion. Only a steadfast faith remained by which they could hope ever to break through its timeless, spanless infinitudes to another world of reality.

The clear dry heat sucked the moisture from their tissues. Within the first hour Andy began to thirst as he had never thirsted before. Left to his own inclination he would have emptied his canteen, but Joe vigorously denied him and would permit him only to wet his lips. That seemed no better than an aggravation. His throat was dry and sticky, his tongue actually swelled in his mouth. For a time his mind dwelled on sweet waters—the dripping bucket rising from the well on the Pennsylvania farm, the rushing cool brook where he and Joe had eaten their first lunch together, even the stale, foul pools in the buffalo wallow back there on the prairie from which he had turned with disgust. Joe seemed to read his state of mind.

"Don't think on it," he croaked, warningly. "That's the way to go *loco*."

Toward noon mirages began to form. A beautiful cool lake seemed to lie directly across their line of march. Andy was deceived by it, as well he might have been, for not only did he think to see its waters and the trees about its border, but its surface seemed to be ruffled into wavelets by a breeze. He uttered involuntarily a cry of relief.

"False pond," pronounced Joe, and sure enough, as they approached, the appearance dissolved, faded away, leaving only the eternal and limitless expanse of desert ash. As the afternoon advanced, more and more of these false ponds took shape. Some of them would have been very beautiful had it not been for the mockeries of the nagging thirst. In one of them a group of moving figures seemed half immersed. With a momentary clutch of the eerie, Andy recognized themselves.

At last the sun withdrew its strength. They made camp. The day's toll seemed to the boy terrible. In the short span of a few hours the horses had gaunted to scarecrow caricatures of the sleek animals of that very morning. They were doled a few quarts of water and began listlessly to crop at the sparse bunches of grass. The men too drank sparingly. They nibbled at the jerky and spread their blankets. There was little conversation.

The next day was worse. Andy had thought he had reached the limit of his endurance, but he found that now he must draw on new reserves. He found them, but they were pitifully small. He husbanded them, withdrawing within himself. Somehow, he felt that the powers at his command were equal to only this, the slow dogged plodding on, that if he were to be called on for even an added ounce of attention he would find that he was unable to arouse himself. Nevertheless he must do so. The animals were weakening. They moved slower, and ever more slowly. They must be prodded on, finally forced on. Two of them wanted to lie down, from which they were prevented only by frantic urging. Andy, sitting dully, wondered where his companions found the necessary energy. Finally one did lie down. They could not get it up again. Through a haze of mere endurance Andy saw the men dismount, consult together. Finally the beast's equipment was stripped from it and piled atop another. They moved on, leaving the horse outstretched on the plain. Andy was too benumbed to care.

Joe and Kelly rode ahead. They looked often at the sun, consulted a pocket compass which Kelly carried, talked together low-voiced.

After that, things became a little hazy in Andy's mind. All he could remember was not to say anything.

Toward the close of the afternoon he was roused by a momentary stop. The straggling little procession had drawn into a group, and the men were all looking toward something. Andy for the first time became aware of a mound rising above the plain dead ahead. He gathered that it was a landmark.

They rode on. The mound looked to be small and only a mile or so distant. Nevertheless they rode the rest of the afternoon before reaching its base. Then it proved to be considerable of a hill, perhaps a thousand feet in height. After they had dismounted Kelly distributed nearly all of the remaining water. Joe was triumphantly jubilant. His direction had been faultless.

"If we'd have missed her, we'd have been gone beaver!" he cried.

There was no water here, but it seemed the spring on the upper Cimmaron was now but a few hours farther on.

The extra ration seemed to revive Andy completely. He could feel his desiccated tissues swelling to a normal succulence. His mind cleared. For the first time he noticed that two more horses were missing. The others were skeletons, scarecrows. This evening they built a fire of the greasewood and cooked themselves a meal. Kelly busied himself making notes. Joe climbed to the top of the mound, and Andy's enthusiasm was enough revived so that he accompanied him.

The prospect spread out before him seemed limitless. To the south the smoothness of the plain was seen at last to be broken here and there by other smaller mounds and buttes raised to visibility by the observers' added elevation. To the north, similarly, stood isolated single buttes. Somehow these individual and separate things restored a friendliness that had been swept aside by the flatness and uniformity. And far beyond these, to the northwest, low, suspended just above the horizon, gleamed a silver strip above an azure base, like a shimmering hazy cloud.

"The Rocky Mountains," said Joe.

The trappers went into camp above Santa Fe to *rub up*, as they called it, before entering town. But about as they were getting under motion again the appearance of a body of horsemen caused them to stop and to draw together in a compact group. They were too old in precautions to omit this simple one before the intention of the strangers should be declared. The soldiers, for such they proved to be, stopped at fifty yards. Their commander rode forward. All were well mounted, with creditable horse harness. All sat their horses with the ease of accustomedness. But their uniforms and accouterments were nondescript, to say the least. Not one of them possessed a long rifle. A few bore old-fashioned English smooth-bore muskets, which looked rusty and out of order, but most were armed merely with lances and a type of firearm Andy had never seen before—*escopetas*, or firelocks, right out of the sixteenth century. A few carried only bows and arrows! Nevertheless Andy thought them, on the whole, a handsome and spirited-looking lot, except that their demeanor was hangdog and sullen.

The commander was, in contrast, a thoroughly dazzling creature. His uniform sagged with gold braid, his long spurs were silver-inlaid, and his sword and pistols sparkled with precious metal. His face also was not unhandsome and would have been prepossessing had it not been for the pomposity of a pride that verged on the ridiculous. He rode beautifully a beautiful horse which he caused to advance by a series of mincing caracoles. The trappers eyed him and the performance with stolid contempt.

Kelly advanced his own animal a few steps. The two greeted one another. The captain spoke at length. Kelly listened without expression. The men became impatient.

"He is desolated to an unbelievable extent," Kelly answered dryly the calls for information, "but he is out here to arrest us. We must give up our arms and follow him."

A short harsh laugh was the response to this.

"Ef that is the only Mexican army he has," drawled Bill Williams, "tell him to send him back a messenger and start recruitin' another. We mout take this one away from him."

Kelly and the captain went into extended conference. The mountaineer produced credentials from Senator Benton which the Mexican perused, frowning importantly. He made as though to thrust the paper into the bosom of his tunic, but Kelly laid an arresting hand on his arm. The captain reared, threw back his head, glared with indignation, half turned his horse to back away. As the mountaineer's iron grip did not relax, he succeeded merely in coming close to leaving his saddle. Kelly spoke quietly and firmly. The paper was returned to him. The captain whirled his horse in its tracks, plunged his long spurs against its flanks, shouted an order to his motley command, and the whole band galloped off in a cloud of dust.

"Well, boys," said Kelly, "we'll just have to 'light and wait."

"Don't we git to go to town?" asked Fitz.

"He's gone to report to the governor. We'll just have to wait."

They dismounted and sat on their heels. They grumbled, but it was evident there was nothing else to do. An hour passed, and another and another. Some of the more reckless were inclined to ride into Santa Fe anyway.

"We kin take keer of ourselves," they asserted confidently.

But this was largely talk. After a time, with reluctance, they unpacked and unsaddled the horses and turned them out to graze. The herd was held close under a mounted guard.

Late that afternoon appeared, again under a military escort, a small sad-looking individual, with exquisite and elaborate manners. He was the first Mexican Andy had seen in civilian costume, and the boy filled his eyes with the picturesque, and dashing details. This man, who proved to be the governor's secretary, or prime minister, or confidential man, greeted all present with punctilious ceremony, which a few acknowledged with curt nods. He sat on the buffalo robe spread for him. He and Kelly talked at great length. The mountain men listened attentively, but without comprehension. Their knowledge of Spanish was limited to the mixed fragmentary jargon of plains dialect. Kelly, on the contrary, proved to be possessed of a fluent command of the language, due, Andy later learned, to the fact that a trapping partner of some years back had been a native of Spain. At the end of an hour the Mexican took his leave with many bows and flourishes.

"We don't go to the *calabozo*," Kelly reported to his companions. "They are evidently very suspicious of us, but the Senator's name gets them. But I'm afraid, boys, you don't get your spree in town. They've got different plans for us."

It seemed that the following day Kelly was to call on the governor to state his business and present his letters. In the meantime—and here Kelly hesitated—the rest of the company was to proceed, under military escort, to Taos, there to await the conclusion of the business. After that they were to get out of Mexican territory by the shortest route. As he expected, this proposal was met by a storm of protest. Nobody trusted the *greasers*.

"Ef they git you in thar alone they'll clap you in the *calabozo* and then whar will you be?" cried Bill Williams. "Look at what they done to Bob McKnight."

But Kelly was firm.

"That's the chance I take," said he. "It goes with the job."

He argued them down at last. Even twelve mountain men could not hope to invade and maintain themselves against the whole of New Mexico.

"We must play their game, boys," said he.

He made them see it at last, though they consented reluctantly and with much grumbling. It was agreed, finally, that if he did not rejoin them within a reasonable time, they should make their way back from Taos to report to Benton.

"This is government business," he insisted, "and they have some sense."

"Mighty little." They were unwilling to concede so much. They had supreme, ridiculous confidence in their own prowess. "Ef'n we stick together." Kelly had to try to take this out of them. He succeeded only partially.

They parted the following morning in an uneasy frame of mind.

"If you want to help me, behave yourselves," was Kelly's parting and earnest admonition. "If you start any trouble, it will just get me in difficulty and won't do me any good."

"Well, they better behave *themselves*," threatened Fitz.

Joe Crane had fairly to be commanded.

"I never yit quit a pardner thisaway," he mourned.

"You do as you're told, Joe." Kelly turned on him sharply.

"All right! All right! But I'm tellin' you, I don't like it!" He spat contemptuously in the general direction of the squad of ragamuffin soldiers who were to escort them. "They better not git funny or they'll be one *military escort* turn up missin'! I ain't collected me no greaser sculps—yit," said he darkly, fingering the tufts of hair on his leggings.

But they found nothing of which to complain either during the two days' trip to Taos or after their arrival there. Andy thoroughly enjoyed the wide sweeps of the green valleys, the singing turbulent streams, the dark snow—clad mountains rising to the skies. They looked very good to him after the savaging he had gone through east of the ranges. He particularly noticed the numbers of sheep and goats, and the corresponding absence of game. At an adobe ranch house they were given goat's milk and a sort of curdle cheese.

They entered Taos grandly, like a triumphal procession. Two or three dozen dogs and as many ragged or naked children furnished the animation. The picturesque element was supplied by the men lounging along the whitewashed house fronts, their bright-colored light blankets thrown across their throats, their black eyes gleaming from beneath their broad hats. Gracefully they leaned against the adobe walls and slowly smoked cornhusk cigarettes, and watched from behind indolent impassivity these strangers. They looked as if they had always been there, part of the town's ornamentation. As a matter of fact they had appeared only a moment before, gathered by urchins' reports of the approaching cavalcade. The romantic element was furnished by a stir and rustling felt rather than heard behind louvers and doors, by the flash of curious eyes, guessed rather than seen. The only difficulty was that the *street* ended almost as soon as it began, so that the triumphal procession effect was brief and transitory. They came to a halt in the middle of a small and dusty plaza, the mountain men leaning on the horns of their saddles and looking curiously about them.

The soldier in command of their escort dismounted and entered the largest of the white adobe buildings. He returned shortly accompanied by a grave, fine-looking man with a grizzled square beard.

"*Alcalde!*" said the soldier, pointing to this individual.

The *alcalde* was most courteous. It was gathered from his gestures and such fragments of his speech as they could understand that the village was theirs to dispose of as they would. Other men, mostly of middle age or beyond, sauntered forward. The young men remained fiercely aloof, smoking their cigarettes against the whitewashed walls. There appeared to be much hospitable urging to dismount. Small boys were imperiously summoned to take the horses. At the knee of each mountain man stood one or more would-be hosts.

But the mountain men were not to be stampeded into precipitate action. All this palaver might be all right, but they preferred to stick together. They were not going to permit themselves to be scattered all over the place by an appearance of hospitality. Somehow Joe made the *alcalde* and the others understand this. They raised their shoulders and spread their hands in hurt deprecation, consulted together in rapid Spanish, finally, smiling gravely in their beards, led the way to a long low structure across the plaza. The mountain men followed, still on horseback. The *alcalde* made a sweeping hospitable gesture.

"*Casa de ustedes*," he pronounced slowly and distinctly.

The mounted men looked at it.

"*Calabozo?*" demanded Joe Crane.

The *alcalde* showed white teeth.

"No—no—no!" he deprecated. "*Cuartel.*"

Joe tossed his reins over his horse's head and dismounted. His rifle in the crook of his arm, he strode to the doorway and peered within.

"Looks all right, boys," he decided briefly.

They all dismounted, and ignoring and even thrusting aside all proffers of help from the mixed crowd that had now slowly gathered, they proceeded deliberately to unpack and unsaddle, each man carrying his equipment within. Andy found that the interior of the building was as severely plain as its outside. It consisted of one large room, dimly lighted by small narrow windows. Across one corner was a blackened open chimney with a hood. The floor was of earth that had evidently been watered, tamped down, and allowed to dry. There was no furniture of any kind. To Andy it seemed gloomy, bare, and none too clean. But the mountain men approved. The walls were two feet or more in thickness, the narrow windows were shoulder high, just right for rifle ports.

"'Gin we got plenty water we kin hold her against three or four of them little greaser armies," said Fitz with satisfaction. "Tell the old boy, Joe, he's got to send us in plenty water—a bar'l anyway."

They piled their belongings against the wall. Bill Williams had stationed himself at the door. Some of the older men, attempting to enter, found themselves barred by the barrel of a long rifle across their chests. They exploded in grieved expostulations, but Bill was inflexible.

"All right—*amigos*," he agreed, "but this yere is our place now, and all others keep out."

But a fresh problem presented itself. The horses. It was self-evident that the animals could not be stabled in the cuartel.

"Take 'em along." Joe's gesture rather than his words indicated the trappers' usual instant acceptance of anything inevitable. "If we need hosses and ours ain't forthcoming, I reckon well know how to git some."

There were no long consultations as to procedure. These men seemed to agree automatically. A word or two, a nod of the head. Two would always remain on guard at the door, *"and sober,"* reminded someone. The others would go sightseeing as they would, never singly, but always by twos. The war whoop was the signal of trouble when all were at once to make their way to the fortress.

"And I don't reckon they's enough greasers in this place to stop ary two of us," observed Joe.

But all these precautions seemed unnecessary. The people were friendly. Andy, wandering about in company with Joe to see what he could see, was everywhere welcomed with smiles and with greetings which he could not understand. Only the younger men, half muffled in their *serapes*, remained sullenly aloof. The reason for this soon was made evident. Everywhere the two Americans went they were aware of curious scrutiny, caught half glimpses of bright eyes peering at them, of girls' figures whisking suddenly away as they approached. Joe cocked his hat on one side and shouted facetious remarks in his bastard dialect. His sallies were acknowledged by subdued giggling. Someone concealed in a doorway shot back at him a volley of rapid in-understandable Spanish that brought forth a shriek of laughter. Joe darted suddenly into the doorway and dragged forth by the arm an old woman struggling but delighted. He held her firmly before him.

"Now *madre*!" he chided her. "What you saying about old Joe?"

He leaned forward and planted a resounding kiss on her cheek. The laughter redoubled in volume.

"Thar!" cried Joe to the concealed world at large. "No trouble to show samples!"

The old woman slapped him, chuckling. Joe leaped into the air, cracked his heels together, crowed like a cock, smote himself on the chest.

"Heap *mucho amigo*!" he cried.

"*Estrellita!*" shrieked the old woman. "*Va dentro la casa!*"

Andy turned in the direction of her attention. A girl had emerged from the doorway into the street. She was a very pretty girl with regular features, mischievous large eyes. Her blue-black hair was plastered shining close to her small head. She wore a short bright-colored skirt and a loose blouse of fine white linen, without sleeves. These, and shoes of soft leather, seemed to be her only garments, for her smooth and shapely legs were bare. A red rose had been thrust over her right ear. Many heavy gold and silver bracelets clashed softly on her wrists. The old woman berated her in energetic Spanish.

The girl thrust one hip sideways and rested a hand on it. She grimaced defiantly at the old woman, and smiled swiftly at Andy.

"'Ullo *yanqui!*" she called. "'Ow you was?"

Joe uttered a howl of delight, dropped the old woman's arm, and leaped in her direction. The girl whisked about with a swirl of her short skirts to vanish inside the doorway. The old woman, with surprising agility, darted after, still shrieking volumes at the top of her lungs. Andy stood alone, somewhat bewildered, in the soft sunshine of the square.

After a few moments, Joe reappeared, shaking his head. The old woman, still talking, pushed behind him as far as the portal, whence she continued her admonitions.

"Plumb evaporated," Joe told Andy. "Now *madre*," he pretended to threaten the old woman with the muzzle of his long rifle. "You talk too much. *Some* gal! Now whar did she larn to talk United States?"

They resumed their stroll, and so passed close to one of the numerous aloof and muffled figures leaning against the wall. Andy, looking up by chance, met the man's eyes. So unexpected and violent was the hatred burning in them that, irrationally, Andy's spirit flared in response. It was as though the lounger had, unprovoked, struck him in the face. Deliberately, he walked up to face the Mexican. For a moment, they stared at one another. Then Andy, recovering, turned away.

"What's the matter with that fellow!" he grumbled, still outraged by the apparently gratuitous hostility.

Joe chuckled.

"Keep yore eyes shinin' when that *hombre* is about," he advised. "Looks to me like that's his gal."

"Well, what's he mad at *me* for?" complained Andy. "Seems to me you're the fellow ought to look out."

"Wagh!" snorted Joe. "She didn't even *see* me till I took after her."

They strolled to the edge of town. That did not take long. The flat-topped adobe houses were clustered, without order, close to the rectangle of the central plaza. The plain about flung upward to snow-capped ranges. The air was vital with the wine of elevation, for the plain itself was higher than most mountains. Then they strolled back again. As they drew opposite the scene of their little adventure, a red rose fell into the dust at Andy's feet.

So magical was its appearance, apparently materializing from nowhere, that for a moment Andy stared at it, and then looked about to see whence it could have come. The young Mexican, still leaning against the wall, took advantage of this slight hesitation. With a sudden and catlike movement, he snatched the blossom fairly from beneath Andy's tardily clutching fingers.

"*Perdón, señor,*" said the Mexican. His eyes flashed with triumph and perhaps with a faint mockery, and his even white teeth showed in a smile that made no attempt to conceal its amusement.

Andy reddened with anger. But before he could act, the girl, Estrellita, dashed from the doorway to snatch the rose from the young Mexican's fingers. She shot at him a volley of Spanish, emphasizing her remarks by a stamp of her foot in the dust, all the while both hands occupied in refastening the rose in her hair. She stamped her foot again, whirled about, and was gone through the doorway again. She had ignored Andy, except that as she turned, she scorched him with a high-nosed contempt. The Mexican shrugged a shoulder and turned away. Joe laid a restraining hand on Andy's arm.

"Mind what Jim said about makin' trouble," he admonished. Then, as they walked on, "You got all the speed of a foundered mud-turkle, ain't you, Andy?" said he in mock admiration.

"Oh, hush up, Joe!" cried Andy. He was thoroughly impatient. He wanted to see that impudent young Mexican again. He particularly wanted to see Estrellita again. Just to get even, nothing more!

The trappers were gathered again at the *cuartel.* They reported a uniform absence of hostility. The military escort had started off on its return journey. For the inhabitants, as possible enemies, they professed a profound contempt. Only Bill Williams interposed a word of caution.

"Just the same, keep yore eyes shining a'ter dark," he advised. "These yere *hombres* is handy with a knife."

They feasted hugely on the provision hospitably brought in at the command of the *alcalde.* As this included a generous quantity of wine, they were moderately content, though several grumbled at a place where men lived together and no good liquor to be had, and no public saloon. As a matter of fact, as they discovered later, there was an inn, or public house of sorts, just at the settlement's edge, but as it was marked off only by a bush hung over the door, and as the trappers were unfamiliar with this convention, it had escaped them. So they squatted in a row against the front wall of the *cuartel* and smoked.

The sun had gone down. The crests of the distant ranges were edged with gold. Above them, the sky had dissolved its hard day surface to a depth of light green translucence. To eastward arched the brief phantom of the shadow of the earth. The atmosphere had softened, so that through it came distant sounds, mellowed and clear, that the day had not permitted.

The plaza filled gradually. Older men and women promenaded slowly around and around the little square. They inclined courteously to the trappers as they passed, carefully restraining too flagrant evidence of their curiosity. Their voices were soft and pleasing.

"*Buenas noches, señores,*" *they murmured.*

Girls walked together in little groups. They wore the short gaudy skirt, the loose *camisita* of linen, much gold and silver. Their hair, sleek and shiny, hung down their backs in two braids. Their smooth and shapely legs were bare, but their small feet were prettily shod in the soft leather *zapatos*. In honor of the evening, each had assumed a filmy *rebosa*, which she wore variously and coquettishly across her head, sometimes across the lower part of her face. Andy's rigid upbringing was at first a little shocked by the fact that they were, one and all, smoking *cigaritos*. He had never before seen women smoking. Their eyes were large and expressive. Some of them were very pretty. At first, the effect of their make-up somewhat disconcerted the Pennsylvania lad, for their complexions had been whitened by a heavy powdering, and their lips had been reddened in a contrast almost too startling. Nevertheless the final effect was subtly stirring in its very strangeness. They drifted by in close groups, trying hard to affect the unconsciousness of the stares of the tall mountain men, pretending to ignore the facetious greetings flung at them. Their eyes roved, snatching hasty glimpses, they giggled, melting together toward a common center, they lingered ever so little before they passed.

The young men, also in groups, strolled in the contrary direction. They, too, had assumed their finery and made a brave show with their low-crowned glazed hats, and their short jackets, and their split pantaloons, and their white linen, and the negligence of their folded *serapes* thrown over one shoulder. As they passed the girls, they bowed with formality. Sometimes, they paused and a short conversation was exchanged, after which each group resumed its sauntering stroll. The mountain men watched with interest a man and a girl who were evidently greeting one another after some absence. The left arm about the waist of each, cheek to cheek, they shook hands.

"Now that *shines*!" approved Joe Crane. "Wonder ef'n I kain't find me an old friend. Seems like I seen that little one somewhere before!"

One by one, yellow lights in the buildings heralded the dusk. From somewhere across the way came a rhythm of half-heard music, intermittent, faint.

The *alcalde* and two of the older men stood before them, bowing courteously.

"*Señores*," said he.

He was trying to explain something, gesturing gracefully and uttering soft-syllabled words. They caught one.

"*Fandango*," repeated Joe understandingly. "He wants us to come to a dance. What say?"

They rose to their feet with alacrity. But for a moment, their natural caution caused them to hesitate.

It was suggested that two be detailed to guard the *cuartel*, where the rifles would be left. In case of trouble the rest could fight their way back to those weapons with their knives and tomahawks and such buffalo pistols as were in their possession. Like to see any lot of greasers stop us! But what two? They brushed the idea aside with impatience. Take the rifles along. Stack them in a corner. Take turns guarding them. Hell! Who's afraid of a bunch of greasers? They're friendly enough, looks like.

They followed the *alcalde* across the plaza and crowded after him into an adobe building. The room was already well-filled. The women sat demurely along one wall. The men lounged against the other or clustered about a rough table at one end. Two guitars and a fiddle were tuning. Home-dipped tallow candles furnished some light and plenty of heat.

The music began. Men crossed the room, bowed before the ladies of their choice, and led them forth ceremoniously. With dignity and with considerable slow grace, they paced the formal measures of a *contradanza*. The mountain men looked on gravely. The music ceased. The girls were returned to their places. With a low bow, the men resumed their own. Cigarettes were lighted.

Ben Tilton and a man named Markey wandered down to investigate the table. Tilton uttered a whoop.

"Yere's likker, boys!" he cried. He held aloft an earthenware cup.

The trappers instantly deserted their corner. They tasted.

"That shines!" they cried jubilantly. "She's got a take-hold to her? *Que*?" they demanded of the man nearest.

"*Aguardiente*," they were told.

"Guess so," they agreed. "Anyway, she shines!"

Another dance began, slow and formal. The trappers paid it no attention. They were busy. Andy saw the girl, Estrellita. In her hair she wore now a tall comb over which was draped the *rebosa*. She moved gracefully, swaying her hips to throw in languid rhythm her short skirt from side to side. Her head was high, her eyes far away. She appeared wholly unaware of the tall young man by the stacked rifles, although the figure of the dance brought her within touching distance. Her partner Andy recognized as the same of that afternoon's encounter. He did not ignore Andy. His black eyes swept the American haughtily. Andy felt his hackles rise. An unreasoning anger swept him.

But now the decorum of the occasion was interrupted. Joe Crane was capering in the middle of the floor. The music broke and stopped.

"That stuff don't shine!" shouted Joe. "Give us something lively. Come on now! Hit the trail!" He flapped his arms at the startled musicians in an expressive pantomime. They hesitated, then broke into a quick tempo. "Come on, boys. Select yore pardners!" He seized one of the girls about the waist. "Stand aside, greaser!" He thrust away her escort of the moment. "You kain't shine in this crowd!"

The figure of the dance broke up in confusion. The mountain men, following joyfully Joe's example, each grabbed one of the girls. Laughing, they pretended escape. The older people fell back against the wall. Some of the younger men scowled and offered to object. They were swept aside.

"Grand right and left! Swing yore pardners!" howled Joe, whirling his own right off her feet.

For a moment, something near consternation seized the assembly. Then, recovering, they entered into the spirit of the occasion. The older people hugged the wall, laughing. The girls pretended to struggle but ended by yielding. A wild sort of quadrille formed itself. Joe howled the figures.

"Sasshay yore pardners! Swing yore pardners! First four forward an' back!"

The Mexican girls caught the idea and followed with spirit and grace. The mountain men stamped their moccasins vigorously, leaped high in the air, cut pigeon wings and monkey shines. The musicians scraped and twanged away spiritedly.

"Go git ye a gal, bub," said Bill Williams's voice at Andy's elbow. "I'll watch the guns. No, git along. Yore young and spry."

Andy did not protest overmuch. His moccasins were already tapping in time, and his very soul swayed with the quick rhythm. Over in a corner, hemmed in by a group of older people, and so overlooked, the girl Estrellita peered forth with excited eyes. He darted to her, thrust aside those who surrounded her, and seized her by the arm. She jerked back. He passed his arm around her waist. With one sweep of his powerful shoulders he swung her in a long arc to deposit her on the open floor and drew her to him closely. She looked up at him in rebellion, but suddenly melted.

"My! You ver' str-rong!" she said.

Andy was panting a little. It was as though something within him had taken off a lid. For the first time he was, by this release, indirectly conscious of how great had been the pressure of the journey, indeed the pressure of his whole harsh and laborious youth. Something bubbled up within him like a strong effervescence. He was wild with its intoxication. And the only possible expression was this dance. Around and about he whirled and pranced. He did not know he was shouting. He swung the girl clear of the floor in the turns, crushed her close to him, and flung her away. Acutely, but somehow impersonally—for this madness of release was bigger than that—he was conscious of the girl's soft, pliant body through the *camisita*.

The music abruptly stopped, probably from exhaustation. Andy came to himself as though awakening. Estrellita, bright-eyed and panting, was regarding him with an enigmatic mixture of astonishment and delight. Andy was dimly conscious of a scattering of applause and laughter from the half-scandalized, half-fascinated, but wholly amused bystanders.

He drew a deep breath and turned to encounter eyes ablaze with hatred. The young Mexican of the afternoon had thrust himself forward. His hand was on his knife. He was saying something.

"Juan!" cried the girl in sudden alarm.

Andy did not understand the words, he hardly saw the knife. But his excited state made him feel the crisis. His fist shot out to crash against the Mexican's jaw.

Instantly, the place was in an uproar. The women screamed. The older people crowded back. The younger Mexicans leaped forward, knives bared.

But prompt as they were, the trappers were quicker. Acting with the automatism bred of many dangers, they were instantly together in a compact group. For the first time, Andy heard the war-whoop, "Howgh-owgh! Howgh-owgh!" Facing steadily in all directions they moved slowly to where Bill Williams, rifle in hand, awaited them. One by one, they backed out through the door. Joe Crane was the last.

"You all better stay put for a spell!" he told the assembly at large. "Wouldn't be no ways healthy for you to stick yore head out 'n that door for a spell."

They did not understand his words, but his menace was unmistakable.

The little group of trappers crossed the moonlit plaza to the *cuartel*.

Once inside its walls, they began to laugh. Andy, who had thought to be in disgrace, was astonished to find himself somewhat of a hero.

"Offhand or with a rest, bub, you shore make them *come*!" cried Joe.

"Don't make no trouble," says Jack. "Wagh!"

However, there was no trouble. Gradually, the Americans were coming to the understanding that these were a genuinely hospitable and gentle people. In this remote mountain village, distant from the politics, sensitive pride, and greediness of the *gente de razón* at Santa Fe, their natural inclination was to friendliness. The incident of the evening was dismissed lightly as an amusing misunderstanding of hot-blooded youth. Indeed the *alcalde* brought with him Juan, and some sort of truce was insisted upon, though as neither party wholly understood the other, the terms were obscure. The result was satisfactory in that the trappers as a body were freed from the necessity of feud.

The entente grew rapidly. Gradually, the Americans abandoned the most stringent of their precautions. The rifles were left in peace at the *cuartel*. No longer did the men feel incumbent to keep together in twos. The new arrangement made for satisfaction, for it is extremely difficult to carry on a successful flirtation in squads of four. The rigidity of convention, at first so formidable, appeared to be a shell, for some of the girls at least proved to be both accessible and compliant. Each man had his sweetheart. Nevertheless, at the *cuartel*, one tall figure always lounged, lazy, sleepy in appearance, but decided in his menace against any who tried to enter.

Word came from Kelly. His business was progressing, but slowly. It might be ten days—two weeks.

"Make it two months, suits me," said Joe.

"Goin' to miss the fall hunt if we don't git along soon," grumbled someone, but the grumble was merely conventional.

Andy was no exception to the general sentiment. The day following his escapade at the *fandango*, he took his courage in his two hands and called at Estrellita's house. The old woman answered his knock. She grinned amiably when she saw who it was.

"*Bienvenido, señor.*" She motioned him to enter.

"*Señorita*," said Andy, "*yo deseo*—" His new Spanish failed him. "*Señorita*," he repeated.

But the old lady needed no more. To Andy's surprise she seemed friendly. He had supposed, in view of her attitude the afternoon before, and in view of last night's performances, that she would be quite otherwise. But she smiled at Andy and nodded at him brightly and reassuringly and made him sit down on a bench in the patio, and departed without objection, presumably to summon the girl. And in a minute or so, Estrellita stood before him, surprisingly subdued and demure, her eyes cast down, her hands crossed demurely before her. She carried a turkey wing as a fan.

"*Buenos dias, señor*," she greeted him, and sat down stiff and sedate.

Andy was a trifle thrown out. He had come with a somewhat hazy idea of making amends. He had expected a rigidly chaperoned interview to be conducted in the face of disapproval, if not of hostility. His excuses were received impassively, with only a slow wave of turkey wing by way of acknowledgment. It is difficult to talk against a blank wall, especially to one whose comprehension of your language is doubtful. Andy ran down.

"Well—I guess—that's all," he stammered, and arose to his feet.

For the first time the girl raised her langorous lids to look up at the tall American, limpid-eyed.

"Yo' go?" she inquired softly. "Yo' no lak Estrellita?"

"Of course I like you!" cried Andy. "But I thought—I've been telling you—about last night—"

"*Yo no comprendo*," said she, shaking her head.

"But I thought—you talk English."

"Sooch a very little," she pronounced slowly.

Andy felt unexpectedly helpless.

"That's tough," he said to himself, but aloud.

"Tough as 'ell—eh?" said Estrellita surprisingly. "Yo' lak talk wid me—no? What yo' lak say—eh?"

"I'd like to tell you that you've got the world beat for looks and go," said Andy, bold behind the screen of her ignorance of the language. She listened with her head on one side, like a parrot.

"I t'ink I lak," she decided. "Yo' mus' tell me Español."

"I do not speak Spanish," Andy pronounced with great distinctness.

"You lak I titch yo'?"

"Very much—yes," said Andy.

She swayed from the bench where she had been sitting to stand facing him. With one hand she touched her shining small head.

"*Cabeza*," she pronounced slowly. "Now yo' say."

"*Cabeza*," repeated Andy dutifully.

She took his great hand in her tiny palm and placed it flat beneath her heart.

"*Corazón*," she told him, then, a trifle impatiently, as he made no immediate response. "You say!"

Andy was too plainly cognizant of the softness of her body and the curve of her young breast but just above his hand. He slipped the hand suddenly around her, drew her to him, and kissed her savagely.

"What do you call that?" he panted.

She tore away, struck him across the face, and was gone. A door slammed. And Andy was alone in the patio, faced by solid doors and barred windows. He tried the doors and peered in at the windows. The house was as though empty. Finally, reluctantly, he went out through the great door into the street. He was in a most confused state of mind. He was at the same time aroused, a little indignant, and very doubtful. Aroused by the strong sex lure of the girl, indignant at her repulse after so much of what he took to be encouragement, doubtful in the belated recollection of the fact that she belonged to a race of whose customs he was, after all, profoundly ignorant. But he was chiefly indignant.

As he moved slowly along the house front outside, he was arrested by a soft hissing whistle. He looked about him but saw nobody. Nevertheless, Estrellita's voice came to him.

"Yo call heem *besito*," it said. "Now yo' say."

Andy looked all about him. Finally he saw her, or rather the top of a head and one eye of her, over the parapet of the flat roof.

"Nodder time yo' come back. I titch yo' more Español," went on Estrellita. There was a flash of a white arm. Something curved through the air to fall with a plop at his feet. It was another red rose. Andy, without competition, retrieved this one and thrust it into his hat.

Joe at the *cuartel* eyed it sardonically.

"Speedin' up, eh, old mud-turkle? Wall, keep yore eyes shining. They's times when ary woman is hard to tell from a catamount or a yaller jacket."

Chapter 7
Indian Country

Estrellita was, of course, just a little devil, a very skillful little devil. Poor, unsophisticated and straightforward, Andy was so easy that his subjection would soon have lost interest had he not been so tall, so strong, so good-looking, but above all, a foreigner, and therefore possessed of the lure of the exotic. The most rudimentary technique was sufficient, and as everyone knows, the basis of rudimentary technique is to keep them guessing. Andy never quite knew where he stood. He left her kind and melting, he returned to her haughty with some mysterious displeasure from which he must win her back. The boy's almost total ignorance of Spanish was a great help to her, a wonderful screen from behind which to take these potshots. Andy was never quite sure what might or not have caused their frequent misunderstandings, or indeed, what in thunder the misunderstandings were! If any! As far as the rest of the business was concerned, the facilities were quite adequate. To be sure, Estrellita's English was very sketchy, consisting merely of fragments she had picked up as a child when, with her mother, she was one of the household of Lande, the adventurer. But her eyes, and her red lips, and her rounded shoulders, and her fluttering expressive hands, and her deliriously lissome body were all in working order. Likewise, there happened to be a moon, a large, calm, desert moon that threw strong shadows on the whitewashed adobe buildings, that floated the world in a magic that drained from it the substance of solidity, so that the distant mountains hung as ethereal as clouds, and the low chaparral of the plains stood as fragile and brittle as frost crystals. Sounds floated like spirits in the delicacy of its enchantment. The stream had left off shouting and was murmurous with little voices. Quiet breezes whispered sweetly to the shivering ecstasy of leaves and grasses. The distant, faint bass notes of guitars throbbed like hearts. One sitting alone could hardly have remained impervious to the unfoldment of romance. What of two sitting together?

The course of true love, as Andy now seriously considered it, ran smooth. Suspiciously so. Andy was too unsophisticated to realize that fact. He knew nothing of Spanish ideas, he knew nothing of *dueñas*, and Estrellita did not *titch* him that particular word. Though, to be just, there were none of that sort of dragon resident in the simplicities of Taos. Estrellita did exactly as she pleased, and had always done so, at the cheap price of an occasional thoroughly enjoyable row with the old woman who happened to be her great-aunt. As for the rest of the small community, she did not bother her pretty head about them, she snapped her dainty fingers at them. They shrugged their shoulders philosophically. They had long known that Estrellita was a little devil.

So nobody did anything about it, though, of course, it was a scandal. But such scandals were not infrequent in the lazy, warmly romantic little town. Later travelers of the Santa Fe Trail speak of them with appreciation or with virtuous horror according to their religious and moral convictions. Except that the *alcalde*, seriously desirous of fulfilling the governor's instructions as to these Americans, did invent an errand designed to remove from the scene the young man, Juan. That seemed the simplest method to avoid trouble. He did not accomplish this without difficulty. Juan did not take it lying down. But an *alcalde* is an *alcalde*, and the Mexican finally departed for the mountains, riding hard.

Kelly arrived from Santa Fe after a little over a week. He proved to be fully satisfied with the success of his mission. The new Mexican governor was inclined to favor the American trade. He would dispatch secret messengers to confer with Senator Benton. Kelly's own report and the rough route maps he had sketched would go forward by the same hands. That job was finished. The trappers could now go north in time for the fall hunt.

"It is only fair to tell you, boys," said Kelly, "that if any of you want to stay here, the game is open now. They no longer object to American residents."

They pricked up their ears at this. The country was virgin, unknown, from their point of view. How about these mountains? Ary beaver? Ought to be rich picking...

But Kelly dashed that.

"They're keeping their own fur for themselves," he told them. "You might get to be a Mexican citizen if you stay long enough. I don't know. But you can stay and grow up with the country if you want to."

Their interest died disgustedly. Git to be a greaser? Not if they knew it! Theirs was the sturdy, contemptuous Americanism of the pioneer. The spree was over. Let's git to the hills! They would set out the following morning.

Kelly had, for his part, been presented by the governor with a short telescope. The trappers were inclined to deride this instrument but Kelly would not agree.

"It'll come in handy to spy for Indians—or for game, for that matter," he insisted. "I'm glad to have it."

Andy drew apart. All afternoon he sat against the adobe wall, somber and silent. Glamour had him, and he was helpless against it. It was not a matter of decision, for reason was buried by sheer instinct. At last, shame-faced, embarrassed, he drew his companions aside.

"I think I'll stay," he told them gruffly.

He had difficulty in making them understand the simple meaning of the statement. Joe exploded with indignation and incredulous amazement. Andy, his head down, explained doggedly. His reasoning sounded lame, even to himself. The trade was opening, and he had money. Here was a good opportunity to establish himself, to be on the spot when the caravans began to come in.

"You aimin' to be a *trader*!" cried Joe. "You quittin' the mountains! You quittin' us!"

Kelly said nothing, but watched keenly.

Andy mumbled on. Desperately he tried to justify himself, to set himself a little right. He might as well have saved his breath. Joe was outraged. Finally, as the tatter's expostulations had no other effect than to drive the boy into a sullen obstinacy, he became furiously angry.

"Hell," he cried. "If any stinkin' Kaw Injin had done me sich a trick, I'd —It's that gal!" he cried. "That Estrellita bitch!"

Andy threw up his head with a jerk.

"Say what you want about me but keep off her!" he warned.

"I'll say what I want about anybody!" began Joe. "Why that little—"

Kelly laid his hand on Joe's arm.

"That'll be all, Joe," he said quietly. "This is Burnett's affair. I'm sorry,

Burnett. I think you are making a mistake. I'll arrange for you to get your share of Senator Benton's fee."

"I don't want it!" cried Andy.

"You'll take it," returned Kelly coldly. "Come, Joe." They left him to himself.

The rest of that afternoon and evening Andy moved miserably apart. No one spoke to him, except in the briefest necessary terms. He was thoroughly unhappy. It seemed that his peace of mind had deserted him forever. But he knew that he could not do otherwise. The thought of Estrellita swept through him like a flame.

In the gray of dawn the mountain men methodically saddled their riding horses, packed the other animals, mounted. They were wild with high spirits. The lazy little town was up and about, to see them off. The trappers shouted gay farewells and leaned from their saddles audaciously to snatch their girls clear of the ground. Some of the latter were weeping. The cavalcade moved.

"*Adios! Adios!*" cried the bystanders. "*Vaya con Dios!*"

Alight morning mist lay over the plain. Into it, the little band slowly melted from view.

After they had quite disappeared, Andy took his rifle and went on foot toward where the river ran through the awesome gorge it had cut for itself across the tableland. He had not much thought of game. He wanted to be alone for a time to ease his sore heart. Later he would go to the house of Estrellita. Somehow, he would make her understand that they should be married immediately, as soon as Mexican formalities would permit. Then, they must move down to Santa Fe to establish themselves in anticipation of the trade. Andy had quite sufficient capital, what with the remainder of his grandmother's savings and his share of Senator Benton's fee. As he was but just past his twentieth birthday, his imagination, started on this line, and extended it with the easy facility of youth. He saw himself in the velvet and linen and silver lace of the country, riding gravely the streets of Santa Fe on a coal-black steed as gorgeously caparisoned as himself. People bowed to him respectfully, greeting Don Americano, the rich and influential merchant, who—Andy was sure of that now, he had been doubtful—sported clipped side whiskers halfway down his cheek. At the edge of town, he brought his horse to a stand before a low, rambling adobe covered with roses. Instantly, from other, more hazily defined buildings somewhere near at hand, a number of *peóns* came running to hold his stirrup and take his horse. A more dignified figure bowed before him after he had dismounted, details somewhat misty, but very important. Brushing by him with a kindly word, his master entered the house to clasp to his arms Estrellita. Add a brief, negligent impression of an interior polished, simple, but richly dim. Also, children indeterminate as to numbers, age, size, or sex. Keep in mind, as a sort of enveloping atmosphere, the grave, worshipful, very Spanish dignity of Don Andrew, *el Americano*, whose benign influence in this sun-soaked country of dreams was becoming, somehow, rapidly patriarchal.

By this time, the sun was over the mountains, and the low-lying mist had disappeared. Andy's spirits were much lighter. And as it now occurred to him that Estrellita must have finished her chocolate, he leaped to his feet and started back toward town. So wholly was his heart drawn in eagerness that he quite forgot the long Kentucky rifle, which he left leaning against the boulder on which he had been sitting. On which act an imaginative person might have moralized as an apt bit of symbolism. A passing horseman, leaning from his saddle a few minutes later to appropriate the piece, had different ideas.

In the meantime, while still a mile from the little settlement, Andy was passed by another horseman at full gallop whom he recognized as the young Mexican, Juan. The latter knew him at the same instant, made as though to rein in his horse, changed his mind, shouted something, undoubtedly derogatory, dug in his spurs, and drove on at full career. A momentary gust of anger swept Andy. He shouted something back to the general effect that Juan was another, and hastened his steps.

The streets of the town were deserted. The inhabitants were still within doors, comforting themselves after the chill of the unwonted early rising, awaiting the warming of the sun.

Andy entered the large gate into the patio. Nobody was about, but smoke arose from the chimney. For the first time, Andy realized that he had not broken his fast. He would get the old woman to give him a cup of chocolate. Perhaps Estrellita would herself make him a *tortilla*. The thought brought to him an entrancing picture,—her face flushed charmingly by the heat, her lithe figure bent as she spread carefully the cornmeal paste on the *camal*, the sheet of copper over the charcoal fire, her eyes sparkling as she explained somehow in her delightful mixture of broken English and slow Spanish that the thinner the *tortilla*, the greater the cook's skill.

"An' see! The mine are thin like *el papel*!"

And her low gurgling laughter when Andy tried it, with the result that his was, "T'ik, lak *blanquilla*."

Whereupon he had seized her and in retaliation had—at the recollection of what he had done a flame of eagerness leaped within him. Without ceremony, he thrust open the door and entered.

On the threshold, he brought up short. The young Mexican, Juan, held Estrellita close. Her arms were around his neck, her face was upturned to his, she was murmuring to him swift Spanish. Her eyes were alight.

She caught sight of the intruder first and tore herself away with an exclamation. The Mexican whirled.

"*Roto cabrón!*" he snarled. "*Te tengo ahora!*" He threw the *serape* about his left arm, bared his knife, and leaped forward like a cat.

Confused and bewildered, Andy could not for a moment collect his wits. Almost too late, he realized that he must defend himself. His hand shot back to the handle of his own knife at his hip.

His wrist was seized from behind, and at the same instant, the folds of a blanket fell across his head.

Blinded, smothered, caught at a disadvantage, he nevertheless struggled desperately. Muffled, he heard dimly Estrellita screaming, shouts, the crash of objects falling. Other hands were grasping at him, attempting to pinion him. He put forth all his strength and managed at last to wrench an arm free. With one last convulsive effort he cast the knife blindly over his shoulder, as Joe had taught him. Even through the smothering of the blanket, he heard the thud of its impact, an exclamation of pain. Then his arms were clamped to his side, his legs jerked from under him. He was snatched bodily from his feet. Still struggling, he felt himself carried for some distance, hoisted aloft. A saddle was between his legs. A rope bound him. Suddenly, his head snapped back as the horse leaped.

And faintly, through the choke of his wrappings, he heard Estrellita laugh.

In momentary expectation of a knife in his ribs or a bullet in his brain, Andy rode on. He was securely bound and could do nothing. He could not even throw himself from the horse. But nothing happened. For five minutes they proceeded at full gallop. Then, the pace moderated to a slow shuffling trot. Thus, for hours.

Andy's first confusion steadied. He could think, after a fashion. Whither was he being taken? For what? Why had he not been killed out of hand? The direst forebodings filled him. All the stories of Spanish cruelty, of torture even, thronged to his mind. His imagination ran riot. But why this long journey? The horses had fallen to a walk. They were climbing. He heard the sound of water. They were in the hills. Why? There was no sense to it.

For a time, the suspense was racking. But as the hours wore on, Andy's more vivid emotions had to exhaust themselves. He fell into an apathy. It began not to matter. He wished they would get it over with.

Then, an illuminating thought occurred to him. Perhaps he was not to be killed after all, perhaps they were taking him to Santa Fe. The *calabozo*, that was it! He remembered Bob McKnight and his long ten years of imprisonment. Andy's emotions veered. He began to curse himself for a fool.

A weary indifference of despair succeeded this mood. Two things persisted in the dulling of his consciousness, the memory of the mountain men melting away slowly in the morning mists, the memory of Estrellita's laugh.

He strained his ears to determine, if he could, the number of his captors. Undoubtedly, they were soldiers. He could hear nothing. They rode steadily, silently. He might have thought himself alone, adrift, bound and blinded on a horse turned loose, were it not that occasionally he discerned the click of other hoofs on the rocks, or caught an occasional muffled exclamation.

The sun waxed in heat and cooled again. A chill crept into the air. It must be getting on toward evening.

At last, the horse he bestrode was halted. Unseen hands loosened the ropes from his saddle and lifted him to the ground. After a time, someone approached and fumbled with the blanket from behind. It was withdrawn from his head. Andy, blinking, looked about him. So certain by now was he of his solution of the situation that his first glance was not to his captors, but to his surroundings. He wished to determine, if he could, how far back toward Santa Fe the day's journey had taken him.

He found himself in a wild and rugged defile of the hills. Great masses of rock towered all about. Scattered and stunted conifers grew from a bare and barren soil. A small stream dashed by. The sky was pale green with the first of evening.

He turned about. A small fire flickered yellow in the gathering dusk. Over it squatted Bill Williams, carefully attending to meat roasting on sticks. About lay or squatted the other trappers taking their case. The figure before him, the blanket in his hands, was Joe Crane! Andy gasped and gulped, trying to adjust his mind.

"Thar, yo' tarnation little idjit," Joe was saying severely. "Yore out of that! And what do you think of yoreself now?"

Relief overwhelmed Andy like a wave. He tried to say something but failed. The only thing he could think of was not to break down and cry like a schoolboy. After a moment, he recovered himself sufficiently to blurt out, "I've been a fool!"

"Wall, that's all right," replied Joe judicially. "You shore have! But I warn't sartin you'd suspicion it."

"I don't know how I could have *been* such a fool!" cried Andy. "How can you ever—"

"Wagh!" said Joe. "I seen a bull elk once"—he pronounced it *ellick*—"that came out all by himself and made war on a mule wagon. An ellick is a pretty *sabe* animal when he's sober, but when he gits tangled up with a cow, he's a considerable of a fool too. No use arguin' with him, jist got to bat him on the head. Then he's like to come to—ef'n he ain't daid." He looked at Andy doubtfully. "Think yore goin' to behave and stay put?" he speculated rather than asked. "Or have I got to tie yo' up again to keep yo' from backtrailin'?" He made his own decision as to this. "Thar's yore rifle," he said, indicating the piece. "I picked her up whar you left her, leanin' 'agin a rock. Now thar's a purty piece of business! Don't you never do nothin' like that again. We done brung along yore horses and possibles, yo'll find them over thar. And yere's yore knife. Three inches more to the left an' I'd have been a gone beaver."

For the first time Andy noticed that Joe's hunting shirt was torn and bloody at the shoulder. Joe brushed aside his concern.

"'Taint't nothing," he disclaimed. "Jist a slice off the hump meat. Purty good flip for a back cast thrun blind. Come and eat."

Andy joined the others, reluctant and very shamefaced. They made no comment. Nevertheless, he kept in the background and slunk about like a whipped dog. His self-conceit was down to zero.

He was glad to spread his blankets. But Joe had one thing more to say.

"Ef'n yore still hankerin' a'ter that little Mexican *puta*—" he began.

"I'm not. I never want to even hear of her again," cried Andy passionately.

"That's all right. But I was goin' to say these yere Crow and Blackfeet gals ain't so bad lookin'. You can git you a squaw up in that kentry plumb easy."

Andy's spirits were enough resuscitated so that he made a playful pass in Joe's direction. But the trapper was serious.

"Jist yo' be good to them and they'll make yore moccasins and keep yore lodge and cook yore vittels and dress yore skins equal to nobody. They's a heap of comfort in a good squaw. And they're faithful and lovin' no end. No foofaraw about them! Next time you get to pawin' the ground and snortin' through yore nose and banging yore horns agin the trees, you remember what I'm tellin' you!"

———

They crossed the mountains of Sangre de Cristo and moved north through what is now Colorado, keeping well east of the high ridges. Thus, they passed through a much high plateau from which rose detached mountain ranges separated by wide plains. The latter were broken here and there by buttes and mounds and low castellated cliffs that terraced the different levels into which the tremendous sweep of clear distance resolved itself. Here were only a few buffalo, but many elk and black-tailed deer, and in some of the higher buttes, Andy saw for the first time the *cimmaron*, the Big Horn, and was told the usual tale of how they habitually leaped down cliffs to land on their horns, and none the worse, and of course, believed it, and spent some time trying to chase one over a precipice. Here were, too, occasional herds of wild horses, mustangs. They were fine animals, free-moving, high-headed. Andy thought them a beautiful sight, but the trappers seemed not to appreciate their presence. "Like to toll off our stock," they told Andy. The air, even in the heat of midday, was a thrill with vitality. The atmosphere was so clear that for long stretches, travel appeared to be on some mysterious kind of treadmill. Andy's scale of sizes and distances was confused, a hill apparently a half-hour distant, so near he thought to distinguish every clump of *sacatone*, turned out to be a mountain, and the clumps of *sacatone*, trees. As for moving or living objects, there was no telling. Might be a group of buffalo five miles away, or a flock of ravens near at hand. It was a big country, and in it at that time dwelled a spirit of loneliness that has since vanished from even the wildest spaces.

It seemed, illogically, that it could harbor no enemy. It was so big, so clean washed, as it were, by the crystalline purity of its atmosphere. But through it, the trappers moved with circumspection. In the morning, before the day's journey was begun, one or another—generally Kelly—galloped in a wide circle ahead, dashing at full speed past the ravines and buttes and folds in the earth's surface that might conceal marauders awaiting the movement of the little caravan. With the same purpose, outriders jogged ahead, and on either flank, a half-mile or a mile afield, but always within sight. Before the horses were spread out to graze at close of afternoon, the country for a mile or so in every direction was thoroughly ransacked. Nothing that moved in all the wide vista escaped keen and expert scrutiny.

"Injin kentry," Joe told the boy. "No, they ain't what you call hostile—'less'n they git a good chance."

The necessary hunting was done in twos, and always in an understood direction. Ordinarily, those assigned the task rode out straight ahead of the proposed line of march. Game was abundant. In its pursuit, Andy took a delight so keen that he was permitted to supply most of the meat. Joe Crane was his companion. From the trapper, he learned rapidly. Naturally keen of eye and observation, his faculties improved, so that several times he earned the mountain man's rare praise for his quickness in catching brief small movements in the crystalline distances.

"That shines!" commended Joe. "Anything that shows big and plain is safe. It's some leetle flicker of a movement behind a rock that says danger."

Nevertheless, the first danger showed both big and plain. It appeared suddenly in the shape of a horseman, silhouetted against the skyline of a low, flat tableland a scant half-mile away. The man seemed to Andy to have sprung from the ground. One instant, the skyline was clear, and the next, there the Indian was, sitting a motionless pony, looking intently in their direction.

Andy's heart leaped in his throat. He looked toward Joe. The mountain man was dismounting leisurely.

"Wall, yere we be," drawled the trapper. "Git ye down, Andy. We got visitors."

Andy scrambled to earth. He was just a little breathless, and his mouth was sticky with excitement. Nevertheless, his eyes were bright with eagerness, and he was relieved to discover in himself a gratifying steadiness. He had not known how it would be.

"Will they attack us?" he asked.

Joe paused in his preparation to examine the lad. Apparently satisfied, he resumed his inspection of his priming.

"They mout," he admitted. "Nobody knows what an Injun' will do. More like they'll try to stampede our hosses. What they'd like would be to rob us and turn us loose afoot. Fur as I know, none of these yere mountain tribes is warrin' agin whites—except Blackfeet." He paused to shade his eyes for a look at the motionless horseman. "Kain't tell yit—too fur. Looks like a snake or a Crow. Mout be a war party. More likely a huntin' party. We'll know purty soon."

He had been engaged in tying his own and Andy's riding animals closely nose to nose with the pack horse they had taken with them to bring in the game. Now, with a turn of the rawhide rope, he hobbled a foreleg of each to the other.

"Thar," he observed with satisfaction. "Stampede that outfit ef'n ye kin, ye varmints." He turned to the boy. "Now, Andy, yo' keep yore mind on what I told you. An Injin likes hosses and he likes sculps, and he'll take them whar he finds 'em when he kin get them cheap. But he thinks it's plumb foolish to git killed doin' it. And he's right and he knows mighty well that when one of these yere talks"—he patted his rifle—"it is one dead Injin. But he knows another thing, that an empty piece ain't wuth a cuss. So don't you go to shootin', no matter what happens. Don't you go shootin' yore gun 'less'n yo hear me fire, or I tell yo' to. Then pick you a good fat chief with lots of feathers and paint to take with you to the Happy Huntin' Grounds, 'cause that's whar you'll probably be a-goin'. Now you goin' to mind what I say—for onct?"

"But I don't see how we're to defend ourselves if we don't—"

"Jist p'int yore piece," interrupted Joe, "like you meant business—when one gits pressin' in too close or looks like he's goin' to shoot an arrow or somethin'. You stand that side the hosses, I'll take this side. Now mind! They'll do their leetle best to tease you to shoot. Don't you do it!"

Andy took his position. The Indian on the skyline had been joined by a dozen others. They rode slowly down the slope directly toward the two men and the three horses. As they drew nearer Joe commented on what he deduced, with a running explanation for the benefit of Andy's schooling, which he never forgot.

"Snakes—or Arapahoes—kain't tell which, chest tattooed, anyway. Huntin' purty, young bucks. Ef'n it was a war party, they'd be painted fur it, and they'd have their gun and bow covers wound round their heads—but watch 'em jist the same!"

At four hundred yards or so, they broke into a gallop. Andy, peering over the horses' backs, could see them leaning forward over their ponies' necks. Some brandished aloft guns or bows or lances. Others carried buffalo robes or other skins which they streamed in the wind of their going. All were yelling at the tops of their lungs. The speed and mass of the charge looked irresistible, as though it must override by sheer weight and impetus. Nearer and nearer it came. Andy was decidedly fidgety. He was held to a semblance of self-possession only by the fact that, across his saddle, he could see the outline of Joe's jaw moving rhythmically and calmly on his *chaw*. At last, when the onrushing cavalcade was within the hundred yards, the mountain man leveled his long rifle. So swift and businesslike was the maneuver that it had its effect, even on Andy. In spite of his schooling as to Joe's tactics, he momently expected the sharp crack of the piece. The effect was magical. The oncoming band split, the ponies whirling to left and right as though executing a drill. The same magic emptied every saddle, as each warrior threw himself to the far side of his mount. They cascaded by to either side, ran straight ahead for a short distance, then swung in on a circle as the riders resumed their seats.

"Lots of fun!" grunted Joe. "Yore turn now. When you p'int yo're gun act like ef'n you mean it, but don't git to pullin' trigger."

The warning was well-timed. Andy found it was one thing to view the rush from behind the shelter of Joe's rifle and the horses, and another to meet it alone and exposed. He was trembling, not from fear, but from over-eagerness to do the right thing. Nevertheless, strangely enough, there was leisure of mind somehow, amid all the pressure of hurry and excitement, to notice all sorts of things. Now that the Indians were on his side, he could see them clearly. Small details registered—as that they guided their ponies by a single line knotted tightly about the lower jaw, that a few bestrode a sort of saddle, but that the most rode bareback with a surcingle, that those who were not waving their skin robes wore them on the lower parts of their bodies held by a belt, leaving the torso naked, that their hair was long and streaming, that their faces were painted, if not for war, then for some fantastic personal purpose, that a few brandished guns, but that the most carried bows and arrows which they continually drew to the head in threat and as often eased back without letting fly. And he found room for a fleeting admiration of the horsemanship that could do all this and at the same time so perfectly guide the swallow-like swoop and turn of the charge. Then the rush was upon him, like a strong wind blowing in his face. It was impossible to hold faith that he, standing there alone, with one shot at his disposal, could avail against it. Nevertheless, with as stout an assurance as he could summon, and with a deliberation he did not feel, he raised the muzzle of his piece. He could not believe that it would work, but it did. As before, every saddle emptied, and apparently riderless horses scurried away to both right and left.

All but one. This man, astride a fine pinto, held straight on, his bowstring drawn back to his ear. Nearer and nearer he pounded, without a sign of fear or hesitation.

Andy met a fierce and flashing eye and stared into a savage black painted face. It seemed that he must intend hurling his mount like a missile right against the compact little group. So apparently direct and undeviating and purposeful was his rush that Andy's mind was crossed by a panic of indecision.

"Hold yore nerve!" Joe admonished him sharply.

Andy set himself like a rock, the silver of his front sight on the middle of his opponent's chest. And just as it seemed the next plunge must bring the collision, the pony's hoofs plowed the light soil in the turn as, with the same movement, the savage dropped behind the animal's barrel.

"Sassy young squirt, tryin' to be heap big Injin," grunted Joe. "Wagh!"

The last exclamation was caused by a further act of bravado on the part of the young warrior. As the pony scampered away, its rider had turned it deftly with a touch of his moccasined foot, swinging it broadside. At the same instant, he had discharged his arrow from beneath its neck. The shaft was launched at random, as a gesture.

Andy found Joe at his elbow.

"Git that fellow!" he cried roughly. "Let's see you shoot!"

Andy did not pause to question the change of orders. Nor did he stop to point out to Joe that there was nothing to shoot at, for of the Indian but one moccasin was visible above the pony's back, and part of his leg below the pony's barrel. With admirable promptness, he did the next best thing. At the crack of his rifle, the pinto went down head over heels, apparently rolling clean across its rider. The latter stirred, attempted to rise, and fell back.

"Load! Load! I'll hold 'em off!" cried Joe, thrusting his own rifle forward toward the Indians, who were returning at full gallop. "That's makin' 'em come!" He raised his voice in the high, harsh war-whoop. "Howgh-owgh! Howgh-owgh!"

The cry was echoed from behind them. Andy, stealing a glance, saw that the trappers' train had topped the low rise. Several of the men were galloping in their direction.

The Indians did not attempt to close. They came in only as far as the fallen warrior whom two lifted between them without dismounting. Then all made off over the tableland whence they had come.

"Good boy!" approved Joe. "You done well. Now you know how to handle Injuns. And that was good shootin', that far and runnin'. Too bad you couldn't take his sculp." He gazed regretfully after the disappearing savages.

"I thought you told me I ought never to shoot," said Andy.

"Not while they's comin' in. Sometimes, when they's goin' away, ef'n they's two of you and one keeps his piece charged. Anyway, that feller got too *tarnation* sassy. Kain't stand for *everything*."

Joe turned. A momentary, sudden physical sickness threw a black film before Andy's eyes. From the broad of the mountain man's back, just below the shoulder, protruded the feathered shaft of an arrow.

"Joe!" he gasped.

"'Tain't nothin'," said the trapper indifferently. "Didn't tech the life."

The trappers rode up and dismounted. Some of them set about disentangling the three horses. Two went to examine the dead pinto. Nobody asked any questions. They did not need to. The details were quite plain to their expert eyes. Kelly and Bill Williams set Joe on the ground.

"Stand fast," warned Kelly.

He seized the shaft of the arrow and gave it a quick, hard tug.

"Won't come," said Joe coolly. "Reckon you'll have to butcher her out. Cut off the shaft, boys. Don't aim to spile this shirt. She's a good shirt."

They cut the shaft and peeled off the shirt. Joe lighted his pipe and puffed stoically while, with his hunting knife, Bill Williams operated. He had to cut deep, for the arrowhead was well embedded. Even then, it came away only with effort.

"Done hit gristle," he grunted.

Joe smoked. Only the acceleration of the smoke puffs belied his complete detachment. Fumbling in his *possible* sack, Bill produced a handful of loose fur, which he bound to the wound.

"Beaver fur," he explained to Andy, who hovered about feeling very sick. "Nothin' like it to stop blood and heal a wound. Got a piece of buckskin, anybody?" He padded the fur with the buckskin and bound it in place with thongs. "Thar you be. Put on your shirt, old timer."

Joe shrugged experimentally.

"Seems like I ain't never goin' to git the use of that shoulder," he complained. "First off, Andy throws knives into it, and then this yere *cabrón*. And he didn't aim the thing, jist chucked her in the air fur gineral results. I don't have no luck!"

Bill Williams looked up at Andy.

"Did he git you too?" he inquired with rough solicitude. "Yo' lookin' mighty white and peaked."

"No. I-I just—" stammered Andy.

"Don't you take on about me," interposed Joe. "Boys, he shore made 'em come! Stood steady as the Rockies till I give the word. And then he took that pony right in the neck, runnin', a good twenty rod. Wagh!"

A week later, without very much ceremony, the little band split up. Each pair or trio had its picked country for the fall hunt. It was agreed to meet at the beginning of the next summer at Henry's Fork. If Sublette kept his promise, and the goods he brought in were not overpriced, they would deal with him. If not, they could float down to St. Louis on bull boats, for a change. Nobody expressed any desire for the Blackfoot country.

"You kin hev the whole of it," said one. "Me, I choose to keep my ha'r."

Shortly thereafter, travel for our three turned almost exaggeratedly slow and cautious. To their left the country flung to the skies in high and glittering mountains through which shortly they must find a pass. In the meantime, they held to the wooded ridges and heights of the foothills and lower mountains. The going was often steep, rocky, obstructed. The worst was through the thicket of quaking asps or popples or lodge-pole pines. The small trees grew close together. Even the horsemen were often put to it to squirm a way through, the pack horses were continually getting stuck. Where high winds had wrought, the trunks lay crisscrossed like jackstraws, and so close together that the horses had to buck-jump as from one pen to another. It took hours to win through a mile or so of this sort of thing. The ridiculous part of it was that a few hundred feet below, perhaps, lay the open river valley, or a plain, or a park across which they could have ridden with ease, but in full sight. Andy would have been tempted, especially when exhausted by hours of bitter struggle. Apparently, neither of his companions even considered the possibility.

Below the summit of each ridge, they halted. The animals rested or grazed while either Kelly or Joe Crane went ahead on foot. Kelly, some time since, had shot a wolf and had taken its skin. He used it now as a blind, drawing the mask over the top of his head which he eased slowly above the skyline. On occasion, he lay on his belly for a full half-hour, squinting through the governor's telescope, before signaling the others to come on.

They stopped in the middle of the afternoon, built a fire, and grazed the horses. The fire, when possible, was made in the dry bed of a ravine sheltered on the side toward the lowland by bushes. If they intended to spend the night there, the camp must be overhung by low boughs to prevent reflection on trees overhead. But ordinarily, after both horses and men had fed, they repacked, traveled as rapidly as possible for an hour or so more, and lay down without fire. This was sometimes uncomfortable, for after sundown, a fierce chill swept from the snow-clad heights.

Even as to the small cooking fires they permitted themselves, they took pains to burn only the odorless and comparatively smokeless wood of the quaking asp, making often considerable excursions afoot for it, collecting and carrying a supply on one of the pack animals when the indications were they would run out of the growth. In his first offer of replenishment, Andy learned something.

"Hold on!" admonished Joe, removing from the fire the billet Andy had placed thereon. "Not that away! Thisaway!"

He explained that a white man ordinarily made his fire so that the logs burned in two at the middle, but that an Indian pointed his logs toward a center and burned the ends. Why advertise the presence of white men?

It was all a queer combination of the most thrilling excitement and an impatience that must be mastered and a vigilance that must never be permitted to relax, not for one instant, even in the face of repeated evidence that these vast and awesome wilds harbored no other human beings but themselves. To his companions this was second nature, but close of day found Andy's capacity for attention worn thin almost to the point of exhaustion. He had to resist a temptation to leave it all to his competent comrades. But he did resist, and so found that daily, his perceptions gained in keenness, tended more and more to become automatic. His eyes, sweeping the prospect, were training themselves to pass over the usual, to stop only on what was unusual or abnormal to such a landscape.

The point of greatest anxiety was the matter of subsistence. It was necessary to kill from time to time, and killing meant shooting. Andy learned to judge country, to estimate the configuration of the hills, and above all, the nature of the blanketing growth—practical acoustics. It was astonishing how properly selected surroundings would smother the sharp crack of the rifle, and how a slightly different circumstance would re-echo it in seemingly unending reverberation. There must be but one shot. If the marksman was not absolutely certain, he should withhold his fire until he was. Andy was proud that, as a matter of course, his companions permitted him this duty in his turn. That was gratifying. His life seemed full of bitter mortifications and compensations like this.

For the first time he learned the resources of the wilderness. The meat supply was eked out by wild fruits. Joe dug camas root which, when boiled, proved to be not unlike a potato. Another root was dried atop the packs, pulverized between stones, mixed with water and sunbaked. Then there were wild onions, and bitter root, and Indian turnips. Andy considered them a pleasing variation, but Joe did not think much of them.

"They're eatin'," he admitted, "but give me good meat."

They tried for a pass across the shining mountains. It was bitter, incredible toil. The horses managed to scramble where Andy would have sworn a goat would have found no foothold. Sometimes, it was necessary to explore for hours afoot, working out inch by inch the sketch of a possible route for a few hundred yards. The canyons pinched out, filled with great boulders and slabs among which rushed white water torrents, finally stood on end so that they were forced to the hogbacks, hoping for a grade that might lead to the summit. Mountain sheep stood on bold elevations and looked down on them. Marmots whistled from the rocks. White goats stepped astonishingly across the face of sheer precipices. Andy shot one of them, but it fell from the tiny ledge, whirling over and over, and he could not get down to where it struck. An eagle closed its wings and dropped like a plummet after the falling body. Andy, looking down into the blue abyss, turned giddy. So they worked their way until sheer cliff interposed, or a precipitous gorge. Then they must return. The nights were bitter cold and comfortless.

The third attempt encouraged them. They emerged above timberline to wide boulder-strewn slopes of grass and flowers. Summer dropped below their feet like a garment. It was still early spring. Willows were budding. Snow water trickled busily in tiny rivulets. The grass was short and new and tender. An icily cold wind sucked downward like a draught.

"Bet we're hittin' her!" panted Joe.

The horses' flanks were heaving painfully. They could flounder but a few steps before resting. The slope was gentle but seemed interminable. To right and left, the great peaks lifted jagged to unbelievable blue, thrusting skyward through the snows.

Andy was afoot, as were the others. He led his horse, and brought up the rear, behind the pack animals. The elevation caught his wind, his heart was pounding painfully, his eyes were strangely blurred. When the horses stopped, he gulped thankfully at the rarefied air to ease his bursting chest. When they moved, he gave all his forces just to placing one foot in front of the other, each step a single and separate exertion, his eyes fixed on the ground immediately before him.

"Yere's the *puerto suelo!*" Joe's cry startled him.

Andy looked up. It was unbelievable. The slope had ended. The little group huddled on a narrow level beyond which plunged the blue of descent. He joined his companions.

He saw, spread out far below him, a tremendous prospect of rolling, tumbling hills, like a chop in a tideway, culminating in remote ranges that rose insubstantial to the height of the eye. The mountains on whose backbone they stood curved grandly to meet them in the blue distance. Viewed from this height, the lower hills, held like water in this enormous cup, looked mottled in various shades, as the darkness of forests yielded to the olive of brushland or the paler green of grass. Immediately below the pass, almost under their feet as it were, stretched a long lozenge-shaped valley, apparently flat. The most of its floor seemed to be grassland, but the meander of a stream was plainly marked by a winding strip of trees. It was what the men of that day called a *hole*.

"Thar's our kentry!" cried Joe with satisfaction. "Ought to be beaver aplenty in every fold of them hills. And I reckon nary white man ever set moccasin thar!"

For a thousand feet or so, the descent was ridiculously easy. The westward slope proved to be more abrupt than that to the east. The horses half slid in the loose shale. The eye could follow a feasible route, apparently all the way down. It was most encouraging.

Then of a sudden, their way was checked by a sheer drop. It was of not over ten feet, but there seemed to be no way around—except perhaps by a backtrack too long to undertake today. For the first time Joe lost his temper completely, announcing in no uncertain terms what could happen before he'd climb back one foot. His tirade was accompanied by vigorous action. The next half-hour gave Andy a new conception of what could be done with horses in the mountains. Each animal was blindfolded. A rawhide rope was knotted about its middle and turned twice about a handy juniper as a snub. Then, with Andy on the other end of the rope to pay it out, Joe led the beast to the edge and shoved it off. Andy had never before heard a horse scream. The animal kicked wildly, turned like a teetotum, bumped the rocky wall, lost a little skin—but landed safely on the lower level where Kelly waited.

"Do you have to do this sort of thing often?" panted Andy, straightening his back after the ninth horse had been landed.

"You do all sorts of things often, ef'n yo' travel in the mountains," said Joe.

But when they came to take stock, it was discovered that there had been one irreparable accident. In some manner, the brass telescope, presented to Kelly by the Spanish governor, had been crushed against the rocky walls. The eye lens was cracked, the brass tube smashed. Only the object lense remained intact. Andy rescued this from the wreck and slipped it into his *possible* sack.

The hole, from the level of the valley, offered a different impression than when viewed from above. What had seemed to be merely a tumble of hills now proved to be themselves quite respectable mountains, so that the place became a long, narrow park, fenced in by apparently unbroken ranges which differed only in that those to eastward were higher and soared upward even beyond the snows. They stood aloof and severe like majestic sentinels, while the others closed ranks in guardianship, like friends.

The plain between them was here a full three miles wide. It was a grass-grown, flower-decked prairie, broken by small groves of trees or patches of high brush where tributaries from the flanking hills came forth to join the river.

They angled to the north, riding boldly in the open.

"Yere's where we camp," Joe explained. "Either they's Injuns, or they ain't. We got to find out sometime."

The grasses stood knee-high. Game trails crisscrossed in all directions, but dim and overgrown. There was much sign of elk and buffalo, but all old.

"They've followed the snow," said Joe.

At a point where a tongue of the prairie opened through the trees to the river's edge, they unpacked. The river proved to be both wide and deep. Its clear waters ran swift. Andy caught the gleam of trout behind the boulders of a riffle, weaving slowly as they held place against the current.

"Now," Kelly told him, "we will leave you in charge for a while. Keep your eyes open. We will go look for sign."

The two trappers galloped off at full speed, Joe to the north, Kelly to the south.

Andy settled himself, his back against the piled-up packs, the long rifle across his knees. The sun was warm and caressing. The light air was cool and tingled in his nostrils. Liquid notes of meadowlarks and robins seemed to float in suspension, and behind them, a steady undertone of cascades falling and the ceaseless busy murmur of the stream. Andy, closing his eyes, could almost imagine himself back in the slumberous summer peace of the old, quiet country. He opened them again to the austere majesty of the ranges.

Close under the frowning walls, on the distant green, steep slopes of talus, his attention was caught by tiny movements which he at last made out to be that of animals feeding—the black solidity of buffalo, the more scattered, lighter brown of elk. Slow-moving cream-colored spots against the black precipices must be goats. A single tiny perfect model of a bighorn stood motionless against the sky. Ravens croaked from the nearby forest. A mother duck, quacking conversationally under her breath, drifted past him down the current, her downy babies bobbing atop the water, light as chips. A long, slim, furtive, shining animal—it was an otter—slipped from the opposite bank like a shadow into the water, leaving no ripple where it submerged. Small hawks held themselves suspended on vibrating wings. Two eagles crossed circles in leisurely soaring far above them. Black and white magpies chattered raucously, without decorum. His spirit lifted in a great anticipation and a great thankfulness that he was here and not back in the little sunbaked Mexican town. It had become as remote as a dream. And the girl. He shuddered at the chill of a recalled escape. Surely he had kind gods!

He had no realization of the flight of hours. The shadow of the hills fell across the valley, and began a slow, relentless march up the eastward slopes. First Kelly, then Joe rode in. They were jubilant. No Indian sign whatever, old or new. Plenty of beaver cuttings. Bear sign, deer in the bottoms—Joe carried a fat young doe across his saddle,—antelope on the plains to the south, a lake with ducks and geese. The fulfillment of the dream that made bearable the harshness of every trapper's life. Virgin hunting ground! Unknown! Unexplored! All theirs! A new Hole!

"Burnett's Hole, that's her name!" cried Joe. "Shut your trap!" he countered Andy's modesty. "Not for you, for your granddad. Wish I had some likker. I'd shore like to git drunk and disorderly."

Chapter 8
The White Buffalo

In spite of the fact that all Indian sign in the newly discovered Hole was of last year at latest, the experienced trappers did not therefore abandon all caution. They made hasty and temporary camp in the middle of a willow thicket, and then spent all their time from dawn until dark exploring, not only the valley itself, but the neighboring mountains, so that, when they had finished, they knew all the possible entrances and exits. Incidentally, they thus obtained knowledge of the fur prospects. Into the Hole flowed a number of tributary streams, all of which supported a teeming beaver population. Kelly and Joe Crane passed on after a gratified glance, but Andy, to whom these animals were strange, would have lingered. The beautiful precision of the treefelling, the uncanny engineering skill evidenced in the placing and construction of the dams, and the very appearance of the swimming animals fascinated him. But his companions pushed on. They rode with a haste almost feverish, using all the horses, turnabout.

"Time 'nuff for beaver when we get set and aimed," said Joe.

But by the end of the fourth day they knew all about the place.

The Hole was a paradise. Protected by the backbone of high mountains to the east, its feasible entrances from the west were but three. Each showed marks of an Indian trace, but unused of late years. The river foamed out of a gorge to the north. It flowed into a lake at the southerly end of the valley, a lake cliff-bound on the two sides. They rode along the flat shore until their way was barred by the black precipice. Kelly dismounted, took off his clothes, and waded out into the water. He cast a comical look back at Joe.

"I wish I knew if you were lying, you old Kaw!"

"I kain't nuther swim!" asseverated Joe vehemently.

Kelly struck out in the long, easy stroke of the practiced swimmer. Andy watched him, skirting the base of the cliffs, until his head was small in the distance. Finally, he rounded a point and was gone. Though by now, the boy had learned to economize on questions, his curiosity bested him.

"Gone to scout where the lake empties out," Joe replied. "Then we'll know *every* way in—and out. Mout save our ha'r."

At the end of a half-hour Kelly returned. He was shivering like a leaf. His body was blue. His hands were shaking so he could hardly buckle on his equipment. He eyed Joe malevolently. Joe refused to meet his eye, but he could not sustain the pressure.

"I kain't nuther swim!" he repeated, quite gratuitously, for Kelly had said nothing.

"Well, someday when you ain't looking, I'm going to push you in where it's deep and find out!" said Kelly vindictively. "That is plain ice water."

He leaped astride his horse and rode off at full speed but returned at the end of five minutes warmer and better-natured.

"It runs out over a waterfall around a bend," he told them. "Mighty near sucked me in."

This finished the exploration. The Hole had everything. The broken country that looked down upon it swarmed with hundreds of bighorn. On the talus or across the hanging meadows, grazed herds and bands of buffalo and elk.

"They'll foller the snow down," said Joe. "Come winter, the bottom will be full of them. Fat meat! Wagh!"

Blacktail deer in every clump of cover. Of an evening they grazed out in the grass openings, does and fawns, one could see them in any direction he looked.

"Bucks on the open ridges a-hardenin' their horns," Andy was told.

The abundance of game filled Andy with a hunter's eagerness to be up and at them. But his companions had no time for mere sport. Grizzly tracks were numerous and large. Thrice they saw the great creatures, once, on a sandbar, within a few yards. But the trappers sheared off and rode around them.

"B'ar meat is poor eatin'," said Joe. "And b'ar fights git you nowhar!"

Andy looked back longingly at the monster nose raised, sniffing after them as a dog sniffs at something that arouses its curiosity.

"Leave them be, and they'll leave you be," said Joe.

There were even a few small bands of antelope on the open plains at the head of the valley, and a village of comical prairie dogs with their attendant small owls.

These were the outstanding creatures, the most remarkable, possessed of the most interest to a hunter, barring, of course, the fur bearers. There were plenty of the latter—otter, mink, marten, raccoons, wolves and their little cousins—the coyotes, lynxes, foxes, all sorts of lesser creatures—but save for the otter perhaps, Kelly and Crane passed them over. It was twenty years before their time. Still, they were interesting to Andy, as were the grouse, the geese and ducks, the loons, magpies, the meadowlarks, robins, the ravens and crows, and the hundreds of unnamed sweet-voiced littler people awaiting their Audubon. The valley was abrim with life, calling to Andy's joyous youth. It was hard to wait upon these maddeningly deliberate preparations.

Kelly and Joe decided to locate the camp in the concealment of aspens near the shore of the lake. For several days, all three labored, hacking down slim, straight logs, and building a crude hut. Until it was finished, they slept in the open. At the end of the day's labor, Joe and Kelly lay flat on their robes, smoking. But Andy liked better the lake shore. There he sat, his back against a boulder.

The prospect before him was noble and full of voices, the blue still lake, the towering snow range to the right, the carved and castellated buttes of stratified red, green, yellow, and purple sandstone to the left, the bottomland of grass, the brilliant stars of single flowers, the spread blue of flax, the spaced groves of cottonwood and willows, the dark pines of the middle slopes with here and there on a projection a single tall fir like a sentinel.

The night drew on. Across the floor of the valley crept long peaked shadows. Level shafts of sunlight touched the upfling of the ranges, gold against the forests, red against the snow. With it came the cold. Bird voices stilled. The chill subdued the voices of the torrents. Slowly fell the imposition of the night silences.

The golden shafts lifted and were gone. The moon gained strength. It touched the high peaks, and they turned insubstantial against the darkening sky.

Andy was young, he was a hardy pioneer, and instinctively, he resented anything that savored of a softening influence. But he could not abstain.

Harden his surface as he might, abundance poured into his spirit and lifted it into expansion. He could not realize the irresistible transmutation taking place within him, a transmutation that, unrecognized for what it was, had already taken place in these very men he so admired and desired to emulate, so that thus, and only thus, rough or gentle, they became of one kin with one another and with the mountains, truly the mountain men.

Joe Crane's voice at his elbow startled him.

"Kind of purty, ain't she?" Joe was saying. "Sort of gits you. No matter how fur away you go, somehow yo' got to come back! Makes up for a lot of hard doin's somehow."

The following morning, they were up early. This was to be an exciting day. For the first time, Andy was to set out the traps he had so long carried in the buffalo skin bag.

The evening before, Joe and Kelly had made some curious preparations. From his *possible* sack Joe had produced a vial made from the tip of an antelope horn scraped thin until it was transparent. This proved to be filled with a queer-smelling mixture which Joe called *castrum*.

"Made out of beaver glands," said he. "Use it for bait. Beaver kain't seem to keep away from it nohow. We'll make a plenty more first beaver we catch."

In the meantime, he divided the supply carefully in three. He and Kelly cut off their buckskin leg gear at the knee, and with their awls and deer sinew, pieced it out with cloth.

"Got to wade to ketch beaver," Joe told Andy. "Kain't go trompin' around on the banks leavin' a scent. Buckskin's all right when she's dry. But when she's wet yo' got enough to make britches for two men and a boy. And when she dries agin yo' ain't got even enough for the boy, and air so tight yo' kain't make a bow for ordinary politeness."

The traps were all examined for rust, the springs tested. Andy turned in aquiver with eagerness for the morning. For a long time, he was too excited to sleep. Then, immediately, it seemed to him, Kelly was kicking the coals together in the early dawn.

The promise was of a gorgeous day. It was bitter cold. In the first light the meadows were seen to glitter with white frost. The horses stood about humped up, their hind feet drawn in. Their shaggy hair stood up with the appearance of fur. Andy's fingers were blue and stiff. He shivered in the chill breeze.

But as they ate, over the great ranges, the light poured in a cascade of gold. A woodpecker drummed vigorously. The horses shook themselves and moved slowly atop a little rise, awaiting the sun.

Kelly rode off by himself. Joe took Andy with him.

Arrived at the beaver stream of his choice, Joe spent a few moments clipping a long stake for each trap. Then they left the horses, and their traps slung over their backs by means of the long chains, the two set themselves to wade upstream against the current. At various strategic points—*slides*, paths into cuttings, underwater entrances to dens and the like—Joe set the traps. He placed them near shore, in just a certain depth of water. Over the pan, he planted long switches, the tips of which he dipped in the little antelope horn vial of castrum. But the stake to which he attached the end of the five-foot chain he drove as far out toward the middle of the stream as it would extend.

"When a beaver is first ketched, he strikes for deep water," said Joe. "Ef'n yo' kin keep him thar, hell drowned shore. But ef'n he kin git out on the dry bank, he'll git away."

In spite of himself, Andy felt a queer pang of pity. He stifled it promptly, but from time to time, it returned.

In a few spots, the water was too deep for this expedient. Joe ran the chain out toward the middle just the same, but attached to it a float stick to mark its position. For the first time, Andy understood the significance of the figure of speech he had so often heard—*my stick floats w'th yours, there floats my stick.*

"That's all there is to this trappin' business," said Joe. "Simple as all git out—once you larn the habits of the critters."

The fur came fast, faster than ever before in all their experience, both Kelly and Joe admitted. This was obviously a virgin field. Even the Indians had not been trapped here, at least for a great many years. The tributaries to the main river were numerous, and all contained beaver. For a while fully eighty percent of the traps did business each day.

The first week Andy found the job wholly and engrossingly fascinating. The second week, although his enthusiasm was still keen, he began to see that it came partly under the category of work. For there was no leisure for anything else. It was a whole-time job. Up at daylight and off to make the rounds of the traps which must be emptied and reset, generally at a new place. The catch must be skinned, tied to a hoop stretcher, fleshed with minute care, and placed to dry. The pelts caught some days before must be examined and given whatever attention they needed. Those fully dried must be taken from the frames, folded properly, laid, or hung in a safe, dry place. When enough of them had been accumulated, they must be squeezed together, by a most ingenious scissors-press of logs and rawhide, into a pack. There were sixty skins to each pack, which weighed about a hundred pounds. Joe surveyed the first one with satisfaction.

"Fifteen or sixteen *plew*," he estimated. "We're gittin' rich fast."

Andy had long since learned that a *plew* was six dollars, but that single fact had never satisfied him. His youth made him reluctant to ask questions that would reveal basic ignorance, as it were, but now his curiosity got the better of it.

"I don't know," confessed Joe. "Allus been that away when you talk of fur. Mout jist as well say dollars, I reckon, but that's the way it is."

But Kelly was better informed.

"In the early days," said he, "a beaver skin traded for four dollars, but a very fine skin brought six, and that came to be the standard of value. The trade was largely French. A fine skin was known as *plus*, which is a French word meaning *more*—that is, more than a common skin."

As is always the case in established routine, the days flashed by rapidly. Andy seemed, to himself, to be always rolling himself in his robe, another day finished. The work was absorbingly interesting, but it was work, in the sense that it insisted on itself, and would not release him to the enjoyment of any of the thousand fascinations the Hole seemed dangling just outside of possibility. The game animals were moving into the bottoms. As he waded the beaver streams, the bright trout darted before him. In spite of Joe's pronouncement that there was nothing in bear fights for a sensible man, Andy's combative spirit leaped to the challenge of the great lumbering grizzlies—white bear, Joe called them. They did very little hunting. A deer lasted them over a week and could be shot almost from before the cabin door. The Boone gun seemed to be out of a job. And there were other minor drawbacks. Discomforts of the business which Andy had not, in his first enthusiasm, noticed now forced themselves upon him— the biting snap of the early mornings, the icy water of the streams. After wading awhile, his feet turned numb, and he was conscious only of a cold ring around his legs, but when he emerged, he had for a time to endure a minor torture as circulation reestablished itself. He was more or less wet all over, and all of the time. In general the weather held fair, but occasionally violent storms swept down from the peaks. Left to his inclination, Andy would have stayed under shelter in the fire's comfort, but since his companions went forth as a matter of course, he had from very shame to follow. And, as anybody who has experienced one can testify, a mountain storm in the fall of the year can be a miserable business.

It must not be understood that Andy was sorry for himself, or that the adventure was becoming in any way distasteful. Quite to the contrary. But it had ceased being entirely a picnic and had turned into a job, which was perfectly proper, and as it should be.

The season advanced with incredible swiftness. The wildflowers were gone, the grasses had ripened. The elk and buffalo and buck deer were working down to the bottomlands. The clear bugling of the former echoed from the cliffs. The aspens had turned a clear, pure yellow in striking contrast to the dark pines. Cottonwood leaves, shriveled brown, whirled down the gusts of wind. Suddenly, the whole valley was alive with swarms of small, busy migratory birds. It was necessary to build a pole corral in which at night to confine the horses, for the buffalo had drawn close about. After dark, the bulls came close to the house and the corral, and pawed the earth in challenge. Long flights of crows appeared high in the air over the mountains to the north, specks in the sky, dipped toward the valley in ragged whirling flight like windblown leaves, only to rise again and disappear over the mountains to the south. The locusts left the grasses to seek food on the shrubs, where they clung torpid.

"Winter's drawin' in," said Joe. "The Cold Maker's comin', as the Injuns say."

He and Kelly discussed the matter seriously and at length. Shortly, with the next storm, the high passes to the east would be filled with snow. If they were to get out of the Hole, it must be soon. The alternative was to winter in the valley. It was an important decision.

If they went out, they lost the month or so that remained of this superlative trapping before the beaver retired to their winter lodges and were frozen in. They already had caught more than their horses could carry over the rough country. It would be necessary to cache part of the take and return for it in the spring. Here were plenty of game, plenty of firewood, all the essentials of existence. On the other hand, it would be very lonesome and monotonous as compared with the rendezvous, where undoubtedly would be gathered a goodly number of the mountain men, not to speak of a few score lodges of the friendly Indians of that region. Furthermore, the wisdom of tempting Providence by too long a sojourn in a hostile country was worth debating. It might be wiser to take what they had and get out.

"Still," Joe pointed out, "we ain't seen ary Injun sign yit. And Blackfeet is no great hands to go projectin' around in dead of winter. Assiniboins, yes, they's plumb fools and likely will start out anywhar in ary weather. I'd shore like to swap yarns with the boys, but I reckon we can git along here without chawin' each other's ears. As long as we got to come back in the spring anyway to git our fur, we mout as well stay and be right on the ground for a spring hunt. We ain't trapped the main river at all. Come spring one of us kin cross the range and git more hosses from the Crows."

The debate was, after all, a matter of form. No true mountain men would ever decide against such hunting as this.

The decision made, Joe at once began preparations to trap the main river. As the volume of water was too great to permit wading, and as it was absolutely essential that the trapper leave no scent on the banks, it became necessary to construct what Joe called a bullboat. Andy found it interesting.

For one thing it gave him a day or so of respite in routine. Joe wanted a number of buffalo skins, and these Andy was permitted to kill, a pleasant hunting interlude in itself. The pelts collected, Joe stuck upright in the ground a circle of light willow poles, bent the ends over toward a common center, and tied them together to form a great inverted basket twelve or fourteen feet long. This he covered with the buffalo skins sewed together. Underneath, he built a slow fire. As the skins warmed, he assiduously rubbed a mixture of buffalo tallow and resin into the seams, which cooled as hard as the dried hide itself. Then he and Andy, working on opposite sides, carefully pulled up the willows from the earth, turned the thing over, cut off the projecting ends, bound on a rough gunwale of willow.

"Thar she be!" said Joe. "That's a bull boat!"

It floated high and light on the water, and carried them both easily and to spare, but Andy had the greatest difficulty in making the thing go any way but around and around. Joe laughed at his efforts until the tears came. The harder he paddled, the farther out in the lake he drifted.

Ef'n yo' don't git ashore by supper time, I'll git Jack to swim out and give yo' a tow!" he shouted.

But, when the time came to use it, even Joe made no attempt to force it against the current.

"She's a downstream boat," said he. "When she has to go upstream, she's got to use legs."

So they built a travoy for the gentlest pack horse and took the bullboat overland to the river's inlet.

As two were required for this sort of thing, Kelly continued work on the smaller streams while Joe and Andy teamed together. They worked the river methodically, dropping down the current, holding their craft by a grasp of the overhanging willows or by a rude stone anchor while they set their traps. Next morning, it was necessary to travoy the boat back again in order to pick up the catch, after which the reset was made, another stage downstream. It took them ten days to traverse the length of the river to the lake.

"*And* repeat in the spring!" said Joe, viewing the piled-up packs with satisfaction.

Winter caught them unawares, in the sense that their personal preparations had been somewhat neglected in favor of business right up to the actual retirement of the beaver. It did not much matter, except that the accomplishment of the necessary provision was made the more uncomfortable. Hunting in the crisp, clean, cool of autumn would have been much pleasanter than in the snow. There were quite a few of these out-of-door tasks to be accomplished. First of all a number of buffalo must be killed, which was not so easy for the reason that most of these animals had drifted over the westerly passes, presumably toward the lower country. The stragglers were scattered and remote. But, besides the meat, to be *jerked* against the possibility of famine, the trappers wanted the hides. From them were to be made winter moccasins and winter coats. And with them the whole outside of the log hut was carefully covered over. When the blizzards began it would be well to have something that would keep out the wind. For the moment, even the two window openings were blocked, which made the interior as dark as a pocket, except when the fire was going in the middle of the floor. The smoke from the latter escaped through a hole in the roof. Andy would have supposed the place would be chokingly unlivable, but as a matter of fact, the lower stratum of air was clean and sweet. This was due to an ingenious cowl or shield arrangement of short poles and skins, which could be turned to suit the wind. It was modeled from, or suggested by, the peak of the Indian lodge. The upper quarter of the cabin, under the roof, eddied with smoke drifting toward the suction of the outlet. Here were hung the bales of skins, the jerked meat, and later, the buckskin when it was ready to be cured.

"We'll have winders when we git to it," promised Joe.

They made a grand raid on the bighorns and the blacktails, carrying in a dozen carcasses on the pack horses. This was an exciting but a very laborious task. Exciting because Andy always loved to hunt and to exercise his skill with the rifle, laborious because each animal must be skinned immediately, on the spot, before it had stiffened and frozen. That was nipping work on the fingers. Kelly and Joe did not seem to mind, but Andy was either not yet as hardened as his companions or was still too young to have gained to the full of the mountain man's indifference. When he hunted alone, he made himself a small warming fire to which to refer those fingers from time to time, an expedient to which he was too proud to resort if either of his companions were with him. As a matter of fact their keen senses caught the smoke smell. They grinned at one another understandingly but said nothing. Andy was doing pretty well. He discovered that sometimes, when the sun was out, the salvaged lens of the telescope, used as a burning glass, was much easier on numbed fingers than the flint and steel.

Under the cliffback of the house, where the sun never reached, they erected a substantial rack. On its pole, beyond the reach of a wolf's leap, the carcasses were hung in a row. There the meat froze solid, and should keep fresh all winter, barring a thawing *chinook*.

"Probably'll be plenty of game winterin' in the bottoms," said Joe. "But they mout move out, and it's jist as well to play safe. And we need the skins now. For buckskin," he explained. "Winter's the time to make us new clothes."

With this end in view, he fashioned a *graining block* of such shape as most readily to expedite the removal of the hair and *grain*. The traps were all carefully cleaned and greased and hung on a pair of elk antlers and pegged to a tree.

If Andy had pictured the winter as a time of enforced and monotonous leisure, a period of waiting in idleness for long days to pass, he was soon undeceived. There was plenty to do, and most of it good hard work. He learned all about tanning hides and making buckskin. After the first buffalo skin was dressed and tanned and softened, the three men set to work with knife, awl, and sinew to manufacture warm and serviceable, though somewhat clumsy, footwear, a great comfort after the thin deerskin moccasins. Another pair of hides made them greatcoats. To the delight of Andy's hidden romanticism he was soon, like his companions, topped with a headgear made of a raccoon's skin, the striped tail hanging down behind. The making of the buckskin was a long and laborious job. He spent hours, under Joe's critical direction, scraping away on the hair and the grain, after it had been loosened in ashes and water, in patiently rubbing into the fiber a mixture of brains and fat, and in stretching and pulling, pulling and stretching, over and over again until the fabric was pliable enough to pass Joe's inspection. The latter process seemed endless.

For a time, Andy despaired of producing anything more flexible than a sheet of tin. But Joe assured him that it could be done, and done at last it was, and the softened fabric hung in the smoke to mellow. Andy was relieved to discover that Joe also thought this job quite a chore.

"Squaw work," said he. "That's the good of havin' you a nice leetle fat Injun gal in yore lodge. Then you can set back and smoke."

Snow fell from time to time. It covered the floor of the valley to the depth of a foot or so, save where the wind bared the exposed flats. The mountains were white and aloof, and seemed to sleep, for the voices of falling waters had been stilled. They built for themselves fantastic architecture of snow cornices undercut by the wind. Here and there, the steep precipices, disdaining the winter, thrust stark and black above the soft mantle. A quiet hush hung motionless like an invisible mist. It held in its substance a quality that seemed eternal until the shattering roar of an avalanche, smoking down from the sheer peaks, let loose in the reverberation of strange echoes. The little streams were frozen fast. Along the banks of the main river, anchor ice crept out from the shore. Beyond it the current turned, dark and menacing, heavy as oil. The sun, when it shone, was weak and dim, ringed widely by the frost crystals in suspension, but shining in the glittering diamonds of reflection from the snow's surface.

In all the valley, there seemed now to be no life, though the tracked pattern of the snow belied that impression. The animals were rarely seen. The deer held close in shelter, leaping away, dim, and ghostly, when almost trodden upon. The small creatures moved furtively and at night. Only busy tiny chickadees and the fluffed-out and unregenerate Canada Jays upheld a vanished tradition of cheerfulness in the very face of awe.

The horses grew long, shaggy coats, thick as fur. They pawed the shallow places in the snow for frozen grasses, they nibbled the bud ends of the browse. But their main sustenance had to be collected and brought to them in the corral, beneath the crude shelter that had been constructed for them. Andy was astonished to see how eagerly they ate cottonwood bark, and how they thrived on that strange diet. It had to be peeled and cut up into short pieces. That was another cold chore. Andy learned that only the round-leaved sweet cottonwood would do, as the horses disdainfully refused the other.

"And look out you thaw it out good," warned Joe. "Ef'n yo' feed it froze, it cuts their mouths and stummicks like knives."

In January, it turned really cold. The snow whined under Andy's moccasins. The men spent most of their time within doors. Joe had made his promised windows of doeskin, rendered translucent by marrow fat, allowed to dry hard, without manipulation. They admitted some daylight. The fire, fed with slivers of pitch pine, aided illumination. Smoky little lamps, constructed of the hollows of buffalo horns, burning melted fat through a cloth wick, added their quota. There was light enough for the indoor tasks.

Andy became a tailor. Under Joe's instruction, he cut out and sewed from the soft aromatic buckskin a proper hunting shirt, made with a large cape, with loose sleeves. It reached almost to the knees, was lapped over in front so widely that a belt enabled the folds to be used as a pocket. He also built himself leggings with fringes, like Joe's. When he had them finished and put them on, he felt himself at last a full-fledged trapper. His garments of homespun were about worn out. Then he learned to make moccasins, and did make moccasins. In fact, he became very sick of making moccasins, for Joe kept him at that job relentlessly. Even with the hard soles of parfleche, they wore out only too rapidly. In time, all three were splendid in new and comfortable garments. The old, shiny, and black and patched, were, however, carefully preserved. In this life, nothing was discarded, it always had some use.

So the days passed, much more rapidly than Andy could have believed possible. The dark interior of the little hut became, to him, a very homelike place. Suspended by a stout cord well above the fire hung always a quarter of venison or bighorn. It swung gently in the rising heat and smoke. Whenever one of the men got to his feet, he started it turning. Thus, it roasted slowly, hour after hour. But when it was pronounced ready, it proved to be the most delicious meat Andy had ever tasted, all the juices sealed within, a faint, aromatic smoky flavor permeating its every fiber. Meat cooked in various ways was their only diet, yet they retained their full zest of appetite and were in good health. This was probably due to the fact that they supplemented the cooked meat with slices of raw liver, which they had saved and frozen at the time of the hunting. *Mountain bread*, Joe called it. Andy sampled it first with considerable misgiving, but found it good. Whether this inclusion of raw meat was due to happy coincidence or to the deep dietetic instinct that seems always to have informed the human race, it is impossible to say. Certainly, these men knew nothing of its virtues as an antiscorbutic.

Spring neared. Freshly loosened rocks clattered down the mountains in landslides. The voices of the waters were liberated again.

The men stirred more abroad. The winter tasks were finished, the new-come chinooks softened the last ragged remnants of the fresh meat hung on the pole. Andy liked to take Knock 'em-stiff, the old Boone gun, and wander up and down the river looking to see what he could see, puzzling out the stories told by the tracks in the snow, spying for indications of the new season. The sun was slowly gaining in power. At noon, in the most exposed places, it even managed to melt a surface on the snow which, frozen by the ensuing night, showed the next day hard and polished as a mirror. The stones and boulders made elbow room all around themselves. But the weather was still capricious, likely at any moment, without warning, to revert to black winter fury from its unstable condition of grace.

On one of these days, Andy made a momentous discovery. Against the whiteness of one of the lower hill passes to the west, he saw a half-dozen black specks moving. Closer approach disclosed the fact that they were buffalo, returning to the valley early from their winter ranges. This seemed to Andy important for two reasons, the animals' instincts sensed a definite change of season, but especially that here in sight was a welcome variety from straight venison.

The animals were few, and therefore, likely to be wild. Andy, therefore, took pains with his stalk. But when it was about half completed, the landscape was blotted out by a most curious phenomenon.

By some freak of breeze or condition, the atmosphere suddenly turned intensely cold, and this cold congealed into a haze of frost crystals that the moisture suspended in the air. All objects more distant than fifty yards or so were blotted out as though by a fog. But the substance of this fog glittered gloriously with millions of diamond points. The sun shone through it dimmed and ringed.

It was beautiful—but disconcerting to Andy, who had lost sight of his quarry. Nevertheless, he pushed forward blindly, and was rewarded, after a time, by blundering straight on one of the animals. He made it out, dim as a ghost through the strange sparkling haze, but plainly enough to define the sights of Knock-'em-stiff. At the shot, it sank to its knees, and rolled over on its side.

When Andy approached, he first thought the beast's heavy coat frosted over by the substance of the fog. Then, a closer examination convinced him that he had shot that rarest of animals, a white buffalo cow. Indeed, so unusual was this albinism that many men lived all their lives on the plains, saw literally millions of buffalo, and stoutly denied to the last that such a thing existed. Nevertheless, here lay an indubitable specimen. It was cream-colored rather than white, and Andy was interested to see that its eyes were dark. Andy had understood that albino eyes were always bleached and pink. For some moments, he bent, examining his strange prize. So, he missed another curious phenomenon of nature. By a second mysterious shift of conditions, the chinook reestablished its power. The haze of frost crystals vanished. It went, not slowly and in eddies, like a fog, but instantaneously as at the command of magic. Again, all the details of the valley and the mountains, near and distant, stood forth in the uncompromising definiteness of the high altitudes.

Andy looked up to see, fifty yards or so away, a small group of mounted Indians watching him intently.

His heart sank like lead beneath the swiftly darting activities of his mind seeking an expedient. It found none. Vague recollections flashed to him of old tales of the heroes of bygone days—his grandfather, Daniel Boone—their apparently miraculous escapes against odds, somehow none of them fitted this situation. His rifle was empty. He could not even, with any conviction, try the customary device of attempting to stand them off with the withheld shot. And anyway, some deep inner instinct assured him it would not have worked with this lot. To his credit, be it said, Andy retained both his coolness and common sense. So when one summoned him in sign talk to approach, he obeyed. It was the only thing to do.

He stopped when a dozen feet from the group, dropped the butt of his rifle to the snow, leaned his elbows on the muzzle, and stared as boldly as he could.

The riders were eight in number. For some minutes they sat motionless, staring back. Andy had full leisure to look them over.

In less disconcerting circumstances he might have been able to admire them as quite the most handsome of the plains people he had as yet encountered. They were tall men, good-looking, with grave countenances of a lofty and not unkindly expression. That of the eldest, he who had signed Andy to come forward, was wrinkled into an appearance almost of benignity. He was a fine old man with a clear direct gaze. Andy was surprised, as their glances crossed, to see that his eyes were not black, but hazel. His long hair was parted in the middle and hung in two braids bound with red beads. The parting had been painted vermilion. It was held in locks by means of clasps made of bone or shell, and through them had been thrust a variety of ornaments—eagle feathers, horizontal, pieces of carved wood and the like. He wore about him a buffalo robe belted at the waist. Its hair side was in, and the exposed surface had been brightly painted with crude figures and designs, the most prominent of which was a huge conventional sun with colored pointed rays. Where it fell away at the neck Andy saw a necklace of the long claws of the grizzly bear. He bestrode a saddle high behind and before, over which had been flung sideways a cougar skin lined with red cloth, the long tail hanging down to one side. From the folds of the robe peeped the muzzle of a long smooth-bore *fuse*.

After several minutes two of the younger men dismounted, and throwing their robes back from their shoulders, advanced upon Andy, who faced them as stoutly and as steadily as he could. He did not know what to expect. Their bodies were clad in buckskin. Bows and quivers in otter skin cases peeped over their shoulders. But in the right hand of each was clasped the *warhawk*, or war club, which with the mountain Indian of that day replaced the traditional tomahawk of the warriors farther east. They took position either side the boy.

He was helpless. Even his knife was inaccessibly beneath the cover of his buffalo coat.

But at a sign the warriors thrust their weapons into their belts. One produced a rawhide cord with which Andy's arms were bound at the elbows behind his back. They lifted him bodily and cast him across a horse's back.

At this moment one of the band raised a cry. There was a sudden excited movement. The horse stirred restively, dumping Andy to the snow. He twisted about to find that the whole band had deserted him and were gathered about the dead buffalo.

For a brief, excited moment, a clamor of cries. Then one of the younger men ran over to him, snatching a knife from his belt. Andy closed his eyes, bracing himself for the fatal thrust. But his bands were cut, he was assisted to his feet, led gently forward.

All had dismounted. Two youths had darted away to the creek bottom on foot. The others had cast off their robes, were fumbling with the bundles slung to their saddle bows. Andy, by now thoroughly bewildered, watched them hastily stripping themselves in the bitter cold, throwing aside their discarded garments, tearing open the bundles, from which came gorgeously embroidered shirts and leggings, carefully folded crowns of erect eagle feathers. He saw, in less time than it takes to tell it, the warriors, in contrast to their previous muffling against the cold, stand forth fully arrayed in barbaric gorgeousness. The two young men returned uphill from the creek, carrying handfuls of dried grass. The chief took it from them, knelt in the snow, and set fire to it with his flint and steel. Andy caught in his nostrils the penetrating aromatic pungency of sweet grass.

In the smoke from the tiny fire the chief washed his hands as though in water, then arose to his full height. He raised his knife toward the sun. The warriors ranged themselves behind him. In all that spacious valley was no movement. A vast solemnity seemed to have been evoked by the old man's simple gesture, so that the mountains themselves paused in the invisible flow of their slow, eternal thoughts. Only the horses stamped softly and blew the smoke of cold from their nostrils. Andy could not understand, but he was impressed.

The chief stepped forward, stooped, cut out the beast's tongue, and stepped back. The others, with an evident reverence, one by one passed their hands, then their knives, through the waning smoke of the dying sweetgrass fire. Then with the greatest care they skinned the buffalo. Until this slow task was quite completed the old man stood rigid, holding the severed tongue at arm's length toward the sun. The detached robe was at length rolled into a bundle.

"O sun!" Then intoned the chief in the Blackfoot language, "*I give her to you. Take her. She is yours.*"

Two of the young men bound the robe carefully to a riding saddle.

It was all bewildering to Andy. But what followed was still more so. For the chief himself, bearing it reverently, restored to him his rifle. He was signed to bestride the cougar skin saddle. Then, he alone mounted, all the Indians afoot leading their horses and chanting low-voiced, the band resumed its way down the floor of the valley, leaving the meat untouched, except for the tongue which the chief carried before him impaled on the point of a spear.

Andy did not know what it was all about, though he could guess part of it. The situation, however, did not seem entirely hopeless. The savages numbered only eight. The odds against the two trappers were not excessive, provided they were not caught by surprise. Andy's rifle was empty, but his voice was in working order. He made up his mind to shout the alarm when the time came. His mind was instantly busy on the details of a plan—how he would try to edge his mount aside, throw himself—The line of thought was checked abruptly. Across the snow converged the tracks of a second, larger band of Indians.

And when they rounded the aspen grove to within sight of camp, he found the whole place in possession of the Blackfeet. Their horses stood in a compact bunch against the cliff, guarded by two of the younger men. The other Indians, to the number of scores, it seemed to Andy, were everywhere. Some were driving in the trappers' horses. Some were examining the traps hung on the elk antlers, or the meat rack, or the bull boat, or any of the other of the simple arrangements. But by far the majority were either going into or coming out of the hut. Bales of beaver skins were strewn about outside. These were the center of a vociferous group.

Andy, even from the height of his horse, could see nothing of the white men.

The old chief shook the spear aloft and said something in a loud voice. The heads of those nearest turned toward him inquiringly. The rhythmical chant, which Andy's captors had never ceased to croon, now rose to full voice. The nearest of the bystanders took it up. This caught the attention of those farther away. They drew near, joined in. In the center of the milling, jostling mob those who had led the chief's horse were unpacking the skin of the buffalo. Andy was left quite alone and unguarded, on the outskirts.

For the first time he was able to see his companions, hitherto concealed behind the crowds about the door. They were seated side by side, their backs against the building. Joe was smoking. Andy dismounted and made his way to them. Nobody offered to stop him. Joe's leathery countenance showed no change of expression, but for an instant his eyes shone. However, that was the only indication of relief he exhibited at the sight of Andy, still alive.

"Well!" he drawled. "What you doin' walkin' around with a weapon in yore hands? Don't you know it ain't polite when you got visitors? Look at Jack and me." An expression of angry disgust flitted across his face. "Caught flat-footed!" he cried. "Old *hivernants* like us! We *ought* to lose our ha'r."

"What happened?" asked Andy.

"Nothin'," Joe had resumed his sardonic drawl. "One minute there was me and Jack. Next minute thar was all of us. By God we got jist what was comin' to us! But I'm sorry about you, boy."

"What will they do with us, do you think?" asked Andy.

"Several things," Joe surmised. "The festivities will begin later."

He was not looking at Andy, but toward the group of Indians who were crowding closer together more and more absorbed in what was happening.

"When I say *go*, jist slip around the corner of the house," said he, "and take for the river. Ef'n we kin get across before they see us, we mout have a slim chance. We got one rifle, anyway."

"She's not loaded, and they took away my powder and shot pouch," said Andy.

"Settles that," observed Joe. He relighted his pipe.

"How come they git you?" he asked finally. "Have a fight?"

"I'd shot a buffalo—in the fog. It lifted suddenly, and there they were. My rifle was empty."

"Never knew Blackfeet to travel winters," stated Joe, as though in extenuation. "But that's no excuse," he added.

The compact group of Indians divided. The chief, followed by a half-dozen of obviously the most important members of the band, approached. He stopped before the seated whites and began an oration in *hand talk*, the sign language. The three watched him attentively, for Andy had by now, under Joe's tutelage, acquired a very workable facility.

They learned that the white buffalo is a sacred animal. That it belongs to the all-powerful sun. That he who kills such an animal partakes in some degree of its sacred character. That the whole tribe to which such a man belonged shared in that favor. He stated these things briefly, with no mark of friendliness. Then abruptly he turned away.

Through the thin clear air, from up the valley, now could be heard the mingled clamor of a multitude approaching. Shortly, around the end of the aspen grove, streamed a confused horde of ponies, dogs, women, children, old men—straggling, noisy, without order. The vanguard stopped, milled about, as the rear guard gradually closed in. There was much shouting back and forth. A sudden stilling to immobility and again the chant arose, full-voiced, triumphant, arms extended upward toward the setting sun.

As it died the mob, with renewed clamor, broke in all directions. The women led away the laden horses. Shortly, in the bottomland below the cabin, the lodges began to stagger erect. Boys, shouting shrilly, drove the horses to the low tableland above.

The men waited apart. When, in an incredibly brief space of time, the new blue smoke began to arise from the lodge cowls, they strode away to their several habitations. But on their way they paused at the camp to shoulder the bales of beaver skins. They took the traps from the elk antlers on the trees. They carried off the little bundles of moccasins, product of the winter's labor. They unhooked from the pegs in the rafters the remaining store of jerked meat. Already the horses, and Buggs, Joe's mule, had been driven off to the main herd. Not once did they vouchsafe the three men, still seated by the door, a single glance. At last they were gone. The whites were left alone, free, unguarded, but stripped clean. The clothes they wore on their backs, and the empty Boone rifle, without powder or ball, were now their sole earthly possessions.

They went inside and built up the fire. It was getting cold. There was nothing else to do.

Kelly was grave and silent. He seemed to have retired to an inner citadel of watchfulness that awaited the event. He shook his head to Andy's questions.

"Don't know," he said briefly. "Seems we're safe for the present. That's all I can tell."

But Joe's unquenchable spirits had revived. He was inclined to view facetiously even his first chagrin at being caught so completely unaware.

"Shore we're all right. Ain't we still got our ha'r? And whar thar's ha'r thar's hope, as the book says. Andy yere's made himself a genuine god. And yo' saw what the old boy said, it's ketchin' to the whole tribe. Ain't we his tribe?"

But Andy did not feel very cheerful. In the old chiefs brief statement he had discovered no trace of friendliness.

"No," agreed Kelly, "they're not friendly. If it had not been for your extraordinary good fortune in running on that buffalo, we'd have all been dead by now. They consider they own this country."

Night fell. No one came near them. They had nothing to eat. Joe grumbled humorously at this.

"I suppose they got an idee gods don't git hungry," said he. "Well, this one does!"

Lacking their robes, which also the Blackfeet had taken, they passed rather a miserable night around the fire. Morning found even Joe subdued and thoughtful. Andy's imagination prowled gloomily among the facts and possibilities of the situation. They might be left here to starve, helpless. They might be turned adrift unarmed to the iron mercilessness of the winter mountains. Joe added a happy thought.

"Mebbe this god-stuff wears off after a while," he suggested. "Somehow my ha'r don't seem so firm this morning." He laid his hand on Andy's shoulder. "I'm sorry, boy," said he. "Us old tough ones—it's no more than we deserve, I reckon. But you—"

"I'm trailing," said Andy stoutly.

Chapter 9
Blackfeet

In spite of the sacred character with which Andy Burnett had been invested by his lucky killing of a white buffalo, his situation, and that of the two trappers, was indeed uncertain. How long this protection would last was uncertain. Whether it would extend to his companions was uncertain. But several things were only too sure. They had been robbed of the most wonderful beaver catch ever trapped in the mountains, they had lost their traps, their weapons, they were very hungry, and there were no prospects of food in sight. The morning wore away. The straggling Indian encampment in the bottom showed plenty of life and activity, but none of it directed toward the cabin. It began to seem that there might well be merit in Andy's suggestion that they were to be left most ceremonially to starve.

But, a few moments before the sun reached the meridian a small delegation detached itself from the teepees and took its way up the slope in their direction.

The old chief walked a few paces in advance. He was dressed in complete buckskin, elaborately and beautifully embroidered with beads and dyed porcupine quills. Over his shoulders hung a cape made of the forelock and mane of a buffalo bull. He carried a short staff from which hung buffalo hoofs which he rattled together softly as he walked. Immediately at his heels strode a warrior bearing the long feathered calumet. He carried also a staff covered over with red cloth to which raven feathers had been attached in a row, evidently a badge of office. Four or five others followed close behind. They were distinguished by their headdresses of eagle's feathers from which protruded the curve of a pair of buffalo horns, and also by their peculiar staffs, which were long and hooked and covered with otter skin into which, at spaced intervals, had been fastened eagle's feathers. Otherwise they were empty-handed.

"Thought they might be bringin' us breakfast," Joe pretended, "*and* last night's supper!"

As the group neared, the chief took the long pipe from its bearer, and pointed the stem forward at arm's length.

"Peace talk," said Joe. "Wall, that's *some*thin'!"

But when the three whites arose and moved forward, Kelly and Joe were ordered back.

"Think before you answer," Kelly advised Andy hurriedly.

"I'll do my best," replied Andy. He took his indicated place, to the right of the chief, on the spread robe, very much troubled in mind, for he realized keenly his total lack of experience in this sort of thing, and the vital importance of steering the right course.

The bearer of the pipe filled it, lighted it, handed it again to the chief. The latter puffed at it in silence. No one moved or spoke. A gush of petition welled up in Andy's heart, a silent reaching out to claim a shadowy heritage, and as though in response his spirit steadied. For a brief mystic moment it seemed to him that somehow he was no longer alone.

The chief extended the mouthpiece of the calumet toward the zenith.

"*O Sun, reveal to us your purpose!*" he petitioned in Blackfoot language.

He offered Andy the pipe.

It was a warm day, the first establishment of the spring chinook. The surface of the snow had softened. As Andy accepted the pipe a heavy drop of water fell from the cottonwood branch overhead directly into the bowl.

The tobacco was extinguished.

So evidently calamitous was this portent that even the white men could not miss its significance. Both Kelly and Joe uttered exclamations of dismay. A stir of awe and consternation swept the council circle like a wind. The chief's face darkened.

Only Andy himself, of all those present, remained undisturbed. His mind was working with a calmness and a clarity and a certainty that later he looked back upon with wonder and a little awe. Without conscious decision he seemed to know exactly what to do. Deliberately, without excitement or haste, he took the telescope lens from the pouch at his waist, extending his right arm above the bowl of the pipe focusing the sun rays.

The dampened tobacco smoldered for a moment, glowed red. Andy puffed strongly the ceremonial thrice, and passed the calumet to the warrior at his right.

The gravity of the occasion was not proof against this miracle. None of the Indians had ever seen a burning glass. It is doubtful if many even noticed that the boy held any object in his hand, and those probably considered it some sort of *medicine* or charm. To them it seemed that Andy had called upon the sun, the Sun, greatest and most powerful of the gods, directly to light the pipe. A murmur of surprise and of awe swept the circle. They clapped their hands flat over their mouths. Only Kelly's quick wits leaped to instant appreciation.

"Put that thing away!" he called sharply to Andy. "Don't let them lay eyes on it again!"

Andy slipped the lens into his pouch.

Ceremonial formality was broken for a moment. The warriors snatched at the calumet, puffing eagerly, avid that the virtue of this miracle might touch themselves. The pipe made the rounds in record time.

But now with a sharp word of command the old chief brought them to order. He turned to Andy once more. He began to question him in sign talk, but now with respect.

"You have great Sun-Power," he said. "The Sun is your father. He holds you in his hand."

He pondered for a few moments, then roused himself.

"What are you doing here?" he asked.

"We trap beaver," Andy replied.

"This is our place. We own the beaver."

"We looked. We saw no sign of men. This place had no men."

"It is our place. White men are our enemies."

"You are enemies of white men," countered Andy. "Why?"

The chief's face darkened again.

"The white men have helped our enemies," he signed swiftly. "The Crows ride with many guns. The Assiniboins ride with many guns. The Flatheads ride with many guns. We have few guns. Why do the white men give arms to our enemies?"

An interruption turned all heads toward the cabin. Kelly had suddenly begun to chant a queer wandering minor cadence, not unlike the melody of the Indian music. And the message of his chant was directed to Andy, and was this.

"Tell him it is because the Assiniboins and Crows are near at hand and the Blackfeet far away. Tell him the Flatheads get their guns not from us but from the Hudson Bay men, and they are our enemies too. Tell him that the Blackfeet can have guns also if they will bring in beaver skins."

After which he continued, while Andy repeated this, to sing on in a string of nonsense.

"It is the medicine song of the white man," Andy replied to the chief's sharp and somewhat indignant demand.

He turned squarely to face the old man.

"We are not your enemies," he signed slowly. "The Sun is our friend. I called upon the Sun and he came from the sky to tell you we are his children. Do not make the Sun angry."

He extended again his right arm toward the luminary, his cupped hand concealing the old telescope lens in its hollow, focusing the burning point of light on the back of the chief's hand.

"Ay yah!" cried the Blackfoot as the fire bit.

He snatched the hand away, examining it with awe. His dignity was broken. He leaped to his feet, gathering the robe hastily about his shoulders, concealing his finery. He stared again at his hand, and strode rapidly away, followed in confusion by his men.

"Boy, I could jist *love* yo'!" Joe's arms were around Andy's shoulders. "Yore wiser'n a he-wolf! Wagh! How'd yo' come to think of *that?*"

Andy looked about him dazed, as though just awakened. He smiled sheepishly, hesitated.

"It sounds foolish," he said. "But somehow I didn't think of it. It just came. It sounds foolish," he repeated. "But somehow it seemed to me I wasn't doing it at all. It was somehow as if someone were telling me, someone wise and—and—well, like my grandfather, like Colonel Boone would have—I don't know—I must be crazy!"

"Crazy like an owl!" cried Joe. "Yo' saved our ha'r. And look thar!" He swept his arm to call attention to two old women coming up the slope, bearing certain articles. "We eat!"

———

The squaws brought with them robes as well as food. The three were now comfortable enough. But most evidently they were prisoners. No guard was set about them, but as Kelly pointed out, at this time of year the mountains were sufficient, and the snow.

Except for a daily provision, delivered by two old women, they were wholly ignored until five days later, when Andy was peremptorily summoned by a ceremonially clad messenger. There was nothing to do but to obey, which he did a little doubtfully. However, he found he was merely to take part as a principal in a ceremony. The hide of the white buffalo had been tanned and most elaborately decorated. Now, afoot, a procession of chanting warriors carried it, outspread, up the valley to the spot where Andy had made the kill. There they hung the robe beneath a tall tripod. The old chief made appropriate remarks. Andy was in the foreground, probably as principal witness. They left the robe dangling in the breeze. There it would hang until it rotted away, or, more properly until, by disintegration, the Sun took to himself the offering. As the Blackfoot piously believed, he had already accepted the dedicated carcass. Certainly it was all gone, save for the skull and a few scattered bones. That numerous wolf and other tracks on the snow might indicate the Sun had had a little help had nothing to do with the case.

The rites finished, the little band returned to camp, all easy laughter and informality. They ignored Andy as though he had been thin air. Evidently, as the favored killer of the white buffalo, his presence had been essential. But that *bought him nothing* further.

They returned, not to the cabin, but to the main Indian camp. Here, in a wide open space left vacant in the middle of surrounding lodges, were seated, in a circle, all the grown men of the band. A small fire burned in the center, on one side of which stood a young man holding a white horse, on each of whose flanks had been painted the rayed effigy of the Sun. Its mane and tail had been shaved clean. Joe and Kelly stood on the other side of the fire. A segment of the circle had been left vacant to accommodate those who had taken part in the dedication. Obeying a signed command Andy joined his companions.

"What's up?" he asked them, low-voiced.

"Don't know," replied Joe, "but I reckon they're goin' to figger what to do about us."

The circle was complete. The warriors sat cross-legged, silent, staring straight in front of them at the ground. They were dressed in heavily embroidered new white buckskin. Some wore the gorgeous crown of eagle feathers. Some a fillet of feathers made suggestively diabolic with curved buffalo horns. Some were bareheaded, their long hair braided and caught into locks by bone clasps, into which had been thrust eagle feathers or carved objects of wood. The faces of some had been painted black, those of others were patterned in colors, stripes of yellow, streaks of vermilion across the forehead, the edges of the eyelids picked out in red. As Andy looked about him he perceived that those comprising the great circle were divided into groups, distinguished one from the other by certain badges or tokens, a war eagle's claw bound to the wrist, the red pole fringed with raven's feathers in a long row, the crooked staff covered with otter skin with spaced eagle feathers, the war club with buffalo hoofs hanging in a clump from the handle end, short-handled rattles. These marked the different fraternal orders, of various dignity, to which a warrior graduated by virtue of attainment. Behind the motionless figures rose irregularly the pointed painted lodges, their pole ends like fingers against the sky. Behind each stood a tall tripod supporting a shield, a lance, a pole from which at spaced intervals swung and fluttered the dried and painted scalps of enemies killed in battle. Here and there among the lodges stood small groups of women and children.

For a long time nothing happened. Then the pipe bearer lighted the pipe and handed it to the chief. He pointed its stem to the four parts of the compass, down toward the earth, upward toward the sky, puffed on it three times, passed it to the man on his right. Slowly it made the rounds of the circle. Then another long pause.

The chief arose to his feet and stood aside. The young man holding the white horse led the animal through the gap in the circle. He threw off the rope from its neck, and at the same instant the chief thrust the point of his knife into the animal's rump. With a great plunge of pain and fright, it leaped away. Up over the low tableland across the plain it raced at full speed. But just as it seemed about to vanish in the low foothills below the mountains, it turned, circled back, at length joined the great band of ponies browsing in charge of boys just within the fringe of willows. The chief, still on his feet, shading his eyes with the flat of his hand, watched intently until the white horse had lost itself in the herd. Then he resumed his place in the circle.

The whites viewed the performance with interest, but as it meant nothing to them, with detachment. Their interest would have been considerably sharpened had they understood. If the Sun—painted on the animal's side—continued on over the mountains the sign would have been clear that he withdrew his power. In which case their lives would have been of little worth. But as the white horse followed the other animals the augury was clear that the god followed also.

Nor naturally did they comprehend the spaced leisurely speeches that followed, though of course they knew their fate was in balance. It was a court of judgment to decide what might be considered a case in equity, if not in law. And like many modern law cases, it was settled on a quibble.

Granted all the signs of power and favor from the Sun, there still remained the inescapable fact that the tribe had sworn enmity against the white man, and that it was known that the Sun considered the breaking of a formal oath a most personal insult. That certainly presented a fine enough distinction to be debated by any Supreme Court of any land. Certainly it provided a good excuse, either way, for the satisfaction of personal prejudice.

Some of the younger men were hostile. Their insistence was vehement, fiery. But the older heads were not so sure. Finally one of the youngest, a youth who wore the eagle claw, the emblem of the *mosquitoes*, the freshman fraternity, as it were, arose to his feet diffidently. He was a young man of pleasing and kindly countenance. It was not his place to speak in the council of great warriors, but he thought the Sun had whispered in his ear, for the brilliance of his inspiration he modestly disclaimed as beyond his own powers. He explained. A guttural murmur of applause followed his suggestion. It was just the sort of fine-spun evasion that pleases lawyers, and Indians seated in council, not too vividly swayed by emotions, are essentially dialecticians.

Truly the white men were enemies. Truly the tribe had sworn to consider them such. Truly to violate that oath would insult the Sun. Truly it was a question no man could decide wisely, whether the Sun would be more affronted by a disregard of his repeated evidences of favor for these white men, or by the breaking of an oath made solemnly to his face. It was a dilemma full of danger. But here was a way out. How does one treat an enemy? One steals his horses, that had been done. One sheds his blood. Why not take some of the blood of these white men without killing them?

Save in the case of a few implacables this brilliant suggestion was received with acclaim and relief. Kiasax, for that was the young man's name, was in consideration awarded the privilege of carrying through what amounted to a bit of true symbolism. The chief handed him his own knife. Kiasax advanced upon the captives, who, ignorant of the decision, gave themselves up as dead men. To their astonishment the young man merely turned back their sleeves and in the forearm of each made a tiny incision. Then the circle broke up. The whites were returned to their cabin. As for Kiasax, he thereby gained great honor, for he was permitted to remove his lodge and his pretty young wife and his baby to the innermost circle of the camp, surrounding the council space, reserved for the great men of the tribe, and he was graduated at once from the juvenile *mosquitoes* to the fraternity of The Buffalo With Thin Horns, to the great envy of the Dogs and the Prairie Dogs and Those Who Carry the Raven, whose orders he should have passed through in normal sequence.

Nothing further happened. The Indian camp carried on a busy and happy life in the bottomlands. The white men waited at the cabin, because for the moment there was nothing else to do. The old squaw whose job it was brought them their food regularly. She was ignorant of, or pretended to be ignorant of, the sign language.

The situation was doubtful, but not so dark as it might have been. There was nothing to do at present but to accept it. After the snows had melted and the summer was well established would be time enough to make plans for escape. No use speculating before then, Kelly pointed out, the conditions were too uncertain.

"If they do not move out of the Hole and take us with them, and if they do not put a guard on us, it might not be too difficult," said Kelly. "If we can make it as far as the range yonder, I'll guarantee they'll have trouble getting hold of us. Once there, we can strike over the shed and make it somehow."

But there were a good many *ifs* and possibilities. Nobody knew just how far this Sun-favor went. It might be, when the time came, that they could walk away in open daylight, and no one would stop them!

"And mebbe not," observed Joe.

Of one thing only were they sure, when the season opened they must attempt escape.

Their resources were few, but might have been fewer. There was Knock-'em-stiff, the Boone gun, and Andy's knife and Andy's tomahawk, and the lens from the telescope.

"Ef'n we could only get hold of powder and ball, we'd be set up," sighed Joe. "Keep yore eyes shinin'. Mebbe'll come a chance."

There were plenty of percussion caps in Andy's possible sacks. The Indians had robbed the older men clean, but Andy's personal possessions, with the exception of the ammunition, they had left intact.

Another evidence that he was held to be in a different category from his companions was soon forthcoming. The three decided to walk down for a look at the Indian camp. Such an excursion might conceivably prove dangerous, but inaction was wearing on them.

"Jist take it easy and keep yore eyes shinin'," said Joe, "and back out quiet if you have to."

At the outskirts of the encampment Joe and Kelly were stopped and ordered back by a warrior carrying the police emblem. He signed to Andy that this prohibition did not extend to him.

Andy hesitated a moment as to whether to take advantage of the implied permission, The thought of venturing alone suddenly lost its appeal. But on second thought he decided to go on. He was curious, he might stumble upon valuable information, it was barely possible he might locate ammunition on which then or later he might get his hands. But principally, and immediately, he took a chuckling and boyish delight in passing Joe with his nose in the air.

Nevertheless, this first afternoon he used discretion, merely wandering down past the outskirts of the encampment, to the river and back again. The numerous cur dogs dashed at him, snarling and barking. Some children tumbled out from behind the lodges to huddle together, staring at him. He spoke to them, and signed friendship, whereupon the youngest fled, uttering small squeaks. The older boys held their ground, their flint-like eyes unwavering, but made no other acknowledgment. At the river were a number of women and girls chattering and laughing. On his appearance they scattered like quail. Over in the center of the village, beyond the blank rounded backs of the painted lodges, he could see many figures moving about, the rising of smokes, he heard the sounds of lively talk and merriment. He did not quite dare intrude into the enclosure as yet, but contented himself by an approach close enough to afford him a glimpse of varied activities. He did not see very much. Men and women were moving about, emerging from the low doorways, stooping to enter. A close-gathered group bent over some sort of game. Small boys and dogs ran about. But the air was sharp, and most of the people were in shelter. Nevertheless Andy gained the impression of light-hearted merriment, of good-fellowship and gaiety quite at variance with his preconceptions of Indian character.

He was inclined, on his return, to poke a little fun at Joe over his especial privilege.

"Seems to me," observed Joe. "I heerd somewhar these Injins fat up their gods a spell to git them good and prime for killin'."

"The old tough ones they just skin alive," said Kelly dryly.

Andy took full advantage of his privileges, however. It was something to do, and it was very interesting. Tentative experiment proved to him that he could wander about as he pleased. Nobody stopped him, nobody paid him the least attention. The Blackfeet did not ignore him, for ignoring is a conscious act. To them he simply was not there. Andy at times was overcome by a weird feeling that indeed he must have died, thrown off all bodily solidity, become invisible, thin air. Or, contrariwise, that this shifting, colorful, barbaric scene itself had no actuality, that he walked in a vision, a dream of his own subjective consciousness. Only the dogs and the youngest children bestowed on him a notice that made the shadow world real. And certain concealed, shy, quick glances stolen by some of the pretty young girls when they thought he did not see them. A tentative greeting he ventured to some of the men did not even gain the recognition of rebuff.

But this complete detachment had one advantage. The ordinary business of the camp went forward without modification or interruption. Andy could look, and look he did, and he found it all so interesting that he came at last to spend nearly all his waking hours in the Blackfoot camp.

He had a good many surprises, and some of his preconceptions went by the board. One was that, as already stated, of Indian taciturnity and gravity. They were a laughing, merry people, given to fun and games. Another was that the squaws were ill-treated drudges. To be sure they seemed to do all the camp work, and some of it was laborious, but they took their time at it, and seemed to enjoy it and to take a pride in it. And they appeared to be well treated, with many evidences of real affection and tenderness. Andy spent much of his time watching their activities, partly because his practical mind found much of interest in their ways of accomplishing things, and partly because, try as they might, they could not quite gain to the men's total detachment. He felt himself noticed, acknowledged as a human being. The eyes of the girls especially fluttered slyly sidewise toward the tall young frontiersman. The things he saw stored themselves in the recesses of his mind, and so gradually he acquired an understanding of Indian methods and Indian thought possessed by few white men, a knowledge that later was to stand him in good stead and to make him famous.

He watched them make the store of pemmican and pack it in the boxes of hardened hides—parfleche, and then spend long hours decorating the boxes until the aesthetic as well as the practical sense was satisfied. He saw them whiten the buckskin by means of a certain fungus, and in later years, remembering this, he saved himself by noticing that fungus had been torn from trees, and so deducing the presence of hostiles. He saw them decorate the buckskin also, with elaborate patterns of beads, each of which was patiently threaded on sinew and sewed on separately, of quills yellowed with a dye made from the moss of fir trees, reddened by a root hacked out of the frozen ground and boiled. They cut wood in the thickets and brought it in. They carried water from the river. This might be called hard work, but they accomplished it singing and laughing and skylarking. They seemed to be having a good time. Of a morning, when the sun was warm, the chiefs and warriors sat cross-legged on robes at the lodges' entrance while their wives made their toilets, plucking carefully stray hairs from their smooth faces with hardwood tweezers, dressing their hair, renewing the paint patterns on their faces. Whenever the man of their lodge brought in game, they dressed it and cooked it.

Nor were the men inactive and lazy, as Andy had understood. To be sure they spent a good deal of their time smoking and talking. Their activities, like those of the women, were intermittent, but none the less effective. The mere question of sustenance was serious, and that was the man's job. The tribe possessed few firearms. Except the rifles taken from Joe and Kelly, they were all smooth-bores, ill kept and badly sighted. Most of the hunting was with bow and arrow. A good proportion of the male population was always afield. Hunting took up much of the time and energy. The surplus of the latter overflowed into horse races, shooting matches with the bow, wrestling contests, foot races. Andy hung about the sports rather wistfully. He was young enough to want to take part. Especially would he have liked to have a try at the races and the wrestling. He wanted too to test his skill at a game quite new to him. A small beaded hoop, or wheel, a foot or so in diameter, was rolled rapidly past the contestants, who shot arrows at it, or thrust at it spearwise with staves. To knock the hoop over seemed to count against the player as much as a miss. There were also seated games with bones or pebbles that passed from hand to hand, but these Andy did not understand. Each of these games had its own song which the contestants, and sometimes the spectators, chanted continuously.

One afternoon a group and a commotion up on the tableland attracted him to the horse herd. The young warrior, Kiasax, was engaged in breaking a pony. The animal was quite wild, indeed a mustang, captured and turned into the herd the autumn previous, but never before handled. When Andy arrived Kiasax had choked the animal to unconsciousness by means of a slip noose, and was *hogtying* its feet together. He loosened the rope. As soon as the beast had regained consciousness he began to beat it over the head with a wolf skin. The pony flopped and struggled in terror, but at last lay quiet. Kiasax untied its legs. The pony lay for a moment, then leaped to its feet, plunging and rearing. Again, Kiasax choked it down, tied it, and beat its head with the wolf skin. After the fourth repetition the horse no longer struggled. Kiasax approached cautiously and laid his hand on its shoulder. Instantly the beast reared and struck. More wolf skin. Kiasax was very patient. Inside the hour the pony stood, trembling, his eyes rolling, but quiet, while Kiasax gingerly cinched to his back the high saddle. He did not attempt to mount, but contented himself by running the animal in a long circle, drawing it gradually to him. At the extreme end of the rope he treated it roughly, tenderly when near. Andy had never heard of this method of breaking a horse, but it was effective. Next day he saw Kiasax riding the animal, which was already as gentle as were all the other Indian ponies.

He returned through the encampment as the first dusk was failing. He had not yet summoned the nerve to enter the lodges, but now be peered within one of them. Its interior was dark except for the embers of the fire in the center. The halflight revealed dim guessed forms in a circle and the dull glow of the pipe as it slowly passed. A woman leaned over and dropped a bit of buffalo fat on the fire. For an instant the flame shot up. Andy saw the muffled figures of men, and intent grave faces, and spread robes and things hanging.

Once a day every child in the village above the age of two was dipped in the icy waters of the river. This had two results, it hardened them to resistance of the severe cold to which the northern winters subjected them, and it made them fearless of water. Too much so, sometimes. One afternoon Andy, wandering idly along the stream's edge, saw an infant of possibly three years toddle across the rim ice and slip into the river, where instantly the current sucked it under. Andy dove after it without hesitation, by a miracle got hold of it, by another miracle extricated himself and managed to hitch his burden out on the thin ice and so to the shore. Before he could think what next to do a young and pretty woman followed closely by a man flew down the bank and snatched the strangling infant from his arms. Kiasax—for it was he—in his turn seized the child. They bent anxiously over it for a moment, then hurried back up the bank again toward the lodges. Andy was left shivering in his dripping garments. They had not even glanced at him.

Nor when next day he encountered Kiasax face to face in the village did the young Blackfoot show the faintest sign of recognition, or, indeed, awareness of Andy's existence. Andy was just a bit sore. After all he had wet down his best buckskins and chilled himself to the bone, not to mention the small matter of personal risk. Joe laughed at him.

"You keep thinkin' Injuns is human," said he.

"They *are* human," Andy insisted unexpectedly. "A lot more human than some people I know. I've been watching them. I like them, I wish they'd like me."

For a moment Joe was shocked, then he thought he had the solution, and grinned.

"Nev' mind," he soothed in mock consolation. "Crow gals is jist as good-lookin'—ef'n yo' git out of this with yore ha'r."

But Andy's heresy from common white opinion was no sex urge.

However, that afternoon his heart was lightened. Passing the willows of the bottomland, his attention was caught by the continuous agonized bleating of a rabbit in distress. Turning into the thicket to investigate, he found himself face to face with Kiasax, who had made this realistic imitation to draw him aside.

There was nothing of emotional stolidity about the young Blackfoot now. He seized Andy's hand and pressed it to his heart. Then, in sign talk so rapid that Andy could hardly follow it, he poured forth gratitude. The Little Warrior was his only son, long had the Water People desired to seize him and take him down to dwell with them. His woman—he supplemented the sign by spoken syllables, Nit-o-ké-man—had seen this in a dream, in the Moon of Wolves. The two of them had made medicine against the Water People, but the power of the Water People was strong, stronger than their medicine. But the Sun-Power of this white man was stronger. Were it not for Andy their hearts, the hearts of Kiasax and Nit-o-ké-man—again he pronounced the names—would have been on the ground.

———

Andy had a friend, a friend of his own age, and as it proved, of his own ardent and eager temperament. Their affinity struck deeper than the mere tie of gratitude. In spite of the differences of their race, their breeding, their civilization, their manners of thought, they took to one another instantly.

They could not meet openly. That, Kiasax explained, was as much as his life was worth. Before the public of the village he could not deviate from the prescribed attitude by the flicker of an eye. But they spent long hours together in private. The lower end of the willow bottom afforded them secure concealment. There was nothing to take anyone to that part of the valley, it was too distant for children's excursions. The sun-bared interlacing windfalls enabled them to break the trail. Sometimes he came alone, sometimes the woman, Nit-o-ké-man, came with him, bringing the child. At their first meeting she had shyly pressed the white boy's hand to her heart. After that she sat apart while the young men talked, silent, her eyes cast down. The Little Warrior tumbled sturdily about.

Spring was drawing on rapidly. Long hours the two young men sat in the sun, exploring each other's minds, a delightful occupation warmed in the climate of genuine sympathy.

At first, naturally, all communication had to be in sign talk. But gradually Andy began to acquire some fluency in the difficult Blackfoot tongue. His eagerness to learn, coupled with a natural aptitude for languages and Kiasax's delight in teaching him, made for unusual and astonishing progress. In return he tried to instruct the young Indian in English, but with less success. Shortly the two were conversing in a queer mélange of all three, fluently, happily, and most of the time without consciousness as to exactly how they were getting their ideas over. But they did get them over, a true communion not only of thought but of emotion. Curiously enough Andy said nothing of this friendship to Joe and Kelly, why, he could not have told.

They had much to talk about. At last Andy could satisfy his curiosity as to the purport of many things he had observed. He learned the significance of the white horse, and its importance to his own fate, and the meaning of the knife incisions. Kiasax modestly said nothing of his own part in that decision.

"Your Sun-Power was great, and wisdom came," said he.

In a burst of confidence Andy showed Kiasax the burning glass and demonstrated its use. He did so recklessly, thrusting aside all thought of his companions' disapproval, could they have known. Kiasax was his friend! He dealt openly with Kiasax!

But the exhibition in no way lessened Kiasax's awe of the phenomenon. It was still supernatural, an evidence of Andy's Sun-Power. The lens was merely a talisman, a charm in obedience to which the mighty Sun came down from the heavens, made itself small, performed the white boy's bidding. He gazed reverently on the focused glowing spot, and covered his mouth with the flat of his hand.

Andy learned that the apparently haphazard headdresses had significance, so that one informed could read in them, as in an open book, of the wearer's deeds. Thus an eagle feather thrust horizontally in the hair meant that its owner had, in sight of enemies, touched a dead or alive foeman with his hand, an upright feather signified that he had killed by a blow of the fist, a small piece of wood, that he had slain with musket or bow, a carved wooden knife painted red, that he had struck with that weapon. On the other hand a feather stripped to the quill except at the tip indicated merely that its wearer had been the first to discover and give warning of hostiles. This was a common decoration, not very highly prized. Still it was a good start for a young and enterprising warrior. A peculiar bracelet—Kiasax wore two—was permitted him who took a prisoner. When a warrior's deeds overcrowded his head space, so that specific mention of each became impossible, he assumed the feather headdress and horns. There were not many such.

These and many, many other things Kiasax explained to Andy, pleased at his eager and genuine interest. Andy himself did not realize as yet the value of what he was learning, did not appreciate that he was slowly absorbing a knowledge of Indian ways and psychology unique among the white men of his time.

In return he tried to give Kiasax some idea of white man's cities, white man's wonders. This was more difficult. The Indian expressed no incredulity, but he covered his mouth.

Andy was not so polite or so tactful in his reaction to some of his friend's statements. As when Kiasax told him of the medicine men, of how the priest, retiring within his little tent, called thunder and lightning from clear skies, and a strong wind, or of how the lodge was shaken violently from no apparent cause, and great voices were heard. He shook his head over this. Kiasax was in no way abashed.

"It may not be so with the white man," he replied reasonably, "but how do you know it is not so with the Indian? You tell me many strange things which happen to the white man. I do not tell you no, though I know they could never happen to the Indian."

On one point only could Andy at first get no satisfaction. It was the most important point of all, and he hammered at it constantly. What was to become of them? For a long time Kiasax would not reply, or only vaguely and briefly.

"I do not know," he answered. "It is a matter for the chief men."

Kiasax was reluctant, embarrassed. It was evident that he knew more than he would disclose. But Andy persisted. At last the young Indian gave way.

Andy's life was safe, he was protected by the Sun. Nobody would dare affront the greatest of the gods by flouting that protection. That was the first bit of information he succeeded in digging out. As to his status, Kiasax was genuinely ignorant—whether he would be captive, slave, or honored. That could not be decided by this small band, it must be settled at the great council of the Blackfeet when they should gather in the

Berries-ripe Moon, over the mountains, where the Cold Maker comes from.

"And his companions?" Andy pressed.

"They will be killed," replied Kiasax indifferently. "At the end of the spring hunting, in the Thunder Bird Arrives Moon."

This was sufficiently definite and sufficiently dismaying to be reported. Andy took his companions into his confidence. They listened attentively, with full appreciation of the situation. The escape must be attempted earlier than anticipated, much earlier than desired. For a number of reasons they would have preferred a later date, the mountains would be more passable, it would be more difficult for the Indians to follow their trail, it would be easier to secure sustenance. It must be remembered that, while the Boone gun remained in Andy's possession, ammunition lacked. They must live on what they could dig and snare. Joe had already collected and laid away a hank of horsehair for the latter purpose. Both the older men seemed to take certain things so entirely for granted that they did not even bring them up for discussion. One was that Andy would prefer to take his chances with them rather than become a sacred man among the Blackfeet, in which they were correct. The other was that they need expect no help from Andy's Indian friend.

As to the latter point Andy differed vehemently—at first.

"Sure, Kiasax is yore friend," Joe soothed him. "I ain't arguin' that. When yo' got a friend among Injuns he sticks same as a white man. He'll do anythin' for yo' he kin do. He mout even die for yo'. He'll do anything but one thing—and that is to go agin the law of his tribe, and especial the religion of his tribe. Dunno as I kin blame him," Joe said fair-mindedly. "Because the minute he does that he's an outlaw, a renegade, he don't belong to nothin'. So 'less'n he's prepared to quit his people complete he ain't goin' agin custom. If yore life was in danger, mebbe. But it ain't. Have yo' traded knives?" he asked suddenly.

"Why, no," replied Andy frankly puzzled. "Kiasax did want to trade, but this is my grandfather's knife, you know, and I know its balance, so I wouldn't do it."

"Wall," drawled Joe, "ef'n an Injun'll trade knives with yo' that makes yo' his brother forever." He arose and fumbled in a crevice in the rafters. "Yere's a skinnin' knife I happened to stick up thar whar she wasn't found. Trade him this. And see how fur he'll go."

Kiasax was greatly pleased. He made a little ceremony of the exchange, drawing blood from his own and from Andy's forearm with each knife in turn.

"Now we are brothers," he said.

But at Andy's proposals he stiffened to the strange Indian stolidity that seems to throw everythin off a hard and polished surface. In vain Andy pleaded that the white men were also his brothers, that he could not accept his own life if theirs were forfeit, that if it came to a choice he must throw his lot with theirs in an attempt at escape, no matter how desperate. He wanted no active assistance. Two things would suffice, a few hours' start and ammunition for the long rifle. Kiasax set his face like flint. For a long time he would not even reply. At last the force of Andy's pleading broke down his defense to the point of grudging explanation.

"No Blackfoot will harm you, my brother," said he. "You are safe. As for these others, they are of your people. My heart is on the ground. But I have my people. If I were to help you, as you ask, they would do to me what is done to one who is false."

"They need not know," protested Andy eagerly. "You can watch your chance. A little powder, a few balls. Who can know?"

"If I am a crooked stick to my people, I must tell them so. I am a warrior, a Buffalo with Thin Horns. I could not live among them and keep this lie in my heart."

He was genuinely troubled.

"Even this I would do for you, for you are my brother, and I have sworn on the knife to die for you. For me it is as the wind. But also Nit-o-ké-man, the Little Warrior, they too. You would not ask this, my brother? I have no more words."

"No," agreed Andy slowly. He did not argue further.

His own generous spirit sensed the full significance of an authentic point of honor.

Kiasax covered his face with his blanket, grieving. Nit-o-ké-man too covered her face and uttered small crooning sounds of lamentation. Even the Little Warrior, subdued by this sudden cloud across the sun, ceased his play and sidled close to the woman's side.

"I understand," said Andy sadly. "But," he hesitated, "you will not tell that we—"

"I know nothing," said Kiasax. "The wind has passed my ears. Aie," he mourned, "my heart is on the ground."

Joe and Kelly accepted Andy's report philosophically. It was as they had expected.

There was no sense in further delay. Already the snows were vanishing. Every day brought danger nearer. Shortly, it might be considered worthwhile to set a guard on their movements, even to confine them. Best be away before the Blackfeet leaders thought it possible they would attempt the mountains.

They sat in the dim light of the fire, making their plans. The first consideration was to leave as little and as blind a trail as possible. Andy told of the windfalls in the bottom on which they could travel to beyond his usual rendezvous with Kiasax. Thence—Joe took up the plan—they must swim slanting down the current as far as a strip of bare talus on which they could land without leaving tracks. Andy shivered in anticipation.

"Thought you couldn't swim, Joe," Kelly reminded sarcastically.

"Man kin do anything he has to," returned Joe, unabashed.

Up the talus, avoiding earth and snowfields. Over the pass as rapidly as possible. It would be difficult, for obviously the pass was not open yet for normal travel. Perhaps impossible. But the Blackfeet would hardly—at least at first—believe they would attempt it. They would search at the start for traces in the lower hills. Once over the summit they must shift as best they might.

How would they live? Horsehair snares. In a game country, perhaps the chance to appropriate wolf kills. The inner part of thistle stalks. Roots. Buds. Pull in your belt.

"Hard doin's," said Joe soberly. "Ef'n we only jist had a leetle powder and ball!"

Other conditions were not the most favorable, even for such a desperate attempt. In order to make way through the windfalls without leaving tracks some light would be necessary. There was a moon, but it did not rise until near morning. However...

So they muttered, exchanging ideas, weighing chances. None of them wanted to sleep.

Shortly after midnight they were frozen to silence by a faint scratching at the door. After a moment Kelly arose, crossed the little cabin in three steps, flung aside the covering to the opening. A figure slipped inside. It was Nit-o-ké-man.

She was completely muffled in a robe. Her head was bare. She hung her head.

"Take!" she said, and without looking up, held to Andy a small bundle which she produced from beneath her robe. He hesitated. "Take!" she repeated insistently. "Ai—ee!" she wailed with a sudden intensity, then with a sudden, quick turning movement vanished. The skin covering to the doorway quivered a moment, hung still.

Slowly, a little confused, Andy opened the bundle. It contained his powder horn, his shot pouch, and a small store of dried meat.

Chapter 10
Assiniboins

It was but a scant two hours until dawn before the late waning moon had risen above the ranges to give sufficient light. To these white men huddling in the cabin the time from midnight on seemed interminable. Every minute that passed seemed a minute wasted. Yet if the escape was to prove successful they must wait. No man can walk the crisscross of bottomland windfalls in pitch darkness. If they were to leave no trail for the Blackfeet they must keep their moccasins from earth and snow.

Their preparations were necessarily simple. Andy loaded the Boone gun. The powder smuggled to him by Nit-o-ké-man was his own, and therefore of good quality. The shot pouch also was his own. This was sheer good luck. Nit-o-ké-man might well have brought the ammunition belonging to some of the old fusees owned by the Indians. Of course they could have made shift. Trade powder burned slow and dirty, but it exploded—generally. The lead of the musket balls could have been refashioned to the grooved barrel. But it would have been an inaccurate makeshift. Here lacked only patches for a proper loading, fit for nail-driving. There were a few in the patch box in the butt, but not many. Joe rummaged the crevice under the rafters to haul out the ragged remains of the garments Andy had long since discarded for his buckskins.

"Thar you be!" he cried triumphantly. "Didn't I tell you not to throw nothin' away—that it shore would come in handy sometime? Cut yo' patches from that shirt."

And when the time came to venture, the old clothes justified Joe once more by *coming in handy* again. They were wetted, then laid craftily in and around the freshly fueled fire. There they would smolder for hours. The resultant smoke, escaping through the cowled hole in the roof, would give the cabin the appearance of habitation, and as none of the Blackfeet, with the exception of the old woman who brought food, ever came near the place, this should afford the fugitives a start of hours, even in daylight.

The morning was snapping with cold. The sky was blue-black, asparkle with stars. Only, over the high eastern ranges, spread the milky extinguishing paleness of the moon. At first the fugitives could see nothing. They stood patiently until their irises expanded, until they could make out, dimly, the markings on the snow's surface. Then, stepping carefully in the old moccasin trails, they stole down toward the river bottom.

All went well for a time. They were nearly past the sleeping village. Then the breeze, which had been blowing steadily downstream, suddenly fell flat, whirled a stray gust in the opposite direction.

A dog barked.

"Down! Down!" hissed Joe.

The three threw themselves on their faces.

But the dog had had a noseful, and he clamored excitedly in the strange mixture of bark and wailing howl peculiar to Indian canines. In two seconds the night was hideous with sound as every other dog in the encampment—and there were dozens of them—joined the chorus. The men flattened themselves close to the earth, cursing steadily under their breaths.

The clamor was enough to wake the dead. The fugitives caught momentary red gleams as opening tent flaps showed the coals of fires within. Against the sky, they made out, here and there, the silhouettes of men peering, listening.

Encouraged by this human reinforcement the dogs redoubled their outcries. Some of the bolder even made short dashes toward the outer darkness, but with hind legs in reverse, ready to scuttle back. They were, however, very bold with their tongues, daring the hidden monster, hurling opprobrious epithets, histrionic, after the manner of dogs showing off their zeal before their masters.

A fox barked sharply in reply, so close to Andy's elbow as almost to startle him into movement. A touch of Joe's hand restrained him. The fox barked again, and yet again. Obviously it returned the dogs as good as they sent. Obviously it gave its contemptuous opinion of dogs in general and these dogs in particular. It defied the whole race of dogs.

The hullabaloo in the encampment trebled in volume. The dogs told the fox just what they would do to him if only stern duty did not hold them. But they did not venture. Deep-seated racial experience had taught them the extreme insalubrity of the wilderness night.

The chorus broke up in a medley of astounded and indignant yelps, through which could be distinguished sharp human language and a dull thud or so as a moccasined foot or a billet of wood found its mark. Evidently the Indians also had heard the fox. Only the original dog, the one whose nostrils had caught veritable evidence, persisted self-righteously in his warning. But his quavering howl too terminated in a sharp *yip* of pain. His fleeing form darted across the skyline to plunge precipitately to the haven of a lodge flap, where presumably he brooded on the injustice of man.

After a few moments the white men rose cautiously to their feet, and so reached the river bank undiscovered.

Joe removed his cap and wiped his forehead.

"Whew!" he breathed. "Thought shore our powder was all wet that time. Good thing I larned to talk fox!"

"Was that *you*?" whispered Andy, astonished.

"What'd you think?" asked Joe sarcastically. "Think I had me a tame fox to foller me around?"

"Let's get on," said Kelly with a touch of impatience. "It's getting to be daylight."

Indeed, the delay had been longer than they had supposed. The sun, in close pursuit of the moon, was filling the sky with an added paleness. Apparently there was as yet no actual light, and yet, dimly, objects about them were becoming distinguishable. Although they had escaped discovery thus far, the check was like to prove disastrous yet.

But it turned out to be good fortune in disguise. The original plan had been to make their way up the river bottom over the jackstraws of fallen aspens, which would leave no trail, then to swim the river. But the new visibility revealed to them a great cottonwood, loosened at the roots by the thaws, and newly fallen in such fashion that it spanned the stream. In complete darkness, they would have passed it by.

"Wagh!" cried Joe under his breath when he saw this. "She's a lucky trip. We gits our powder and ball, we gits our jerky, now we gits our bridge!" His irrepressible spirits were bubbling again. "No cold water for this child!"

He untied his moccasins and slung them about his neck.

"Barefoot holds better'n parfleche," said he. "Take em off, Andy."

"And hurry!" urged Kelly. "We're in plain sight of camp."

The crossing was a ticklish business, for while the tree trunk was thick, the dark water thrust against it strongly. Its whole length was aquiver. Andy had to use great will power to hold his attention away from the whirl and boil of the rushing current. He felt that if he yielded for the fraction of a second, he must topple into giddiness. He gave his whole mind to reaching one bare foot sideways to the left, bringing the other bare foot alongside, over and over again, sidling slowly like a crab. The log seemed of interminable length. He did not dare look up to see what progress he had made. He was among branches around which he must squirm and still retain his upright equilibrium. The trunk had divided and become small. Its trembling had increased to a veritable swaying. Then from the corner of his eye, he saw the beach. He made a single desperate leap sideways. He was ashore.

Hastily retying their moccasins they ran rapidly down the stony stream bed past betraying snowfields to a point where naked talus afforded them an unmarked ascent. Up this they toiled as fast as they could climb. It was full daylight. The camp was directly across from them, distant by only the width of the stream. If any early riser were to emerge from one of the lodges, were to glance in their direction, discovery was inevitable. They scrambled desparately, gasping for breath, their hearts pounding in their breasts. Andy's legs were leaden. He felt that he could not lift his feet another dozen paces, and yet, paradoxically, he seemed to himself to be raising his knees absurdly, inordinately high, an illusion of exhaustion.

"Wagh!" exploded Joe, suddenly. "Down! Down!"

They dropped behind a talus block, breathing heavily.

At the very instant of their disappearance, a devilish outbreak of shrieks, cries, yells, and whoops, punctuated by musket shots, burst from the village across the way. Andy gripped his rifle and peered around the edge of the talus block. At first, so certain was his preconception of discovery, he did not understand what he saw. He was aware merely of a confusion of figures running about. Joe's comment focused the situation for him.

"Told you she's a lucky trip!" exulted the trapper. "Now they're so busy they won't *never* pay us no attention!"

It was now clear that the Blackfoot camp was the subject of a surprise attack.

"Assiniboins," said Kelly after an attentive examination.

"Who'd have thought they'd ever git west the divide this time of year!" Joe marveled.

"Not the Blackfeet, evidently," said Kelly. "They're caught as flat-footed as we were."

The Assiniboins had crept up on foot, and had at a signal, made a concerted rush from three sides. The Blackfeet, caught totally unprepared, awakened from sleep, catching up what weapons were next their hands, stumbling scattered from their lodges, were pounced upon before they had gathered their wits to offer defense. For a moment or so, the slaughter was almost unopposed. Then here and there, single champions, reckless with desperation, began to fight back. Many of them were overwhelmed, but not before they had done some damage. Others made head and slowly forced a way to coherence in small groups. The din was fearful, for to the cries of the warriors were added the shrieks of the women and the wails of the children.

The Assiniboins were darting alertly and eagerly about, doing just as much damage as they possibly could in the briefest possible time. That was what they were there for. They kept after the individual warriors just as long, and only as long, as the odds were overwhelmingly in their favor. As soon as a Blackfoot succeeded in struggling to the nucleus near the chief's lodge, they abandoned him for easier prey. If enough Blackfeet survived and got together to warrant a counter attack, then the Assiniboins would withdraw. They were comparatively few in numbers. If they could wipe out the camp without a pitched battle, well and good. If not they would be abundantly satisfied with the scalps they could take and the destruction they could inflict. In the meantime others of the band would be gathering the horses and running them up the valley toward the low passes to the north. That was the method of Indian warfare.

Joe, watching critically the course of events, explained these things to Andy in running comment. Kelly, at the other side of the talus block, occasionally added a word. Both the older trappers were calm and obviously pleased with the shaping of events.

"Told you she was a lucky trip!" Joe kept repeating. "Everything laid out to order. We'll jist cache right here until the Blackfeet put up a real fight. Ef'n we move now some stray mout look up and see us. When the real fight starts all hands will be too busy. Set still, Andy, we'll tell you when."

This was directed at Andy's obvious restlessness. The younger man could not share his companions' cool detachment. The affair was dreadful, agonizing. From inside the lodges women, little children ran shrieking, were overtaken by bounding Assiniboin warriors, felled by blows from the terrible *Warhawks*. Brave men, fighting bravely, went down overcome by the press of numbers, and their bleeding scalps were brandished in triumph. Lodges toppled, came down with a crash, enveloping their floundering inmates, who were pounced upon and slaughtered out of hand. It was a nightmare, in the rapid and confused movement of which no detail could be seized and held, on no single incident of which the eye could rest long enough to catch an outcome.

Then suddenly one situation leaped from chaos very clearly. A tall warrior emerged from the interior of one of the lodges dragging a woman by the hair. These figures Andy distinguished plainly, so plainly that for the moment all else of the swift terrible confusion faded into a mere background of commotion. Details irrelevant and unimportant registered on his mind. For example, somehow he had space of leisure to notice such small things as that the Assiniboin wore a white buckskin cap, that he was naked to the waist, that he wore a peculiar necklace made of wolves' tails, that his warhawk was decorated with feathers. There things registered instantaneously, as a lightning flash reveals. Andy saw at the same time that the woman was Nit-o-ké-man.

Motion seemed suspended. The warhawk was raised for the blow, but did not descend. Andy appeared to himself to be moving with a cool deliberation in an ample leisure. He thrust forward the muzzle of the long rifle, he assured a careful sight on the Assiniboin's head, he slowly squeezed the trigger. As he did so a story told by his grandmother recalled itself in complete detail, how in the siege of Boonesborough Colonel Boone had dropped a sharpshooter from a distant tree—*a notable feat*, the old lady had said. As a matter of fact Andy flung the rifle to his face and fired as the butt touched his shoulder. The savage wilted in his tracks. Nit-o-ké-man tore herself from his dying grasp and darted back into the lodge.

Andy was down the slope of the talus running along the beach. Faintly in his preoccupation he heard Joe's astonished voice behind him. Somehow he was across the log. Somehow he had reloaded as he ran. Somehow he was yelling at the top of his voice. These matters seemed to have nothing to do with himself.

His sudden appearance for a moment struck the turmoil flat. Straight through the paralyzed Assiniboins he darted to the lodge in which the Blackfoot woman had taken refuge.

He had no chance to look within. The Assiniboins recovered promptly from their first surprise. Andy found himself beset. The foremost he killed with a shot, then clubbed his rifle and laid about him. For a moment he swept a space clear. An arrow thudded into his left shoulder. He leaped backward with a roar so formidable that again his assailants paused.

Andy faced them in the brief respite. His left arm was numb and useless. He dropped his rifle to the ground, and his hand sought the knife at his belt. The Assiniboins ringed him close, stooping for a last rush. Andy saw them all clearly, individually. His mind, back of the great excitement that sustained him, was working clearly, coolly, in a strange hypnotic calm. The occasion pressed, was a matter of split seconds, yet he seemed to have all eternity for decision. Outside and beyond the ring of warriors and some fifty feet or more distant stood a man apart. He too wore a cap of white buckskin to which he had attached upright a pair of buffalo horns. His face was painted black. He took no part in the fighting, but watched.

Why he selected this man Andy could not have told—certainly this Assiniboin was no immediate threat, as were the others—but he swept back his arm in the long overhand throw he had so often practiced, and the knife flashed, turning over and over, to bury itself hilt deep in the warrior's neck.

A loud wail burst from the throats of Andy's assailants. One leaped forward and struck Andy a glancing blow on the head. The next instant they were swept aside by the rush of the Blackfeet. Andy's clarity broke. He stood helpless and bewildered in mind. He saw a confusion of struggling bodies. He caught a glimpse of Joe's tall figure, of Kelly laying about him with a warhawk. He heard wild yells of triumph as the Assiniboins gave way, scattered running in all directions. He was feeling giddy, a little sick.

Then Joe was pounding him on the back. The trapper was wildly excited.

"Quit that, it hurts," protested Andy.

But Joe was with difficulty dissuaded.

"That's the quickest, fastest, longest shot I ever see mortal man make with a rifle!" cried the trapper. "That's the longest, straightest throw I ever see made with a knife! Boy, you do make 'em *come*!" He thrust a mass of hair and blood enthusiastically into Andy's lap. "Thar's yore sculps, four on 'em," he exulted. "I took 'em fer ye."

"Good lad," Kelly was saying quietly. "Killed their chief. That's using your head."

Andy shuddered and thrust the scalps violently from him. The world was very confused. He fainted away.

When he came to he found himself on a robe in the lodge's interior. For a moment or so he stared at the smoke hole, unable to figure out just where he was. The voice of Nit-o-ké-man oriented him.

"He has ceased from dying," she cried joyously.

Andy turned his head. Though his mind was still strangely confused, it was clearing, but as it cleared he became more and more painfully aware of a throbbing shoulder and an aching head. He saw Nit-o-ké-man kneeling at a cooking pot over the fire. Beyond her sat Kiasax, and by him, bolt upright, stood the Little Warrior. Kiasax head was big with a bloody bandage.

"You have been dead a long time, my brother," said he. "I too was dead"—he touched his head—"but I have heard. Your Sun-Power is great but it cannot fill the whole of your heart. I have no more words."

"What has happened?" asked Andy.

"I do not know. I too have been dead," Kiasax repeated.

Andy listened. From the outside came no sounds save a thin low wailing. He arose to his feet, steadied himself, went to the lodge opening to look.

The camp was empty of men. The presence of the women was attested only by the mourning from within the lodges whither they had carried their dead. The slain and scalped Assiniboins lay as they had fallen. The dogs prowled furtively among them. Overhead wheeled ravens, materialized from nowhere at the summons of no one knows what mysterious perception.

Andy cocked his ear to a faint clamor over the tableland. It increased. Then around the end of the willow thicket swept a dozen men on horseback. At their head rode Joe Crane. He was yelling at the top of his voice. He brandished his rifle in one hand, waved a handful of scalps in the other. The pony he bestrode ran recklessly unguided, its ears flattened, its head extended, its nostrils wide. The Indians at its heels were pressing him close, both in speed, in excitement and in noise. After a brief interval came Kelly, jogging soberly. He too had somehow reclaimed his rifle, which he carried across his saddle. A larger number of Blackfeet afoot jogged tirelessly alongside him.

The cavalcade swept the village like a whirlwind, plowed to a stop. Joe was afoot. He rushed up to Andy, enveloped him in a mighty bear hug, scalps, rifle, and all. Andy nearly fainted again from the pain in his shoulder. He half hit, half shoved Joe so mighty a buffet on the chest that the trapper's hold was torn loose and he staggered back several paces. The

Indians, who had also dismounted, and were crowding close, laughed delightedly at this exhibition of strength.

"Lay off, you old idiot!" growled Andy. "I've got a hole in me."

"Wagh, I forgot!" But Joe was unabashed. "Boy! That was a fight! We made 'em come!" He slapped the nearest warrior so mightily on the back as nearly to overset him. "Hey, old hoss?" He crow-hopped in absurd caricature of the war dance, leaped in the air to crack his heels together, crowed like a cock. The Blackfeet crowded close, laughing, as much excited as he. Andy could get no sense out of anybody.

Kelly had ridden up and dismounted. Small boys swarmed from the lodges to hold the horses. Women followed them. The men who had been running afoot joined the shouting, exulting mob milling restlessly before the lodge door. Hands brandished scalps aloft. A score of voices shouted, declaimed, chanted. The noise was distracting. Yet somehow below it, through it, persisted the thin low wailing of the hidden women mourning the dead.

Andy was suddenly invaded by a deadly weariness. He could make nothing of it all, except that a victory had been won. Joe was hopeless. His caperings had become a center about which a rough impromptu dance of triumph was forming. The young man suddenly abandoned it all with a gesture of despair.

But Kelly was at his elbow, cool, collected, smiling faintly.

"Come inside, lad," he advised.

They entered the lodge and sat side by side on the robe. Kelly recounted, accompanying his recital by a running translation of sign talk for the benefit of the young Blackfoot.

Andy's knife throw had turned the tide of battle. The death of their chief had cast the Assiniboins into a momentary confusion. Before they could recover, the Blackfeet had gained the upper hand. Furthermore their plans had been wholly upset by a clever bit of strategy. A small detachment of the Blackfeet had avoided the fight to execute a swift movement in capture of the attacking party's riding horses, which were being held convenient for the retreat when the time was ripe. Kelly did not mention the fact that this thought was his own. The raiders had to fight it out afoot, which was no part of their original intention. The sudden injection of the white men into the melée had upset all their calculations, which, naturally, had not taken such a reinforcement into account. Nor could they have foreseen the moral effect of that reinforcement, with its deadly long rifles, which had been promptly restored to their owners. In fact the whole of their strategy had blown up. Such of them as survived had made their way to the willow bottoms where they were being hunted down one by one. In the meantime a sufficient band, mounted on the enemies' own ponies, had followed the trail of the horses.

"They'll recapture them," said Kelly confidently. "You can't drive loose horses very fast. They leave a plain trail, and there can't be many men in charge of them."

The triumph had been complete. Kiasax's eyes glowed with gratification, though he made no comment.

Nit-o-ké-man stood before them, smiling shyly, offering each a wooden bowl filled with a savory stew of venison. Andy accepted it eagerly. To his surprise he discovered himself to be suddenly very hungry.

"This is something like!" he cried to his companion. "I'm starved!"

But Kelly expressed a gratification over and above the mere satisfaction of appetite.

"Better than you think," said he. "Once you have eaten in an Indian lodge you are a guest, and a guest is sacred from hurt or theft. I have known them to sleep in the snow outside while guests occupy the lodge. This is the best news yet."

However that might be, Andy found the food most grateful.

"Well," said Kelly, after the bowls had been emptied, "we're back again. We'd better collect that wild Indian of ours and get back to the cabin. What next?"

But when Andy would have departed, Kiasax would have none of it. Staggering weakly to his feet, his hands on Andy's shoulders, he forced him gently back to the robe.

"No, my brother," said he. "You are now a dweller of this lodge."

The pursuers returned bringing back the stolen horses. The camp formalized to ceremony.

The fallen lodges had been erected again. The warriors disappeared within, to emerge after a few minutes in their oldest clothing. Their faces were painted black. They seated themselves in two long lines facing each other, a wide space between. Under their breath they hummed unceasingly a low and mournful chant. The three white men were instructed to take places in one of these lines. A youth appeared from the direction of the horse herd leading a white pony. Its sides had been marked with designs in red. After a short pause the old chief arose to his feet. By signs he instructed Andy to mount the pony. An ancient squaw thrust into his hands a long peeled staff from which dangled four tufts of hair. Obeying a signal Andy held this aloft at arm's length.

The chief began a recital in a loud singsong voice. Andy could not understand all that he said, but he gathered that his exploits were being recounted, one by one. As the chief's voice ceased, at the end of each episode, drums tapped, the bearers of rattles shook them in corroboration of the testimony. Thus four times, once for each scalp. Then Andy dismounted and resumed his place.

"Countin' yore *coups*," explained Joe. "Makes 'em official-like."

Joe and Kelly had next their turn, followed by those of the Blackfeet who had that day killed an enemy or taken a prisoner or performed a deed noteworthy enough to be counted as a *coup*. The ceremony was the same, except that each told of his own feats.

When all had finished, the chief arose to his feet again. He supplemented his speech by sign talk so that the white men should understand.

"The will of the Sun is plain," said he. "When these came among us our eyes were dim. We could not see. Now they are clear. We looked upon these men as enemies, deceived by the color of their skin. Today they have fought for us. They are not our enemies. Their hearts are the hearts of our people. They are our brothers. Our hearts are theirs, our country is theirs. We are Blackfeet." He washed his hands in a fire of sweet grass and drew his forefinger across the forehead of each in turn. "I pronounce them Blackfeet." He raised both hands over Andy's head, palms down, "I-tam-api shall he be called," he said solemnly. "I-tam-api—Happiness. I have no more words."

He sat down. All eyes were turned toward Andy.

"Git up," urged Joe under his breath. "Say somethin'."

Andy arose to his feet. His eyes were misted, he choked.

"O chief," he pronounced slowly in the Blackfoot language, "my heart is lifted from the ground."

A low murmur of surprise and amazement arose. The chief raised his arms. "Great is thy power, O Sun!" he cried. "Thou hast given him also our tongue!"

An old man shuffled into the center, holding aloft a peeled white wand from which dangled tufts of hair. Drums tapped in broken rhythm, a shrill squeaking pipe struck up a wandering minor air, the rattle bearers shook their rattles. The scalp dance had begun, and would continue for hours. Every able-bodied human being in the village would take part—except the mourners for the dead. Andy stopped to look down with pity on one of these women. Her unbound hair had been sprinkled with ashes, she held her hands before her. One of the fingers had been chopped off at the first joint in token of grief. As he started on again he felt a touch at his elbow. Nit-o-ké-man was looking up at him eagerly.

"You come back, to our lodge, to stay?" she asked.

Andy was embarrassed. He had taken Kiasax's statement as figurative. He translated and explained to his companions. Kelly was emphatic.

"Of course you must do so!" he insisted. "It would be an insult to refuse!"

So Andy reassured the young woman, and she returned pleased to the dance.

The three white men on reaching the cabin experienced a wonderful surprise. Evidently during the performance of the ceremonies someone had been very busy. A fresh fire burned. The bales of beaver skins hung under the roof in the smoke. The moccasins they had made in such numbers during the past winter had been laid out in rows atop their own robes. They looked about them, identifying one by one their simple belongings. Nothing was missing—the traps, the tobacco—Joe pounced on this eagerly—the powder and lead, the small store of trade goods, even their discarded, patched, and shiny buckskins. The restitution was complete, or nearly so. A few small items lacked, mostly from the trade goods, and generally such *expendibles* as tobacco, powder, or vermilion. But other things had been added, possibly in payment—a beautifully beaded *possible* sack, moccasins decorated with dyed quills, and the like. Andy's bed and his personal belongings were missing.

"They've moved you to the young Blackfoot's lodge already," surmised Kelly.

Neatly arranged around the fire were a number of curious contraptions. Short pieces of willow had been split halfway of their length and cleft over other short pieces, clothespin-wise. These puzzled them.

"Looks as if the children had been playing," Kelly surmised.

But Joe, who had picked one up, had an inspiration.

"Hosses!" he cried. He held the toy so that the cleft bit was vertical, and sure enough, it became a rough representation of a man on horseback. "This means they've give' us back our hosses!"

"Too many," said Kelly doubtfully, but in the event Joe proved to be right, and the new members of the tribe found themselves the owners of a score of ponies besides their own.

As dusk fell Andy returned to take his place in his new home. The fire in the lodge was burning bright with buffalo fat. Kiasax and Nit-o-ké-man awaited him. As he stooped beneath the entrance flap they came forward to greet him. Each took a hand and led him to a low wicker chair back covered with a skin. When he had seated himself Nit-o-ké-man handed him his filled pipe, held a coal to the tobacco. She smiled shyly and directed his attention to a beautifully decorated robe spread over a low bed frame.

"For you," said she.

One by one she touched with her forefinger various objects laid out orderly across the robe—a suit of whitened buckskin heavy with bead and quill work, moccasins solid with beads, a circlet of white wolf tails atop a magnificent coronet of eagle's feathers.

"For you," she said of each.

She laughed happily at Andy's expression. Her shyness was gone. She was as eager as a child. Nothing would do but he must take off his present garments, array himself in this gorgeous and ceremonial costume. Andy demurred, then tried to make her understand that at least she should leave him in privacy for the change. He shifted as hastily and as modestly as possible. The embarrassment was all his. Both Kiasax and Nit-o-ké-man were as unselfconscious as children, exclaiming in astonishment at the whiteness of his skin where the sun had not bronzed it. Then Nit-o-ké-man knelt before him and painstakingly painted his face. Her lips were pouted prettily in the absorption of her task, she held her sleek head critically sideways, studying her effects. At length she was satisfied. Andy arose to his feet. Kiasax carefully fitted to his head the eagle crown. They stood back, laughing delightedly over his appearance. Nit-o-ké-man handed him the long rifle. Kiasax signed him to follow. The two young men left the lodge.

Andy found that he was in for a round of calls. First they visited the lodge of the chief, whom Andy for the first time heard named as Mat-o-suki. There they smoked. Abundant food was brought. They ate. Everything was most dignified and ceremonious. Andy enjoyed the experience. He felt that he must present a very fine appearance.

From there they proceeded to the lodge of the next in importance. More smoke. More food. Andy had eaten heartily of Mat-o-suki's spread.

But he was forced now to eat more, for Kiasax gave him to understand that a refusal would be insulting. Another lodge, still more smoke, still more food. After the fourth repetition the situation became serious. Just about as he was beginning to despair, Kiasax instructed him in a convention that saved his life. In each lodge were other guests, men of lesser importance. Andy learned that after the first taste, if he so desired, he could present the nearest of these men with a small bit of wood, whereupon the one so designated would, as his substitute, empty his bowl for him. Next day Andy must redeem his tokens with some small gift. In his present overstuffed condition he felt that they would be cheap at the cost of all his possessions!

At last the ceremonial visits were over. The two young men returned to their own lodge. Nit-o-ké-man arose at their entrance.

"Ai-ee," she murmured. "My men have returned." She stood before the white boy, looking up at him. He towered over her, head and shoulders, and the tall crown of eagles' feathers exaggerated his height. Both she and Kiasax, somehow, seemed to find this discrepancy funny. They commented on it, but so rapidly that Andy could not quite catch the joke. But he joined delightedly in their laughter. His heart expanded. A warmth enveloped him that was not wholly due to the dim coziness of the lodge.

"I-tam-api," Nit-o-ké-man said softly, "I-tam-api. Is he not a great warrior?"

I-tam-api—Happiness! Andy was only just twenty-one.

Time flowed by with the swiftness of water after a thaw. Lo, it was summer!

The white men had resumed their trapping, in which a certain number of the Indians joined. There were streams enough and beaver enough for everybody. This kept them pretty busy. However, they found time to see a great deal of the Indian life, to take part in it almost as fellow tribesmen. But the prime of the fur was over, the spring hunt had finished. The Blackfeet must move north to the summer council under what are now known as the Tetons. The whites must get to the rendezvous if they were to determine the disposal of their furs. The necessity came as a bit of a shock to all concerned. Somehow, each had, without thinking, taken for granted the other's company. The white men told Mat-o-suki of Sublette's proposed trading expedition, and urged him to lead his band to the rendezvous to barter the Indians' spring catch, which was now considerable. Mat-o-suki pointed out that his band was too small for such a journey into the country of the Crows and the Assiniboins. In return he suggested that it was really not quite clubby for the three new members of the Blackfeet to absent themselves from the convention under the Tetons—he wanted to show them off, as was right and proper. Kelly pointed to the bales of fur, which must be disposed of. The chief suggested that to the west were other white men, not so far away. The Blackfeet had nothing to do with them, but the Flatheads traded there. These white men, said Kelly, were King's men, enemies of the Americans. Mat-o-suki acknowledged this, but wanted to know if the two older men could not do that errand to rendezvous, leaving Andy with the tribe. After all, Andy was the show piece. Andy vetoed this. He could not desert his comrades.

"But," he added, "in the Leaves Will Fall Moon I shall come back. I swear it, by the Sun." He cast a glance at Kiasax, silent and somber in the circle. "Shall I not seek my brother and my sister? Shall I leave empty my place in my lodge?"

"Good!" said Mat-o-suki. "And our other children?"

Kelly nodded, saying nothing. But Joe laughed out loud.

"Me?" he cried in English. "With all them beaver yere waitin'? Jist try to keep me out! Besides," he added drolly, "ain't I jist gittin' that little fat purty one to thinkin' I'm a heap big Injun? You tell him to save her fer me, and I'll be here!"

Andy translated this. The men laughed. Even old Mato-suki's grave countenance broke into a smile. The little fat pretty one, who, with the other women, had been listening at a respectful distance outside the circle, dove for the shelter of a near-by lodge. The women cackled delightedly. Joe grinned at them all.

Two days later the encampment was broken up. For a time the whites and Indians were to travel in company. It seemed there was, farther to the north, a lower and easier pass to the east. The lodges came down, the travoys were packed. Amid a confusion of cries, laughter, the barking of dogs, the tribe moved up the valley.

The first day's travel was in the happy-go-lucky, go-as-you-please style incident to a country where no danger was feared. The older men rode ahead in small groups, dismounted as the fancy took them to sit and smoke. The younger men and the boys swooped about the country at full speed, skylarking, dashing regardless through the throng, stirring up trouble among the stray horses and colts, pursued by shrill protests from the women. Dogs ran after them, fought among themselves, dodged irate old squaws. The long loose procession flowed along in a curiously eddying current, stringing out, overtaking, coagulating, stringing out again. The clamor was continuous. Only the three whites marched their outfit with any coherent compactness, Kelly leading the horses packed high with the beaver skins, Joe bringing up the rear, Andy cruising about to head in any of the animals inclined to break away. Over the low passes to the north they climbed, and so into another and smaller valley. Near the close of the afternoon Mat-o-suki stopped in the flat of a stream. Slowly the others drew up to him. Here and there a favorite squaw took her stand, holding aloft a lance as the gathering point for the family. The new camp took form.

But the following morning this engaging informality was abandoned. Camp was struck, the horses packed expeditiously. Then, instead of setting out at once each was ready, the various families and fraternities gathered in separate groups and stood waiting. The men were all dressed in their best and most ceremonial gorgeousness. Except for the barking of the dogs, complete silence reigned. Only at a signal from Mat-o-suki did they set forth. And the manner of their riding was this:

In front of each group, and on its finest pony, rode proudly a young girl in beautifully decorated buckskins. Against her right stirrup she bore a thin pole, ten feet or more in length, its tip decorated with brass trinkets, or a flashing mirror, or a gilt ball, or perhaps a nosegay of bright flowers. Behind her rode the head of the family or the clan, in full panoply, carrying his lance and shield. Behind him, again, the women and children and packs. The younger warriors brought up the rear. They rode in silence, eyes front, looking neither to right nor left.

At the end of an hour Mat-o-suki stopped and faced his pony about. The tribe gradually closed in back of him. When all had reached the place and stopped, Mato-suki spoke.

"Here the trail divides," he declaimed in a voice loud enough to be heard by all. "There is the pass to where the Sun comes from"—he pointed his lance. "My brothers have many horses, many beaver. Yonder is the country of the Crows. But the Sun-Power of I-tam-api is strong. You will pass through the country of the Crows, We, your brothers, will make medicine for you." He signed certain young men in the background, who drove up a number of laden horses. "Here are more beaver,' he continued, "which my young men have taken. Take them. Trade them for us, and in the Leaves Will Fall Moon bring us that which the Americans will give."

This was surprising, and just a little disconcerting.

The three whites consulted hurriedly. Considerable responsibility attached to such a commission.

"Look here," objected Kelly, "you'd better tell him there's more than a chance we may not get through, that we may not get back."

But Mat-o-suki waved this aside.

"That is the affair of the Sun," said he.

"All right, if he wants to take a chance," decided Kelly. "But what does he want us to bring him?"

At Andy's translation a babel arose, presumably from the owners of the skins. Even the women dared lift their voices in urgence of their desires. Mat-o-suki silenced them by a lift of the hand.

"Bring guns and powder and lead and knives and tobacco," said he, "and other things which our brothers will know."

"He's shore got a trustin' natur'," said Joe sardonically. "Thar's many a plew in them bales. Yo' tell him that," he insisted. "Tell him mebbe we won't come back a'ter all."

"If my brothers do not come we will paint our faces for the dead," said Mat-o-suki, unmoved.

"Dog-*gone*!" blustered Joe when this was translated. "Yo' tell him he's a tarnation trustin' old fool. No, needn't tell him that. Dog-gone! Ef'n enybody'd told me I was goin' to like an Injun like a white man I'd a-crawled his hump! An' yo' know what you're a-doin', Andy, you tarnation little squirt you? Yo're makin' me out a *trader*."

"That's a rattling good notion, Joe," said Andy quietly. His face was grave. Suddenly he seemed to have matured, to have taken leadership. He turned to Mat-o-suki with an air of authority. "We will do these things," he told the chief. "And this also we will do. In the Leaves Will Fall Moon we will bring the trade for this beaver. And we will bring also other trade—beads, and paints, and axes, and kettles, and fire steels and red cloths and blue cloths"—a low murmur of admiration came from the attentive women—"and many other things. Some of these will be *on the prairie* to show my heart is big for my brothers. Some I shall give for the skins you will bring in. I have no more words."

He grinned at Joe as he translated.

"So now you *are* a trader!" said he.

"Dog-gone if I ain't!" cried Joe.

They gathered the laden animals and rode away. A chorus of farewells followed them.

"Come back! You will come back, I-tam-api!" they pleaded.

Suddenly Joe wheeled his pony and dashed back.

He snatched the little fat pretty one from the ground, implanted on her startled face a resounding smack, set her on her feet again.

"So long, folks!" He waved a long arm in general.

They toiled slowly up the slope of the low pass. The Indians stood where they had left them. From time to time Andy turned in his saddle, waved his hand. They did not answer the signal. His last look, from the *puerto suelo*, showed them motionless, still in the same place.

The three white men camped that night just over the summit on the eastward slope. After supper Andy left the fire and climbed to the saddle of the pass.

It was a gorgeous evening. The air was crisp with the chill of altitude, but from time to time a wandering sweet warmth, astray from the distant plains, touched him inquiringly and passed on. It was the time of the rising moon. Already that luminary was above the horizon. As the daylight drained away it took serene possession.

Andy sat on a rock and fell into a reverie, his chin in his hand. Past events plucked the sleeve of his musing for recognition. Each required its own space of dignity, so that the multitude of them made for themselves an imposing past that had no relation to the calendar. He saw every detail of his first meeting with Joe Crane in the woodland glade, but he saw it microscopic, small, dwindled by the immense distance of experienced time. Yet he had left the Pennsylvania farm only a little over a year ago! It seemed impossible. It seemed impossible too that the raw lad he recalled himself could be the same as him who was now sitting the summits of the Rockies, of a moonlight night.

From this vantage point he could look both ways. To the eastward were the foothills and the prairies and the great rivers of the plains. He looked across them with his mind's eye, leaping in imagination to the seaboard, then following back again. To him the white man's civilization seemed at that moment like a flood dammed back by the wilderness, waiting to overflow and take possession. Finger-like its first small trickles were feeling their way, like leakages, into the country prepared.

He turned his eyes from the moon-bathed east to the shadowed west, and at once his spirit stirred. Those tumbled ranges held in their folds and recesses something that the groping fingers had banished from the plains. It called him powerfully. The Unknown! There was his land, there the obscure destiny of his blood and breeding called him. For a moment he gave himself up to his dream.

But his mind, tugging insistently, drew him back to what it pronounced its reality, calling upon him to face facts as they were. He could not deny the logic of his mind. His way must lead, not through the dream, but through the reality. By a distinct effort of the will he recalled a picture that had faded. It was of a little old lady, in a Boston rocker, by the open window of a Pennsylvania farmhouse. She was awaiting, she had been awaiting, patiently his return. Thither led his way. At the thought of her a gush of affection welled up in Andy's heart. Yet, disconcertingly, into the serenity of the night jangled a dissonance, sweet bells out of tune. Andy was disturbed. He mentally castigated himself for his disturbance.

And then a curious and beautiful thing happened. Over the little troubled surface of his uneasiness the spell of moonlight poured, mystic, wonderful. Andy seemed to himself to be holding very still in a stillness that was not merely of the body, but of the mind and soul as well. And this stillness released in him strange quiet powers of perception. Things presented themselves and stood before him serene for his contemplation, and quietly withdrew. He saw them in their significances.

The first of these things that presented themselves was a sure conviction that the picture he had evoked was no true picture, that no little old lady sat now in the Boston rocker by the open window of the Pennsylvania farmhouse. His grandmother was dead. Andy was as certain of this as if he had learned of it by a sure messenger. The certainty held itself before him until the first sharp shock of recognition had given way to the flow of a strange and exalted peace, as the acceptance of something grateful to her and desirable and long desired, whose exaltation he must share. Then it faded and a flood of love bathed him. He was surrounded by it, permeated by it, uplifted by it, transformed by it as the soft moonlight transformed the world at his feet. His spirit soared in an eager uprush of response. It lifted him for a brief moment or so into what seemed to him a personal communion. The terms of that communion were very simple, an abstraction almost, the essence of two things—a deep and satisfying approval, a mighty uplifting inspiration to a destiny foreordained. It filled him as breath fills the lungs, flowing to him as a great wind from sources mysterious but not quite unknown. For at the same time the third conviction came to him, but rather an impression than a conviction, of his grandmother, and more faintly, aloof in the background as it were, of old Gail Burnett—perhaps of Boone himself.

It was tremendous, but mercifully brief, for the content of it was too great for long human endurance. It lost strength, drained away. Andy awakened to his normal self slowly as one coming to consciousness. He looked about him still a little dazed. The mountains had become mountains again. The rock on which he sat was a piece of granite. The air was cold. Somehow be was not surprised to look up at Joe Crane, standing at his elbow.

"Wall!" observed Joe. "What do you think yo're a-doin' up yere—mountain man?"

Part Two
Mountain Man

Chapter 11
Council

By 1823 and 1824 the fur trade west of the Mississippi was balancing in unstable equilibrium. The old order was changing, and a great many people who were accustomed to it were disgruntled. Others approved.

Andy Burnett, carrying his grandfather's long rifle from a Pennsylvania farm, happened to his mountain experience just at the moment. In order to understand, it will be necessary to review a bit of history, to picture a situation. But that is no great task, nothing west of the Mississippi was dull in those stirring days.

Up to the time of Andy's first sight of the Rockies, the situation was very simple. The lower Missouri and its tributaries were traded and trapped in some sort of organized fashion by companies formed for the purpose. The earliest of them had been Manuel Lisa, the Spanish American, who had built the first posts, and had died in 1820, leaving behind him a reputation for square dealing and irascibility. In its latter years his enterprise had been known as the Missouri Fur Company. He was succeeded by Pilcher, a man of sufficient enterprise to push back as far as the mouth of the Big Horn River, where he built his outpost fort. By 1822 he is said to have had three hundred men on the upper rivers. Some of these were trappers, some were executives and clerks and *engagés* in the various posts, some were in charge of transport, some were traders whose business it was to search out the Indian encampments. The Trade was well organized and busy and profitable. It was also exciting and passably dangerous. Whiskey, or what was called such, was a big item in the barter and a disturbing one. Because of it, and for many other inevitable reasons, matters were always aboil. There was on the part of the Indian tribes drunkenness and treachery and surprise attack and thieving raids and all the rest of it, as also hospitality and welcome and friendliness. The trouble was that no man knew which to expect. The Arickarees were the most uncertain. The village that one day would hail the trader's keel boat with delight would attack it viciously the next and with no known reason. The Mandans were steadiest, but no lone white traveler ever felt quite at ease, even with the Mandans. Therefore great pains were taken never to become a lone traveler. The annual supply expeditions from St. Louis were well armed and strongly manned. The posts were of stout construction. They conducted their affairs circumspectly after a safety-first routine, admitting but a few customers at a time, obtaining their meat and wood and such necessities guardedly. Those whose business led them far afield—the trappers and the itinerant traders—went in companies. These bands were not numerous enough to defend themselves against determined hostility, but were sufficient to discourage wanton aggression when determined hostility lacked. For it must be understood that as yet the Plains Indians were not concertedly inimical.

And far over the western and northern horizons, similarly, the great British Company carried on its trade. It had united with the Nor'westers, and it had crowded out Astor.

But these conditions obtained only on the outskirts, as it were. Within their wide thin encirclement lay the vast and unknown area described as the Great American Desert Unknown save to a handful of daring men who annually disappeared into its mysteries, and annually returned bearing rich furs and tall stories. They were the mountain men.

Where they went nobody knew but themselves. What dangers they ran, what countries they traversed, what peoples they encountered could only be guessed by the disappearance of familiar faces. Their numbers were sparingly recruited from the ranks of the most adventurous. They were trappers, not traders.

Indeed they entertained, at this time, a profound contempt for and distrust of traders. They preferred to make the long and difficult journey to St. Louis in order to dispose of their catch, rather than seek the nearer posts. They were bitterly jealous of invasion, and eyed with suspicion any symptoms of extension toward the mountains.

In general they lived at peace with the tribes. Too few in numbers to arouse suspicion of encroachment, their presence was viewed by the

Indians with a certain toleration. At worst they were in danger only from stray marauding bands, always willing to pick up easy scalps or plunder. At best, they took Indian women and moved freely within certain districts, almost as members of the tribes. In any case there was no general hostility to them as white men and interlopers. Nevertheless their existence was precarious enough to develop in them a wariness and craft and independence that made of them a class apart.

Such was the equilibrium which was now to be disturbed. It was evident that the monopolistic isolation of these few could persist only as long as the lower country was undepleted. But as the beaver there became scarcer the organized trade was bound to go farther afield.

The mountain men felt this, but did not understand its inevitability. They resented the portent of invasion. They were restless before the shadow of its threat.

What might have come of it in the way of opposition, complicated by the influence of the trappers over the mountain tribes, it would be difficult to say. But at this moment the Trade took a new turn. General Ashley organized a brand new expedition for the purpose of trading, and traffic, not in the zealously guarded Rockies of the mountain men, but in the comparatively virgin country just to the east. Sublette, himself a mountain man to a certain extent, was diplomat enough to make plain that he intended no encroachment. The trappers under his command would confine their activities to the upper waters of the Missouri. And the mountain man would be able to sell his furs and obtain his supplies, practically at St. Louis prices, at the expense of a journey, not of several thousand, but of a few hundred miles only. The mountain man was in some respects a simple creature, swayed by his emotional prejudices. The personal element bulked large in his psychology. He knew and liked General Ashley. Ashley's head men, such as Sublette, Henry, and Fitzpatrick, were of their ilk, of themselves rather than of the hated professional trader class.

Andy Burnett reined in his mount below the skyline and advanced afoot. At the summit he drew a wolfskin over his cap, and slowly thrust his head above the ridge. A hundred paces or so below, the small cavalcade awaited the results of his inspection, the mounted men sitting their horses idly, the laden pack animals improving the opportunity to crop at the short alpine grasses. It was well to exercise caution. The pack horses carried a rich take of beaver skins, the men were but four, an easy prize for wandering Crows or Assiniboins.

For some minutes, the young man's eyes swept the prospect below him, then focused to a detail. After a moment, he signaled his companions. They dismounted and joined him. All four scrutinized the distant object of his attraction.

"White man," pronounced the young Indian at last in the Blackfoot tongue.

The others made no comment.

Then, at last, Joe Crane arose to his feet

"He's right," he muttered in English. "That boy's shore got good eyes."

"How do you know, Kiasax?" asked Andy.

But Joe answered, rather impatiently.

"Legs hang down straight. Never saw these Injuns ride long stirruped."

They remounted and boldly crossed the skyline. The distant figure had come to a doubtful stop. Andy drew to one side and wheeled his mount back and forth in the friendship signal. Then they descended the slope.

The three white men and the young Indian approached the stranger steadily and observantly, saying nothing. The man awaited them in stolid silence. He sat one horse and led another. The beasts were sleek and well rounded, for the new grass was strong, but their tails and manes were curiously ragged and short, the tails especially gnawed to the very stumps.

"Hard doin's thar!" Joe Crane muttered to Andy. "Starvin' times!"

The rider, however, was thin to the point of an emaciation which his long hair and beard only partially concealed. He was clad in a strange mixture of buckskin and cloth, the former blackened and shiny with wear, the latter ragged to the point of disintegration. But these clothes he sat in, and the saddle he sat upon, and the two horses were apparently his whole possessions. He carried no rifle, no robes, no utensils, no supplies, or equipment of any kind.

"Good-mornin'," greeted Joe as they rode up. "How are ye? Stranger yereabouts, eh? Got ary meat? Well, we got a hind quarter of *cimmaron*. Come along, camp with us, and eat and talk awhile."

The stranger croaked in his throat like a raven. His eye was wild and unsettled. As though he considered the croak sufficient, or perhaps because he found his voice too rusty from disuse, he made no other response. He wheeled and joined the march.

All the rest of that day they rode together in an apparently incurious silence which the varied activities of an extreme vigilance were not quite sufficient to explain. The main body plodded along slowly at a methodical two miles-an-hour gait. But always two, and sometimes three, of the travelers were circling far afield, urging their ponies at the swiftest gait possible, rummaging the pockets and folds of the hills, scrambling to the top of commanding elevations for long looks abroad, searching the earth for signs wherever its rocky surface softened. When the ponies tired, fresh ones were saddled from the little bunch that trotted about among the sturdier pack horses. When these outriders returned to the main body, or their circles crossed afield, they exchanged terse tense comment on the immediate business in hand, which was to get safely through an alien land. They had no leisure of mind for extraneous chatter. That must wait. This was serious business. They paid no attention to the visitor, who, on his part, paid no attention to them, but rode dully, all watchfulness now relaxed, his chin sunk in his long beard.

Toward the middle of the afternoon Kelly, who was ahead, stopped short, dismounted. The others converged on him as rapidly as possible. He had come upon horse tracks.

The ground was hard and flint-like. They could make nothing of them. But while they were bent in examination, they were jerked upright by the sound of the shrill Arapahoe war whoop. Around the curve of a butte a mile away charged a half-dozen horsemen.

Instantly the practiced mountain men leaped to their preparations for defense, seizing the rawhide ropes wound about the horses' necks, with them tying the animals closely nose to nose, in threes and fours, so they could not run away. Rapidly, but without flurry, they bent themselves to the task. The job was insistent on their attention. They did not spare a second glance toward the attacking party. This came first. The stranger was as active as the others, and when the last horse had been secured, without direction he gathered the ends of all the ropes together.

That shines!" Joe approved him, as he leaped to his post outside the circle.

So quickly and coolly had this maneuver been executed that the speeding horsemen had covered no more than half the intervening distance.

"Why, there are only six of them!" cried Andy.

"Must be a big party somewhere in back, watch out," said Kelly.

The riders were bending low behind their ponies' heads. Straight on they came. Joe Crane was getting restive.

"They's gittin' purty far from home and mother!" he muttered. "Ef'n they come clost enough let's pot the lot. We got plenty time to load afore the main gang can git to us. No use to hold our fire."

Kelly was puzzled. This performance was contrary to all tenets of Indian warfare. There must be some trick, new even to his long experience.

"Better go slow," he advised, then amended his idea. "You and Andy can fire. Kiasax and I will hold back."

But at this moment the riders straightened in their saddles, and discharged their guns straight up into the air. This is the most obvious of the many conventions of peace, for it is evident that an empty gun is harmless. And with the discharge came a roar of hearty laughter. The Arapahoes were seen to be white men, who now trotted to the group and dismounted hilariously.

"You tarnation idjits," growled Joe, "yo're a-goin' to git yore fool heads shot off ef'n you keep on with sich monkeyshines. Me and Andy was jist about to cut loose, and ef'n we had—"

But the boisterous newcomers refused to be impressed. They slapped backs and shouted gleefully over their reckless joke.

"Come on! Turn loose yore horses, you Injin fighters. We got meat and water. Whar ye headed? Sublette's outfit? So are we! Wharabouts you expect to diskiver him? Got ary likker?"

"Whar in tarnation you expect we'd git ary likker?" Joe was disgusted.

"Wall, yo' got Injins and a prisoner, by the look of him, and hosses and sich like nat'ral curiosities. No harm askin'. How's yore ketch?"

"Kain't you see? You got eyes." Joe was still grumpy.

"Ef'n them's all beaver," said the other.

"They are," replied Joe shortly. He unbent a little. "Whar you been trappin', and whar did you winter?"

"Same as usual. Got to hunt us a new hole next season. Gittin' caught out. I s'pose you been with yore pet Blackfeet." A tinge of envy crept into his voice. "Lord! I'd like to have yore luck!"

"Try it," said Joe.

"Not me! I like my ha'r right whar she's a-growin'! No Blackfeet in mine!"

The word seemed to arouse the stranger from the lethargy into which he had fallen.

"Damn Blackfeet to hell!" he croaked rustily, but with surprising energy.

"Hullo! Got a voice, eh, old timer!" exclaimed Joe. Both men looked at the emaciated scarecrow curiously.

"What about Blackfeet?"

But the stranger had retreated again into dull silence, nor did repeated effort elicit another word.

The trappers' camp had been cunningly chosen for concealment and protection. The newcomers' horses were unpacked and unsaddled, and turned out to graze with the others. There was a great deal of chatter, a rapid interchange of news. The Arapahoes were said to have found buffalo this year in the Bull Pen, the Snakes had starved on roots, and were dangerous, there was little game in the mountains, for some reason, except up toward the Yellowstone, the grass on the Bow was dry and scarce, nothing but bull beef near Belle Fourche, so they say. Two of the six men knew Andy, had been with the original Taos party. He had not seen them since then. He had to confirm and expand and correct the rumors as to his miraculous favoritism by the dreaded Blackfeet. They listened to him eagerly, commenting only by an occasional throat-scraping "Wagh!" Their eyes shone at his description of what every mountain man dreamed of, a virgin beaver country, untouched, untrapped. They frankly envied him and his companions, and said so. How about the country farther west? South of the Columbia? Some said there were good trapping streams there too. Some said there was nothing but desert. How about the Injins down there? Suppose there were good beaver streams, how you going to get your fur out? Nobody really knew. Jist have to go see sometime. Mebbe next year...

Andy's eye fell on the stranger. He sat against a rock, collapsed, his dull eyes looking straight ahead. Andy sprang to his feet, snatched from the fire a ramrod on which half-cooked meat was roasting. His heart reproached him. In the excitement he, and all the others, had forgotten.

For a moment the man seemed sunk and unaware. Then, suddenly, ravenously he seized the ramrod. He stuffed the meat into his mouth in great chunks, swallowed it, choking, half-chewed. He uttered eager animal-like noises. Gradually the talk fell. The attention of all men turned to him. He was oblivious of them, wholly and greedily occupied.

"Better call a halt," someone advised at last. "He'll done kill hisself."

Kelly took the ramrod, still half full. He had to use considerable force. The man clung to it, objecting with strange inarticulate noises. Suddenly he relinquished it and fell back against the rock. He looked about him as though just awakening.

"Someone got any tobacco?" he muttered.

He puffed at the pipe, his eyes half closed. As he showed no present indications of confidence, attention fell away from him. These men would not ask questions. They returned to their own affairs. Always the talk veered, from whatever the subject, back toward the mysteries of the beyond. Merritt said there was a river, flowing into the Pacific Ocean, that cut through the high Sierra. It must rise somewhere to the south and west. He even knew the name of it, the Buenaventura. Now, if a man could just strike the headwaters of that river and follow it down—

"They's no sich river," interrupted Halsey positively. "If there had been the Spanish would have foilered her *up* from Californy. That stands to reason."

"Mout be rough whar she heads through the Sierra."

They proffered equably the pros and cons. The argument melted into vagueness. Only way to do would be to go see. Perhaps they might some day. If there were such a river there should be beaver...

"Wall, how about this yere big salt sea they talk about out beyond the Utes?" challenged Merritt again. "What you think of that?"

That was nearer, or was supposed to be. This discussion was more animated.

"Ask yore Blackfoot, Andy," suggested Merritt at last. "Mebbe he knows something about it."

A sudden stir returned their attention to the stranger. His eyes were open and blazing, staring at Kiasax.

"Is that Injin a Blackfoot?" he croaked in his hoarse voice. Without waiting for a reply he leaped to his feet and cast himself blindly at the young Indian's throat. Kiasax, almost caught unawares, nevertheless slipped sidewise like an eel, seized the stranger's wrist, whipped it behind the man's back, and so held him immobile in a grip against which struggle was useless. But indeed of struggle there was little. The sudden burst of energy had exhausted the stranger's feeble strength. After a moment Kiasax relaxed his grip. The man sank to earth like a filled sack. Kiasax looked down at him for an instant in lofty scorn, then quietly resumed his place.

The men looked at one another. Finally, Joe Crane spoke up.

"Look yere, stranger," said he authoritatively. "Yo've had a full belly and a smoke and a sit down, and that's enough for ary mountain man to find his tongue. If so be yo're a mountain man," he added. "What happened to ye? And whar yo' hail from? And how come you got no rifle nor possibles? And what for you try to climb the hump of one of the party that picks you up, Injun or no Injun, Blackfoot, or no Blackfoot? 'Bout time, seems to me, you declar' yoreself!"

A murmur of assent ran about the little circle. The stranger collected himself, with a visible effort.

"If you'd a-been through what I've been through, you'd do the same," he half apologized in his hoarse voice.

"We're listenin'," said Joe Crane.

The party of which this man was one, it seemed, had circled into the Blackfoot country farther north. For some months they had trapped with considerable success without encountering any Indians. Then one day the Blackfeet appeared. They visited the trappers' camp, which seemed friendly.

"There was only twenty-eight of them," said the stranger. "I counted them."

"Was there ary women? How were they painted? Never mind, go on," said Joe.

They had left, still professing friendship. But for some reason the white leader, whose name was Immel, was uneasy. He insisted that camp be broken. They set out in some haste down the Yellowstone. Nothing more was seen of Indians. Some of the men grumbled at leaving so early such good trapping grounds. But Immel had authority, he and a man named Jones. Then, just as they thought themselves safely away, they were ambushed in a rocky gorge.

"So narrow we could only go single file," explained the stranger.

Someone spat contemptuously.

"It was the only way through," insisted the narrator, "and Gordon—he was our hunter, and he was huntin' ahead for meat—he went through ahead of us all right. We saw him."

"Sure, they *let* him through, to toll you on!" remarked Kelly.

The attentive mountain men grunted agreement. But even then—only twenty-eight Indians—how many in the white party? Twenty-nine? Ary white man should lick ten Injins!

"They was hundreds of Injins, thousands," asserted the stranger earnestly.

Kiasax grunted. They turned toward him.

"You know about this, Kiasax?" Andy asked him in Blackfoot.

"These white men were in the country of my people," replied the young Indian. "They shot the game and caught the beaver. The game and the beaver belong to my people."

It seemed that he had accurate knowledge of the whole affair. The first small band had made haste back to the main tribe, had collected some four hundred warriors, had patiently trailed the white party down the Yellowstone to the favorable spot for an ambush.

"We killed the two chiefs," said Kiasax calmly, "and five more, and wounded four. These and the other white man made a raft and crossed the river. But we took all their horses and their traps and their beaver. We did not know of this man. White men must keep out of our country. We will kill them."

"We are white men," Andy pointed out.

But Kiasax shook his head.

"You three are Blackfeet," said he obstinately.

"H'm," observed Andy. "He has heard something about it," he told the others. Andy did not consider it wise to elaborate.

The narrator, who had fallen behind the main body, doubled back and escaped. He had lost his outfit in swimming the river. Since then he had subsisted as best he could. They questioned him. Why had he not gone straight on downstream to Fort Benton? He feared the Indians. Attempting a roundabout route to the same end, he had lost himself in the mountains. The trappers considered gravely. From their point of view it was a curious tale, for no one of them but could have better extricated himself. But one explanation could be valid. However accustomed to or skilled in a trapper's life he might be, this was no mountain man. Their silent deliberation moved logically to the next conclusion.

"Look yere, stranger," Joe voiced it bluntly. "Yo're no free trapper. Who you workin' fur?"

"I'm a Missouri Fur Company man," stated the other simply.

A dead silence followed this admission. The men looked at one another.

"Now look yere, stranger," Joe spoke up after an interval. "Yo've had hard doin's, and I don't aim to rub salt in sores, but don't you know you were gittin' out of yore territory? Don't you know this yere is our kentry, that we done found and explored and we don't look kindly on no outsiders?"

"I don't know nothin'," returned the company man stoutly. "I jest go whar my partisan tells me."

"I expect that's right," agreed Joe dryly, and with a slight contempt. "Wall, we kain't turn no white man adrift. We're goin' over Belle Fourche way lookin' for Sublette. When we git thar you kin go on back to yore boss. And you might kind of tell him, next time he wants to send yo' out to the mountains, that they ain't so good. That right, boys?"

The others nodded a somber assent. Only Kelly seemed to find some humor in the situation.

"That's exactly, word for word, what Kiasax, on behalf of the Blackfeet, would tell these others!" he remarked privately to Andy, as the conference broke up.

———

Sublette was not at Belle Fourche, nor was there any sign of the promised fort. A small group of trappers were already on the spot awaiting him. The situation was most unsatisfactory. It was now too late to begin the long difficult journey to St. Louis, at least with any expectation of returning that season. The men were burdened with many skins, they lacked, and must have, the essential supplies. The next nearest point where such could be procured was at Fort Benton, near the mouth of the Big Horn River. To trade there, the outpost of the Missouri Fur Company, whose constant encroachments and persistent advances the free trappers so resented, was like bitter medicine. But what else? A man must have powder and ball and tobacco and a few *possibles*. To say nothing of a *good time*. So they took up their march.

They were now strong enough in numbers to proceed boldly and comfortably, with only the ordinary precautions. Kiasax, the young Blackfoot, would go no farther. Already he was too deep into the country of his tribe's hereditary enemies. So he cut out his ponies, and took his outfit and turned back, quite alone, but entirely confident. The tribe's skins he turned over to Andy Burnett to trade for him, as he had done the year before.

"You will find us, I-tam-api, by the Lake of Bright Stones in the Berries Ripe Moon."

Some of the men were inclined to grumble resentfully over the failure to establish the promised fort. But most took it philosophically. They knew Ashley, they knew Sublette. No blame probably attached, but they were uneasy lest something had happened to throw the whole enterprise overboard. In that case, what? Resume the long journeys to St. Louis? Or trade with the *enemy*? They argued the point, on theory, and some of the arguments became quite heated. Especially Joe Crane and a red-headed giant named Tilton stirred up bad blood that already existed between them. At the beginning they were not widely apart in actual opinion. But Tilton happened to make a careless and harmless remark to the effect that if Ashley wanted the trade he'd better be on the spot or he'd lose any chance he might have had to establish himself. Joe caught this up and extended it by implication to hint at disloyalty. Tilton, who really did not care much either way, was forced to the opposite side by sheer contrariness. Shortly Joe became a *renegade Blackfoot* and Tilton a *company spy*, with an adjournment to the prairie imminent. But Kelly and Merritt intervened.

"You're ridiculous, both of you," said Kelly. "You neither of you know one thing about it. Anything may have happened. A ten-year-old child would suspend judgment until he found out. I'm ashamed of both of you, going off half-cocked like this."

Neither took admonition gracefully, but Kelly had the authority of prestige among these men, and Merritt's slow-moving taciturnity, when definitely ranged, was formidable. Nevertheless the quarrel smoldered, and was likely to culminate in sudden violence at any chance. Joe was stubborn to Kelly's private reasoning.

"I don't aim to be trompled by no red-headed woodpeckers," said he.

But the next afternoon a lone horseman came into sight riding across the prairie.

"It's Fitzpatrick, he allus rides humped over like that," a keen-eyed trapper identified him. "What for he wants to lose his ha'r ridin' around in the open thataway?"

"Don't you worry about Fitz," said Halsey. "When he rides in the open, they ain't but jist one reason, they ain't no Injins in fifty mile. That old coot kin smell 'em furtherer than an eagle kin see."

The lone rider rode up leisurely to the halted party, reined in his horse, threw one leg across the pommel of his saddle, squirted a stream of tobacco juice at a passing beetle.

"Howdy, boys," he drawled. "Where away you bound?"

"How are you, Bad Hand," said Kelly, giving the man's Indian name. "We're angling over to Fort Benton. Looked for Sublette at Belle Fourche, but he's not there. Where *you* bound?"

"Lookin' fur you boys," replied Fitzpatrick placidly. "Figgered you might be goin' Benton way. Aimed to cut yore trail." He squinted at the sun. "Let's jist camp and talk it over."

"Where's Sublette?" called Halsey.

But Fitzpatrick did not reply. He turned his horse's head and led the way to the left where a thin fringe of stunted junipers marked a break in the plains, a queer figure, his knees high from shortened stirrups, the tail from his wolfskin cap wagging rhythmically to the stepping of his horse, his long rifle in its fringed case crosswise before him, a buffalo ham tied to his cantle bumping against his thigh. Nor would he vouchsafe a further word, so that the men at length ceased to question him.

Only when camp had been made, the meat roasted and eaten, the horses grazed and secured, the pipes lighted, did he condescend in his own due time to break silence.

"You boys better not go to Fort Benton," then said he. "Yo' better stick to yore own folks."

"Well, we want to, Fitz," rejoined Kelly, "but where are they? We've got to trade somewhere. Where's Sublette? Where's Ashley?"

"Over yander." Fitzpatrick waved his pipe stem vaguely toward the east.

"What they doing there? How far? What's it all about?"

Deliberately, with aggravating indirection, Fitzpatrick at length gave his news.

Trouble. The keel boats of Ashley's second expedition had fallen into difficulties from the start. Big fight with the Arickarees. Lost a lot of men, a lot of horses, a lot of goods. Delay and loss all along the line. Nevertheless Henry, with eighty men, had pushed on to the mouth of the Yellowstone. There he also had been attacked. Lost four men and twenty-two horses. He had begun a post, but this reverse decided him to abandon the post and push on up the Yellowstone. Near the mouth of Powder River he had come upon the Crows and had bought more horses. Sent Provost and a few men over the Rockies to see what they could see. Hadn't heard from them yet. Henry was still up in that country searching for a site for a post. The main expedition was on the river.

"Better let me take you thar," drawled Fitzpatrick. "It ain't so much fartherer than Fort Benton." He cast an appraising eye at the packs piled about. "Good ketch, boys."

But, it developed, the great bulk of Ashley's trade goods had been lost. Quite frankly, from them he could not pay in full for the furs.

"We kin let you have a plenty of powder and lead, and tobacco," drawled Fitzpatrick in his detached manner, "and mebbe a few possibles yere and thar. 'Nuff and more to git on with for another winter. Next season we'll bring yo' back full vally of yore furs."

"Mebbe we won't be yere next season," spoke up someone.

"The old man ain't licked, yit, not if you boys stand by him," proceeded Fitzpatrick, paying no attention to this remark.

"How about Indian trade?" spoke up Andy, thinking of his consignment from Kiasax. "Kettles and blankets and knives and vermilion and such?"

"Purty well cleaned," confessed Fitzpatrick, after a deliberate inspection of this youngest member.

A dead silence fell. Fitzpatrick smoked calmly. The situation was confusing, dismaying, the choice difficult. On the one hand, only a vaguely sensed and not yet developed threat to these men's independence from the fur companies, an equally vague and undeveloped loyalty to an enterprise still amorphous, a demand for a sale on sheer credit, a procedure utterly foreign to their type of thought, a gamble on the integrity, the solvency, the ability, and above all the tenacity of men personally known to few. On the other hand a sure and certain trade, the bird in the hand.

"Ary likker?" someone broke the silence.

"Some," said Fitzpatrick. "A few here's-hows, but no drunks."

He arose, knocking the ashes from his pipe.

"Wall, thar ye be!" said he, and ambled away to his saddle robes, spread out as a bed.

The ensuing discussion began calmly enough, but soon grew heated. It was a hard thing to ask. To wait a year on an off chance, to trust the entire proceeds of a harsh and grinding toil to a vague and indefinite future, above all, to forgo that season of profligate and joyous carousing whose anticipation had been the leaven of hardship. Only profound trust in their own kind, and an equally profound prejudice against all others made it even worth discussion. The affair was emotional. Few besides Kelly were capable of a broad enough view to vision the far-reaching politics of the decision. And on an emotional basis it was finally decided.

Ben Tilton, Joe's red-headed enemy, was from the first loud and swaggering. He'd worked hard for his furs, he'd be damned if he was going to throw them down no rat hole for ary man. They were his, and he'd take them where he could get the most from them. To hell with Ashley, or any other man.

"And first thing yo' know yo'll have a flock of these yere *mangeurs de lard* traipsin' over into that kentry of yores yo' tuk two years to find, and then whar'll yo' be?" cried Joe Crane, instantly and automatically on the other side.

Tilton allowed he'd know what to do with anybody who came traipsing about any of his country.

"Shore!" Joe spat contemptuously. "Yo'd jist fight the whole United States Army ef'n yo' had to!"

"Wall, they's plenty more beaver kentry ain't been teched." Tilton had to recede from his lone defiance of a whole organization. "And I know how to find it. And I won't have to turn into no renegade Injin to stay in it nuther!" he ended darkly.

Again Kelly had to interpose his authority to prevent a clash. But in sheer obstinacy Tilton and Crane made the issue clear-cut. Tilton was going to Fort Benton. Crane was going to Ashley. And as Tilton's turbulent disposition had at one time or another embroiled him with almost every man present, it came about naturally that the next morning, he and the rescued derelict rode off together in one direction, while all the others followed Fitzpatrick to the east.

At the river was already quite a gathering, for others besides Fitzpatrick had been sent out to gather in the free trappers whenever possible and wherever they might be found. A great council was held. Like the Indians, they sat in a circle, like the Indians, they smoked gravely for some time in decorous silence. Then Ashley addressed them, telling them briefly what they already knew. The previous year's expedition unsuccessful. Started with trade goods in keelboats. Almost immediately lost one, containing $10,000 worth of goods, on a snag. Nevertheless, some progress, a post built. This year, no better. Nevertheless, he was not broke. Next year he would be back to establish himself. In the meantime, if they cared to trust him, he would take over their furs. He would pay them, either through credit in St. Louis banking firms, or in trade the following summer. He sat down, and *engagés* passed tin cups of whiskey among the trappers. This was not in trade, but *on the prairie*, as a free gift was called. When all had drunk, Ashley once more rose to his feet.

"I am glad so many of you are here," said he, "for I wish to tell you what I have decided. This new company of ours will not trade in opposition to any other unless that other invades its territory. Let the Missouri Company, or any other, have the whole of the Missouri River Valley. I relinquish that to them. I'm going in for the mountain country." He paused. "And one thing more, I shall make no effort for Indian trade. As far as I can, I shall get my furs from white men."

"Wagh! Wagh!" The trappers bent their closer attention.

Rapidly, Ashley expanded his idea. The Indian trade was uncertain, hazardous, and increasingly based on liquor. Indian trapping was unproductive as compared with the efficiency of the skilled whites. Indian loyalty to one company or trader as opposed to a rival was undependable. Of course, he would not refuse such trade. If Indians brought furs into the posts, he would take them, but he intended to send out no trading or drumming-up expeditions to the tribes. Perhaps the white trappers could get hold of them. Ashley would be ready to furnish the trappers' trade for that purpose. He proposed to send out his own men to trap the fur, but above all, to contract to take the fur of those already on the ground, the free trappers. They stirred a bit uneasily at the first part of this statement. After some hesitation, Bill Williams arose to his feet.

"I got a purty good trappin' district," said he. "Done tuk me goin' on two year to work her out. I'd hate like p'is'n to see yore hired trappers come trailin' in ater me, cleanin' out my fur."

"That goes fur me!...And me!...Me too!" cried several.

"If a man is in any district getting the fur, that is enough for me," stated Ashley emphatically. "No one I have anything to do with is going to interfere. But there are more beaver streams out yonder. There must be. Provost and Henry are already afield. We shall search them out." He looked about him at the attentive, bronzed faces. "All we need to push further west is posts near enough so that the fur may be disposed of and supplies obtained. Is not that so? That is why some of you men have not already gone farther. Is not that so? It isn't the Indians who have kept you back. Well, I shall build such posts. I shall send men to look for the new country. Perhaps some of you would like to be of the number? Ah, I thought so!" Ashley laughed delightedly at the eager lightening of the faces.

"Now," he resumed after a moment, "I need your advice. You know the country better than anyone else. I want your opinion as to where the necessary forts should be built."

Here was a problem! A buzz of discussion burst forth. Two or three talked at once at Ashley. Other small groups argued heatedly among themselves. Strange and unknown names, rough maps traced in the earth by means of sticks, a babel of confusion. Andy, his eyes bright with a sudden inspiration, leaned to speak in Joe Crane's ear. Joe clapped Andy on the back.

"That shines!" he cried. "Tell him about it!" He tried to drag Andy to his feet. The lad hung back, red and protesting, in a panic. Joe uttered a war whoop that stilled the chatter.

"Yere's a boy got the right idee," he told Ashley. He thrust Andy into the circle.

"Why, sir," hesitated Andy, as there was no other way for it. "It was just a thought came to me, that I told to Joe. I doubt it is of much worth. I am but new in the mountains."

"Let's have it," encouraged Ashley.

"I was just wondering, sir, why you should build forts or posts at all."

"Not build forts? What do you mean?"

"I know that is what all traders have done. But why do you need them? You said, sir, you did not think to trade with the Indians, but only with us of the mountains. But that can be done all at once, unlike the Indians, who come in for the trade at any time that suits them, and so must be accommodated the year round."

"Proceed," urged Ashley briefly.

"Why, that is all, sir. But it seemed to me that if you appointed a meeting place in the summer where all could gather, bringing their furs, all purposes of the trade could be accomplished, and the expense and difficulty and danger of maintaining a fort could be avoided. And there is also this, sir, the place of meeting each year could be shifted according to the best convenience of all, for the center of trapping moves here and there. That's what I was telling Joe, sir. I expect it's foolish," and Andy, confused by the silent attention of so large a gathering, dropped back to his place, and slyly punched Joe for his pains.

Ashley considered thoughtfully, then struck his thigh a mighty whack.

"But the lad's hit it!" he cried. His eyes searched for Andy, who, sensing renewed public notice, had disappeared. "Who's that fellow?" he asked. "Where is he?"

"He's the Blackfoot man," answered someone.

"Oh, yes!" Ashley was enlightened. "Well, he has a head on his shoulders. I want to talk to him later. He has the idea. A rendezvous. That's it!"

The assemblage of scattered free trappers was rapidly being drawn into the coherence of that unity which is always the product of an idea. Already the beginnings of ordered resistance fronted the advance of the Missouri Fur Company and the more powerful Astor interests. Though not yet named a definite organization had come into existence, facing east!

They talked at length. Swiftly, minute by minute, the project took to itself the substance of manifest bodily form. The place for the first rendezvous was decided upon. July was to be the time. It was planned that Jedediah Smith should, with an adequate party, push out into the Snake River headwaters to see what the Flathead country might offer. At length came a pause. Ashley caused the tin cups to be refilled. He arose to his feet.

"This is the last drink you'll get until next year, boys," said he. "And here's a toast to drink it to."

He paused and held his cup aloft.

"The Rocky Mountain Fur Company," he proposed solemnly, "and its godfather, the Blackfoot man," he added more lightly.

Chapter 12
The Surround

Andy Burnett, splashing slowly upstream in inspection of his beaver traps, was suddenly overtaken and passed by an old duck and two full-grown flappers. One of the latter almost brushed his elbow. It is not the nature of wild ducks to lose one fear except in a greater fear. Andy looked about him appraisingly, waded diagonally to the bank and tossed, as gently as he might, the long rifle to the cushion of a low bush. Then he reached upward to grasp the overhanging sycamore branch his first appraisal of the situation had disclosed. It was not strong enough to support his whole weight for long, but it sufficed, aided by a quick supple twist of his body, to swing Andy several feet across the grass bank. He looked back critically. Only a scattering of sprinkled water from the legs of his garments marked where he had broken trail. This might be sufficient for sharp eyes. Andy retrieved the rifle and slipped back downstream a few rods. He sat on a log, well within the screen of alders, and listened.

For some time he heard nothing but the rare autumnal half-songs of birds, the rustle of the breeze, and the low chattering voices that always accompany fast water in undertone. Then fitfully, intermittently, his sharpened senses became aware of occasional breaks in the rhythm. Someone was, indeed, wading up the stream. Andy slipped behind his log. Nearly opposite him a small aperture in the foliage looked through to the surface of the water. Here Andy would get a fair sight at the intruder.

But while the latter was yet some distance downstream Andy's intent scowl of attention dissolved to a grave smile of amusement. He reseated himself on the log, laid aside his rifle, filled a pipe, which, however, he did not light. His ears had caught one sound that determined his action. It was the quick high chirk of a pine squirrel. Pine squirrels may only rarely be seen in mid-stream, and in such circumstances, they never chirk.

Andy waited on the log. Now plainly could be distinguished the slow spaced interruptions of the smooth current's flow as the unseen wader made his way upstream against it. Andy's buckskins blended into his background, he held himself still as a graven image. The opening in the leaves was small, so that only for the briefest moment could the eyes of one passing align themselves with it. Nevertheless he was instantly discovered. He grinned again in appreciation as the young Indian checked, then turned to the shore, thrusting aside the screen of leaves.

The newcomer was a young man of pleasing and open countenance, naked save for breechclout and moccasins, of about Andy's own age, which was in the early twenties.

"Welcome, Kiasax," the white boy greeted his friend in the Blackfoot tongue. "You have sharp eyes."

"Greetings, I-tam-api," returned the Indian. "But if you will sit in plain view, you must be seen."

"I heard your signal. What do you hear? Are our people in the valley?"

"I am alone. I have come to seek you, my brother."

Andy produced from the buckskin sack his burning glass, and with it proceeded to light the tobacco in his pipe. Kiasax watched with enormous respect. The tobacco well alight, Andy passed the pipe to his friend. For some moments the two smoked in silence, turn and turnabout.

"The buffalo have not come," the Indian at last rewarded Andy's patience. "There are none. Our young men have looked far to the Cold Maker's country, to the country whence comes the Sun. Sai-yi has made medicine. There are no buffalo."

"That is bad," said Andy.

He did not need to be told how bad it was. To the buffalo the Indians looked for their very livelihood. On its flesh they depended for their winter subsistence, on its skins and sinews for their houses, their clothing. Lack of it meant poverty and privation, perhaps even famine if the not infrequent scarcity of other game happened to coincide. The season was already shortening. Soon winter would close in.

"All signs are bad," continued Kiasax. He arose from the log, hunted about for a moment, returned with a small black and green cricket cupped between his hand. Andy knew the insect. Its Indian name was He-Who-Points-Out-the-Buffalo. Kiasax took it gingerly between his thumb and forefinger and held it out before him at arm's length. It squirmed about frantically, seeking to escape. Finally the little creature gave it up, ceased struggling. Its long antennae quivered, lifted slowly. The young Indian watched it, his lips parted in complete absorption. The horns waved about, came to rest, pointing straight up.

"You see!" cried Kiasax. "It is always thus! Are we eagles that we can seek the buffalo in the skies? Ai-ee!"

He cast the cricket from him with an abrupt gesture, reseated himself. For some moments he remained sunk in gloomy abstraction.

"I have come to seek you, my brother." He roused himself at last. "There are those who say this is because of you. They say the Sun has withdrawn his favor. He has darkened his face because of you. He is angry because the Blackfeet have taken white men in their country. Sai-yi makes much talk. He has made medicine. He says his medicine tells him these things. His heart has always been bad. He has not liked it that the Sun has favored you."

Andy nodded. He had been well aware of the old medicine man's jealousy.

"Some of the young men follow his medicine," went on Kiasax. "They have struck the post. They have taken no scalps. The young women will not look at them."

"That is bad," said Andy thoughtfully. He arose abruptly. "Come, Kiasax, we must talk of this."

The trappers' camp, in the willow bottoms, was unoccupied except by Pai-ó-to-ki. Joe had married her the winter before, *the pretty little fat one* as he had called her. Now she kept his lodge with great pride, made Joe extraordinarily comfortable. Joe on his part treated her with a rough, rather shamefaced tenderness that was entirely genuine. Kiasax did not deign to take Flying Woman into his confidence, but Andy briefly detailed to her the situation. She was much distressed, covering her face with her garment, for she understood instantly the choice she must make should her white man be banished. Nor did Joe Crane and Kelly, when they came in, fail to appreciate the full significance of the affair.

"We've got to do one thing or the other," Kelly summed it up. "Get out or go at once to the village and see this out. If we stay here and do nothing about it, they'll be down here to murder us in no time."

Joe cursed heartily the necessity that took them from the beaver streams just at the height of the fall trapping. It meant the premature finish of the whole season, for by the time the powwow was over it would be too late to return. However, his annoyance did not blind him to necessity. Five days later the three trappers, Pai-ó-to-ki, and Kiasax, with all their worldly goods, including their traps and fur bales, rode into the bottomland where straggled the Blackfoot village. Their reception was mixed. Some greeted them joyfully, but from others they received black glances or met covered faces. Pai-ó-to-ki erected Joe's lodge near the riverbank. Kelly and Andy left the disposal of their own camp until later, but when they returned their lodge also stood in place.

The three white men at once sought out old Mat-o-suki, the head chief. He received them politely, formally. They smoked. Mat-o-suki evaded all questions.

"There will be a council," he told them.

They left his lodge uncertain whether he was for them or against them. This was disconcerting, they had relied on him.

The drum began to tap in summons. There was a stir among the lodges. Many of the warriors bad begun to deck themselves at once on news of the white men's arrival. Others delayed until the last minute. But slowly the circle filled, each man taking his place with his own society. There was no compulsion of attendance. But when Mat-o-suki at length lighted the ceremonial pipe, each sub-chief, looking down the line of his fraternity, could count full ranks of all those at present in camp—the Buffalo Bulls, the soldiers, The Buffalo With Thin Horns, Those Who Carry the Raven, the All Crazy Dogs, the Dogs. All were there, and in full membership, all but the Mosquitoes. These youngsters were not sufficiently considered to take part in so important a council. The three white men were given places on Mat-o-suki's left. This was no bad omen, or at least it indicated their case was not pre-decided.

After the pipe had passed, the business of the day was taken up. This was ostensibly the lack of buffalo and what was to be done about it. Numbers of men spoke. Each was listened to in silence and with decorum, without marks of either approval or disapproval. Any interruption would have been considered very bad form. Later in history this custom was to lend much false cheer to missionaries, who mistook it for endorsement of what they said.

But the agenda shifted from the ostensible to the real object of the council when Sai-yi arose to speak. The medicine man, or more strictly the Sun Priest, had been eaten by a secret jealousy of these white men's prestige as encroaching too nearly on his own. He had not dared give this jealousy rein. The signs of the Sun's favor had been too strong. He dared not, in the first freshness of their wonder, stand against the plain portents. But now the withdrawal of that favor, as evidenced by the present buffalo crisis, gave him his opportunity. It was the old, but ever new, story. No administration can be overset in prosperous times, no administration can stand in adversity, even miracles can lose the potency of novelty. The full freshness of wonder to the beholder is gone forever at the moment the first airplane's wheels leave the ground.

The Sun had withdrawn his favor from his people. The most powerful and reliable medicine was powerless to unveil his face. Why was he angry? What had his children done that he should frown upon them? Their consciences were clear. In no ceremonial of respect had they failed. He, Sai-yi, as Sun Priest vouched for the full performance of his duties. He called upon Mat-o-suki to bear witness that in no respect had the people sinned. These were a virtuous and a pious people. Sai-yi enumerated one by one the basic precepts of conduct. One must be brave and cunning in war. One must not suffer his women or his children to want. One must never betray a friend. One must resent and revenge insults. One must venerate and obey the old. One must fear and propitiate the Bad One. One must not fear death. He paused and added impressively, one must defend the hunting grounds against encroachment. In what had they failed, that the Sun should be angry? He paused again for a dramatic half-minute. The Blackfeet were the enemies of the white men. Never had they permitted the white men in their country. The Sun had shone upon them with his favor. Now they had broken this trust. There were no more buffalo.

Mad Wolf went on at length, detailing the glorious deeds of the Blackfoot confederacy in defense of this principle. He told of fights against the Flatheads, the Assiniboins, the Arapahoes, the Crows, the Shoshones, others of their hereditary enemies. He told over one by one the whites who had attempted the forbidden territory. For the first time the three listening learned authentically the fate of men who had disappeared. Sai-yi ended in a grand and boastful and patriotic description of the defeat and massacre of the Missouri Fur Company expedition under Immel and Jones, on the Yellowstone River. He sat down, wrapping his robe about him. The case was opened.

After a suitable pause, Kiasax took the floor.

He began by recounting the deeds and portents that led to this first exception to the ancient rule. The killing of the White Buffalo by Andy, his power to call down the Sun and make him small to light his pipes and his fires, the great fight with the Assiniboins in which he and his two companions had of their own accord returned from escape to rescue the Blackfeet, to war on their side. Kiasax was very dramatic and detailed in all this, but it was, after all, what everyone knew, and was the obvious case for the defense.

"It is true that we have said in council that the white man shall not come in our country," he argued. "But these are not white men, but our brothers. We have said in council that they are Blackfeet, like ourselves. One has taken one of our women to his lodge. We smoke the pipe under the same tree with them and walk the same path to the spring."

Sai-yi, his face eager with malignancy, could hardly restrain himself for the ceremonial pause.

"My brother says these are not white men but Blackfeet!" he shouted, extending his arm. "He says that though their skins are white their hearts are red. How are they red men? Has any one of them gone forth to fast alone? Has one of them lived hungry until the Sun has showed him the vision of his medicine? Look upon their breasts. Will you see there the medicine bag? Which of them has danced in the Medicine Lodge the Four Days' Dance of Endurance? Look again upon their breasts! Will you find there the scars? What made them Blackfeet? Words! Words said, not in council, by me, Priest of the Sun, but idly, in the wind. Would such words make of one of our young men a warrior? You speak of Sun-Power. It is well known that with every white man comes a cloud of evil spirits. Who knows the power of those spirits? Or in what disguise they come? These men come into our country. They trap our beaver. They take them away on the horses we give them. And we give them also our beaver, that we have trapped ourselves, that they may bring back to us from the white men, there in the country whence comes the Sun, rifles and cloth and many things which the white men have given our enemies but not ourselves. What do they bring back? Words! Next year! And next year we will give them more beaver, and they will not come back. My brother says they have done the things he tells of for love of the Blackfeet. I think the Sun has veiled his face from his children because they are fools!"

"Tarnation!" Joe muttered at this. "That's bad!"

Kelly shook his head. The failure of Ashley's expedition to bring in the trade, and their entrusting to him their own and the Blackfeet's furs on credit against next year, were beginning to look disastrous.

"I am the Sun Priest," Mad Wolf cried. "I have made medicine, and I see the sky overcast with clouds. I see no buffalo. He"—he stretched his arm toward Andy—"let him use his Sun-Power. Let him fast and see his vision and learn his medicine. Then let him show us the buffalo! If his heart is red, let him show us the buffalo! I have no more words."

The three white men, returned to their own lodge and agreed that the situation had become serious. Sai-yi by no means had matters all his own way. There were many genuinely friendly to the trappers, many still in superstitious dread of their Sun-Power. But the opposition was strong. Inevitable jealousies, primitive distrust, envy, and above all the childlike susceptibility to the appeal of mere change—all these enlisted themselves on the side of the Sun Priest. So close was the deadlock, so violent were the emotions engendered, that the whole controversy came not far from civil war, or a schism in the band. But Mat-o-suki spoke in decision.

What Mad Wolf alleged as to the reasons for the withdrawal of the Sun's favor might or might not be true. His accusations of embezzlement of the season's furs might or might not be true, but the season before I-tam-api had brought back the trade as promised, so now they carried guns, and the white men had never spoken with forked tongues. However, in one thing Sai-yi had uttered straight words. The white men had never become red men through the usual ceremonials and tests. Nor had they each discovered the secret ingredient of his medicine, as the red man does. Obviously, the next thing in the program was to rectify these omissions. After that the question of Sai-yi's challenge to find the buffalo.

"So I reckon we'll have to go starve in the timber two-three days," said Joe resignedly. "I reckon I kin see a vision in less'n that."

The first rite they were to undergo was very simple. Each would inhabit a pole-and-branch lodge, built apart for the purpose, without food and without drink for four days, by which time the giddiness of exhaustion should cause them to see visions. In one of the visions the Sun would reveal to each the special ingredient of his own personal medicine. This might be almost anything—the leaves or twigs of some plant, the powdered bone of some animal, the feather of some bird, anything at all—but it became to that man sacred, and he must carefully conceal its identity and carry some of it always with him in a pouch slung about his neck. Of its especial uses Andy was to learn more thereafter.

Kiasax and some of his young friends accompanied Andy to his lodge of retirement. From its apex they hung a buffalo skull, a kettle, and various furs and robes. These would be left as offerings to the Sun, and until they had rotted into the ground no man, Blackfoot or other, would ever disturb them. Andy was touched to the heart, for the value of these offerings attested his friends' affection for himself. Kiasax wanted to contribute his new rifle, bought in the last year's trade, by far his most precious possession, but from this Andy dissuaded him. The young Indian finally substituted an eagle crown, scarcely less valuable in his eyes. Andy himself, on inspiration, contributed the four Assiniboin scalps Joe had insisted were his. He hated the things and was glad to be rid of them. The magnificence of this sacrifice greatly impressed his Indian companions. They left him with a warm glow at his heart. Whatever the enmity fostered by the Sun Priest, these were true friends.

Andy lived as patiently as he could through the four days. Nothing remarkable happened. Hunger did not bother him. He became very thirsty indeed, but not to the point of light-headedness. Since his mind was not exalted in anticipation of visions, he had none. Most of the time he lay on his back, staring idly at the buffalo skull and the other things swaying gently above him. He tried to puzzle out where probability had led the buffalo but gave that up. He wished he knew more about their habits of migration, but if Joe and Jack Kelly, who knew the topography of the plains, were at a loss, how could he make an intelligent guess? Kiasax had not proved helpful. Kiasax told him that the great herds poured out of a hole somewhere in the south and went north to the Cold Maker's land where they were all eaten by the gods, a fresh batch each year. This was comforting from the conservation standpoint but had slight bearing on the present situation. He slept as much as he could. Even the urgency of the crisis faded in ineffable boredom.

The afternoon of the fourth day wore on. At sunset the drums began to tap. Andy heard footsteps approaching. And at the last minute an idea came to him. He sat bolt upright, examining the inspiration. It might work.

At the council fire the fraternities were already seated, waiting. Andy was led to his place. Joe grinned at him.

"Ary visions?" he asked ironically. "Git yore medicine? No?"

"Not a vision," replied Andy. "Only think I could think of was that I wanted a smoke."

"Wall, that'll do."

"What?"

"Tobacco, that's yore medicine." He grinned. "Mine's a good slug of likker, but I don't know whar I'll git it." He composed his face as Mat-o-suki approached to present the small buckskin pouches which each was to fill with the secret ingredient. The council circle waited in silence while the three white men withdrew for this purpose. Joe and Kelly seized upon the first things that offered. Andy accepted the suggestion as to the tobacco. All three took the chance to get a drink of water, which was strictly a bootlegging operation, but nobody was watching.

"I don't know what good this hocus-pocus is going to do us," confessed Kelly, "but we'll play the game and hope for the best. At least it gains time, and anything may happen."

At the council circle Andy found that Kiasax, as his adopted brother, had been appointed to instruct him in the proper procedure. The two squatted together in the center before a flat ceremonial dish. In it the young Indian reverently deposited a number of prescribed substances—common earth, sands of different colors, the ashes of specified plants, portions of the bones of certain animals and birds. All these had their symbolic meanings, which Kiasax explained in a low voice. Then he turned his back, the warriors veiled their eyes. From the medicine pouch about his neck Andy sprinkled in some of his *secret* personal medicine. Under Kiasax's instruction he stirred the mixture.

Sai-yi advanced to the center of the circle. It was his function as priest to interpret from the resultant combination of colors whether or not, for the moment, the beneficient influence or the evil influence was in the ascendant. If the medicine was bad, the mixture would be carried outside camp and buried, no one touching it, and the enterprise in hand abandoned. If it was good, it would be parceled out among the warriors, who would, during that particular enterprise, wear it as a charm. This put the game strictly in Sai-yi's hands. Unhesitatingly he pronounced the medicine bad.

But Andy would not be defeated without a struggle. He boldly challenged Mad Wolf's decision on the ground that this was white man medicine which a white man only could interpret. It was a flimsy argument, but a sufficient rallying point for his numerous friends. Long and passionate discussion. Again the threat of civil war or schism. The issue was clean-cut, conservative against radical. Mat-o-suki looked troubled. Andy seized the moment of confusion to arise to his feet.

"Brothers," he began, "Sai-yi says this medicine is bad. Sai-yi is Sun Priest and knows medicine. But he does not know my medicine. I say it is good. There is one way to find out." He paused a long dramatic minute, looking from one face to the other, then shot his arm to its full height, pointing toward the northeast. "The Buffalo are there!" he cried. "I see them there, like leaves of grass! Let my brothers journey there and see. If it is not as I say, then my medicine is bad."

He spoke with an air of confidence he was far from feeling, but so strongly simulated that his hearers were impressed.

"How far, I-tam-api?" asked Mat-o-suki at last.

"Very far," replied Andy.

"Five suns?"

"Farther."

"Ten?"

Andy calculated rapidly.

"More."

"But that is in the land of the Assiniboins!"

"That is so, O Mat-o-suki."

A low murmur swept the circle. Bold enough in war and raid, the Indian, accompanied by his women and children, is much like a dog, brave in his own country, but timid when out of it. And the hunting of the buffalo required the presence and assistance of all the band, male and female, old and young. Andy seized the moment of hesitation. The buffalo are there, he stated emphatically. Take it or leave it. Plenty or starvation. The Sun has spoken. Are his children brave men or women? After which Andy too indicated he had no more words and sat down.

"How come you think the buffalo are thar?" Joe asked him, low-voiced, as the discussion begun.

"Don't," answered Andy briefly.

"Good lad," approved Kelly. "Gains time."

They voted at last to make the test. The issue was decided by the very hot heads among the younger men who had formerly been most urgent against the trappers. Assiniboin country! War perhaps! Scalps! Glory!

"Well, so much to the good," commented Kelly in relief. "I hope to heaven we run on buffalo. If not—"

"Well look that trail over when we come to her," said Joe cheerfully. "But look yere, son, seems like to me yo' ain't much of a lawyer. Or mebbe yore a tarnation good one. You made big talk about white man's medicine bein' different from Injun medicine, and the whole pint of the argument, as I made it out, was that we're Injuns and not white men."

"I thought of that." Andy grinned. He waved a hand to call attention to Mad Wolf's figure striding angrily to and fro. "And I'd lay a small bet that he's kicking himself because he has just thought of it, too."

Artistic balance would require that they journey to the country of the Assiniboins, and there find the buffalo to the complete discomfort of Sai-yi. But things rarely work out that way in real life. As a matter of fact, they came upon the buffalo not ten days out, which, as to the controversy, settled nothing. Sai-yi's adherents called attention to the obvious fact that the buffalo were not as far as Andy had said they would be. Andy's partisans pointed out that they were in the general direction the white man's medicine had indicated, the exaggeration of distance was trifling. They had a little the best of it, for here were buffalo! And that was the important point.

They camped in the bottomlands well back from the herds. Andy was to see his first buffalo hunt on the grand scale, for now the year's supplies were to be laid in. It was quite a different affair from the ordinary and occasional expeditions for fresh meat. Andy had taken part in a sufficiency of those. He was by now an excellent buffalo hunter, according to the methods of both races. He was skillful in stalking and so selecting his terrain that his *shooting from a stand* often resulted in six or eight beasts down. He learned from Kiasax that in open country, and the game disturbed, it was often possible to approach within close range by imitating the clumsy motions of a young bear or the sneaking, prowling gait of the wolf, all this without any disguise whatever. He had, with a half-dozen or so of the younger men, taken part in buffalo *runs* from time to time. These were most exciting, and somewhat dangerous. His rifle was too light and too long for the best results at this form of the sport, he had none of the large-calibered pistols often used for the purpose, so he adopted the short strong Indian bow. Kiasax made him one, and a sheaf of buffalo arrows, with wider blades than the war arrows, the quicker to *bleed the buffalo down*. To ride at top speed over that rough and boulder-strewn prairie, seamed with dry water courses, pock-marked with holes, would have been exciting enough and dangerous enough in itself. But to do so in clouds of dust, dodging back and forth among stampeding thousand-pound animals blinded and maddened by the contagion of herd fear, was either the height of exhilaration or the height of terror! The rider would take no thought of his going, his whole attention was concentrated on picking his animal and in driving, at arm's length, his short broad-bladed shafts as deeply and as accurately as he could into the side of his quarry. For the rest he depended on the power of his *medicine* and his pony. It took a headlong reckless boldness, an entire disregard of possible consequences of which the modern steeplechaser or fox hunter knows nothing.

That more hunters were not killed or maimed in this heedless rush was due more to the horses than the *medicine*. The pony it was who, amid all the excitement and distractions, kept his head, watched his footing, checked and turned aside from the impassable, tense to recognize the obscure, almost imperceptible, movement that preceded a lunge by the maddened buffalo alongside which he raced almost within touching distance, and to leap sideways out of danger. He needed no bridle, no directing rein. A touch of the rider's leg, he identified the object of pursuit and followed it tenaciously in all its twists and turnings without further guidance. It was hard, fast, intelligent work, and performed with the same eager zest every polo player or cowboy would have recognized. Disregarding legend, the Indian pony that could, in one *run*, kill four buffalo was considered very good. A *six-buffalo horse* was remarkable.

Naturally a good buffalo pony was highly prized. It was never turned out at night with the main herd but was tethered close to its owner's lodge.

But, as Andy soon discovered, this, as the big hunt of the year, was to be conducted on very different lines. The control of the tribe passed from the hands of the chiefs. The fraternity of Dog soldiers took charge. They designated the camping place, far from any chance of disturbing the herd, pitching a lodge in the center which became their barracks and which they inhabited as a body, apart from their own families. Their wood, water, and food were here brought them by the people. They imposed and preserved the most rigid and arbitrary discipline. Without their express permission no one was allowed to leave the confines of the camp. Even excursions to the near-by stream for water, to the adjacent thicket for wood, were made under their escort. The boys grazed the horse herd only when and where designated. Kiasax told Andy that if anyone so much as stepped foot out of lines, his dogs and ponies would be shot and his lodge cut to pieces. No one did so. It was true martial law.

Each day, the most skilled hunters rode forth, not to hunt, but to arrange conditions for the hunt. It was desirable to kill as many buffalo as possible. In order to do so, it was necessary so to distribute the different components of the main herd so that the hunting of one band would not alarm and drive away all the others. A general stampede would end matters in a single day. This was undesirable. To that end various furtive and subtle enterprises were undertaken. Discreet and distant and brief appearances, the burning of grass, circles far to windward so that a faint scent should move but not too greatly alarm. The mass was skillfully maneuvered, herded, without its becoming aware of that fact. The appointed headhunter, Pi-ta-makan, decided these things, but from his opinion, appeal could be taken to the Dog soldiers.

When matters were arranged the entire camp was up before dawn. The hunters, on their best ponies, rode upstream under the protection of the cut banks. The women and old men and children held themselves in readiness for a summons by messenger when they should be needed for the butchering. Some three or four miles above camp the party of hunters dismounted in the bottomland, there to shiver as patiently as possible in the nipping air while Running Eagle and a few chosen men advanced cautiously to spy out the country, to determine whether or not conditions and distributions had changed. The afternoon before the situation had been ideal. A segment of the great herd were frequenting a narrow valley with many lateral ravines. But this morning they had moved out of the valley to the tops of the tablelands adjacent. Pi-ta-makan considered that they could not be hunted there without serious danger of disturbing the main herd. Several of his men dismounted, sneaked through the grass on foot, and at judicious intervals, showed brief glimpses of themselves, so brief that they were not identified as human beings, but long enough to catch the buffalo's attention. Thus, partly because of this delicate and gingerly herding, partly because of natural drift back toward water, the herd was returned to the valley floor. Running Eagle and his assistants slipped over the hill, back to the main body of hunters.

Immediately, on his signal of permission, the company split to right and left. When near the unsuspecting herd, one by one small squads, each under its captain, or corporal, made their way to designated stations, until the quarry was entirely surrounded on all but the windward side. The white men had been separated, Andy had been assigned as one of five under the leadership of Kiasax. Firearms were considered to be too noisy. Most of the Blackfeet carried bows. A few were armed with lances, but these latter were mostly Dog soldiers to whom a certain percent of the kill came as a right. The individual hunter preferred arrows because by them he could prove ownership of dead buffalo.

When all had taken their places, Pi-ta-makan rapidly swung in his own party to close the gap, and almost as the startled buffalo raised their heads to the tainted breeze, lifted his voice in signal for a concerted charge.

The buffalo, turning to flee downwind, away from their first alarm, brought up short before the fluttering yelling mob at their faces. They wheeled sharply to the right, about-faced to the left. They were surrounded. In confusion they made short individual dashes, now this way, now that, ended by huddling, crowding toward the center. The herd was *milled*. Around and around the horsemen rode, discharging arrows at a few yards' range, dashing in to thrust deep the long lances. Dust rose in clouds. The buffalo bellowed. The riders yelled. The younger and more daring swooped fairly into the press of brown bodies, wheeling away like falcons before the lunge of the maddened bulls. The harassed buffalo crowded, threatened the nearest of their tormentors with short vicious dashes which, however, they relinquished as soon as they found themselves alone. A number broke through the ring and lumbered away. They were not followed. To do so might alarm the main bodies over the hills. They could be seen toiling heavily up the slopes, their tongues hanging, their flanks heaving, their eyes wild in the terror of their escape.

It was all over in ten minutes, though so crowded with action was each second that the time seemed to Andy much longer. Over a hundred dead buffalo lay crowded in an area not a hundred yards across.

The triumphant hunters sat their ponies while coolly Running Eagle made a detailed survey of the field, counting the kill, estimating how much time the women would require taking the robes and meat. He glanced at the sun, waved his hand in dismissal as he decided there was not time for another surround that day. Some of the younger men, who had been watching him with leashed eagerness, looked disappointed. But there was no appeal. They drew aside and dismounted.

The women, riding and leading horses, streamed up the valley in ragged procession. As they arrived, they flung themselves from their ponies, darted here and there among the dead buffalo, identifying the arrows of their men, establishing volubly their claims. Some carcasses showed two arrows, or more, of different hunters. The position as respects vital spots was supposed to decide ownership. Voices arose in shrill dispute. Not only the claimants but every woman within hearing took part. The men, seated aside, their ponies' halters in their hands, disdained even to be aware of these gusty quarrels. Usually the bickering died eventually into resentful mutterings, but occasionally Pi-ta-makan intervened. He alone had remained mounted. When it seemed to him that the quarrel had lasted beyond all decorum and efficiency, he thrust his pony into the group, leaned over a moment in scrutiny, stretched forth his coup stick and lightly touched one of the disputed arrows. That settled it.

Already in the grass not so very far away, on the hill edges, lurked the gray wolves, their ears pricked, waiting impatiently. Coyotes and the little kit foxes weaved restlessly about. Overhead wheeled the ravens, gathered the vultures. Sharp-eyed young warriors had long since departed for commanding hilltops where they lurked in the grass, spying for a possible enemy informed of their presence by this unavoidable advertisement of the killing. They were still in what they considered Blackfoot country, but the land of the Assiniboins was just over the horizon.

The women worked with the speed and skill of long practice. Shortly, their immediate tasks finished, the first of them, leading their burdened horses, were straggling back toward the encampment. By sundown the valley was deserted by all humankind, given over to the wolves and foxes and birds. From the dusk, gathering like a mist in its cup, arose a pandemonium of croaks, snarls, growls, shrieks assaulting the quiet of the evening sky.

Thenceforward the meat camp was very busy, a place of hard work. The jerky must be cut and dried, the pemmican of pounded meat and dried berries and marrow fat prepared and poured into its parfleche containers, the skins fleshed and dried and given the preliminary dressing which would preserve them until the winter's leisure, the sinews and other valuable by-products dissected out. Running Eagle and his chosen assistants were afield, sizing up the best conditions for another surround. Skilled and trusted scouts ranged cautiously and far against the menace of enemies. Nevertheless there was time for feasting on fresh meat and for dances and jollifications. It was a light-hearted time. The grim specter of famine had been exorcised. No matter how hard the labor of the day, evening found no one too tired to take part.

There was nothing ceremonial or symbolic in the dancing. It was for fun. Andy had never heard of a cotillion dance, a *German*, nor, in all probability, had most of the world. But here, had he known it, he was seeing just that thing.

The dance was begun by one woman. After a few steps she selected a partner. They danced together, separated, and each picked other partners, *but not for themselves, for each other!* And so on until all were afoot. At a signal those together at that moment seated themselves and the man kissed the woman. The humor of the situation was to get together those least likely to want to kiss one another.

A variation was the eating dance. The couples, when they separated, selected their partners by bringing them something to eat, as the later civilized dancers of the cotillion offered favors. Thus at the end each had something to eat in his or her hands, which at a signal must be consumed.

This constituted the sole refreshment for the evening, a sort of supper dance. The more incongruous the offering to the recipient, the better the fun. An old toothless squaw mumbled a large bone, a notoriously heavy eater looked disconsolately at a tiny morsel of tripe.

There were only two conventions. All must take part, all must be accepted in good humor.

In the daytime, while the women worked at the provisioning, and while Pi-ta-makan and his hunters were abroad, the men amused themselves with horse racing and other sports. The races were more for speed and agility than for endurance. The contestants, starting from a stand, dashed to touch a certain tree and back to the starting line. There were considerable jostling, collisions, some bad falls at that tree. Or they ran to touch a heavy horizontal pole, suspended breast high, and back, whereby some, who could not check in time, were swept from their saddles. Or they must run to where rawhide strips had been laid parallel, ten feet apart, hop the pony completely into the area thus enclosed, and return. If the pony did not place all four of his feet within that space, or if a single hoofmark showed beyond the farthest strip, he was automatically disqualified.

Andy had not much success against these skilled horsemen, but he joined heartily in the laughter. He excelled, however, in the wrestling, and was unequalled at throwing the knife at a mark. Indeed, so remarkable had become his skill at the latter art that his accuracy was supposed popularly to derive from the Sun.

But with all this light-hearted gaiety the rigid camp discipline continued to be strictly imposed. The lodge of the Dog soldiers still stood in the center as its symbol. Some of the youngsters, especially those inclined to courtship, were coming heartily to hate the sight of it. They would be delighted when at last it should be struck.

Within the next week or so they accomplished two more successful surrounds. The wants of the band were fully supplied. Each family had its desire. A certain percentage had been given the Dog soldiers, a certain further percentage had been set aside for the widows and orphans. Pai-ó-to-ki, Flying Woman—Joe's *little fat pretty one*—and Nit-o-ké-man, the young wife of Kiasax, gave Andy and Kelly to understand that their share also had been cared for. At the same time they lectured Andy on his bachelor estate. They did not quite dare tackle Kelly.

"We have taken your robes for you, I-tam-api," Nit-o-ké-man admonished him, "but that is not our business. Our business is to take the robes for our own men."

"I am sorry you did it," protested Andy. "I was not hunting for myself. I can kill enough for myself in the mountains. I do not need the robes."

"It is fitting that you have robes," Nit-o-ké-man interrupted him severely. "You are a Blackfoot warrior and you must have what is fitting. My heart is lifted, the heart of Pai-ó-to-ki is lifted, to do this thing for you."

"Ai-ee," agreed Joe's wife.

"But," Nit-o-ké-man was emphatic, "you should have your own woman to make warm your lodge."

Andy recovered himself, and since human nature is the same everywhere, he told his tormentors that if he could find another Nit-o-ké-man, another Pai-e-to-ki, he would follow their advice instantly, but there was no more such. Which of course sent them into shrieks of laughter, under cover of which he fled.

Joe did not find the suggestion impracticable.

"There's a lot more purty ones," said he, "aside my woman and Kiasax's. Look about you. Use yore eyes!"

"But I don't want one!" protested Andy. "Why are you all pestering me? Why don't you get after Jack, here?"

"Jack?" Joe laughed shortly. "He's sot. When it comes to squaws, he's one of these yere misanthrops." Joe's vocabulary sometimes included the most improbable words, which he invariably mispronounced. "Yo're too young to git that away."

Suddenly Andy felt that there was a conspiracy against him. He was beset. A pressure seemed to be closing on him from all sides. Every time anybody looked in his direction, he thought uncomfortably to feel an expectation. The men seemed to him to be withholding approval of him until he, as a Blackfoot warrior, should establish himself with a family. As for the young girls, with whom he had joked so freely and familiarly, he imagined calculation in every eye, and he took to scuttling around corners when a bevy of them hove in sight. This was in his imagination, of course, but his imagination was vivid and was, subconsciously, deeply alarmed. Andy's woman-time was not yet come and the deep instinct back of his destiny stirred in his defense. He had a horrible and vivid dream of himself at bay, like a shaggy old buffalo bull, and the girls swirling around and around him shooting arrows at him.

Kelly was at first enormously amused, then he took pity on the lad.

"Don't pay any attention, they're just joking you," said he.

He talked at length in a sensible vein, and Andy agreed with him, and even laughed at himself. But however his mind assented, his deeper instincts refused. This refusal took the form of a new restlessness.

Yesterday this life with the tribes from which other white men were barred had seemed to him fully satisfying. Suddenly new possibilities called. They stirred beneath the threshold, then rose one day to recognition as an idea.

"Jack," he said to Kelly, "don't you think it would be fun sometime to take a trip out west?"

"You'll never find better beaver country than right where you are," Kelly pointed out.

"No. I suppose not," Andy had to agree. It took him some time to outflank this entirely common sense objection. "Might be a good idea between seasons to look around, though." He returned to the attack. "We'd always come back. I'd hate to leave Kiasax and the rest. Perhaps he'd come with us."

"What for?" asked Kelly bluntly.

"I don't know," confessed Andy.

"Look here," Kelly put it to him squarely. "How could you be any better off than you are? You are a trapper. You want beaver, and you want beaver to sell so you can make money. Well, here you are. You are in the best beaver country I ever heard of. You have it practically all to yourself. No other white man is going to trap it out for you. You have a good and honest market within reach. You are laying up money in St. Louis. You have firmly established yourself with a people unfriendly to all other whites, what more do you want?"

"I don't know," muttered Andy.

"And what better can you expect? What is there out further west? You don't know that country, nobody does. There may not be a beaver in a thousand square miles of it. There may be no game even. What do you know about the Indians? If you do find fur, what are you going to do with it? Isn't that so?"

"I guess it is," Andy agreed reluctantly.

"Well, what is your idea?"

"I don't know. I reckon I'd just like to go see."

"So would I," said Kelly unexpectedly.

"Huh?" Andy was startled.

"So would I," repeated Kelly. "There is no sane reason for doing so, but you and I are the same kind of damn fool."

Andy stared incredulously. The older man was entirely serious.

"How about Joe?" he asked at last.

"Oh, Joe!" Kelly was contemptuous. "He'll holler his head off, but he'll go."

Suddenly Andy's spirit was filled with the wild exultation known in its purity only to the small boy on the eve of the glorious fourth.

"We can always come back," he said in answer to an inner reproach. "To Kiasax and the others," he explained.

"Sure—if we get back," said Kelly.

Boylike, Andy was all for starting at once as soon as they had returned to the base camp and could collect their outfit. But Kelly shook his head. Winter was coming on. And he pointed out, certain obligations must yet be met. There was the matter of the postponed pay for the furs the Blackfeet had entrusted to them last season, the trade for which Andy was yet to deliver. In his excitement Andy had forgotten that. The expedition must wait until after the rendezvous. But after the first small dash of disappointment Andy found the prospect of another winter with his friends, another spring season in the rich beaver streams, not unpleasing after all—with the Great Adventure warming the horizon of the immediate future.

It was agreed, on Kelly's insistence, that nothing be said to Joe as yet.

And Flying Woman? Andy had not thought of her.

Kelly shrugged. That would take care of itself when the time came.

"We can always come back," Andy repeated to himself with a faint stirring of dismay.

Sai-yi had subsided, at least for the time being. No opposition can stand against prosperity, and the ponies were laden. The subject seemed forgotten.

Only Joe was a little curious.

"What was the idee, Andy?" he asked. "How come you knowed the buffalo was here?"

"I didn't, I tell you," Andy repeated. "I just shook the dice on it."

"Wall," said Joe, "yo' shore got luck. That's all I kin say, but yo' allus did have luck." He cogitated, then a new thought occurred to him. "But didn't yo' overplay yore hand?"

"In what way?"

"When you told them the buffalo was up in the Assiniboin kentry."

"Oh, that!" Andy laughed. "Well, I'll tell you. I remember when my grandmother found out something my grandfather had forgotten to do or something he had done that she didn't like, and began to get after him about it, he'd always try to head her off by digging up something *she* had done and starting in to scold her about that. It never fooled her any. I can see her now. She would tap the arm of her chair with her thimble and fix him with her eyes—she had the snappingest black eyes!

"'Look here, Gail Burnett,' she would say, 'don't you try to distract attention by raising a dust in the northeast corner!'"

Andy laughed again, and there was a touch of tenderness in the laughter.

"I remembered that. I thought that even if there were no buffalo the Assiniboins might raise so much of a dust in the northeast corner that Saiyi and his lot would forget all about us."

"Wagh!" exclaimed Joe, profoundly admiring.

Andy arose and strolled to the edge of the traveling camp. A group of girls crossed before him, making bright eyes. He did not even see them. He dropped the butt of the gun to earth and crossed his elbows on its muzzle. Below him lay the dark fringe of timber marking the bottomland. From it rose the plain to its clear-cut edge against the sunset sky. Steady-eyed he gazed into the golden glow. Like the swoop of a falcon his aroused imagination leaped on over the curve of the earth—to the West!

Chapter 13
The Raiders

The ambition and enterprise of General Ashley in over-leaping the old fur country and establishing himself in what was then the extreme west marked distinctly a new fling forward. The grounds he occupied with his new trading company were already known, to be sure, but only to the scattered free trappers, the mountain men. Now, in some mysterious manner, the mere presence of the Rocky Mountain Fur Company seemed to release these men's energies for further exploration. To be sure as yet the company operated only informally under that name, and its occupancy consisted merely of its annual rendezvous and the activities of its hired trappers. The country was just as wild, just as remote as it had been. Nevertheless a new restlessness stirred in the wind.

Andy Burnett, Joe Crane, Jack Kelly, returning with the annual *trade* to their friends, the Blackfeet, were all afire with it. The only whites privileged to the Blackfoot country, which was rich in untrapped beaver streams, they should have been satisfied with their lot. As to fur, they could certainly hope to do no better elsewhere.

But at the rendezvous a first half-determination was hardened by a chance-met Crow chief with whom Andy made friends. He had a knack of making friends with Indians, mainly because he genuinely liked them. For that same reason, they genuinely liked him. As was natural, being full of the subject, Andy inquired as to the Crow's knowledge of the country west of the Divide.

"That," signed the Crow, "is the country of the Utes and the Shoshones. It is not the country of the Crows."

At first, he was discouraging, but discovering that Andy's enthusiasm was proof, he unbent to a little practical advice. Andy sought out Joe and Kelly.

"He says he knows where there are lots of beaver," he told them. "It's on a river west of the Divide, toward the south. He does not know where the river goes, he was down there once with a war party. But he says there are lots of beaver, more beaver than he ever saw anywhere before. He says you don't need traps to catch them, you can get all you want with a club."

"I've heerd them tales afore," grunted Joe, who was still hanging back in favor of his comfortable lodge and his Blackfoot wife and the sure rich gains of the Blackfoot country.

But Kelly went with Andy to talk to the Crow. The latter elaborated the details. He smoothed a place in the sand, and on it, with a pointed stick, drew rough maps to illustrate what he told them. Here was the Big Yellow River—the Missouri—and here, far away, whence came the Sun, was where the River of Soft Sands left it.

"The Platte." Kelly nodded.

The Crow swept thisaway with the flat of his hand.

The Platte branched, then forked again. After some discussion of localities and landmarks, Kelly at length identified one of the forks as probably a stream known in its upper reaches as the Sweetwater.

Very well! One followed up the Sweetwater until it became small, until it disappeared. Here were no streams, only the wide prairies with the mountains far to right and left. And then one came to a small trickle, that grew as it took in other trickles, until it too was a stream. This was the Siskadee Agie. If one followed its course the mountains fell behind. Thus Andy and Kelly, studying attentively, heard first of the stream later known as Green River, and of South Pass through which was to pour the great westward migration of the covered-wagon days.

Kelly was impressed. The Rockies directly west of the Blackfoot country were high and rugged. The Crow's description was detailed enough to seem authentic. Worth trying, anyway. And now that a real objective had been defined, Joe's reluctance gave way little by little until, at last, he became the most enthusiastic of the three, which was typical of Joe. He wanted to start out at once, brushed aside Kelly's common sense as to the rashness of winter travel, grumbled at the decision to wait until spring.

They returned to the Blackfeet with the proceeds of the fur. Next spring, even before the last snow had melted, they were on their way.

The separation had not been easy, though the Indians did not actively oppose the expedition. It had been sufficient to tell them that the whites' *medicine* had called them to a long hunt. No one went against his medicine. Of course they would return. Nevertheless, Flying Woman, Joe's wife, went about with her blanket across her face. Kiasax and Nit-o-ké-man were grave and sorrowful. At odd moments Andy's heart was gripped by a pang sharper than he would acknowledge, even to himself. But he told himself, he was coming back. This was just an expedition. Depression could be but momentary. It could not persist against the flooding uplift of the anticipation of new things.

They rode away at last toward the southwest. A sharp and nipping wind of late winter or early spring stung the inside of their nostrils. A thin veil of snow still dimmed the earth, but through it glowed the pale green of new grasses. Horned larks, heads low, ran across the bared spaces. Overhead were exultant far cacophonous cries of geese flying north.

It was not an easy journey. The grass was still too short for full strength. The horses weakened. The country, while devoid of the rugged terrors of the higher mountains, nevertheless presented difficulties enough. For a time, they threaded their way through sandstone buttes and cliffs, striped in strange colors, cut into domes and precipices, heaped in confusion, a labyrinth, a maze, without trees or shrubs, a barren land. Beyond that they entered upon vast plains of sagebrush. The banks of the rare water courses were white with alkali, the water almost undrinkable. Horses and men sickened from it, became gaunt and weak. The grass was sparse, and grew only in bunches here and there. Game was scarce, an occasional band of antelope, a grouse or so. They were even glad of the smaller rodents. But the most wearing enemy was simple space. Before them, the gray sagebrush dipped smoothly to the lowest point, and rose smoothly again to the skyline. It seemed that one should cross it in a few hours. It took days. Plod as doggedly as they would, they seemed to be getting nowhere, to be caught in a sort of treadmill.

Nevertheless at last, and unexpectedly, they came to a beautiful valley, sunk below the general level, in the bottom of which were groves of veritable trees. Through the trees they discerned flashing waters. They descended into the valley. The stream was wide and clear, flowing over a rocky bed. Though thin snow still covered most of the ground's surface, here and there the sun had melted it away in patches.

"Buffalo grass!" cried Joe, delighted. Here was heartening nourishment for the horses, for the dry buffalo grass cures, over the winter, into rich forage. "And sweet water!" he cried again, as he scooped up a sample in the hollow of his hand.

They camped for several days, recruiting their animals' as well as their own strength, for there was game aplenty in the bottoms. It was a pleasant place, but across the west the mountains ran in what looked to be an unbroken white wall.

"Told you that Crow was lyin'," said Joe, suddenly pessimistic again. "Now we got to wait fer the spring thaw, jist like I said. Never git through them snows."

"Well, we can pull up closer, can't we?" said Kelly.

They traveled up the course of the Sweetwater. The way was easy. At most times, the valley was several miles wide, and again it narrowed to a matter of yards. But never was their progress barred, or even seriously impeded. Were it not for the steady tumbling of the stream, and the deepening snow and the colder air, they could not have told that they were climbing at all. The high mountains had disappeared, save for occasional glimpses, below the rising folds of the terrain.

The nights had turned bitter cold, the horses were again eating the bark of the sweet cottonwood. The Sweetwater had dwindled to a narrow runnel. The snow deepened. Over its surface had been frozen a glittering crust, through which the horses floundered and plunged. The Sweetwater had been lost beneath it too, and when at last they had won to wind-swept high prairie, whence the snow had been blown, the Sweetwater had disappeared.

For a long time they rode across the rolling prairie country, the frost rime over the snow and thick on the low bushes. The plains, to the eye, seemed nearly flat, but the slow, labored breathing of the horses indicated a relentless ascent, which a glance back confirmed. And then, suddenly it seemed, they began to see things ahead. An immense plain dropped away before them, rolling in undulations, broken by buttes and flat-topped mesas and isolated towers and temples and domes, pale mauve with the atmosphere of distance. Kelly stopped his horse.

"We're on the western slope of the Divide, boys," he said.

They exclaimed in wonder and delight. It seemed incredible that they should thus easily have crossed the Rockies. The Crow chief had certainly been right thus far. They pushed on joyously. Now they were descending, though the grade was barely apparent to the eye. But the horses breathed easily, and the surface of the snow was softened at noon. By nightfall they had reached a flowing spring. There was no fuel, but there was grazing of a sort for the horses, so they stopped. By evening of the next day they had come to flowing water, and wood, and a ledge of rimrock where Andy shot a deer. Their camp this night had fresh meat and a fire, and so they were comfortable and could relax and talk it over.

"We must be on the headwaters of the Siskadee Agie," said Kelly. "I suppose it must flow into the Pacific. Think of that!"

"The Crow did not know. He had gone down it only a short way," said Andy.

"I hope he's right about the beaver," said Joe.

They smoked for a time.

"That's the easiest mountain pass I ever saw," observed Kelly after a while. "You wouldn't know you were in one. *Like a prairie*, that's what the old fellow said, wasn't it? You'll see a lot of travel through here some day, folks wanting West."

"And we're the first!" cried Andy.

Kelly grinned at him.

"How about the Crows?" he suggested.

"Yes," Joe spoke up unexpectedly, "and how did they git to find it? Trails made by buffalo—or nobody-knows-what walkin' on four legs, afore them, of these yere prehistoric monsters they talk about." He settled himself on the broad of his back and puffed tobacco smoke straight up. Joe was in a dissertative mood. "More I see of it, more this bein' first business looks funny," said he. "Jack's right about it. This is the easy way. Time'll come when there'll be a lot of people use this pass. You could take a wagon through it right now." He paused to contemplate the image he had evoked. But even the mood of his fancy could not have foreseen the plodding thousands of the Oregon Trail, nor beyond them the glitter of lights and puffing of locomotives as the Overland puffed slowly up its serpentine grade.

"Well, we're the first white men, anyway," insisted Andy, stoutly.

"Shore!" agreed Joe. "And when the old, original hemastodon come on the tracks of the gyasticutis ahead of him, he probably said, *Wall, I thought I was ahead of everybody, but yere's that old cuss! Wall, anyway, I'm the first critter with ten-foot tushes that ever come through here.*" Joe sat up suddenly and pointed his pipe at Andy. "Yo' kin allus be first of something ef'n yo' want to be, son. I bet yo' twenty-five year from now some fat squirt or other will be braggin' his head off because he's the first white man to come through yere with a plug hat on! You see!"

Next day they followed the creek down. It joined a larger stream. They followed that. The country was still high and arid, but as they descended, the spring arose to meet them. The snow softened, thinned, disappeared. New grasses showed a pale verdure. The topmost tips of the occasional cottonwoods and willows and box elders were tinged with green, as though sprinkled by some passing sower from above. The soil deepened and softened.

Joe and Kelly, who were riding ahead, stopped in examination of a patch of sand. Andy joined them from the rear.

"Thar yo' be, Andy. Thar's yore first." Joe indicated numerous hoofmarks half-defined in the soft earth.

They examined them with care, circled wide for prints in soil more favorable for the reading. It was necessary to determine whether the signs were made by a herd of wild mustangs, or by animals under human control. If the latter, they must be wary, for the disposition of the people of this country was unknown.

"Loaded horses," said Kelly shortly, then, after a short search farther, he was able to point to a distinct moccasin track. The three gathered close about to see what they could make of that. After a moment, Joe threw back his head and laughed aloud.

"Pore old Andy!" he commiserated the latter. "Yo' ain't even the first white man! And this fellow's a greenhorn at that!"

"How do you know a white man made it?" Andy protested.

"Take a good look," advised Joe.

Andy did so, but had finally to shake his head.

"An Injun," explained Joe relishingly, "gits on his horse from the right hand side. So do you, so does I and Jack and ary other old mountain man. Why? Because it's the handiest every way. But most white men git on from the left hand side, like this fellow done. Never seen an Injun do that. Use yo're eyes, bub!"

"I never thought of that," muttered Andy abashed.

"Oh, yo' got one-two things to larn yit, but yo're comin' on." Joe chuckled, making the most of his triumph, for by now Andy's plainscraft left him few such opportunities.

"I'd like to know who's ahead of us." Kelly was a trifle put out. "There's quite a crew of them."

"Wall," said Joe, "I reckon we'll just have to ride and find out."

They caught up with the white men below another fork, where the main river had grown to considerable size. To our voyagers' relief, the party proved to be of their own men, trappers whom they had left the autumn before. They greeted one another boisterously.

"Glad it's you, boys," observed Joe as he dismounted. "I was afeared it mout be some of Pitcher's outfit. Who's yore boss?" he inquired, recognizing several of Ashley's men.

But it seemed they were all on their own, in a way of speaking. That is to say, Ashley had supplied them their necessities on credit, but that was the extent of his risk. He was to be repaid out of the proceeds of the trapping—if any. Ashley was too deeply involved, his new company was as yet too precarious to justify him in sending out exploring expeditions. But he was more than willing to encourage private enterprise. The Crow chief had talked to others besides Andy and his companions.

Fitzpatrick proved to be, if not the boss, at least the old he-coon of the outfit, as someone expressed it. He and Jedediah Smith had collected together these volunteers. Most of them were mountain men, a few had been members of Ashley's expeditions, recruited in St. Louis, and so had slighter experience. It was one of these latter who, had mounted his horse from the left. But all were of the eager and adventurous type, and at this moment, all were bubbling with enthusiasm in a manner unusual to the ordinarily sober-sided frontiersmen.

The Crow chief had not lied. The valley of the river and its tributaries swarmed with beaver. The felled cottonwoods lay like windfalls. The dams and the conical beaver lodges fairly crowded one another. It was entirely possible to get together quite a respectable fur catch merely by shooting, and right in broad daylight at that! As for trapping—it was simply a case of how many one could handle! And plenty of country for everybody.

"That's right," Fitzpatrick corroborated, in answer to evident though unspoken doubt. "You'll see for yourself."

This party had left the mouth of the Big Horn very early, and had had the devil of a journey getting through as far as Wind River. There they had left Jed Smith, a half-dozen of the original party, and the weakest horses.

"They'll move over later as far as the Sweetwater," said Fitzpatrick, "and wait thar for us. Jad got clawed by a b'ar last year and he ain't too pert. But we're workin' on shares, and they kin trap the Sweetwater and git the stock strong for when we go out. Want to come in with us? Or do you aim to go on your own hook?"

"We'll come in," said Kelly promptly, without waiting to consult his companions. "Don't you see?" he explained to them later, "We'll get our share of the fur just the same, and if we don't want to go back with them in the fall, our share will be taken care of. Leave our hands free."

That season was a hilarious one. The main camp moved slowly down the river, shifting location as the main streams and the tributaries were trapped of the first cream of an absolutely virgin country. In the morning, the men separated, each hunting and trapping the territory of his choice. There was no friction, for there was indeed enough for everybody, and to spare, and again to spare, and one place was as thick with beaver as another. All one had to do was to set the traps, and none too carefully at that. These were unsophisticated beaver. If one had to set foot ashore, all one had to do was to splash water over his trail, perhaps scatter a few drops of *castrum*. By the time the last trap was set, he could return to the first, certain of a catch. And it was actually a fact that from the cover of the willows, these expert riflemen collected many a pelt by means of a bullet below the ears. This suited Andy, who loved nothing better than to exercise his skill with Knock-'em-stiff, the old Boone gun. When a man had accumulated a backload, he hurried to camp with them, dumped them down before the skinners, and hurried back again. The hunting was as near as that!

The majority were afield, but a few were detailed each day to keep camp, to skin and care for the fur, to make up the packs. They took turns at this.

Within a week, they had taken four packs! It was unheard-of, unbelievable! And beaver selling at six dollars the pound! It was not wonderful that this was the best-natured body of men ever encamped together, that spirits ran high, that quarrels or even differences of opinion were absolutely unknown. The thin air of altitude was like wine, the sun shone through cloudless days, the spring came on apace. No man was ever tired. From the long, hard day, he came in at dusk fresh as at dawn. The campfire under the cottonwoods shone bravely. Beaver tail, venison ribs, an occasional duck or goose. Tall yarns, jokes, songs, brave hearts. Every man was a fine fellow. Sound, sweet sleep, and a new glorious day!

It was amazing how the packs grew. At this rate they would have all the horses could stagger under in less than a month. How surprised Jed Smith would be to see them come ridin' in so far ahead of the expected time! And what a story to tell him!

At first, they made camp as for a hostile country, arranging it in the form of defense, driving in the horses each night, and posting a strong guard. But time went on. In all their wide wandering afoot in pursuit of the beaver, not one had come across Indian sign, new or old. It was a lonesome country. They seemed to be the only human beings in all its vast extent. And the very exhilaration of success gave them confidence, for where everything was so right, how could anything go wrong? Fitzpatrick and the other old-timers were too wary to abandon all caution, but it seemed senseless to take the animals off the rich bottom grasses, and four men should be a sufficient guard for them.

If the sentinels had been sufficiently vigilant, this reasoning might have proved to be correct. It was just before dawn, at the quietest time of the night. The nocturnal birds and animals had finished their business and had ceased crying. The breeze from the plains had established its equilibrium of temperature and had died. The voice of the stream still murmured on, but at the lowered note that comes with the chill of the mountains. A light mist arose from the river and spread over the bottomlands. It was the suspended hour of the twenty-four, when men asleep sink into the deadest unconsciousness, and the faculties of men awake lie at their lowest.

Suddenly, the quiet was broken by a burst of shrieks and yells and the rapid beat of many galloping hoofs. The trappers, snatched from deep slumber, sprang up half-awake. Out of the mist swept a whirl of dim horsemen, bending low over their ponies' necks, waving robes, yelling at the tops of their voices. The younger, less experienced white men, dazed, ran about in bewilderment, shouting questions to which nobody paid attention. The mountain men seized their rifles and fired hastily into the whirlwind of shadows. It was all over in an instant. The dim figures swept in and out in a wide circle, a few arrows whizzed-floo-*plunk!* floo-*plunk,* they were gone. And with them, the horse herd. The white men stood there still but half-awake, listening to the diminishing beat of hoofs, the yells of triumph growing fainter with distance.

———

Here was a pretty situation! The newcomers to the country were wild with rage, the older mountain men were more disgusted than angry. They kicked the dying fire together. No, Fitzpatrick sarcastically reassured an excited Ashley man, there was no danger. The Shoshones would not come back. Why should they? They had everything they wanted. The mountain men repressed the excitables. Maybe the horse guards were asleep, maybe not. What difference did it make? That wasn't the point. The thing was done, wasn't it? Quit hollering about what might have been, and let's see what to do. Andy admired again, for the dozenth time, the directness of these men's processes.

Some were vehemently for following the Indians at once. Fitzpatrick withered them.

"That's what they expect," said he. "That's just exactly what they're ready for. Never do what the other fellow expects you to do."

"Well, what are we to do? Lie down and take it?" cried someone. "And what good is our fur, less'n we kin git it over the Divide?"

"Wall," drawled Fitzpatrick, "we come fer beaver, didn't we? And yere's plenty beaver. We got our traps and our rifles and our possibles. The season's comin' on. Pretty soon the fur will be past its prime. If we got any sense at all, we better go right ahead ketchin' beaver. If it comes to that, Jed Smith's got hosses. We kin cache our take and go back and git them when the time comes. And we can git more horses from the Crows. Ought to make it afore snow time. It's gittin' on to daylight. Let's cook up some breakfast."

"Well, I don't like the idee of ary Injin stealin' me afoot thisaway and doin' nothin' about it," grumbled the Ashley man, unconvinced.

"Me neither," agreed Fitzpatrick, "but beaver ha'r is only prime for two months, and Injin's ha'r is prime all year round."

There was sense in this, and even the hotheads came to it. They continued with the trapping, and as the take continued undiminished, they gradually recovered their good humor. Nevertheless, each man had tucked away in his inner consciousness a grudge against the Shoshones, and later, should opportunity present itself for getting even, you may be certain it would not be neglected. That the victims of the reprisal might be quite innocent of—and ignorant of—the original raid would have nothing to do with it. A Shoshone is a Shoshone. It is but fair to add that this system of responsibility by a whole tribe or a whole race for the crimes of the individuals was a tenet of Indian policy also. The eventual deadly hostility between red man and white, culminating in the great wars from the middle of the century on, had its inception in just such small incidents as this. Although the trappers under Fitzpatrick had accepted the situation with the usual common sense directness of the mountain man, that did not prevent a considerable volume of grumbling around the campfires. Nobody relished the situation. These Shoshones had made a lot of unnecessary hard work and trouble.

So when, after numerous private consultations, Fitzpatrick and Kelly offered a suggestion, it obtained an instantaneous acceptance.

"The beaver are prime yet for a few weeks," said Kelly, "and we could probably make up a few more packs. But here's the point, it's a long, hard journey back to the Sweetwater where Jed Smith is keeping the horses. And when we get there, we've got to go on and find the Crows. We've got more weight than Jed's horses can carry. And the Crows might be most anywhere. We'd have to get to hear of them somehow, and then trail them down, and trade for horses with them. It might take the rest of the summer."

"So you reckon we ought to quit and start out now?" queried someone. "Why can't some of us go for horses and the rest—"

"No," interrupted Kelly. "What I want to say is that Shoshone country is no bigger than Crow country."

"And it's just as easy to find Snakes as Crows," drawled Fitzpatrick.

Kelly elaborated the idea. In this high and semi-arid country, the trail left by the raiders and their booty would be plain, and would remain so until obliteration by next winter's snows. The Shoshones would have fled rapidly for a while, but they would not go forever. Eventually, they would circle back to their village. Why not go get the horses? By now, the Snakes would feel secure, and would have withdrawn the scouts that undoubtedly had been detailed at first to watch the white men's movements.

One and all, the men acclaimed the idea boisterously. There was not a dissenting, not even a questioning, voice. No one pointed out that they numbered just fourteen—to go out against a nation. Couldn't ary mountain man lick ary ten Injins that ever stepped? Nor that they proposed invading an unknown country afoot. Couldn't ary mountain man take keer of himself in ary kentry this side of hell? Anyway, they told themselves, they intended to come back, and these yere Snakes ought to be taught the lesson that they could not monkey with white men and get away with it. Save trouble next year. They chuckled and slapped one another on the back. The swarming beaver were from that moment forgotten, for here beckoned adventure, and not one of these men could ever resist that call. And not one of them even paused to consider the sheer audacity of the enterprise.

Next morning they were up at daylight, busy as the beaver themselves. After some search a suitably dry location was found in the middle of a thicket. They set to work digging a hole. In lack of spades they used their knives and sticks, sharpened and hardened in the fire. The earth they laid carefully on spread robes and skins. When the excavation was some eight or nine feet deep, they ran a tunnel or *drift*, slanting upward, of sufficient size to contain all their furs and the other items of their equipment. They lined the drift with cut poles, thatched its interior with grass. When all the goods had been packed therein, they closed its opening with another thatching and with more willow poles. Then they dumped back the earth to fill the original hole. The surplus was carried to the river. After which Joe Crane and Fitzpatrick, working alone, did a most artistic job of reconstruction, such as a modern builder of museum habitat groups might had envied, replacing grass, twigs, young growths, obliterating the smallest traces, until they were satisfied that even the keen-eyed Indians could see nothing amiss. Then, to make the job complete, they moved upstream a quarter mile and as carefully arranged misleading artificial indications.

"Don't want to overdo it," muttered Fitzpatrick. "Jist a leetle yere and thar. Now let 'em dig! That's what I call a good cache! Now everybody remember the landmarks."

They set forth that instant. There was no sense in delaying, even though the day was well advanced. Each man carried his rifle, his *possibles*, and a store of dried meat. That, with the addition of two traps for the whole party, was all. Every other item of equipment and property had gone into the cache.

The trail, as Kelly had surmised, was as easy to follow as a highroad. There had been no rain, and fifty or more horses leave plenty of indications. After the first rush the Shoshones had scattered widely, as was the Indian habit, to confuse immediate pursuit, but later had reassembled. The trail led out over the arid plain. Five days of steady marching swung it back to the mouth of that very affluent down which the trappers had journeyed in the spring. From here on it followed up the Green River. And from here the indications were that the thieves had concluded themselves safe from pursuit. Their camping grounds were now so close together that the white men, though afoot, easily reached one from the other in a day. It began to look as though the Shoshones were getting near home.

The pursuing party moved with more caution. All day they lay concealed. At dusk they set out, marching steadily until dawn. The moon was full, and its clear, white, and abundant light showed the trail plainly. Fitzpatrick and Joe Crane moved far in advance of the main party as scouts. Up to now the trappers had, after due and careful inspection of the country, ventured an occasional shot in supply of fresh meat. Now they fell back on their reserve supply of jerky, helped out by what could be taken in the two traps. Thus they marched for three nights more, in silence, but with unabated high spirits of anticipation, like small boys toward a melon patch.

Shortly after midnight of the fourth night Joe Crane arose from the shadow of a boulder to bring them to a halt. They gathered eagerly about him.

"Jist ahead, boys," Joe told them, low-voiced, "the whole kit and caboodle. About a mile."

They followed him out of the riverbed to the top of the bluffs. Andy's heart pounded in his breast. For what seemed to him an interminable time he followed the man ahead of him in the single file. Then his nostrils caught the faint acrid smell of wood smoke. At the same instant Joe turned to sign for added caution.

They crept to the edge of the bluff. Fitzpatrick was there, lying on his stomach, looking over.

The moon was full and high. The floor of the valley was plain to see. In a bend of the river stood the lodges of the village, stark white and black in the moonlight. The embers of scattered fires glowed red. Some hundreds of yards beyond the village, and upstream, grazed peacefully a large horse herd. Beyond the herd again was a thick dark fringe of heavy brush.

For some time the trappers lay flat, gazing down, registering carefully all the details of this quiet scene. Then at a signal from Fitzpatrick they wriggled cautiously backward, rose to their feet, retired farther to the shadow of a great rock, gathered close in council.

They were fourteen, and they were about to go afoot against the power of a tribe. In case of repulse or premature discovery they had no stronghold, no reinforcement to which to retire. Their own slender chance of success depended on the smooth interworking of a whole series of fortuities, each one of which was itself a minor miracle. One cannot blame Andy for a shortness of breath, nor for a bit of exaggeration in the eagerness with which he bent his head to listen to the whispering.

But Joe and Fitzpatrick and Kelly and the older mountain men seemed to discover in the situation nothing but a cause for congratulation.

"Jist laid out fer us!" Joe chuckled.

Rapidly the plan was explained. They would steal past the village to the cover of the thick brush fringe. Under its concealment it should be possible to get right up close to the horse herd. Then each man was to get hold of a horse, mount, and at a signal stampede the whole herd right through the village and off downriver and away! Just like that! All that was necessary was to get by the village without arousing the Indians—or their dogs, then to crawl up to the horses without alarming them, then to get hand on one, to scramble aboard bareback, and to stick on in the ensuing wild rush. If a dog barked, or if one of the half-wild ponies became frightened of the sinister crawling figures, or tore loose from its would be rider, or if the latter failed in his leap for its back—or any of those things—well, nobody seemed to think of that, nobody apparently but Andy. He thought of it aplenty, and his tongue was dry as wood in his mouth.

"How about the wind?" he ventured to inquire, remembering the whiff of wood smoke he had caught a while ago.

"Sucks upstream—in the bottoms," whispered Joe. "All right? Well, let's git a-goin'."

They slipped by the Indian village successfully, keeping close to the bluffs, circled to the left until under the cover of the brushy strip. There they drew together again as a group, whispering their exultation. They tightened their belts, slung their rifles across their backs by means of rawhide thongs they had prepared for the purpose.

"When yo' git you a hold of a hoss, even ef'n it's by the tail, *you hang on!*" Joe advised Andy earnestly. "No matter what happens, don't let these devils git you."

Andy nodded without speaking. This was an occasion when, in his case, the Blackfoot phrase was literally true, he had *no more words*.

They crept into the open on their hands and knees. The nearest horses threw up their heads, pricked their ears forward in inquiry of the crawling shapes. One stamped his hoof and snorted, whereupon all the herd awakened and crowded together. The trappers had counted on this, that their crawling figures might be mistaken for wolves, in defense against which horses crowd together in a compact body, heels out. The commotion aroused the dogs in the village.

The moment was at hand! The trappers leaped to their feet, stooped low, ran as quickly and directly as they could to the nearest bunch of milling ponies, trying to get within grasping distance before the animals could identify them as men, and so make off. On that success depended. Andy was frankly frightened. The chances looked so slim to his imagination that he finally switched that faculty off completely. He concentrated on the moment, and therefore his impressions were both confused and full of astonishments. He was astonished that he was actually so close to loose horses at night, he was astonished they did not run off the moment the men got to their feet. He was astonished that he was not brained by the hoofs aimed viciously at him as he ran in, and he was supremely astonished to find himself actually grasping a handful of mane, to discover that he had somehow scrambled successfully across the pony's bare back. At that a wild exultation surged up in him. About him plunged and jostled and snorted the horse herd. There was a good deal of noise. He found himself yelling with the rest. Suddenly the stampede surged, started. Andy was with it, part of it. He had no control, naturally, of the animal he bestrode. Though he was by now an excellent rider, he found that in these particular circumstances sticking on was about all he could think of. Across the tossing heads and heaving backs he made out here and there the figures of his companions swept helplessly, like himself, in the ungoverned torrent of the stampede. In the back of his mind flitted a wonder whether all had been as lucky as himself.

Down through the middle of the Shoshone village poured the cavalcade of maddened ponies, urged to frenzy by the yells of the trappers. They were blind with panic, regardless of obstacles. Lodges went down, fires were scattered. Andy had a brief impression of heaving and tossing, of screeching women, crying children, of dogs dashing frantically, of warriors shouting and bewildered. He saw these things across waving manes. He caught the flash of a rifle or two, and spared a fleeting admiration for the bold horseman who could unsling and discharge his piece. Andy was wholly occupied with the highly desirable feat of staying atop his flying mount. Then, as suddenly, the village was behind them. They were thundering down the valley, scrambling up the flanking hills, streaming out over the spectrally moonlit plain.

For an hour the horses ran wildly. The riders had no means of controlling them. But at last the headlong speed began to slacken. The panic was fading and the long run was beginning to tell. Shortly they fell into a jog trot. Several of the veteran mountain men succeeded in looping thongs about the jaws or noses of their mounts, and thus gaining management. These helped the others. Shortly the men were in command. They rounded in the strays. Fitzpatrick pushed ahead as *point*. Two others swung to right and left as flankers. The remainder brought up the rear as the *drag*. Instead of a disorderly mob, the affair became a directed herd. They headed south. By this time each had made his count. Not a man was missing!

The night paled. It was morning. All that day they pushed ahead as rapidly as the tiring animals could travel. Undoubtedly some of the horses must have dropped out during that frantic stampede, and undoubtedly these strays would be picked up, in time, by the Shoshones. It behooved them to burn the trail. At sundown they rested but were off again by midnight. Traveling thus, with the minimum of rest, they were back at the cache by the evening of the third day. Thus ended one of the most fortunate and one of the most audacious raids in the history of the West.

"Well," remarked Fitzpatrick, surveying the wearied horses snatching eagerly at the rich bottomland grazing. "That's what the gineral would call purty good business. What percent profit would you call that, Jack. Anyway, we larned them Shoshones!"

———

They had been out twelve days of very long hours each, on short rations, and nine of them afoot. The horses must eat, but these men of iron had no leisure to feel fatigue. While the ponies recuperated in the bottoms, men stood vigilant guard, other men scouted to the north against the remote possibility of close pursuit by the Shoshones, the rest of the trappers worked hard all night uncovering the cache, preparing the packs for a departure at dawn. By sunup they were in the saddle and away.

Obviously it would be madness to retrace their route up the Green River. By that way the avenging Shoshones must come. So they took up a little tributary toward the east. When they came to the end of that, they struck boldly across an undulating desert country toward a horizon impossibly remote. There was no grass, no wood, no water, no game. There was no known destination. All they had was the sun by day and the north star by night. The sun was scorching hot, the night turned bitter cold. At nightfall they stopped for a single hour, then went doggedly on again. Near morning they unpacked. Until daybreak the horses were privileged to sleep, if they would. But they wandered restlessly, pawing the desert sands. Already they were gaunt and thin, for though the hours of actual travel had not been many, they were hours long and close-packed with the famine of necessities. They moved slowly, stumbled. Every man realized fully that but one more day was allotted. Not one voiced that knowledge. Straight forward into the unknown. Stout hearts.

By sunrise the sagebrush had begun. Just before noon the country lifted to hogbacks and swales. The slopes became steeper, and by that the more toilsome. As they neared the crest of one of them, one of the ponies lifted its head. The others pricked forward their ears. A chorus of neighing rose in the thin air. And every man lifted his voice in a wild yell of triumph, and perhaps of thanksgiving. They topped the rise. In the hollow below them meandered a thin fringe of green willows and cottonwoods. Across the way rose remembered buttes and tablelands. They had reached the upper waters of that tributary of the Green down which, early that spring, they had entered the country. South Pass was but just over the skyline.

That night they drank deep of the clear fresh water, feasted on new killed venison. The horses rolled and grazed knee deep in the grass. A few days later, *fat and sassy*, very much on the swagger, they rolled proudly into Jed Smith's camp on the Sweetwater.

Jed was well, quite recovered from his wounds. His horses were in good shape, and his men. But with him also was a fresh expedition under Sublette, down from the Big Horn, waiting there to see whether Fitzpatrick could report anything worthwhile.

Worthwhile! The campfires blazed far into the night while the tale Was told. Look at that for beaver! And plenty more. Easy travel. Simple as the back of your hand! All but the Shoshones. Damn the Shoshones! But I reckon we made them come! Won't be so brash in the future! What's the news outside?

"Pretty good," said Sublette.

Henry had gone downriver with a boatload of furs from the Big Horn. Expected to return by winter, bringing supplies with which he would head over this way.

What next? They talked it over. Smith and Sublette were on fire over the stories of the new country. It was still early. By moving promptly they could get across the Divide. But how about these furs? They must be got out somehow. Fitzpatrick had an idea. Why go 'way across the plains to the Missouri?

"Bet a man could float down the Sweetwater to the Platte," said he.

Nobody knew, but it was worth trying. So they shot him buffalo and built him two bullboats, and Fitzpatrick and a few men loaded aboard the furs and set blithely off down the river in their cockleshells. They had no slightest idea of what lay ahead of them, whether of shipwreck in unknown gorges or defiles, or of death at the hands of unknown peoples. They carried with them the entire wealth of the company, the loss of which meant the loss of a year's hardship and risk of life. Nobody bothered about that. As a matter of fact the party did win through, but not in the bull boats. Those cockleshells made the length of the Sweetwater all right, but near its confluence with the Platte were wrecked in the roaring rapids of a gorge. Some of the furs were lost, but a proportion were recovered and carried overland, more than sufficient to discharge the debt to Ashley for the outfits and supplies advanced in the spring. Still it is something to play better than even with any game as stern as this! And the stories there were to tell!

Andy and Kelly and Joe Crane turned away as the second bull boat floated from sight.

"Wall, thar we be!" remarked Joe. "We shore done things this summer. Fat doin's, and hard doin's too. Times when my belly thought my throat was cut. Times when it felt like I'd wore my legs down six inches a-walkin'. My old lodge is a-goin' to look good to me. I'm jest goin' to lay back and smoke and look straight up and let leetle Pai-ó-to-ki bring me things to eat. Look good to you, Andy?"

Andy was embarrassed.

"What is it, bub? Spit it out," said Joe, looking at him curiously.

"Don't you think it would be fun..." Andy hesitated. "Well—Jed Smith and Sublette are going back. We didn't more than begin to look over that country. In the spring they'll be starting out for somewhere. By the time we get here they'll be gone. Let's go back with them."

Joe took his pipe from his mouth and stared in astonishment.

"Who, me?" he asked at last. "Not any! I'm a married man!" he said virtuously. "And how about Kiasax and the rest of them? Don't you aim to see 'em?"

Andy was distressed. He launched into confused disclaimers. Next year, of course...

Kelly laughed.

"My boy, you go with Sublette," he advised.

"I don't want to quit you. I wouldn't for a moment think of it. Only I sort of hoped that perhaps—"

"Why, that's all right. We'll be back in the spring. I know how you feel. Joe and I have been partners for years, but we don't follow each other around like squaws. That right, Joe?"

"Shore!" Joe veered unexpectedly.

"You'll certainly come in the spring?" insisted Andy.

"Sartin shore. We'll be there. But I kain't see what fur you want to winter down thataway when you got a good warm lodge and fat eatin' only just across the range."

"I don't know," said Andy. "I suppose it is foolish, but—"

"Thataway floats yore stick," said Joe.

Chapter 14

Wandering Foot

General Ashley, undaunted by the failure, or the very partial success of his first expeditions, had undertaken yet another. With keelboats, well laden, he started up the Missouri. As far as Fort Atkinson all went well. There he transferred to pack horses, and with them headed for the distant Rockies where should be awaiting him his own trappers and the free mountain men, with their season's catches. The general prayed fervently that these should be large and of fine quality. The furs he had managed to salvage the previous year had no more than sufficed to keep his credit going. He was deeply involved. If he was to be privileged to carry out his plan of an opposition, in the mountains themselves, to the advancing forces of the American Fur Company, he must gain some measure of immediate success.

Indeed the general seemed born to misfortune. Indeed his partner, Henry, utterly disheartened by yet another disaster, was on the point of giving up in disgust. Certainly no man had made more gallant sorties into the vastnesses of the Yellowstone or been more discouragingly or more repeatedly in disaster. He was ready to sell out and quit the fur business. Later Ashley did buy him out! On him and Sublette rested the great moral responsibility they had assumed, to hold the Rockies for the mountain men.

It was touch and go. At prevailing prices a single good season would put the new company firmly on its feet. But another failure would be complete.

Ashley was no novice on the plains. He was wise in Indian lore. His orderly habit of mind, coupled with his military training, had led him to organize and discipline his marches into a precision no band of free trappers had ever voluntarily assumed. This was more necessary in the former than the latter case, however. Ashley had recruited a large proportion of his men by means of advertisement:

TO ENTERPRISING YOUNG MEN

The subscriber wishes to engage one hundred young men to ascend the Missouri River to its source, there to be employed for one, two or three years.

Which brought to him the boldest and most adventurous, but not always the most experienced. Therefore the informal, tacitly understood precautions sufficient to a band composed entirely of veteran mountain men must be supplemented by more rigid regulation in this mixed company. Ashley fully appreciated this. On the march all men had their places assigned. He himself rode at the head. Near him a lead mule, especially picked for steadiness and speed, carried the records, contracts, company books, and the like. After him the pack animals with the goods, each one of which had in charge a man whose sole job it was to take care of that beast, no matter what happened. Followed then the hunters and trappers, each with his own saddle and pack animals, and at the rear Hachter, the *Little Burgeway*, Ashley's most trusted second-in-command. No man, save the appointed scouts and hunters, was privileged to leave his position until the day's journey was ended.

Ashley himself, with the advice and assistance of the old hands, selected the camping sites. Halting at the spot where his own shelter was to stand, he appointed a place to each as he closed up, so that by the time the Little Burgeway had brought in the rear a complete circle had been formed. The horses were unpacked, their backs carefully examined and treated when necessary, the goods piled in the center of the ring. Until dark they were grazed under strong guard, but by nightfall they had been picketed, also inside the ring, or hobbled closely.

Nor was there anything haphazard about the organization itself. The men were divided into messes in appropriate proportions of trappers to camp keepers, each of which was a self-sufficing and responsible unit.

In the morning, the Little Burgeway was the first afoot, shouting what would correspond to First Call on the bugle, "*Leve! Leve! Leve!*"

And in five minutes or so, the Reveille, "*Leche lego! Leche lego!*"

When everyone was supposed to turn out, dressed and equipped. Again, the horses, under guard, were allowed to graze, but before they were sent out, a rider circled the camp at full speed to rout out or disclose possible marauders.

Certainly Ashley, considering well the conditions and the average of materials with which he had to work, took all precautions.

Nevertheless the wily Pawnees managed to get through them. One morning found the party possessed of all its equipment, all its trade goods —and a half-dozen or so only of its horses! The rest had been driven off in a surprise attack by these most adroit of prairie thieves.

It seemed the final blow. Without transportation the trade goods might as well be in St. Louis—or in China, for that matter—and the fur on the backs of the beaver. For the first time Ashley was profoundly discouraged. The season was advancing. Unless he could in some manner get his hands on sufficient fur at least to keep his creditors quiet, the game was up. Henry's last take was not sufficient. Other resources seemed negligible. The free trappers had gone off on a wild goose chase of their own over the Divide, nobody knew where. The chance of their finding anything worthwhile was too slim to be considered.

Nevertheless Ashley went through the motions. He detailed some of the party to return to the Missouri, where they were to try to get hold of more horses. The rest were to remain encamped with the heavy baggage. Then Ashley himself returned to St. Louis to see what he could do. That was not much, as he soon discovered. So, as a sort of sideline, as it were, he ran for governor of Missouri, and was defeated in the August elections. Which made it complete.

About this time a battered old bull boat containing five men drifted into Fort Atkinson, a post on the Missouri River near its fork with the Platte. The inhabitants strolled to the shore. Every newcomer was a matter of interest, though bull boats with stray traders or trappers from the comparatively near-by districts were not unusual. The crew edged the unwieldy craft to the banks and stepped ashore.

The leader looked about him.

"Ary Ashley man yere?" he asked.

Several recognized him.

"Howdy, Bad Hand!"

"Howdy, Fitz!" They crowded to greet him. "Where you from?"

But Fitzpatrick was noncommittal, and his companions proved equally uncommunicative. The bystanders looked them over curiously. They were hard-bitten mountain men, to a man, and from the condition of their clothing and equipment it was evident they had been long afield. Their expedition, whatever it was, could not have been profitable. The bull boat was empty, save for small necessary equipment and a partly consumed quarter of venison.

"Ary Ashley men yere?" Fitzpatrick repeated his question.

As curiosity was apparently not to be satisfied, someone gave him the information. Five or six or so of Ashley's men were somewhere about. Collecting horses. Here's one now. Oh, Jim, someone wants to talk to you.

A keen-looking young man of about twenty years stepped forward. Fitzpatrick surveyed him attentively.

"You an Ashley man?" he asked at last. The young man nodded. "Whar's yore boss?"

"I'm in charge," replied the youth.

"Wagh!" Fitzpatrick looked him over again. "What yo' say yore name is?"

"I didn't say. But it's Bridger, Jim Bridger."

"I'm Fitzpatrick."

"Yes, I know."

"Wall, I want to talk to you."

They drew aside. The group of loungers gradually broke up. The four who had come in the bull boat squatted on their heels and waited in the fathomless patience of the mountain man.

"Whar's the gineral?" Fitzpatrick wanted to know.

Bridger explained at length. The older man listened without comment until the tale was finished. Though ignorant of business details his shrewd mind grasped the general situation clearly.

"Wagh!" he exclaimed at length. "Bad. Fur's goin' to mean a lot. Wall, I got it, and a plenty more whar that come from."

"Where?" asked Bridger.

"Mouth of the Sweetwater. Balance of my men waitin' thar with it."

"You come all the way from the Sweetwater in that bull boat?"

"Shore, and down the Sweetwater from the head. But we couldn't make it with the furs. Lost a lot of packs as it was. How many horses you got? Huh? Not enough. Got to git us some more. Then we'll go back and git us the fur. Kin we git 'em?"

"Sure," said Bridger confidently.

"Wall I'll write a letter to the gineral. Then we'll start."

"Sure," repeated Bridger.

Which was all that, for the moment, was said of the first attempt at navigation of the Platte from its headwaters on the Continental Divide.

Fitzpatrick wrote his letter, collected his horses, and set out for the mouth of the Sweetwater, where awaited him the rest of the party with the furs. It was a good letter, for in spite of its crude style it drew a picture. It told of the newly discovered easy pass over the Continental Divide, it told of the Green River and its abundance, and it speculated on what lay beyond. Ashley's vivid imagination was rekindled. His original intention had been to open trade on the upper Missouri and Yellowstone, perhaps pushing over to the upper Columbia by way of the pass through which, a short time before, Lewis and Clark had made their way. That was the direction of all his former and ill-starred efforts. Now, just as he was about to give it up, here was offered him a brand new territory from which were absent, seemingly, the elements of Indian hostility and the enmity of rivals. He could hardly wait to take possession. Somehow he managed more credit. Even before Fitzpatrick's return he had arrived at Fort Atkinson, ready and eager to set out.

He found the party he had left afoot on the prairie, with the trade goods, well and in good spirits. They had even managed to get together quite a respectable number of beaver skins, both by trapping and by trading with wandering bands of Indians. They were getting a little tired of wild game by this time, and had been looking forward to Ashley's return. The season was almost finished—it was now early in November. They would undoubtedly proceed to the comfort of winter post, there to enjoy the supplies their leader would have brought.

But their first enthusiastic welcome came quickly off the boil when they discovered that not only had Ashley brought no supplies, but that actually he proposed setting out at once for Green River. The leaders among them pointed out that winter was coming on, that the distance must be near a thousand miles, and as naturally they could not go upstream by boat, the route must be both rough and unknown. How cross the Divide? How find feed for the horses? How, for that matter, find supplies for the men? Latterly the game had departed, and no one knew where the buffalo were.

But Ashley overcame the objections. They could get supplies to do them well enough, until they found the buffalo, from a village of the

Pawnees, about fifty miles up the valley of the Loup. One by one he met the arguments, if not always plausibly, at least eloquently. His insistent enthusiasm was undoubtedly spurred by his secret thought that with him it was now or never. Among those who listened were men whose names later were to become famous over all the West. Besides Fitzpatrick and Bridger, whom we already know, there was, for example, young Robert Campbell, a tenderfoot, here present only because, after a hemorrhage of the lungs, his physicians had sent him to the prairies to die. But so tenacious was his quality that not only did he refuse to die but became so mighty a mountain man that some years later, after Ashley had made his fortune and wished to retire, he, with Jedediah Smith and Sublette, bought him out and took over the Rocky Mountain Fur Company. There was also present a man of wholly different type, a mulatto named Beckworth. He turned out to be an example of that rare combination, the tremendous braggart who actually does things, the man of action alloyed with more than a dash of the charlatan and the showman. He attained to a chieftainship of the Crows and took a prominent part in their long struggle with the Blackfeet. In fact he became too popular with his adopted people, and so met his end, for in his old age he wearied of mighty exploits and announced his retirement to peaceful pursuits in another part of the world. The Crows gave him a farewell banquet, at which they paid him great honor. Incidentally, they also poisoned him. This, they explained, was no mark of disesteem. On the contrary. They ascribed their success to the cream-colored chief, and if they could not keep him alive, they wanted at least his bones. At this time he too was a tenderfoot, essaying his first trip to the mountains.

Black Harris was another very much like him. He too was a teller of tall tales, all about himself. According to their own recorded accounts he and Beckworth between them killed more Indians than at that time inhabited the plains. As seems to be the habit of old-timers in all times and in all lands, they threw in a damsel apiece, fighting Amazons of incredible beauty, for good measure. Nevertheless Black Harris too must have been a good man of his hands, for later we find Sublette more than once picking him as his sole companion for long and hazardous winter journeys, and Sublette was no man's fool, nor swayed by sentiment. Nor must we forget Baptiste La Jeunesse, nor Claymore, later one of Ashley's partisans.

These and a score more listened and doubted and finally assented. On the morning of November 6th they broke camp and started up the Loup River toward the Pawnee village. Scouts were dispatched ahead to warn the Indians that the white men were on their way.

But Ashley's evil star seemed still in the ascendant. That very afternoon the wind turned to the northwest. By night it was snowing. Morning disclosed a white world, and the great flakes still sifting down. The wind strengthened to a blizzard.

By now the food was almost gone. It was a starving struggle for both men and horses. A half-pint of flour was the daily ration, the snow was so deep that grazing was impossible, and the sweet cottonwood grew sparsely. No matter, in the Indian village would be warmth and feasting aplenty. Cheered by this vision they struggled on through the deepening drift.

On the third day the three scouts returned. The village of the Pawnee Loups was deserted.

Hard doings! Starving times. The horses gnawed off one another's manes and tails. The men killed one of the poorest of them in order to survive at all. For twelve long days they persisted, struggling forward against the cold and the snow and the blizzard wind. They made twelve miles! Several of the ponies weakened and died and were eaten. Then at last they gave it up. They turned south and retreated to the valley of the Platte. Here were game and fuel and forage for the horses. They thawed out around veritable fires at last, ate their fill of elk and deer. A day's rest sufficed these iron men. They headed up the valley of the Platte. And in ten days of bitter travel they came upon a village of the Grand Pawnees. These Indians informed them that their friends, the Pawnee Loups, were farther upstream, on their way to their wintering grounds at the Forks of the Platte. At the same time they were strong in their advice to give it up, to settle down until spring. Beyond was no fuel, no horse feed. They must surely perish.

Nevertheless Ashley pushed on. The blizzard continued. Half the horses died of cold or of starvation. They found the Pawnee Loups. Then at last they paused. Ashley called a council. He informed Bad Axe, their chief, that he wished to rest for a fortnight, that he wanted to trade for twenty-five horses, for buffalo robes to keep his men from freezing, to buy meat and beans and dry pumpkin and corn, to be permitted to live with the tribe for a short period of recuperation. Bad Axe was friendly. He agreed to furnish these things. At the same time he expressed his opinion that the white men were crazy.

At the end of ten days the party was recuperated, both in strength and in spirits. Bad Axe had fulfilled his promises. They started again, two days before Christmas.

This time it seemed that the evil influence had withdrawn. The weather was clear and sparkling. The valleys were literally covered with buffalo. But the night after Christmas it began again to blow and snow from the northwest. In spite of their new buffalo robes the men suffered severely. Some of the horses had lain down. By morning they were so far gone with cold that they could not rise. When lifted to their feet they were unable to stand. Finally they were abandoned to the wolves. The expedition went on as best it could.

They could not have gone on at all had it not been for the presence of the buffalo. Those animals broke trail through the snowdrifts, by now impassably deep without such aid, and their pawings exposed enough of the frozen grass to keep the horses alive. That was about all, though, and Ashley began to fear he would have to lighten packs, when at the opportune moment, to celebrate the new year, they came to a grove of sweet-bark cottonwoods on an island. Here they rested for one day, feeding their animals. They would have stayed longer, but the cottonwood bark gave out. They found no more for nine days, then, again when about at the end of their resources, came upon another island of the same sort. Fate was grudging, but at least she was relenting just short of complete disaster.

Ashley was not following quite the route Fitzpatrick had taken with his bull boats. On the advice of his friends, the Pawnee Loups, he was ascending a more southerly fork of the Platte. Therefore when they had at last reached the foothills of the Front Range, in the first part of February, they made camp in a grove of cottonwood and willows, there to remain for three weeks while men explored for a possible pass. Game was again scarce. They had to fall back on the provisions bought from the Pawnee Loups. But there was plenty of wood, and forage for the horses, and the weather behaved. The country was still, as Ashley wrote later, *enveloped in snow and ice*, but the air was clear and sharp with the inspiring tang of the high country. To the south rose a huge mountain which Ashley judged to be no more than six or eight miles distant. We now know it to have been Long's Peak, and that it was not less than thirty-five miles from Ashley's camp.

The pass was found, or rather the way through to the real pass.

They started again on February 26th. For three days they struggled in the ranges which, they knew, must be but the first barrier. The Divide must he beyond. Only by the most incredible toil were they able to make way at all. No man could have been blamed for discouragement. If these were the foothills, what must face them beyond, in the crossing of the main range! Nevertheless there was no despair, nor even grumbling. Your true man of the open grumbles plenty over annoyances, but when real difficulty comes along, he ceases to complain. Indeed if his troubles get to be bad enough, to be complete enough, he begins to find them funny!

Nevertheless the end of that third day was grim. Bruised, abraded, shaken, without fuel, without forage, the mountain *frozen and torpid, affording nothing on which an animal could subsist*, the outlook was gloomy. Nobody knew how long a journey it would be over the main range in the best of conditions. But this they did know that if they could not make it in one dash, they could not make it at all. Horses must eat. Already several of them must be helped along, *like an old woman* as someone expressed it. They might easily have turned back to the safety of their cottonwood groves, there to await the springtime. They elected to go on! That decision was the end of their troubles, for the time being. It almost seemed as though Fate yielded in chivalry to the stout hearts of her antagonists. An hour's climb brought them over the foothills. Instead of the rocky precipices among which they had been struggling, the ascent became easy and unobstructed, in fact so gradual that they hardly knew they were climbing at all. The snow thinned. Everywhere were bare spots, already turning green. Buffalo and antelope grazed in the valleys.

Which was a plenty for ary mountain man or mountain hoss!

They had crossed the mountains, to be sure, but not yet the Continental Divide, as they soon discovered. As a matter of fact they had merely passed from the country drained by the South Platte to that drained by the North Platte. So they turned northwest, angling along the Rockies, looking for a way through. But this was a picnic. The game increased in number and variety. The slopes were covered with buffalo, antelope, mountain sheep. Small tributary streams were alive with beaver.

This, one would have thought, was what these men were seeking, a new and untrapped country. Surely here they could have taken a good spring catch and resolved all their troubles. As a matter of fact they did move very slowly, averaging no more than five or six miles a day, stopping over a day or so here and there, and some of the heretofore unburdened horses had to go to work as the store of peltries increased. Indeed there was no sane reason for not here remaining. Except one thing, the challenge of that glittering mountain wall to the west. They had started for Green River, and Green River it must be.

So next we see them toiling over a high rough country without fuel. Water they obtained by melting snow. They had left the land of beaver and of plenty behind them. Jim Bridger found a pass, similar to South Pass just north. By the first of April they were on the west slope of the Continental Divide. A wandering band of Crows, returning from a raid on the

Shoshones, stole some of the horses. Nine men pursued the marauders and recovered some of the horses. Ten days later they came to that fork of the Green down which Fitzpatrick and the free trappers had journeyed the year before. They named it the Big Sandy. After following it down for six days they became impatient and struck across country. On April 18th they at last made camp on the banks of Green River. They had been gone one hundred sixty-six days from Fort Atkinson, they were the first to cross this country in the dead of winter, they were the first to travel this segment of what was later to become the central overland route to the Pacific. Little they thought of that! Two things were uppermost in their minds.

"Said we couldn't make it! Wagh!" growled Black Harris, in contemptuous allusion to the dire predictions of white men and red. "Wall, yere we be!"

"Bring on yore beaver!" cried Bridger, shaking his traps from their coverings.

———

They trapped slowly on down the Green, with all anticipated success. It seemed that with only a moderate patience and industry and persistence a sufficient catch might be accumulated to resolve all financial difficulties. But Ashley's active mind day after day contemplated the simple phenomenon of water running downhill. Where did it go? After he had asked of himself this question long enough, why, naturally, he had to find out! The riverbed angled to the southeastward. Possibly it broke through the Divide, emptied at last into the Gulf of Mexico. In that case, and if cargoes could be floated down its whole length, New Orleans was likely to become the headquarters of the fur trade in place of St. Louis. And what a glorious outlet for this new country! In no time Ashley had persuaded himself that he ought to do what he wanted to do. It was not too difficult to forget his debts for the time being, and the necessity of meeting them. Those debts were a long distance away, and their maturity dates in a future whose remoteness was compounded of both space and time. Besides, Sublette was out somewhere, Jedediah Smith also. Burnett and Crane and Kelly would undoubtedly bring in rich trade from the Blackfeet. Ashley did not know then that the three last-named were also suffering from an attack of the wandering foot.

"Fitz," said he, "I'm going to give you six men and send you upstream to find out where it rises. You ought to find good trapping. Claymore, you and another six can strike out toward that range of mountains to westward. Harris can find out what's in that other range to the southwest. And all of you try to get news of Sublette and Smith. Now we'll have to use all the horses the Crows left us, so we'll have to cache the goods. We'll build me a bull boat and I'll float them down to some suitable place, say a hundred miles or so downstream. I'll cache them there and mark the place. That will be our rendezvous. We will meet there about the middle of July. Spread the word among all the Ashley men, and also any Indians who are friendly enough and who wish trade."

Now that was businesslike! Most of the men would be properly employed in gainful occupation. Only six would accompany Ashley in the bull boat. And probably they would find good trapping somewhere. Ashley persuaded himself that he was looking beyond the present to the future, in a large general way. Probably he was. But deep in his heart he was wild to find out whether the water went downhill.

So they built the bull boat, and loaded in the goods, said farewell to the three horse parties, and shoved off. But they had hardly rounded the bend when they realized that they were carrying too much weight. It was all right in perfectly smooth water, but the smallest riffles slopped over the rail. So they stopped and made them another bull boat.

Nothing is more delightful than downstream travel. The boat slips along silently. The country is undisturbed. Each bend is an exciting revelation. One comes upon things suddenly and unexpectedly. Ducks preening in a solitude for the first time broken, knee deep elk or deer lost in the suspension of slow animal contemplation, a clownlike bear grubbing and snuffling as he upturns the sand for lily roots, long lines of shaggy buffalo filing methodically to the water's edge for drink. None of these creatures could believe their eyes. They stared incredulously at the strange, silent, smooth-running apparition, snorted, stamped, were seized by sudden panic. Sometimes it was very funny. In their haste of departure they jostled and collided and splashed and scrambled. Even the smaller birds and creatures were astounded. The tiny, black-cowled chickadees examined them, bright-eyed, then swung themselves beneath the twigs to see if the thing would look any different upside down. There was no hurry. There was little work. The weather was fine, the springtime was in full flood. Game was abundant.

By the last of the month they came to the base of a lofty mountain covered with snow. Here a good-sized stream ran in from the west. It seemed to Ashley a suitable place for the rendezvous, so he landed and cached the bulk of his trade goods and made the marks by which he had agreed to designate the meeting place.

Thus he had accomplished his part of the general plan. It was now only logical that he and his men should stop here to trap their quota. It was not only logical but imperative if the full measure of his financial responsibilities was to be met. But the water still flowed downhill.

So with a pause of only one day they launched the lightened bull boats and again floated away.

But toilless travel and peace of mind here abruptly ceased. Not half a mile below the cache the mountains pinched in, the channel narrowed, the current accelerated. Ahead they heard the wild and tumultuous shoutings of turbulence. It was too late to turn back. Into a narrow dark gorge, whose walls rose perpendicular to a height of fifteen hundred feet or more, they swept uncontrolled. The water dashed white against the black and splintered boulders of a formidable rapids. Round and round whirled the bull boats, dipping, rushing forward, escaping collision with the rocks only because they were so light that the backwash flung them aside. Occasionally their passengers were able to help themselves momentarily by a lightning shove of pole or paddle to avoid the bared teeth of destruction. Most of the time they were the helpless playthings of the roaring unleashed forces of the river. And when at last they were spewed out into quiet waters, with a pleasant little park on the margin of the stream, each thanked whatever gods he knew.

But they were unable to land at the pleasant little park. The current, though smooth, was too strong. It swept them helplessly past and shot them into a second gorge, cleft as though with a knife through the mountain. Another miracle brought them through this also. Once more the river played them its little joke, offering to their dizzied eyes a delightful pleasance past which it drew them by its power. A third gorge, a third wild and terrifying ride, a third miracle. This time they emerged into bright sunlight, a wider open space, a gentler current.

Although they had come only about ten miles, and fast ones at that, they needed no orders to paddle ashore. Seasoned to danger as they were, these mountain men, they stamped their moccasins gratefully on the solid earth. They looked back at the gorge and the white water tumbling from it, looked at one another, laughed.

"Reckon this child's willing to call it a day," drawled one.

"And I reckon we're not goin' to go back the way we come," supplemented another.

"We can go back afoot—over the mountains," said Ashley. "We will have to. What say, boys? The farther we go the farther we'll have to come back." He wanted to be fair. "Nobody knows what's ahead."

They glanced up at the mountains, they turned their eyes downstream, and they looked at one another.

"Hell," said the first man at last, "I ain't no landlubber, I'm a sailor man."

"The country looks like it's more open ahead," agreed his companion. "Let's see whar the dang thing goes."

The next morning they relaunched the bull boats. The river was very crooked. They could not see ahead. It was also very broken and filled with rapids, caused by rocks rolled from the sides of the mountains. After the experience of yesterday these were nothing. The crews laughed and shouted in high spirits. But at the end of twenty miles, from the darkness of another mountain cleft, the river spoke to them in no uncertain terms. They paddled hastily ashore before the suction could get them. They had learned their lesson.

"Reckon the old man is talkin' to us this time," said one to another.

They made their way afoot, cautiously and with some difficulty, to where they could see what it was all about. A great landslide had blocked the whole riverbed, and over a tumbled barrier of rock masses the stream rushed in a twelve-foot waterfall. They unloaded, attached long lines to the empty bull boats, turned them loose, braced themselves for the shock of their plunge. The light craft landed smack in the pool below, eddied and tugged, floated quiet. They carried the baggage down piece by piece, reloaded, floated away.

"We larned her that time!" they exulted.

Ashley painted his name and the date on a rock. Forty-four years afterward Major Powell of the Geological Survey found the inscription, still legible. But the date was so blurred that Powell misread it, and names Ashley as some obscure hunter rescued by the Mormons! Such is fame.

Shortly they came to a beautiful pocket in the hills, surrounded by high mountains with green hanging meadows. It was five or six miles in diameter, lush with grass, pleasant with groves of cottonwood and willows, alive with game. They stopped here for a rest and a hunt. Later this place became celebrated as Brown's Hole, the site of Fort Davy Crockett, a rendezvous and wintering ground for hundreds of trappers and literally thousands of Shoshones. Now they left it alone with its elk and bear and *cimmaron*. But ten miles farther downriver they came to a spot where had encamped several thousand Indians at least. Many of the lodges were still standing, and in perfect preservation and intact, for the usual covering of skins had been replaced by cedar bark, and this had been left in place.

This was interesting. They wondered who these people might be, and when they would be met.

Certainly not in the course of the river, that much could be guaranteed. It was just one canyon now after another. Some they passed by unloading and *lining* the bull boats, others they ran. They were becoming more skillful and more reckless. These canyons are now named Flaming Gorge, Horseshoe, Kingfisher, Ladore, Whirlpool Cayon, Desolation Canyon, and many others. At length things became a little too thick even for these hardy men. They landed at what is now the mouth of the Uinta River and cached most of the goods they had brought with them thus far. The bulk, of course, had already been landed and left behind at the place designated for the rendezvous in July. In the lightened bull boats they turned themselves loose and shot into the maw of Desolation Canyon. They made the astonishing distance of fifty miles safely, then they were wrecked aplenty. They swam ashore. Jim Beckworth, the mulatto, helped Ashley to the beach, and bragged about it the rest of his life until the assistance became a rescue. They dried out and congratulated themselves that they had left their stores. The bull boats had overset but were intact. However, everybody, including Ashley, thought they had come far enough. The river had bent decidedly to westward. It seemed now highly improbable that it emptied into the Gulf of Mexico. Ashley had discovered that, go as far as you like, water continues to flow downhill. He was satisfied.

They tramped back afoot to the mouth of the Uinta. To do so they had to take to the back country in places. Thus they ran across their first Indians. These proved to be Utahs. The Shoshone country had been left to the north. They were powerfully built and intelligent looking Indians, but lacked sartorial magnificence. In contrast to the Plains Indians they looked to be stricken with poverty. Some wore buckskin shirts, a few had robes or a ragged blanket, but the majority wore only the breech clout and moccasins. Their arms were bows and arrows. The leader carried a flintlock trade musket for which, however, he had no ammunition. When Ashley signed to ask him where he had procured it, he pointed northwest and made the sign for white man. Ashley found the letters *H B C* stamped on its barrel. He loaded the piece and handed it back. The Ute immediately and joyously shot it off into the air. He seemed much pleased at the noise.

They were entirely friendly. Indeed they seemed overjoyed to see the white men and danced about and shouted merrily. They examined all the white men's possessions with the greatest interest and curiosity but did not beg. Ashley presented the chief with a dozen charges for his musket. The Ute returned the compliment with a basket of grass and sunflower seeds parched and pulverized. They smoked and talked by signs. The Utah chief confirmed Ashley's wisdom in turning away from the river. It continued its course to the southwest, through rough mountains, and grew bigger and wilder and more turbulent until it dropped 'way down below the earth into a painted country where the sun dwelled. The chief explained it all very carefully. The sun was the big chief, the moon was his squaw, the stars were their children. Unfortunately the sun has a bad habit of eating his progeny. So when he gets up in the morning they hide, and do not come out again until he has gone to bed at night. They do not fear their mother, the moon. But once a month the moon paints her face black and goes into mourning for her lost children. Then the sun gets his chance and gobbles up enough stars to keep him going. He is really shaped like a snake, but you cannot see the snake. What you see is his stomach full of stars. He goes to bed in a great hole in the ground. The hole fits him so closely that he has to crawl right on through and out the other end. That is why he comes up in the east. But the painted country was where he crawled in. That is where the river went. Not a good place to go, for a man would there surely be swallowed by the sun. Thus Ashley had news of the Grand Canyon of the Colorado, could he have interpreted its imagery. There was little game in that south and west country. The Indians of that region were poor. They ate roots and fish and horses. The white men had done well to turn back. Yes, there were plenty of horses. They ran wild. Yes, the chief could get horses for the white men. He did so, taking in exchange powder and ball for the old Hudson's Bay fusee and such small knickknacks as Ashley had brought from the main stores and had rescued from shipwreck.

Jubilant, convinced that luck had turned at last, they rode to the mouth of the Uinta, dug up the little cache. They were ready and equipped.

The site designated for the rendezvous lay north and a trifle to the east. It had taken them some three weeks to float downriver from that point. A vivid recollection of the terrifying canyons through which they had been bumped and jostled by the torrent recalled to them the fact that they would have to do some pretty strenuous mountain travel to get back. It was well to be about it promptly. That was the only sensible thing.

But here was the valley of the Uinta angling off to the northwest. It did not appear to offer any great difficulties. How about following it up? Ought to see where that comes from, now we're here. To be sure it would lead them far to the west of where they wanted ultimately to be. On the other hand, perhaps the going would be easier.

One of the men had climbed a peak after *cimmaron* and reported that a big range of mountains, running east and west, seemed to drop off to flatter country at its western end. Why not go around that end and outflank the high rough country, come into the rendezvous from directly west? They managed to persuade themselves that this was a sensible thing to do. Deep in their hearts they knew better. There was no guarantee that the travel would be any easier, indeed no guarantee that travel would be possible at all. The farther north one went, the rougher and higher the ranges. Only one thing, really, was certain, it was much farther.

From Ashley's point of view such a fling westward was sheer folly. His business was to be at the rendezvous at the appointed time, to devote his whole energies to getting together just as many peltries as he possibly could, and then to transporting them to St. Louis as directly and as expeditiously as he was able. Otherwise he was just plain broke, and his associates with him. So, naturally, the little band of horsemen and their pack animals turned up the Uinta valley toward the west.

With the acceptance of this her final challenge to the stoutness of their hearts, Fate smiled at last. That decision marked the turning point of Ashley's fortunes.

They found they could not quite outflank the east and west range of mountains, but the passage through them was easy. They came upon a large river flowing west, and speculated upon it, and decided it probably was the Buenaventura, said to flow into the bay of San Francisco. Only with reluctance did they abandon the idea of following it down to the Pacific. Later at the rendezvous Bridger reported that he had found its mouth and that it flowed into an arm of the sea. He knew it was the sea because the water was salt. Nobody then could realize that he was probably the first white man to set eyes on Great Salt Lake, that the Pacific was over eight hundred miles away on an air line, that the Buenaventura was pure myth.

But down this river, later to be known as the Weber, they did travel for fifty or sixty miles. They might have continued down it to its mouth, in Salt Lake, in spite of their virtuous resolutions. But one afternoon the scout, riding ahead, discerned a solitary horseman in the middle distance, and was at the same instant himself perceived. The two at once set their horses at full speed toward one another, in the universal habit of the plains. Whether friend or enemy, the thing to do was to close at once, or at least to get near enough to discover the other's tribe and intentions. So when within a hundred yards the two recognized the fact that both were white men. They pulled in their horses and jogged together. They recognized each other without outward surprise.

"Hullo, Jake," said the newcomer. "Where you from and what you doing here?"

"With the Gin'ral. He's comin' back yander." He jerked his head to indicate. "You alone, Andy? Whar's Kelly and Joe Crane?"

"Don't know. I wintered with Jed Smith. They went back to the Blackfeet. They were coming to join us this spring at Green River, but Jed decided to go west. We went 'way over into the Flathead country."

"Ary beaver up thar?"

"Beaver everywhere."

"Reckon the Gin'ral will be glad to hear that. I suspicion he needs plenty beaver this year."

"Well," said Andy, "we got some. But we are looking around mostly. We got quite a lot off some Hudson's Bay Indians that had lost all their guns. Shoshones robbed them. They were pretty desperate. But they had nine hundred skins." Andy chuckled. "Jed made a bargain with them. He agreed to feed 'em and take 'em to where a Hudson's Bay man named Ross was located, and they were to pay him with the skins."

"Nine hundred!" exclaimed Jake. "Would they do that?"

"What else could they do? They had to do it or starve—or get gobbled up by the Shoshones."

"Wall, that bargain was some—fer Jed. Did he do it?"

"Sure! He's a man of his word. We cached what we had and the nine hundred, and quit trapping and started out. Joke was that just two days later, we ran into a party of Hudson's Bay men who'd been sent out as a rescue party!"

"Then what? Did Jed give 'em back the skins?"

"Well, what do you think?"

A slow smile overspread the trapper's leathery countenance.

"Go ahead," said he briefly.

"Jed said he'd agreed to take these Indians to Ross, and he was going to do it. A bargain was a bargain. So we all went together. Ross didn't like it much, but by and by he had to laugh. You know Jed." Andy threw back his head and laughed full-voiced. "He's got the nerve of the devil. What do you suppose he did next?"

"You tell," said Jake.

Ross was just setting out to a Hudson's Bay Company Post up past the Flathead country. Jed said he thought we'd go along, too. Said he wanted to *view the country*, and wanted to learn something about how the British traders worked."

"No!" cried Jake.

"*Yes!*" Andy chortled. "And what's more we did it, and we spent a month up there, till near Christmas."

"How did they act about that?"

"I reckon they were none too pleased," confessed Andy, "but they treated us all right. I'll say this for them, they've got a good outfit, and most of their Indians like them. They told me they don't let them use liquor, for one thing."

"Don't believe it," said Jake bluntly. "They use a plenty of it up north."

"Yes, I know. I talked about it with Peter Ogden. He was boss there. He said it was because they couldn't get the fur where other traders used liquor too."

Jake clicked his tongue against his teeth skeptically.

"Everybody knows you kin make better trade with likker," said he. "Did ye winter thar?"

"No," replied Andy. "We stayed there a month. Then Ross started out again, and I reckon Ogden told Jed we'd about wore out our welcome. Anyway we went eastward with Ross for a while, and wintered in a stream they called Salmon River."

"Whar's Jed and the outfit now?"

"Up north somewhere."

"Ain't you with him now?"

"No," said Andy. "Come spring we started out trapping and ran into Sublette and his party by accident. They'd been all over farther north and had wintered up there. Called the place Cache Valley. Last I saw of them, they were sticking together. They wanted someone to go hunt up Provost's party and tell him where to meet us, so I said I'd do it. He was going to cut across to the west. I came down this way and found him. We got a camp just downstream a ways. Now, how about you, where you been?"

But Andy was not yet to hear this tale. The remainder of the party rounded the bend of the bluffs. He guided it to Provost's camp, where again he must repeat what he had in the way of news, this time to Ashley himself. The general and Provost listened keenly to what he had to say, though, of course, Provost had heard it before. Ashley, however, pursued his inquiries more closely. After Andy had finished the story he had already told the trappers and he was subjected to a searching cross-examination.

"No," replied Andy, "the British were not established. Their headquarters were still near the mouth of the Columbia. This expedition under Ross was a small one, an exploring party. But a larger party under Peter Ogden had trapped this spring, farther north. Somewhere between one and two hundred in the party." Andy did not know what luck they had had, but he had been told they expected to take fourteen or fifteen thousand skins.

"Indeed!" said Ashley thoughtfully.

He brooded for a moment. "Do you know about where he is?"

"I think I know," spoke up Provost.

"What does Ogden give for beaver?" asked Ashley.

On this subject Andy could talk length, for this had touched his interest closely, and what he had learned had aroused his wonder. The company paid one dollar for prime pelts!

"That looks mighty little when we're getting five!" submitted Andy.

"A dollar in trade?" Ashley wanted to know.

"Yes, sir. And seemed to me like their goods had a pretty good price on them. Maybe it was all right, they have to bring it a long way. But I did hear Mr. Ross bragging that he'd got six-dollar beaver, China prices, for goods worth sixpence."

"How do the trappers like that?"

"They don't know any different. It's what they are used to. The company outfits them and gives them what they want. On credit. And takes fur to pay at the end of the season. Some of the men complained they could only just keep ahead of the debt."

"I see," said Ashley. "What Kind of men they got?"

Andy chuckled.

"They've got gentlemen, white men, and hunters," said he.

"How's that?"

"That's how they divide them up. The gentlemen are the ones in charge—like Ogden or Ross. The white men are clerks or young men in training. The hunters are all the rest. A good many of them are white men too, but they don't rank as such. There's three white men with Ogden," he added dryly.

"You seem to have taken a good deal of trouble to learn about all this."

"It's interesting," submitted Andy. "Why, sir, when one of these outfits starts out from Fort Vancouver—brigades they call them—the gentleman is all rigged out with cocked hat and brass buttons and ruffles and satin waistcoats and high boots and pistols and maybe a sword. Reckon they don't last long, or else they pack them away. I never saw any. But that's what they say."

Ashley wanted to know more. He was especially particular to know about the hunters. A good many Iroquois Indians from somewhere back east, Andy told him. They were a sullen and mutinous lot. Some French. A good many half-breeds. A scattering of old Nor'westers and Astor men, who had transferred allegiance when the companies amalgamated. Ashley questioned him for a good half-hour. At the end of that time, he seemed to have made up his mind to something.

"Burnett," he said briskly, "I want you to do an errand for me. I'll pay you, of course. I want you to find Sublette and Smith for me and take them to the place I have appointed as rendezvous. I'll draw you a map. Tell them, and the others who meet them, that I shall be back as soon as possible. I think Provost and I shall try to get in touch with Mr. Ogden. He seems to have a great many very cheap skins."

"I don't think you can buy any of him, at any price," volunteered Andy.

"Why not?"

"He is some sort of officer in the Hudson's Bay, a high one, I understand."

"Well, I think I'd like to talk to him. I am obliged to you, Burnett."

Andy, dismissed, walked away, leaving Ashley and Provost alone together.

"We don't go to rendezvous, then?" asked Provost.

"Not yet."

Provost hesitated. He, with Sublette and Jedediah Smith, was close to the new company's affairs. Indeed, he had every reason to believe that he was destined to partnership, and when, some years later, this hope was frustrated, his chagrin drove him into bitter opposition. But at this moment he had just reason to believe himself high in Ashley's confidence. The present financial crisis was well known to him. He, as well as Andy Burnett, knew well the intense loyalty the Hudson's Bay inspired in her servants.

"I don't believe you'll gain by it. It's a wild goose chase, General. The boy is right. Ogden won't sell, at any price, no matter what the profit."

"Etienne," said Ashley emphatically, "we must have beaver."

"I know that."

"Do you know the motto of the Hudson's Bay Company?"

"Don't know as I do."

"Well, it's Pro pelle cutem."

"Does that mean anything in United States?"

"It means a *skin for a skin*. It's a pretty good motto."

He looked at Provost. Provost looked at him.

"There's nineteen of us and a hundred and fifty or so of them," suggested the partisan at last.

"One gentleman and three white men," Ashley reminded him. "The rest are *hunters*."

"What you got in mind, General?" asked Provost bluntly.

"Just to go see," said Ashley.

"The boys won't like startin' west and the rendezvous east."

"I think you can handle that."

"Well," Provost admitted reluctantly, "maybe I can." He shook his shoulders. "Reckon we're travelin' west."

Chapter 15
Rendezvous

The encampment in the river bottom had sprung up almost overnight. Each day brought its increase, almost each hour. Down the grassy valley of the bottomlands, over the skyline of rim rocks, along the winding tributary of the Green, new parties appeared. If they were white men, they came in full speed, as fast as their ponies could step it, waving their rifles and blankets like Indians, yelling at the full power of their lungs. The fringes on their black and shiny buckskins snapped in the wind of their going. Some of them had weighted the fringes with bullets of lead, or ornamented them with rows of hawks' bills, or little bells, and these things jangled together. The tails, too, on the skin caps danced merrily. A few of the wilder spirits had even assumed, for the purposes of this grand entrance, Indian war bonnets, which they had packed all this distance, or had gone to some other childish extreme of barbaric play-acting. Or, rather, it would have been childish against any other background than the year of *splendid wayfaring*, of hardship and danger, from which they returned. Emerging from that confused and dim magnificence of emprise, these bizarre figures rode somehow in appropriate caparison.

They swept down upon the encampment pell-mell. The ponies ran unchecked and unguided, heads stretched, nostrils wide. Behind them, at a distance, the pack animals hurried as fast as they were able, fearful of being left behind, too conscientious in their long training to cut loose and run, regardless of the integrity of their burdens. Into the scattered encampment they plunged, among the tents and lodges, reckless of what they hit or overran, discharging their rifles in the air! Women screamed and ducked aside, children scattered like quail, Indians composed their countenances to stolidity, tall trappers arose, cursing or laughing, snatched at the riders or the riders' mounts. The ponies, sensing that the goal of their wild race had been reached, plunged to a halt, milled around, threw up their heads, racked away at a high swinging trot as soon as their saddles were empty, halted again, restlessly puzzled. For a time, nobody paid them any attention.

Some of their riders vaulted lightly from their backs without troubling to check them. Others came down with a thump, unhorsed by a grasp on arm or leg. Immediately, they grappled with the men who had thus laid them low, rolling about on the ground in a bear hug, pummeling, shouting epithets. The blows were heartily delivered, the epithets luridly insulting. They had to be. Nothing less could be expressive of this high point of the year.

The first exuberance over, they still continued for some moments, pounding one another admiringly on the back, shouting in one another's faces. Then gradually, they fell apart in pairs or little groups. The pack horses came up and wandered about uncertainly. Some of those already encamped were provided with Indian wives, perhaps the rear of the newcomers was brought up by a woman or so. These began without orders to take charge of the animals, to unsaddle them, unpack them, perhaps to erect a lodge or so for their men, or for the unattached guests. The trappers had no time to fuss with such things yet. They were too busy. They sat about on their heels, smoking, gnawing on fat ribs of roasted meat, talking thirteen to the dozen, pouring forth the jumble of question and of news that a year of slow taciturnity in a hard and lonesome land had stored up within them.

Confusedly, in fragments, the mosaic of the tale was patterned. It was too wide-flung in scope and in incident for any one man's telling. Men's minds were too exultantly ebullient for understanding. All that might come later, in the slower, soberer leisure after effervescence had overflowed. There was a large impatience of details as yet, and still, each man was filled with details which he must tell. They shouted snatches at one another, questioned and did not wait for answers. The thing was too big for them. They must spill over, in a grand general spree of some sort, a safety valve, a relief of pressure. Not until then could they settle down to cases. If they only had some likker...

Anybody heerd of the Gin'ral? When was he likely to git in?

Burnett had run across him up northwest a ways. Andy repeated his story for the twentieth time. Ashley and Provost were certainly on the way. This was the place of the rendezvous, all right. Yes, he said he'd be here by July. Well, nigh onto July now, isn't it? Said he had plenty of trade, did he? Well, let's hunt the cache, kain't be fur away. The proposal was greeted with derision. Suppose we ain't looked? Ashley is no *mangeur de lard*. Wise old he-coon. Ary man, or Injin, finds his cache has got a good nose.

So, the newcomers finally settled down with the others. The waiting was not unpleasant. There was plenty of game. Fat eating. Tobacco a bit scarce with some, but they divided up. Plenty to talk about.

They found that, in one respect, the sum total of achievement had been remarkable. This was the first full season beyond the Continental Divide. In a brief space of time, they had covered an enormous extent of unknown territory. Jedediah Smith and his men had been up Green River, over to the Snake, down to the Columbia, to the Flatheads, and back to Utah, where they had accidentally run into Sublette's party. Sublette had been to the southwest to the Bear River, which they trapped all summer, had rounded the Wasatch Mountains, and had, in the person of Bridger, discovered the Great Salt Lake, and had completed the circle to Cache Valley, where they had met Jedediah Smith. Etienne Provost and his band had gone south, then west, crossed the Bear River to the Weber where, Andy reported, he had fallen in with Ashley, and was still out with the general's party. The three other groups under Fitzpatrick, Claymore, and another, into which Ashley had divided his original expedition, had also ranged wide over the expanse of country toward Salt Lake, and were now returned, each with its story. Among them all they had swung back the gateway of the heretofore impassable mountains. And at this moment McLoughlin, the great Hudson's Bay factor on the Pacific coast, was congratulating himself on British security there forever.

"For all coming time," he was telling a visitor, "we and our children will have uninterrupted possession of this country, as it can never be reached by families but by water around Cape Horn. Yankees? As well might they undertake to go to the moon!"

Within forty years, ten thousand wagons, in a single season, rolled over the long obliterated tracks of the Ashley men!

No thought of their successors crossed their minds now. As far as the country itself went, they were interested in two things. It was rich in beaver, and the British were pushing into it from the west, just as they were entering it from the east. Jedediah Smith had run across a small band of Hudson's Bay trappers. He had found them destitute, to be sure, and had generously relieved them of their entire catch, some nine hundred skins, in exchange for succor. Purty slick of Jed! And this year, one of their big bugs was headed in, name of Ogden. Had a big party. Burnett knew something of that. How about it, Andy?

Yes, that is right, Andy told them. He is said to have somewhere between one and two hundred men with him.

They whistled mournfully at this. That's a power of men. That many would clean out a district pretty fast. Why can't they stay back where they belong?

"Hell," said Hartley, "there's country enough back there for a thousand men to trap and never run across one another. She's a big country, I tell you."

But they shook their heads. They did not like it. They had moved west of the Divide to get rid of the Missouri and American Fur companies. Seems like they ought to have *some* place to theirselves! This last from a new arrival.

"The general headed out to find Ogden," said Andy. "That's when I left him to find the others and tell them where to rendezvous. That's what's keeping him."

"That so?" The late arrival brightened. "Wall, I reckon the Gin'ral will handle him."

"Sure!" they agreed comfortably. "He'll handle him. Wisht he'd come on in. I could use a slug of likker. Sure he's got cyards, Fitz?"

Fitz was sure. That was good. Hadn't had a game of cyards since the devil grew a tail.

They were really quite comfortable and happy. The encampment was taking on considerable size. It straggled down the river bottom for a mile or more, its extent augmented by several small villages of Utahs and Shoshones who had come in, drawn by the rumored trade, and who were dwelling quietly and amicably together.

There was much visiting back and forth, among white men and red, renewing old acquaintance. Joe Crane and Kelly had come over from the Blackfoot country. Joe had with him Flying Woman, his Blackfoot wife. They were looked upon just a little askance by certain of the trappers. There was no open hostility, merely a slight but noticeable withdrawal. Joe was inclined to bristle, but Kelly was philosophical.

"What can you expect?" said he. "The Blackfeet are as hostile as ever to all whites in their country. Naturally, since we are the only men allowed in there, we are resented a little."

"Especial since we git the beaver." Joe grinned, recovering.

"The Blackfeet are just as bad toward the British," Andy contributed. "Has there been trouble on our side this past year?"

"Not what you call real trouble," said Kelly. "But nobody's tried very hard to get in. Man, name of Holley, sneaked in around the edges. He made out a while by putting his traps out nights and taking them in before daylight, and lying hid all day."

There was considerable resentment against the Blackfeet. They were the only people with whom it was impossible to make any arrangement, either to trap or to trade. It was felt that Kelly or Crane or Andy should be able to do something about it. In vain they protested that their standing was purely personal, that they had no influence whatever on policies. After a time, since the most were basically fair-minded, this was acknowledged, though grudgingly. Some day they'd get together and go in there strong enough to trap whether or no, and the Blackfeet could go to hell if they didn't like it. Then whar'll you be? Reckon ye don't aim to fight agin white men, do ye? And ef'n ye don't, them Injins hist ye quick!

"He's right at that," Kelly acknowledged in confidence. "When the time comes to take sides, we're through."

Andy was troubled. He liked the Blackfeet, he had close friends among them. Indeed, he had a sneaking liking for all Indians. He was clear-eyed. He recognized that from the white man's standpoint they were thieves, that they were touchily and inordinately vain, that they were treacherous, selfish, revengeful, cruel sometimes to the point of fiendishness, that they lived by foolish and relentless war. He had no illusions as to the *noble red man*. But Andy dimly sensed that there was also a red man's standpoint. For instance, leaving aside the type of robbery under arms which was the breath of life in their nostrils, and pilfering from the alien, he could not but see that they were honest, more honest as a race than the whites. They fulfilled their promises—to one another—to the letter, theft—from one another—was a major crime, but seldom committed. They were hospitable. A guest waxed fat even at the expense of the host's fasting, his belongings, his person were sacred. Certainly, they were brave. They had their own ideas as to what constituted silly recklessness or foolish chances, to be sure, but that was common sense. Certainly, they were deeply and reverently religious. Andy was cursed by the necessity of taking the other man's point of view, he could not help it. Possibly, the point of view of the red race was a lower one than that of the white race, but he was beginning to entertain a sneaking notion that perhaps the individuals, on the whole, lived up to it better. Which raised a nice philosophical point that resulted merely in Andy's confusion of mind. He was no philosopher. At this point, he gave it up. But he did like Indians.

In this, he was almost unique. A great many of the trappers, such as Joe Crane, liked individual Indians, or certain small groups or bands of Indians. A great many more of them got on well with Indians in a rough-and-ready fashion, fighting or fraternizing with equal zest according to the circumstance of the moment. But Indians, as a race apart, were to be considered objectively as one considers any other phenomenon of nature. And already a class was building up that later was to become numerous. These were professed Indian haters, *Indian killers*. Sometimes, their attitude was based merely on a low and bestial racial antipathy. More often, it grew from exasperation over continued petty annoyance—valuable traps persistently stolen, horses raided, highway robberies which left them naked on the prairies, or the more deadly feuds engendered by the killing of a partner or close friend. After such an episode, often bloody retribution was visited at the next opportunity and on Indians innocent of even the knowledge of the outrage. These men were implacable, and looked with fierce contempt on the effeminacy of any sympathy whatever for the *red devils*. Often, they joined in with one tribe in their wars on other tribes solely for the satisfaction of killing Indians!

So we see Andy, in this interval of waiting, often among the lodges of the Shoshones or the Utahs, smoking gravely with chief or medicine man, exchanging views and news in the swift sign talk. Among the former, he found many belonging to the band that had the season before raided away the horses at Green River, and who had in return been raided by the trappers to the loss not only of the plunder but of their own animals as well. He discovered in them no hard feelings because of the episode, and on the contrary, a genuine admiration. In spite of this, and of the murder of some of Provost's men farther north, the Shoshones were inclined to be friendly.

He learned of curious beliefs, and was inspired with what amounted to real curiosity to find out whether these beliefs were general or local to these tribes.

For example, the custom of scalping. It seemed that scalps were, to these people, not merely a trophy of prowess. To scalp an enemy meant annihilation of his soul. If a man was killed, but not scalped, he became for all eternity the servant of his slayer. Each was condemned to suffer forever in the future life the mutilations inflicted in this. It was a dreadful doctrine, but it explained many things. That was why a brave enemy was scalped, but a cowardly enemy, sometimes, was not. One can manage a cowardly servant, but not one of sufficient spirit. The soul of a dead man escapes through his mouth, so that one who meets death by strangulation is earth-bound. A man killed in the dark dwells eternally in darkness, which is why, the priest explained, it is bad medicine to attack before dawn. These things were intensely interesting to Andy, and he told them to his companions. Joe was not impressed.

"Look out you don't git to be an Injun, Andy," he warned. "That's bad medicine for shore. Oh, yes," he acknowledged, as Andy's glance strayed toward Flying Woman. "Injuns is good enough people sometimes. But they ain't white folks."

In all the careless, idle concourse of the river bottom, Sublette and Jedediah Smith alone were preoccupied with responsibility. They examined carefully the combined resources of peltries brought in by the various bands, counting and listing the beaver skins available for trade, not only by the white trappers but by the Utahs and Shoshones. Closely familiar with Ashley's affairs, they had a very accurate notion of what would be required to save the enterprise and set the company in a sure solvency for another season's trade. Their conclusions were discouraging. Although the total catch was an imposing one, the St. Louis commitments were heavy. Furthermore, they must consider the returns as practically complete. The parties still out under Ashley's direct command were small. Andy Burnett's report of their condition when he had last seen them had not indicated they would bring in any appreciable number of pelts. Smith and Sublette agreed that the outlook was not brilliant, but they shared their anxieties with none, and the happy-go-lucky picnic in the valley of the Green continued on until the appointed date was at hand.

Then, unexpectedly, Ashley returned, and at his tail, a long, ragged procession that continued and continued to emerge from the rimrock until fully half a hundred men had come into view, and with them, a swarm of laden pack animals. As they rode nearer, Ashley was recognized, and Provost, and the American trappers who had started with them. But who were these others? They were a wild-looking lot, but wild in some subtle alien fashion. Small differences in equipment or in arms did not escape the appraisement of sharp eyes, to be sure, but the strangeness was not a matter of externals merely. Its outward seeming came from within. They were definitely foreigners. A few wore red sash belts, and by these, the wise ones identified them.

"*Canayens*," said they. "Hudson's Bay men."

The strangers bunched together as they neared the encampment, riding in soberly after the American trappers who had already charged away in their impetuous fashion. At the river, they turned off to one side and began to erect their lodges and unpack their numerous horses.

Ashley greeted Sublette and Jedediah Smith aside from the general jubilation and row. He was in high spirits, blowing away his associates' immediately expressed anxieties with a laugh.

"See there!" he cried. "Over by the river! Fourteen thousand five hundred beaver skins! And prime! You never saw better! Ogden's men come in to trade with us! Our troubles are over!"

"How did you get them?" Smith, who knew the breed, marveled.

"Told them what I'd pay," said Ashley simply.

"And what about Ogden?"

Ashley's face became exaggeratedly expressionless. He stared straight before him.

"There are several ways of skinning a beaver," said he.

That might be. How this beaver was actually skinned has always been made a mystery, though desertion because of discontent is an adequate explanation. Whether because they were ordered to silence, or because there was really nothing more to tell, Ashley's men never went beyond the general's statement. Andy learned nothing further from them. But he heard plenty elsewhere, especially in later years. The stories varied. Ashley had found Ogden destitute and had taken his furs for the relief of his necessities. This was probably a confusion with Jedediah Smith's performance with the Iroquois. He had stumbled on a cache of Ogden's furs and had appropriated them. This was likely an offspring of the trappers' resentment against the British invasion.

"Got no business pushin' so fur east. Their kentry's out Columbia way —let 'em keep out of our'n!"

The same sentiment was responsible for the story that it was a plain hold-up, a robbery by force. The disparity of numbers was glaring, though one might believe almost anything of the audacity of hard-bitten mountain men. But outside of that, the yarn is absurd. Such a high-handed performance would have been shrieked aloud through the halls of international diplomacy. As a matter of fact, neither the Hudson's Bay Company nor Ogden himself ever went into details.

Andy heard these stories as of certain knowledge from people who never crossed the Missouri until years later. He grew tired of denials and speculations. The most absurd was that Ashley had debauched and stupefied Ogden's men with whiskey and laudanum. This continued to exasperate him to the last.

"How could he?" he cried, "The general had cached most of his trade goods at the rendezvous. He lost most of what little he took with him when his boats upset. Where would he get whiskey?"

At any rate, the beaver was skinned. Fourteen thousand five hundred, prime. These, with the season's catch of the various parties, were not only sufficient to lift Ashley's debts, but assured him a comfortable fortune. The Rocky Mountain Fur Company was a growing concern.

They dug up the cache and carried its contents to a great lodge that had been erected to serve as a store. This did not take long, for there were many willing hands. They stacked the flat wooden kegs, with their sides curved to fit a pack animal, reverently in a corner, patting them affectionately. There were two piles. The kegs of one contained genuine whiskey, the other *spirits*, which meant plain alcohol. The latter were in the majority. This was the most compact form in which liquor could be carried, for it could be *cut*, diluted down with water as far as the traffic would bear. It was the usual trapper and Indian tipple. The whiskey was reserved for the more important officers—or those who cared to pay a very high price.

It was announced that trade would not begin until the next day. However, in the meantime, a vessel of liquor was prepared of diluted alcohol *on the prairie*, gratis. Certain of the Shoshone and Utah chiefs were summoned and included in the ceremony. Their tin cups, too, were full, but the dilution was greater than in the case of the white men. The Little Burgeway justified this to Andy. Andy enjoyed the Little Burgeway. He was indeed little—a rotund, active man with a high voice, but decisive for all that.

"Liquor affects Injins more than white men," said he, "so it *ought* to be weaker."

Andy and Jim Bridger had been appointed by Ashley to assist, not only in this first free distribution, but also in the trade to follow the next morning. He had noticed that neither of these lads had helped themselves as freely as the others.

When the ceremony was over Ashley called them, together with Sublette, Smith, and Campbell, into the trading lodge. The group, under his direction, segregated and laid aside a certain amount of goods and two kegs of alcohol.

"These are for the Hudson's Bay men yonder," he said. "I want them carried to their camp immediately." Sublette surveyed the pile.

"Is that what you're paying for those furs, General?" he asked.

Ashley nodded. Sublette gave vent to a low whistle.

"I got them practically for a song," said Ashley. "And Hachter," he instructed the Little Burgeway, "you get some sort of receipt. That finishes the transaction."

Hachter grinned understandingly.

Next morning the trade began briskly. Sublette had already listed the number and quality of each man's pelts, and had determined the value of his credit. For beaver skins, he was allowed five dollars. Two otters equaled one beaver. No other furs were then considered worthwhile.

Against this credit, the trapper drew for his necessities and desires. Besides such essentials as powder, lead, caps or flints, blankets, knives, axes, traps, tobacco and the like, he had, considering everything, a wide field of choice. If he were gastronomically inclined he could buy tea, coffee, sugar, flour, bacon, dried fruit, even raisins. If he were tired of doing everything for himself, he could get iron, copper, or sheet-iron kettles, cloth or flannel, buttons, and thread, with which to make himself clothes, bridles, spurs, horseshoes and nails, handkerchiefs, looking-glasses, razors, soap, a host of most strange and unexpected items of a civilization long since faded into remote distance. For those who had squaws was a wide choice among the *Injin goods*, despised by the white bachelors. And you may be sure the ladies saw to it they had what they wanted before their white man had balanced his account. For her, there was scarlet cloth and blue cloth, calico, and ordinary cotton, and little bells and worsted binding and beads with which to ornament. She must, if her man was to save his face among her people, possess sufficient vermilion for her complexion, finger and arm rings, colored kerchiefs, bright ribbons—a host of astounding items to be seen in this day and age west of the Rockies!

Everything was open and aboveboard. As far as money went, a man knew what he had and what he was going to get. Prices were fixed and were not varied. To be sure, they were high, but why not? These goods had come a long and difficult journey, uninsured. Powder cost two dollars a pint, but it was worth it. And a man knew what he was getting, he could take it or leave it.

That was for white men. When their wants had been supplied—or their credit exhausted—and it came to Injin trade, that was different. Then figuratively, the price tags were removed. That's where the trading came in. Sometimes, you could get a prime beaver skin worth six dollars for a pair of steel bracelets that had cost a dollar a pair, and a drink of diluted alcohol amounting to, perhaps, ten cents. The alcohol came first. It took only an accurate clerk to attend to white trade, it required a shrewd reader of desires to handle the Injins to the best advantage.

Hachter possessed that tact and that shrewdness. Interested in this phase of his business, Andy volunteered to continue his assistance, and was accepted. His duty was to parcel out or to weigh out the commodities each desired, while Hachter computed the prices against the credits. This was not a very complicated job. Each man knew accurately what he wanted as far as necessities went, the variety of other things was not so extensive that it took long to make a choice. Nevertheless each customer liked to dawdle, to linger a little. Hachter kept them moving without appearing to do so and without offending anyone's sense of his due leisure. Each invariably ended his purchases with a small quantity of liquor, which he took away in a canteen or a gourd or perhaps a bladder. This was usually whiskey. The kegs of alcohol stood almost untouched.

A few of the men had very little credit, and in some cases, none at all. The anticipated cards had been busy the evening before. Beyond the limits of their credit, Hachter advanced the barest necessities only—powder, lead, caps, tobacco, perhaps new traps, or knives. This was a debt, to be repaid next year. He refused anything else. Andy was surprised to discover in the rotund little man with the squeaky voice an uncompromising decisiveness. One or two of the rougher men were inclined to bully it a bit. But Hachter paid them no attention.

When the last of the trappers had finished this preliminary business, a messenger was sent to the Indian villages to announce that trade was open. The entire red population moved up—men, women, children, and most of the dogs. Some, a minority, carried furs for barter, possibly an equal number, mostly women, stuck close to them to see that their desires, too, were considered in the exchange, the majority merely came along for the ride or on the off chance of begging something, either from the whites or the more affluent of the Indians themselves. All these people squatted themselves silently in a ragged half-circle in front of the trading lodge. They did not speak, they did not move, they stared. In the lodge opening sat Hachter. He did not speak, he did not move, he stared back. A nirvanic aloofness seemed to have replaced for all eternity the former bustle and activity. Nothing at all happened for at least half an hour. Then Standing Wolf, the Shoshone chief, abruptly arose, stalked across the intervening space, and flopped down at Hachter's side. The latter filled a pipe, lighted it, and passed it to his visitor. Turn and turn about they smoked. When the tobacco had been burned out, Hachter signed to Andy. The latter brought forth one at a time the items of the present Hachter had determined upon as appropriate to the occasion, and laid them before Standing Wolf, namely and to wit, fifty rounds of ammunition for that potentate's old brass-bound fusee, eight small plugs of tobacco, a knife, a package of vermilion, and a yard of cloth for a breechclout. He added, after a proper pause, a handful of bright beads, and a length of figured black and white cotton cloth known as a *cotillion*.

"For your woman," signed Hachter as to this contribution.

Standing Wolf made no sign of satisfaction, though this was a magnificent present even for an important chief. But his lady was not so stoical. She came forward, gathered up the plunder, and retreated, with every symptom of frank delight. Standing Wolf was next presented with a standard-sized liquor cup filled to the brim with so stiff a mixture that his eyes moistened as he gulped it down. After which he retired in favor of the Utah chief, with whom the process was repeated.

All this deliberate ceremonial consumed time. By now, it was near sundown. But the trade had begun, and it must continue. Men came forward with bundles, which they silently opened for inspection. Hachter sorted over their contents, appraising the skins, a slow and careful process, for he must make no mistakes in quality. In the meantime, the Indian, invariably with a squaw at his elbow, was inspecting the assortment temptingly displayed. She talked a lot, and he made no sign that he had even heard her. When Hachter had made up his mind the bargaining began. The white man gave in barter just exactly what he had to, and no more. But first, he offered each new customer a cupful of the stinging trade liquor. Occasionally he refused to deal, and bundled the would-be seller out, furs and all.

"He'll be back," he told Andy, "when the liquor works."

But one man at a time was admitted to the trade lodge. Jim Bridger stood outside to see to this. He and Andy seemed to be the only two, besides Hachter, to feel any responsibility to the occasion. In the trappers' camp, bright fires burned, about which moved dark figures. Ashley, Sublette, Smith, Campbell, old Fitzpatrick, the leading figures of the enterprise, had retired to the privacy of Ashley's lodge. In these modern days, they probably would have been reported *in conference*. They had taken with them the supply of genuine whiskey for safekeeping. Hachter was very grateful for the assistance of the two young men.

"You boys are a help," he squeaked, "and I surely appreciate it."

"Did you expect to do this alone?" asked Andy incredulously.

"Oh, I'd handle it," the trader assured him. "Sublette is going to relieve me later. And if he's too drunk, there's always Jed Smith. He's religious, sorta. He don't drink. Consarn those wolves, they've took all the good whiskey. I could do with a little drink right now myself. I'm getting tired, sorta." He turned to shake his head decidedly and to hold up three fingers as a counter-proposal to the deliberate bargain of the moment. A sudden curiosity beset him. "Whyn' you boys join the celebration?" he asked. "You aren't getting paid for this."

"I want to see how she's done," replied Bridger. "May want to do some tradin' myself someday." Andy nodded, he had no present intention of going into the business, but his curiosity was catholic. And this scene was fascinatingly full of color, the wavering fire flames, the spread array of trade goods, the blanketed savage, the play of light and shadow on metal, bright color, and gleaming eyeballs.

"Here," said Hachter, coming to a sudden decision. "You take charge for a few minutes. Kick that fellow out if he gets funny."

He disappeared. The customer prowled about. Only once did he, tentatively, reach out as though to pick up some object for examination, but withdrew his hand at Bridger's growl. Hachter bustled in, carrying a coffee pot. He set out three liquor cups and carefully filled them to the brim.

"No thumbs in this, boys," he said cryptically. "I think we've earned this, though it don't pay to drink on this job. Whiskey's good, but it makes you too bold." He tossed off his portion at a gulp. "They're having quite a party over there," he confided, wiping his mouth with the back of his hand. "Can't blame them. Best trade I ever saw. They'll be rich men. Wish I was on shares. Oh, well!" He looked at Andy and Bridger. "What's the matter? This is the good stuff. I took it away from those wolves over there. They can't hog it all. Don't you boys drink?"

The two looked at one another, embarrassed.

"Sometimes," said one.

"Not just now," said the other. As a matter of fact, both Andy and Bridger were always remarkable for their sobriety in a wild age and a wild country and in consequence, were occasionally, but very temporarily, underestimated by rough and unthinking strangers.

"Well," observed Hachter, "Jed Smith's religious, too." He carefully poured the contents of the two cups back in the coffee pot.

A white man entered, thrusting aside the hesitating Indian buyer of the moment.

"Gimme four gallons," he demanded brusquely, then, Hachter turned to consult his book of credits. "Oh, I'm good for it!"

"I suspect so," agreed Hachter equably, but without hurrying his search.

"Whiskey," added the trapper.

"No whiskey," said Hachter, without looking up.

"Not till tomorrow."

"Why not?"

Hachter jerked his head toward the leader's lodge.

The visitor swore gustily.

"Well, make her Panther P'is'n then. But mind ye, none of yore Injin mixes, yo' little runt."

"Run along and have yore party, Mulford," squeaked the Little Burgeway, impatiently.

Mulford's eye fell on Bridger and Andy.

"Come on, boys," he invited hospitably. "My treat! Big doin's!"

"So do," advised Hachter. "Things will go slow for a while now. I aim to snatch me a little sleep."

Drunken men are immensely diverting to themselves and to one another, but not very amusing to one who remains sober, or nearly so. Mulford's party was not so bad at first. The men sipped the liquor from the conventional or standard liquor cups, and talked or sang. The quality of the talk and the singing became all the more pleasing to its participants in exact ratio to its actual deterioration in quality. Two or three talked at once, and the others listened just sufficiently to catch a cue to begin their own bragging. These ordinarily silent, direct men held forth after the manner of Homer's warriors. Each had a lot to say about how brave he was and how many hardships he had suffered and how many narrow escapes he had had. Each had killed dozens of Indians and hundreds of grizzly bears. Each was paramount favorite with the Indian girls, could outdrink ary man on earth. Each possessed the fastest-riding animal, without exception, that had ever been foaled. Even Joe Crane, carried away by mob psychology, claimed loudly that distinction for Buggs, his raw-boned mule. This gained general attention, expressed in a loud laugh.

"Wall, anyway, he's the stiddiest." Joe had to back down from a position too absurd, even for alcohol.

Fortunately for the peace of the company these wild claims came in bunches, so that nobody really paid any of them any attention.

"An ef'n you don't believe what I'm sayin'," each concluded his recital, "I'll prove it!"

The proof offered was medieval in spirit. The protestant was ready to run a race, or wrestle a fall, or shoot at a mark, or fight if preferred. One comparative pacificist was willing to leave the question of his integrity to a game of *cold sledge* with the cards! Only occasionally now did some particularly picturesque narration catch general attention for a few moments. As when Old Man Goddard opened up on a real—or mythical—voyage he had made toward the southwest. The southwest was then the land of mystery. Nobody knew quite what to believe of it. Old Man Goddard gave them plenty of material for choice. His leathern old countenance never changed expression, his lank jaws seemed never to cease their slow champing on his quid, his steady, young blue eyes calmly—and successfully—challenged expression of disbelief. He had traveled with a certain Jules Lefourey, who was dead, but on whom he constantly called for corroboration.

"Ef'n Jules were yere now, *he'd* tell you!" asserted Old Man Goddard convincingly.

"Ary man here ever see a carcagne?" inquired the veteran. "Wall, they's a plenty down yander. Talk about yore grizzly b'ar!" The old man's expectoration of contempt completely quenched an aspiring young flame in the fire, "Why a carcagne'll jump right into camp, and you settin' thar by the fire, and grab yo're meat yore roastin' and make off so fast yo' don't see nothin' but a streak, like a lightnin' flash made out of shadder. I seen one once plain, though. He had a head and shoulders like a wolf, and the rest of him was b'ar."

"Did you shoot him?" asked Andy.

Old Man Goddard turned, surveyed the lad deliberately for a moment, and turned back.

"Not this child," he condescended to reply, after a crushing silence. "He's bigger than a buffalo bull. And when he yells, I tell you, everything *stops!*"

He chewed rhythmically. They waited.

"They's some white Injins down in that kentry," he resumed at last. "They live in a big city on a prairie in the mountings. The tops of their houses is all made out'n pure gold. The cliffs all around is about two thousand foot, straight up. They kain't git out of thar, and nobody kin git down. Munchies, they call them."

Gold roofs! They pricked up their ears. Injins—even if white! Might be pickings there! They pressed eagerly, even though somewhat skeptically, for details.

But Old Man Goddard veered off, became vague, discouraging, changed the subject as soon as he could. He'd tried to go back. Never could find the place again. Took some men with him. Clumb half the high peaks in Ameriky but couldn't find hide nor ha'r of them. Spent months at the search. No use.

At this, the skepticism became vocal. Old Man Goddard fired up. If they didn't believe him, he had a Munchie coin he had found on top of the cliffs. Jules, who was raised scientific, said it had Latin words on it. The coin? He'd lost that when he was raided by Apaches back in '17. But he hastened to change the subject, the strangest thing he'd seed down thar was a putrefied forest!

"What's that?"

"A putrefied forest," repeated Old Man Goddard firmly. "Sure as my rifle's got hind sights! It was dead of winter. One day we crossed over a divide and came on a perairie whar was green grass and birds singin' and leaves on the trees! This was February, mind ye. Our hosses was like to die when they see the grass. Hurrah for summer doin's, sez we. I ups with old Ginger and clips the head off'n a grouse. I finds it was stone. And Jules lets drive at a cottonwood with his axe *shurk-k-k*, and off snaps a piece of the blade! We looks at the hosses standin' thar shakin' like they was cold, an' I'm doggone if'n the grass isn't stone too, and it bruk off like the stems of clay pipes! Jules was raised scientific, like I sez, and he says it was putrefied."

"Didn't she smell bad, then?" asked someone after a tactful silence.

"Smell bad!" Old Man Goddard snorted contemptuously. "Wasn't they froze? A polecat wouldn't smell bad ef'n he was froze! And what's more," he added, "ef'n you don't believe it, I brung away a piece of the wood."

"Lose that when the Apaches raided you?" asked someone dryly.

Old Man Goddard favored the questioner with his slow stare. Then deliberately, he fumbled in his *possible* sack and produced a bit of petrified wood, which he offered for inspection.

"See," he pointed out. "She's got the bark on her, Wagh!"

They passed the fragment from hand to hand. There it was, indubitable. It was too much for them.

"Let's have another drink," someone proposed. They crowded forward. Old Man Goddard chewed away in his slow rhythm. It was a moment of triumph, but his leathern countenance did not change.

Andy and his new friend Jim Bridger were enjoying the show. They had not been able to dodge the initial proffers of the Panther P'is'n without giving serious offense. The harsh liquor warmed them and expanded their hearts and their appreciation. Old Man Goddard was a wonder! Hachter was a wonder! Jedediah Smith was a wonder! Everybody in the world was wonderful! Jim Bridger told of his visit to Salt Lake and how surprised he was to find he could sit upright in the water without sinking. That was a tremendous joke on old Jim! They dissolved in laughter over the joke. They could not get over it. And just as they had managed to reclutch their gravity, Jim added that the shores stank. That set them off again. Somehow, that extra detail was just too much! It was irresistibly comic. Mulford stood before them.

"Drink her up!" he was insisting. "Drink her up, I tell ye. Do you want to make me out a ring-tailed gollywop, at my own party?"

Somehow, it seemed highly undesirable to make anyone out a ring-tailed gollywop if it could be avoided. So they accepted the brimming liquor cups and drank her up, as requested.

The lights were bright, the singing sweet to poignancy, the conversation brilliant, though a trifle confused. A great many wonderful things were awaiting a trifle of focusing. This could be attended to at any moment, but was not quite worthwhile. It was pleasanter to bask in the large general comfort of expanded consciousness.

But now Andy felt a considerable attention directed his way. He concentrated. Joe Crane was capering about, doing his imitation of a crowing cock, leaping into the air, and clapping his heels together three times before hitting the ground. He was bragging at the top of his lungs, but for once, not about himself. Andy realized at length that he was the subject. That was why he had been called to concentrate. He listened gravely.

Joe was boasting most particularly about Andy's shooting. He detailed a few of what he claimed were the boy's most notable feats. Some of them were based on facts, some were pure figments of invention. It did not matter, for in both cases, the results were the same. Of the innumerable Indians, Andy, had slain in battle, not one but was took plumb atween the eyes, of the thousands of animals he had laid low, few were killed save on the dead run and at extreme distances. Whenever anybody hooted a doubt, Joe met the situation by the simple expedient of increasing the range.

Andy listened in a spirit of detached appraisal. The precise instances Joe was shouting had somehow escaped Andy's memory for the moment. Doubtless they were in that large and expanded area of his consciousness which he had not focused. But he approved gravely of the general trend of the recital. He was filled with an overmastering indignation at the derisive skepticism of some of the audience. It made him mad that anybody should doubt good old Joe! That idea took charge of him. The fact that this was a question of his own prowess escaped him completely. Andy was a modest lad by nature. But to imply that good old Joe was a liar! Or that Knock-em-stiff, the historic Boone gun, could not drive a nail as far as you could see it —or farther! Andy was on his feet, vehemently backing Joe.

They laughed sarcastically, and the more they laughed, the more the point at issue swelled until it filled the universe with its importance. At length Joe, with a wild whoop, leaped the fire and disappeared into the darkness. But the laughter at his apparent retreat had hardly died when he was back, brandishing the long rifle.

"Yere ye be, Andy!" he cried. "Load her up, load her keerful. We'll larn 'em! Wagh!"

Andy seized the piece and the horn and shot pouch. To his surprise he found that this loading business had been left out in that unfocused area. He had to use tremendous strength of mind, tremendous concentration to bring it in. And when he had moved the process of measuring the powder, placing the patch, driving home the bullet into definition, it became tremendous. The simple movements necessary assumed a spaced and pompous deliberation that took all his vital forces to attend, crowding aside to a periphery infinitely remote from all else that the universe contained. When the loading was finished Andy returned ponderously to the immediate surroundings as from a distance. That was the way things were moving now, ponderously.

Joe was flourishing a small billet of wood, possibly six inches square.

"Plug her, Andy!" he cried. "Plumb center! Larn these yere beavers what shootin' is!"

He capered away to the limit of the flickering illumination thrown by the fire, faced about, and thrust the bit of wood between his knees.

"Thar ye be!" he cried. "That's what I think of Andy's shoot'n'. Plug her, boy!"

"Sure," muttered Andy, "I'll plug her."

He raised the Boone gun and tried to take aim. The sights seemed dim, and somehow confused. The silver bead of the front sight divided, moved apart until there were two beads, drew together again until there was but one. This was an interesting phenomenon, which Andy paused to consider curiously and with entire detachment. Its bearing on his present effort did not concern him at all. The hind sight too was acting queerly. It expanded to twice its natural size, blurred into a fuzz, and then contracted. This too was an intriguing prodigy of nature. While Andy was still contemplating it the reflex habit of his trigger finger discharged the piece.

He came into full possession of his faculties with a shock. Joe was capering about holding up the split billet, which had been sent spinning from between his knees, and which he had retrieved. In some miraculous manner Andy's sure instinct had functioned without his knowledge or volition. He stared about him a moment, then lurched into the darkness and was physically sick.

On trembling legs he staggered to his lodge. His brain whirled, but he had become suddenly and entirely sobered. He threw himself on his blankets and covered his head, trying in vain to shut out the clamoring vision of what by grace of Providence he had escaped. Flying Woman, Joe's Squaw, was bending over him solicitously.

"Napi-awh-ki—white man's water—no good," said she. "You sleep."

"No good," agreed Andy with a groan. But he could not sleep. Too vividly he was haunted by the picture of Joe, his kneecap shattered, and lying here in this lodge, a thousand miles in the wilderness. Outside, the sounds of the revel surged and fell like the beat of a storm.

Chapter 16
Rendezvous—Continued

The great spree at the Green River continued. That does not imply a continuous state of top inebriation on the part of everybody. The thing rose and fell like a tide. But somebody was always whooping it up, just as somebody was always just falling asleep, or waking up, or eating, or quarreling, or pulling off a little private concert of his own. Nobody was ever completely sober. On the other hand, few were so drunk as to be out of control. These iron men could consume astonishing quantities of liquor before the effects became apparent.

Such was not the case with the Indians. One measuring cupful of even the much-diluted trade liquor seemed to awaken to life a personality hitherto dormant and unsuspected. That personality demanded, with all the strength of the most imperative instinct, an immediate and continuous repetition of the dose to the point of stupefaction. It was, once aroused by the first drink, a craving as insistent as that of a drug addict. There was no question of denying it, or of controlling it. More liquor must be had, at any price, at any hazard. After two or three drinks Hachter was able, by judicious denial, to get almost anything he dared ask for the alcohol mixture he dispensed. Nor could he buy now with any other goods. That trade was finished, as far as the Indians were concerned.

The business was for the most part of *consume on the premises*. Andy Burnett, sobered and scared by his narrow escape the night before from crippling his best friend, avoided the trappers for the moment, and helped the Little Burgeway. The lodge was continuously crowded with Indians, in all stages of drunkenness, jostling and elbowing, thrusting forward their offerings in barter, each demanding instant attention. Hachter had barricaded himself behind a rough counter. He was perspiring freely, and looked tired, but he kept his head amid all the confusion, and retained control in a loose sort of way, sensing the temper not only of the crowd but of the various individuals, thrusting back some, beckoning others forward, guiding the situation with sensitive fingers as one guides wild horses. Andy had not been there five minutes before he realized that there was a lot more in this trading business than merely passing out some things in exchange for others.

Hachter was grateful for both his help and for his company. He kept up a running conversation of comment, in relief from long nervous tension. It developed he had a definite philosophy of intoxication.

"Long as you keep things running along smooth, Burnett," said he, "you won't have any trouble. An Injun is good-natured enough, and they're mostly all alike. White men are different. Some get crying drunk, some get quarrelsome, some get singing drunk, or sentimental, never can tell unless you know them. An Injin is wild and noisy, but he ain't mean. Only thing is, he's touchy. Got to watch out his feelings don't get hurt. Can't look cross-eyed at him. Got to keep your eyes shining. If he gets his back hair sticking up because he thinks you're neglecting him, then watch out! Keep looking 'em over, and spot the ones that think they've been waiting long enough."

While he was talking Hachter never ceased activity for a moment, flipping open the offered peltries, abstracting what he decided was the price of a drink, after a keen appraisal of his customer's condition. The offer was an ultimatum, take it or leave it. Sometimes, but not often, the Indian attempted to haggle, but half-heartedly. As a usual thing the savage seized the cup and drained it without further parley, swept up the rest of his belongings, and gave way to the next.

Hachter drew the liquor from one of several kegs placed on the counter. The contents of the kegs varied in their degree of dilution. The drunker the Indian the weaker the liquor served him. Andy noticed that in some cases Hachter thrust his thumb into the cup, diminishing by that much the amount that it contained. He understood now the mysterious interchange of the day before, when the Little Burgeway had offered himself and Jim Bridger a drink, and had assured them that there were *no thumbs in this*. Once or twice Hachter reached below the counter for an especial cup. Andy, examining it, found that melted tallow had been poured into the bottom to cut down its capacity. He ventured, hesitatingly, to doubt the strict honesty of this procedure. Hachter was astonished.

"Why," said he virtuously, "too much liquor is bad for Injins!"

It was a grinding, exhausting, nerve-racking business, especially as the Indians grew drunker, more *touchy*, and therefore more inclined to quarrel. All were armed. At times tension was stretched fine, close to the breaking point. One savage in especial, a brawny creature with his face painted black, became more and more truculent. He thrust others aside, bullied them, shouted, danced about. Hachter could do nothing with him. The little man was annoyed.

"Hell have 'em all going," he complained to Andy in his high voice.

"Don't give him any more," suggested Andy.

But Hachter shook his head.

"I'd hate to risk that," said he. "Guess I'll have to fix him."

He stooped beneath the shelter of the rough counter for a moment.

"Here, you big idiot," he said in English. "Take that."

The bully seized the proffered cup and drained it at a gulp. He brandished his warhawk, lurched about, shouldering aside those in his way. Hachter watched him anxiously. But in a few moments his movements became more uncertain. He groped his way toward the entrance to the lodge but changed his mind, lay down on the ground, and fell sound asleep. Nobody paid him further attention. They stepped over and around his prostrate body until finally, finding him too much in the way, someone rolled him through the door into the open.

"Laudanum," Hachter briefly answered Andy's question. "Don't know how I'd make out without it." He wiped the perspiration from his forehead.

The noise and the heat were terrific. Andy's head swam. It was a nightmare.

A white man entered, thrusting the crowding Indians aside unceremoniously. They gave way without protest. It was Joe Crane on the crest of the wave.

"Sot her out, old timer!" he cried. "An' see you give me good stuff!"

"You giving the party, Joe?"

"Wagh!" agreed the trapper. "Done lost her on a hoss race. Hullo, Andy. Come on!"

Andy demurred. He was horrifiedly off parties after last night's experience. Joe seemed to have forgotten all about it.

"I promised to help Hachter," said he.

Joe would have none of it.

"Hachter's gittin' on all right, ain't you, Hachter?" he asked.

He reached over to grasp at the little man's neekband.

"Come on, you little runt," he cried. "Close up shop for a while and come to my party."

Hachter avoided him.

"All right, Joe. I'll be there pretty soon. You run along and start things." He caught Andy's eye. "I'll bring Burnett. You run along."

"Wall, see you do, or I'll be back to git you!" promised Joe, aiming a playful blow at the Little Burgeway that would have knocked him through the back of the lodge if it had landed.

He shouldered the keg and lurched out.

"One side, you red devils!" he shouted at the Indians. They gave way, laughing, shouting back, then crowded forward again. Hachter looked after him and sighed.

"I'll give that fellow some laudanum too if he don't watch out," said he. "Lord, I'm tired!"

Sublette thrust himself through the Indians.

"How you making it?" he asked. Andy had not laid eyes on him since the day before when he and Ashley, together with Robert Campbell and Jedediah Smith, had disappeared into the general's lodge together with the keg of real whiskey. He was surprised to see that the young man was clear-eyed and alert, in full command of all his faculties. Evidently the party was not quite as *some* as Hachter had implied, at least as far as Sublette was concerned.

"Pretty good," said Hachter.

Sublette looked at him keenly.

"You're about played out," he accused. "You ought to have been relieved long ago. But there isn't a man who knows anything about it sober enough to trust. Think you can hold out another two hours? Some mighty important questions we've simply got to decide, and the general is set on getting away."

"I reckon I can," agreed the Little Burgeway.

But Sublette was not satisfied.

"Your eyes are like holes in a blanket," said he irresolutely. "You've got to have rest. Here, I'll take charge. You go get you a sleep. Stop on your way and tell the general."

Hachter started to protest. Andy intervened.

"Let me," he suggested.

Sublette's piercing gray-blue eyes swung to meet his.

"I'm sober," said Andy. "And I'll remain so."

"What do you know about this business?"

"Nothing," acknowledged Andy, "except what I've watched and seen. But I'm willing to try. I know Indians pretty well."

"That's right. I remember." Sublette nodded. He hesitated a moment, then produced two silver-mounted pistols from the belt around his waist. "Take these, but don't use them unless you have to...come, Hachter. Nay, man, I insist!"

Andy found himself alone, trading liquor with the Indians.

The situation was disconcerting, ridiculous. Andy had placed himself in it on impulse. Now he could not get out of it. He was no teetotaller, and had no general convictions on the subject of liquor. Nevertheless he had sense enough and stability of character enough to see what too much liquor could do to a man. He had had a demonstration of that the evening before when, under the influence of Panther P'is'n, he had shot the bit of wood from between Joe Crane's knees. He shuddered at the memory of it. He was getting a pretty good second demonstration of what it could do now. Hachter was giving less and less of weaker and weaker tipple in exchange for the skins. Andy had tacitly pledged himself to a continuance of the policy. It looked perilously close to cheating. Hachter did not seem to think so, neither did anybody else. It was accepted trade custom, sanctioned by long use. What alternative? Give them full strength in full value? That certainly *would* put them crazy, or out! No use thinking of trying to trade anything but liquor now, they would not have it. No use to refuse. Dangerous. They would tear the place down. Besides, it was his business to get the fur. The whole thing was too complicated for Andy's simple and direct mind, so he did as he usually did—heaved overboard the whole question, and addressed himself to the immediate present.

He got on surprisingly well. The Indians liked him. Still it was no sinecure. Trade was brisk. Some of the savages were near the point of irresponsibility. Their eyes rolled in their heads, and they brandished their weapons in a muddled and purposeless abandon that might easily become dangerous. Andy watched them anxiously. He fingered the vial of laudanum, but he had no idea of the dosage. He should have thought to ask Hachter. He did not want to kill anybody.

Joe Crane was in the lodge, very drunk, and one or two others. He had come to find out why Andy and Hachter had not come to his party. Hachter's absence at first claimed all his attention.

"The little runt!" he cried. "Whar be ye? Yo' kain't hide out on me."

He was determined that Hachter must have concealed himself somewhere in the lodge for the express purpose of insulting Joe. The trapper insisted on searching the place, ferreting about under the bales of furs, behind the kegs, rummaging over the few remaining trade goods, prying into nooks and crevices too small for the concealment of a chipmunk. He was a nuisance, getting in the way, scattering things about in confusion and in temptation of theft by the Indians. Andy expostulated in vain. Finally, when Joe, failing everywhere else, showed symptoms of an intention to cut open the carefully pressed bales of peltries, Andy had to jerk him away bodily, and none too gently.

With a howl of outraged astonishment Joe whirled on him.

"Yo, goddam white-livered farmer yo'!" he shouted. "I'll cut yore heart out!" He fumbled at his belt for his knife.

Some tension snapped in Andy. He hit Joe squarely on the point of the jaw, and behind the blow was all the force of long-pent exasperation and nervous strain. The trapper went down like a log.

For the split fraction of a second the affair hung in balance. Anything might have happened. What between the drink-crazed savages on the hair line of outbreak, and Joe's two inebriated and truculent companions, there was the making of a very pretty massacre. But Andy's rage swept it away, beat it down, scattered it in all directions. Like most deliberate natures, he was slow to anger, but blind to consequences once aroused. He forgot all about the silver-mounted pistols in his belt. By the sheer blast of dynamics he drove them out of that lodge, red man and white, and they tumbled before him like frightened schoolboys. It was most unorthodox. If William Sublette had been there he would have said it could not be done. Possibly it had never been done before.

Then Andy went back and sat down and gradually subsided, and was filled with compunctions and a small but growing alarm. Joe, one of his best friends in the world! And what would happen now? What would the Indians do, once they had recovered? What, for that matter, would Joe's friends do? Everybody was pretty drunk. Andy was not thinking much of himself. But he had been left in charge, and this was how he had handled things! He was very downcast.

What should he do? Call Sublette and the others. That was the sensible thing—before anything more serious happened. Indeed, it was almost the obligatory thing. But Andy's slow and dogged obstinacy forbade. He had started this, he would see it through come hell or high water. His straight level eyebrows drew down. He seated himself on a keg and waited.

Nothing happened.

Gradually his tension of exasperation relaxed. He went to the door of the lodge and looked out. The capricious and semian inconstancy of drunkenness had passed him by for the moment. Joe's two companions had brought him to with a gourd of water in the face, whereupon that hardy citizen, filled with some new idea, had staggered off to try it. The Indians, their heads a whirl, had weaved their way to their own encampment to beat up a squaw or so, or race a horse, or fall asleep as the case might be. Andy was completely forgotten.

The scene was animated, to say the least, and noisy. Obstreperous mirth, whooping, howling, quarreling, singing, mounted Indians dashing into and through the encampment, yelling like fiends, the barking and baying and snarling and howling of the savage wolf dogs, the incessant *crack! crack! crack!* of rifles, and the occasional *wham-boom!* of a smoothbore fusee—it seemed that the very cup of the heavens must be reechoing with the row and the racket. But that mystic and poetical sense with which Andy had been compensated for some of his slower qualities knew better. Only just aside awaited the wilderness. Its serenity absorbed, hushed, deadened like felt. Undisturbed and unaware, the mountains brooded on in the unfolding vision of a million years. Deep in the clear waters of the river the trout and the grayling and the whitefish hung motionless against the current. Frog voices and whippoorwills intoned their unhurried accompaniment to the largo of the evening skies. Strangely comforted and relieved of his anxieties, Andy returned to his upturned keg.

Night fell and the evening wore on. Indians returned, demanding more rum. Andy served them. Gradually the lodge became again the center of potential trouble. Hachter did not show up, and Andy could not leave his charge unprotected in order to search him out. He had to do the best he could. The brawny savage with his face painted black had recovered from the dose of laudanum and was back again. He swaggered and threatened and was apparently always on the point of making real trouble. Andy wished he knew the Shoshone language. Only the Indian habit of supplementing talk, even with members of their own tribe, by fragments of sign language occasionally gave him a clue as to what it was all about. The big man flourished his warhawk, shot arrows into the ground at his feet. Andy became wholly fed up with him. At length the continuous strain brought its reaction. He fell into a fatalistic mood. If the fool went too far Andy would give him a ball from one of Sublette's silver-mounted pistols. Until then, let him rave.

And anyway another crazy idiot showed up who seemed a much more immediate threat. This was a small man, with vermilion stripes painted across his face. He rushed into the lodge, a knife in his hand, talking at a great rate, and obviously very angry. Darting toward Andy he tore and cut and slashed the turf at the young man's feet, and then rushed out again. Andy watched him narrowly, his hand on his pistol butt. The incident passed off without further trouble. But in ten minutes the Indian was back, repeating the performance, and at intervals thereafter all the rest of the evening. It was nerve-racking. Andy never knew what instant he might work himself up to actual attack. But always he confined his warlike demonstrations to the inoffensive sod. After a dozen repetitions Andy was strongly tempted to tap him on the head with the butt of the pistol and have it over with. But he held unto himself. It would never do to precipitate a row. He wished heartily that Hachter would return.

And just about as he had reached the limit of patience and was dangerously near to ruining the trade and his reputation as a trader, Hachter was back, very apologetic.

"I just fell dead asleep and couldn't seem to wake up," he explained. "This is hard business sometimes. It wears on a man."

"I know that!" agreed Andy fervently.

"Any trouble?"

"No real trouble. Close to it at times. There's one little fool that comes just short—here he is now!"

The vermilion-painted savage was back, dancing and howling, flourishing his knife, finally tearing and slashing the ground at Andy's feet.

"That's the one! I'd like to have one crack at him!" pleaded Andy.

Hachter spoke to the man in Shoshone. The man replied briefly, then dashed out, whooping and yelling, still on high. Hachter laughed until he had to wipe his eyes.

"What's the joke?" demanded Andy at length.

"Why, he's your friend!" cried Hachter. "He says he's been protecting you all the evening!"

"Looks like it," said Andy, kicking a toe at the slashed-up ground.

"He says he was showing how he was going to treat your enemies if they bothered you!" Hachter, at the sight of Andy's face, went off into another paroxysm of laughter.

"Oh, Lord!" cried the lad disgustedly. "I'm going to bed."

By next morning things were very considerably off the boil. Andy had slept the sound sleep of one nervously drained dry. He had not known when the noise had died down. Now he lay on his back in the lodge, staring up at the white wood smoke eddying fantastically across a bar of sunlight. From the branches of the big cottonwood just outside came the soft contemplative crooning of mourning doves. Over beyond, a pony nickered sharply. Clear-voiced meadow larks experimented with new songs. Beneath the accents of sound the river gabbled in a hurried and confidential undertone. In contrast to the redshot murky pandemonium of the night before, this was full of peace, and Andy soaked it up as his bodily tissues soaked up the first water after a desert *scrape*.

By and by he turned on his side and looked about him. Joe was back, and sleeping. Flying Woman was moving about. She caught Andy's eye, and smiled at him. Andy yielded to a sudden impulse.

"Pai-o-toki, come here," he commanded. "I want to talk to you. Sit here. Now," he resumed as she sank to the robe at his feet, "tell me this. Why do you not drink napi-awh-ki, the white man's water?"

"Blackfeet do not drink napi-awh-ki," she replied primly.

This was something Andy had not known, although he had twice wintered with that people. But it was a fact. Later the use of liquor was reserved for the chiefs. Still later the Blackfeet went to the other extreme. Which might, or might not, be made into some sort of argument as to inhibition, prohibition, and the like.

Andy pondered. His mind worked slowly but very surely. He was verging toward some sort of idea.

"But the women of the Shoshones, they do not drink napi-awh-ki," he proffered.

"It is the business of man to fight enemies and to bring game to the lodge," said Flying Woman. "It is the business of woman to feed her man, and make for him robes and clothing, to take care of what her man brings her. Is not that true?"

She paused for Andy's assent.

"If a man brings in no meat, if he runs away, leaving his lodge and his woman to be taken by the enemy, then he is no man. He may not sit in council. If a woman leaves the meat that her man has brought in to spoil, or her man to sleep beneath ragged robes or wear mean garments, then she is no woman. Is not that true?"

"This is true," acknowledged Andy. "But I asked—"

"Now think of this, I-tam-api," pursued Flying Woman. "If the man hunts the beaver and brings them in to the lodge, is not that the same thing as bringing in the black sand for the gun, and the white man's cloth, and the knife, and the axe, and the red paint for his face, and the kettle for his food, and all the other things which the white man gives for the skin of the beaver? Is not that the same thing, I-tam-api?"

"I suppose so," agreed Andy.

"Well, then!" Flying Woman completed her simple logic. "If the woman drinks up the beaver skin, instead of buying these things, is not that as though she left the meat to spoil?"

Andy surveyed the small, earnest figure with admiration.

Joe sat up with a prodigious yawn. They turned toward him.

"Ef'n yo' could bring in yore river I could drink her dry," confided Joe.

Flying Woman, understanding his gesture though not his words, presented him with a gourd. He drained it with noisy gulps and flung it aside. "That shines!" he cried. "Some doin's!" said he. "How yo' feelin', Andy?"

"Fine," said Andy. "How are *you* feeling, Joe?"

"Wall," confessed Joe, grinning ruefully, "*purty* fair. I made me a big diskivery, Andy, that I never knew afore."

"What's that?"

"Sleepin' is very bad fer a man. Wust thing a man kin do."

"How do you make that out?"

"I've proved it," stated Joe. "Looka yere, last night I was feelin' fine, top of the world, never better. This mornin' I'm feelin'—well—not so good. What's happened atween last night and this mornin'? Nothin', exceptin' that I been asleep. So I tell ye, sleep's bad for humans!" He rubbed his jaw thoughtfully. "I'd like to know who done this to me."

"I did," said Andy.

Joe turned to survey him in astonishment.

"You, Andy! Was yo' drunk?"

"I was cold sober. And, Joe, I'm just sick about it. I—"

"Tarnation! Wall, it feels like it was a good one!"

"Joe, you don't know how sorry I am."

"Wall," said Joe, "ef'n you done it, and ef'n you was cold sober, I must have been needin' it bad."

He thrust aside the buffalo robe, arose to his feet, shook himself vigorously.

"Didn't nothin' drop off?" he inquired. "Wall, I reckon I'm all thar! Let's marvel out and view the survivors. Some doin's! Wagh!" He chuckled. "Didn't poke Jack Kelly too, did ye?"

"Was Jack drunk, too?" asked Andy, with a faint shock of disappointment. Somehow, he could not associate Kelly's compact efficiency with that sort of thing.

"Why, of course," said Joe, equally astonished at the question. "Whar was yo'? Last I see of him he was makin' a speech or speakin' a piece, or somethin'. Old he-coon of a speech, too, only it was in some furrin language so we missed the cute of it."

The encampment had fallen back to a quieter pace. Men lay about in the sun, gossiped, yarned, made plans, played cards, drank a little. They had a good time. Nobody was bothered with regret or remorse. Those admirable sequences of debauch are largely physical, and these iron men could not be affected so easily. Indeed their psychic equilibrium was rather comfortably stabilized/The whole affair was in the nature of a safety valve, blowing off pressures stored by hardship and danger and unremitting tensities. I think no element of morality was involved. Andy's instinctive perception sensed this and gave it just valuation, but his simpler rational powers were not sufficient to lift him from puzzlement. So, as usual, he gave it up.

Downriver, the Shoshones and the Utahs were drifting sullenly away. They had no more skins to trade. They were even more instinctive than Andy. All they knew was that their peltries were gone.

The leaders, Ashley, Sublette, Smith, Campbell, perfected their plans apart. Hachter yawned in the trading lodge, attending to the spasmodic trade that still persisted. Men with credit remaining filled out their needs or their ideas of luxury. A very few, Andy among them, arranged for deposit of the surplus in St. Louis. There was considerable card playing. When enough felt energetic there was horse racing, wrestling, target-shooting. Fresh meat was supplied by specified hunters. They made a game in determining who must perform this task. A pipe was filled with tobacco, lighted, passed from mouth to mouth. Each must take from it three visible puffs. The man in whose hands it happened to burn out completely had to furnish the meat. Its distribution was affected in an orderly manner. The animal brought in was thrown down before the Little Burgeway's lodge, and there cut up under his supervision. The meat was then divided into piles, their number corresponding to the number of messes, a mess for each four individuals. This accomplished, the first passer-by was halted and instructed to turn his back. Hachter laid his hand on one of the piles.

"Who shall have this?" he demanded in a loud voice.

"Number six," replied the arbiter at random, and to mess number six it went.

Thus, there was no favoritism.

In the evening, things livened up. Somebody with credit remaining usually gave a party. Until the last evening of the rendezvous, these parties never came near to equaling the first burst of reaction. Nobody got drunk, that is, not very drunk, but everybody was comfortably *prime*. They told stories, or sang, or played games of chance. Kelly's recitations were very popular. They liked to listen to him as he drew from his college lore fine old rolling ballads of Scott's, or Milton's sonorous lines. They even urged him to repeat some of his *furrin' stuff*, and relished with a childlike appreciation of beat and cadence the Latin of Vergil or the Greek of Homer. But Kelly had to be *prime* before he would oblige, after which he sat in a black meditation which shrugged aside intrusion with a savage impatience.

But now these days were finished. Ashley had perfected his arrangements, had traded for enough horses to transport his furs. The trappers began to give mind to their own plans, to prepare leisurely for their far-flung scattering until the next rendezvous. That, it was decided, was to be in Cache Valley, the pleasant game-haunted vale which Jedediah Smith had discovered up yonder, to the northwest, and where he had ventured the season before. It was a bold fling, away from the old grounds, out toward the vague region purported to be controlled by the Hudson's Bay Company. The old opposition they had left far in the rear, over the eastern horizon. New lands, new explorations, new rivals! Their eyes shone in anticipation.

Fifty men were to set out with Ashley on his journey, of whom, however, thirty were to bring back the horses after the general had reached the river and so would have finished with them. Among the twenty who would continue on to St. Louis were Sublette and Jedediah Smith, but they were immediately to return. To the surprise of both Joe and Andy, Kelly announced his intention of joining the party. Kelly's black mood had been growing on him.

"I've been in the mountains now a good many years," he told them curtly. "I must go back."

He would not argue with them.

Of the other men, each—or each group—had his own ideas, his own pet park, or hole or trapping district. Joe, with Flying Woman, was going back to the Blackfeet for the fall hunt and the winter. Andy made up his mind to accompany them. A quiet season with his old friends appealed to him after nearly two years' absence. He wanted to see Kiasax again, Nit-o-ké-man. He wanted to see how the Little Warrior had grown. At the thought, his heart warmed within him. He did not think of the beaver.

Each man, before he set out, was required to go to Hachter, the Little Burgeway, and from him receive a statement of his credit. Few of them wanted to do so, or desired the statement.

"Sure, she's all right. I'll take yore word for it," said they.

Nor did Ashley himself attach any great importance to the procedure, he was perfectly aware how little documents counted with these men. But that was the quirk in Hachter's methodical mind, so he was humored.

Andy found himself in company with Mulford, the man who had given the first big party when Andy had nearly shot off Joe Crane's legs. Mulford was grumbling about the necessity of wasting time on such foolishness. Andy was poking fun at him.

"What's time to you?" he asked. "Where you going that you're in such a hurry?"

"Wall, I got a long way to go," returned Mulford. "I'm aimin' to trap 'way over yander. And besides, how about Hachter? Ain't it wastin' time for him, makin' out all them dozens and dozens of bills? Makes my head ache to think on 'em."

"Oh, he likes it," said Andy. "Where did you do your trade last year?"

"Didn't come out. Got ketched in a windfall and bruk my laig, and had to lay over."

"Then you brought in a two years' catch," observed Andy.

"Part. Got raided a year ago last spring and lost part of my spring ketch. Then I had to get out of that kentry and cross over the mountings..."

He went on, encouraged by Andy's genuine interest, to unfold one of those long stories of persistence, hardship, suffering, and sheer dogged courage which never failed to enlist Andy's profound admiration, and this in spite of the fact that the lad's own experiences had by now equaled the best of them. Somehow he had never quite the same point of view toward his own adventures. They were just part of life. These others were heroic. In fairness it should be added that Mulford did not see them so. He was just exchanging the time of day. He did not think he had come out so badly. He had lost two toes in a blizzard and had had about a third of his furs lifted. He had not starved much, except just now and then. But what could a man expect in a country entirely unknown?

"I got her located now," he told Andy. "She'll git me more beaver next year. I brung in a hundred and twenty pounds, all prime."

About six hundred dollars for two years' work! The thought brought Andy up short for a moment. He had never considered it in quite those terms before. He ousted it with an effort, turned his back on it, refused it mind room. Next thing he'd be looking at his own situation sensibly.

Hachter had Mulford's account ready and handed it to him. The trapper stared at it, frowning, his lips moving slowly, as he spelled out the items. When he had come to the end, he looked up puzzled.

"Shore this comes out right?" he asked, hesitating.

"What is there about it you don't understand?" asked the Little Burgeway. "Aren't the items correct? Here, let me see."

"No, I reckon they're all correct," said Mulford hastily. "I ain't doubtin' you got 'em down all right. Anyway, I wouldn't know if you hadn't. But I kinda thought I'd have—mind if Andy added her up fer me? He's got book larnin', too."

"Go ahead," agreed Hachter. "He won't make it any different."

"No, I reckon not," said Mulford deprecatingly, but he thrust the paper into Andy's hand.

Andy read the document slowly. It ran in part as follows:

- JULY 2—Liquor $8.00, Feast $4.00, Ditto $4.00, shirt $8.00.
- JULY 3—Liquor $11.00, Feast $2.00, knives $4.00, powder $12.00, balls $18.00, flints $1.00, tobacco $15.00, kettles $5.00, axe $3.00, trap springs $16.00, blanket $12.00, sugar $2.00, coffee $18.00, tea $10.00, suit clothes $70.00.

"That's the day I bought my possibles," observed Mulford, over Andy's shoulder. "Looks all right, though I was a leetle drunk, and can't be shore." The account added a number of other items—thread, hard biscuit, salt, handkerchiefs, awls, a tin cup, some rice, and the like. After that, the statement continued with a certain brief monotony:

- JULY 4—Liquor $14.00. Ditto $3.00. Ditto $12.00.

with an occasional *feast $4.00* by way of punctuation. The last item ran:

- Liquor and keg $27.00.

"I aim to take that with me. Mout want to do a leetle light drinkin' come winter."

"You'll have it all drunk up afore you're two days out," predicted the Little Burgeway.

"I mout," agreed the trapper placidly.

"What do you want me to do about this?" asked Andy puzzled. "What do I know about it?"

"I just want to know if it's right, what it says there, at the bottom. Does that mean I ain't got nothin' more comin'? Don't seem reasonable with all them beaver. Add her up fer me, Andy."

"Little less than nothing, Mulford," corrected Hachter dryly. "You owe the company a little. But, of course, that's all right."

Andy sat down to the job. Hachter watched him sardonically. Andy was no expert accountant, and his *book larnin'* was of a more sketchy character than Mulford suspected. After losing track three times of how much to *carry*, he gave up exact balances in favor of a more or less rough estimate.

"Looks all right to me," said he, returning the invoice.

"Is that so! Wall, wall!" Mulford was plainly nonplussed. He stared at the bit of paper as though accusingly for a moment, then with a grin, oriented himself to this unsuspected state of affairs.

"Oh, well!" he cried jauntily. "Easy come, easy go!"

Chapter 17
Lowered Swords

The next three years after the first rendezvous in the Green River comprised in many ways the golden age of the Western fur trade. To be sure it had been carried on, and successfully, for many years before. The Nor'westers, the Astorians, the Hudson's Bay Company, other organizations east of the Rockies had written brilliant pages of history. And it was destined to continue as a major interest for nearly twenty years to come. But the exploits of the Ashley men had in them a dash of knight-errantry that lifted them almost into the realm of myth and fable.

The success of Ashley's company was spectacular. It upset all the steady close-figuring authorities in the St. Louis fur markets. Not only did his yearly expedition bring back beaver skins in unbelievable quantities, but their quality was such that the term *Ashley beaver* came into use as a synonym for the top grade. Men's minds were fired as later imaginations kindled over the stories of California gold. The equanimity of the great and old established fur companies was disturbed, they prepared to push farther back. New, wildcat companies of adventurers were formed in all parts of the country and among all classes of men. Some of them were composed of reckless irresponsibles. But back in New England, Nathaniel Wyeth, the son of an old Boston family, left his ice business to gather together twenty-four solid Puritan citizens and to set out, trusting in Providence and native common sense, to do business in the Rockies. Even such foredoomed affairs of ignorance had no difficulty in filling their ranks. As for Ashley and Sublette, they were overwhelmed by applicants. They could pick and choose. About this time, an advertisement appeared in a Missouri newspaper that:

—a boy about sixteen years old, small of his age, but thick-set, light hair, ran away from the subscriber, to whom he had been apprenticed to learn the saddler's trade...all persons notified not to harbor, subsist, or support said boy under penalty of law. One cent reward will be given to any person who will bring back said boy.
DAVID WORKMAN.

The boy against whom Mr. Workman made this magnificent one-cent gesture of disdain was named Christopher Carson. There were many such.

The whole frontier east of the Rockies was restless and astir. The rival companies were coming more closely to grips. The American Fur Company had built its string of forts up the Missouri Valley, was consolidating its trade, was trying—as yet in vain—to push into the Blackfoot country. Kenneth Mackenzie came in on its behalf from the upper Mississippi. He was brave and enterprising, hard, severe in discipline, fond of pomp and display, jealous of his dignity. He wore always a uniform, affected great state, invited few to his table, but beneath the pomp and circumstance he was shrewd and vigilant to extend his company's power. On the whole he succeeded well. The frontiersmen respected but hated him. His men were loyal and secretly a little proud of him, but feared him like the devil. He had no regard for human life. Hearing of an attack by Indians on one of his trading parties, his first inquiry was as to the horses. It seemed that the horses had all been killed or driven off, but every man was safe.

"Damn the men!" said Mackenzie. "If the horses had been saved, that would have amounted to something!"

If an employee became crippled beyond usefulness, he was turned out, or made to feel so unwelcome that he left. Even the Indians took pity on some of these men. Lapenteur tells of finding Joe Ramsay thus among the savage Assiniboins. In spite of these qualities, or perhaps because of them, Mackenzie's administration prospered. Visitors of importance found him most hospitable and charming.

Doubtless he was harassed by emergencies at which we cannot begin to guess. The country was becoming overrun by itinerant independent traders. They were worse than the organized and responsible companies. The latter would be dependent, as was Mackenzie himself, on government license to trade, which could be revoked for cause. The small independent traders came anyway. Some of them had what Mackenzie called the impudence to build little log posts of their own within a mile or less of the company's forts. Mackenzie did not dare run them out by force. Everything he did must be at least in color of law. It was illegal to sell the Indians liquor. Later it was illegal even to bring liquor into the Indian country. Nevertheless no trade could be done without it. It is probable that the big companies might have abandoned its use could they have done so. But if one man used liquor, the rest could do nothing. *Liquor we must have, or give up!* wrote a trader to his chiefs, in despair.

These individual traders tried to undermine one another as well as cut into the business of the larger companies. They played petty politics among the tribes. Each supported some favorite sub-chief of his own, from whom he hoped influence. That made for dissension among the Indians themselves. Each vilified the others to the savages, so that gradually a general impression gained strength among the Indians that all white men were bad. Did they not tell bad things of one another?

Few of such irresponsibles lasted long. When it came to running out opposition Mackenzie gave his own traders carte blanche, instructing them to pay anything for beaver, without regard to profits, and to use any necessary amount of liquor. Thus in some instances he paid as high as twelve dollars for pelts. It became a simple matter of who had the most resources, and as to that there could be no question. But it was expensive.

"It has cost me something to secure the Indians to me!" commented Mackenzie ruefully.

Once be had broken one of these smaller rivals, he was very cocky, and would not even listen to offers to sell out. But often headquarters, at St. Louis, was more politic, and bought in some of the more important ex-rivals, to Mackenzie's openly expressed disgust.

Some of the independents who had thus failed in the business took service with the company, some set out as trappers, others wandered restlessly from tribe to tribe. *Indian killers* became more numerous. Men joined certain tribes temporarily so that they could go to war and indulge in this propensity. They looked on all Indians as *varmints* to be eliminated on sight. They made for trouble wherever they went. The prairies were becoming more and more uncertain, more and more dangerous.

The posts built by the company were fortresses, with blank outer walls, enfilading bastions, a narrow passage commanded by cannon between an outer and an inner gate, all dwellings and stores and shops facing in toward the spacious enclosure. They were capable of withstanding any siege by Indians. Within them was a whole community of activities, presided over, in considerable style, by the overlord and his associates. There was here no necessity for the extreme of rigorous simplicity imposed by the wilderness. We hear of linens and silver and fine wines and a sort of feudal dignity. Hamilton, the Englishman, at Fort Union, each year received boxes of fine clothes from England. He went polished, scented, and oiled, with ruffled shirt fronts, a gold chain about his neck, and always a colored silk handkerchief hanging from his pocket. To him all Indians were beasts. He was rumored to belong to a noble family, and that Hamilton was not his real name. We hear, as time goes on, of distinguished visitors, lavishly entertained at one or another of the company's posts—Audubon, the naturalist, Prince Maximilian of Wied, many others. They came in with the spring boat, and lived in the upper story of the fort with the commandant and his clerks. Above them, on the battlements, were the Indian women and the children of the whites. About the courtyard, whose center was occupied by the huge hide press, French *engagés* beat out the skins and pressed them into packs. Along the walls lounged the trappers and traders, gossiping, smoking turn and turn about the long-stemmed native pipe, gambling at cards. Someone played, rather sweetly, a flute. Their Indian wives strutted about, gay in paint, beads, bells, bangles, the *foofaraw* of trade. Hunters came in with deer and buffalo. Indian dogs hovered about the open gates, eager to enter but afraid to do so. Beyond them a fringe of lurking coyotes. Against the outer walls leaned Indians, clothed in buffalo robes, sulky, forbidden to enter unless invited to do so. A six-pounder commanded the gates. Other six-pounders, and some smaller pieces, perched on the walls. In one of the bastions stood a brass telescope through which the sentry could examine the distance for suspicious-looking signs. If he discovered any such, he must signal the herdsmen and the woodchoppers in time. Not that attack on them might reasonably be expected, even from tribes normally hostile. They wanted trade, and would not be likely to spoil the chance of it. Whiskey, or what passed as such, could be had, a pint for each beaver skin. A pint made one good drunk.

In the bottomlands, below the fort, the distinguished visitor could see the teepees of those tribes. Sometimes there were a great many of them, as high as fifteen to twenty thousand. They were for the moment friendly because they wanted to trade. Nevertheless the visitor would be wise not to visit too freely the encampment, at least, not without suitable and experienced escort. There was always a chance that some young fool had just purchased his pint. Better to study them when they came into the post.

Usually they were moderately reliable, and might be admitted in small groups into the main court. But if there was any doubt, they would not get beyond the vestibule between the outer and the inner gates, whence they must deal through wickets. In any case the six-pounder was ready for action. The life was colorful, interesting, but so confined that in time it became monotonous. To be sure there were, but a short distance away, marvelous swarms of game. The post's hunters were continually out among them after meat. Nothing could be more thrilling than a hunting trip. But it was dangerous. A man could not go alone, or with too few companions, not unless he was very experienced, and then only in daily peril of his life. Each notable had his shy at it, of course, but the necessary preparations were so elaborate that these excursions were never many times repeated. Better leave that to the paid hunters. There was plenty to interest one at home, what with the trading, the coming and going of trappers and partisans, the endless councils with the chieftains.

These were unending. Each week, almost each day, brought its quota of visiting native dignitaries. They ascended the short ladder to the sacred second story, and sat about on the floor of the big room, and smoked ceremoniously, and drank of the trade liquor offered, and talked their business in slow-spaced speeches. Yellow Wolf reports trade to be had at his village, a partisan must be sent there. He-Who-Jumps says that the Comanches, heap mad, have dug up the hatchet, and warns the whites away from their country. Peeled Lodge Pole has come in to excuse his people, who have stolen some of the fort's horses, and promises there will be no repetition of the offense. He claims he speaks with a single tongue. And after the last of these had gone, there were the long discussions, over the evening port, of the company's affairs and policies and plans. When one from the outside had lived for a time in the busy intimacy of the post's microcosmos, there grew in his mind an exaggerated idea of its all-pervasiveness. Its power and influence seemed so to fill the land as to give an impression of an administered and occupied country. This was an illusion. The spaced and isolated posts were connected with one another, and with their parent civilization on the lower Missouri, by the slender umbilical cord of the river. Through its channel flowed their life. Outside them, untouched and untamed, was what for decades to come was to remain the Wild West.

Nevertheless a network was being slowly spun, its strands wide apart and slender, but ever more comprehensive. Fort Union was as yet the outpost. But Mackenzie was looking farther afield. Repeatedly he urged his directors to allow him to cross the mountains. As often they denied his requests. "Let the others break the ground," they stated their policy, "then we will move in and occupy. Await the moment!" Restrained in this direction, Mackenzie made repeated attempts in the direction of the Blackfoot country. They failed.

In comparison with this restless stir of the germ of a new civilization east of the Rockies, the Ashley men, west of the Divide, were still in an earlier historical period. It was as though the great mountains were a barrier in time, damming back the steadily mounting flood of a new era. There the mountain men wandered singly, or in small groups, over a vast extent of unexplored country, rummaging out their beaver streams, losing themselves for months in the parks and passes and defiles of the ranges, reappearing for the period of their rendezvous, squabbling or fraternizing with tribes not yet made actively hostile, meeting unknown deaths, accomplishing unknown triumphs, only vaguely aware of the rising tide beyond the barrier that must soon absorb them into a new life or thrust them aside. Comparatively few in actual numbers, their accomplishment was nevertheless astounding, not so particularly in their rich harvests of fur as in the wide fling of their wandering.

The winter after the rendezvous at Green River passed. Spring burgeoned forth. Gradually the scattered bands closed in to the next appointed meeting ground, in beautiful Cache Valley, northeast of Salt Lake. It was a large gathering this year, over a hundred white trappers, many of whom, like Joe Crane, had Indian wives. Many of them had wintered near the mouth of Weber River, together with over a thousand Shoshones, or Snakes, who had, as a tribe, decided to be friendly. Thence they had explored Salt Lake in bull boats, and had helped the Snakes in a little exercise battle with the Blackfeet in which everybody fought until they got hungry and then called it all off in favor of a feast. Many of the Snakes came to rendezvous. By July Ashley had arrived, having dragged with him a six-pounder brass cannon, the first wheeled vehicle to cross the Divide. Andy Burnett and Joe Crane had ridden in only a few days before. They had wintered with their friends, the Blackfeet. It would have been nearer and handier for them to have made their annual trade with either the Columbia or the American Fur Company, down the river, but they were mountain men, and remained loyal to their kind.

The take of beaver skins was this year rich beyond all precedent. Counting his profits General Ashley realized that he possessed an independent fortune. After consultation with his associates he made an announcement. He had sold out to William Sublette, Jedediah Smith, and another named David Jackson. He was going to retire from active trading in the mountains and realize along-cherished ambition to run for Congress. That did not mean, however, that he severed all connection with the enterprise. He would continue to represent the company in St. Louis. He would dispose of the furs sent in, and would buy for them their supplies. He would not perform these services for anybody else. He concluded by thanking them all in the most heartfelt terms for their loyalty.

They were stunned. Were they not *Ashley men*? In that name had they not greatly dared beyond their own un-united capacity? For the moment they felt scattered. The *Gin'ral* had been their symbol of cohesion. For the moment they could not rally to the mere abstraction of the *Company*. Some of them remembered the terrible mid-winter journey, the perilous descent of Green River in the bull boats, recollected Ashley's fortitude and courage and persistence. They were much affected, much moved. Jim Beckworth, the mulatto, wept openly, and no man's derision called him to account, then or thereafter.

But after the first flattening of dismay they rallied. Both Sublette and Jedediah Smith were some he-coons at that! Dave Jackson was all right too. Leastways he was a good proper mountain man. Later they named a Hole after him, up under the Tetons. And the Gin'ral wasn't quitting them completely. He was back of them still, keepin' an eye on things. Hurrah for the Rocky Mountain Fur Company! They all got drunk to equalize their mingled feelings! They saw Ashley off on his long return journey, cheering wildly and firing their rifles in the air.

The new partners put their heads together. They were in practically undisputed possession of a vast extent of rich trapping country. The Snakes were friendly. The British, over the sunset horizon, were inclined to attend to their Western affairs. Their excursions up the Columbia were few. Anyway, the mountain men knew how to handle the British. Hadn't they proved it? The Blackfeet were still an annoyance. No one knew when a raiding party might be encountered. They stole irreplaceable traps, and horses, and lifted scalps when the chance was favorable. But this was foreign territory to them also, and they had their uses. Their implacable hostility interposed a buffer against the pressure of the Astor men from the East. Surely the mountain men stood in possession of all heart could desire.

Nevertheless the restless and ambitious spirits of the leaders were not satisfied with the immediate present. This new district, as far as the *Grand Lake west of the Rockies*, as they called it, had proved to be a new trapping country rich beyond all expectation. How about beyond Grand Lake? There seemed to be no reason why that should not be equally productive. Nobody knew anything about it. There lay the possibility of future expansion. The partners talked it over. What wealth of fur might there be waiting? What mountains, what streams, what paradise of pleasant valleys untrod by white man's moccasins, unawakened by the echoes of white man's rifles? And was it not there, in the blue of the unknown, that the fabled Buenaventura River must rise—the mighty stream whose waters flowed westward to empty into the Pacific? Down its current the furs might be floated to the Californias, there to be transported to the markets by the New England trading ships. Big business that! Brand new! A project to fire the imagination of these audacious men.

Obviously such a challenge could not be ignored. The main body of the trappers could attend to Green River, the Bear, the Weber, the Wasatch Mountains, all the newfound territory. But Jedediah Smith called for volunteers to go find out. There might be nothing in it, he warned them. Here was a certainty. They rose to the idea with a whoop. He had to select his party from a crowd of volunteers. He picked fifteen. One of those chosen was Andy Burnett. They set out with fifty horses.

———

Jedediah, Andy, and Silas Gobel got back in time for next summer's rendezvous at the southern end of Bear Lake. They had one horse, one mule, no beaver skins. The horse and the mule were so feeble they just managed to carry the little camp equipment.

But they had a story to tell. South boldly from Salt Lake. A barren, open, desert country. Wide-flung, uprising to horizons incredibly remote, like the hollow of a great outspread hand. Short brittle mountain ranges, that looked as empty as pasteboard, bare of vegetation, but clothed in soft veils of the desert country—amethyst, mauve, pearl, lilac, purple-bordered in the deep canyon chasms—until the hot noon sun stripped them naked. Flat-topped mesas, castellated buttes, changing shape momently as the travelers looked at them, throwing up pinnacles, absorbing them again, reaching long arms toward one another until between them arched abridge, pacing the slow transformations of desert magic. No life save the jack rabbits and ghost-like antelope, and the straight-rising columns of signal smoke in the hills. They ate the jack rabbit and the antelope, and found scant water high toward the summit of the ranges and sparse forage for the horses. But the people who had made the smokes they could not come upon.

Then a small river flowing north which they ascended southward. On it they encountered a band of Indians clad in rabbit skins, poor, ill-armed, abject, who looked on the white men with respectful awe. But there were no beaver, no buffalo. A barren and unproductive land. The Buenaventura, the trapping country must lie beyond. So, on they pushed, passed the headwaters of the stream, crossed a divide, came to other headwaters, this time flowing south. Mountains to the left of them, a sandy desert to the right of them, perforce they continued down the stream, for water they must have. There was not much else. Even jack rabbits were scarce, and the horses became gaunt and weak from lack of grazing. They wandered widely in search of a mouthful here and there in the everlasting sameness of cactus and of stunted acrid shrubs. So for twelve days. Then their stream emptied into another and larger river. Smith took his bearings, thought it over, and with a truly marvelous instinct for topography came to a correct conclusion. He identified the river as the Siskadee, the Green, on which, hundreds of miles above, he had rendezvoused two years before. Obviously they had missed the Buenaventura.

What now? Return as they had come? Or ascend the Green back to their old trapping grounds? Those were the safest, most obvious things to do. Nothing profitable to be gained in this barren waste. For some days already they had been living on horseflesh.

They continued on downstream. Perhaps the country would improve. Perhaps they would find game, beaver again. Perhaps they could cut the Buenaventura at or near the mouth and follow it back. Perhaps—oh, lots of things! They still had the most of their horses. Hosses ain't so bad eatin'.

They were now, though of course they did not know it, on the east side of the Colorado River, not far from the Grand Canyon, and traveling due south. Horseflesh was all very well, but soon they were down to a minimum of animals for carrying purposes. All of them had known hunger many times in the past. Now they met it again, face to face. Nobody knew where this river went, or whether the character of the country was likely to change. Certainly they did not want to go south, but water they must have, and they did not dare leave its course. So south they went. And just as even stout Jed Smith acknowledged himself *about destitute*, they came to a fertile valley, well timbered, fifteen miles or so wide, in which dwelled a race of Indians who called themselves Mojaves, and who bartered with them for more horses and such unbelievable luxuries as corn, and beans, and pumpkins, and watermelons, and wheat. The horses they had stolen from the Spanish, the seed of the foodstuffs they had brought in from Spanish settlements. They were friendly, and they told the trappers of California.

This was a pleasant interlude. The men rested and ate, the horses rested and ate. They waxed fat and *sassy*, and their spirits revived. At the end of two weeks, they had forgotten their troubles and hardships. With two of the Mojaves as guides they crossed the Colorado where now the Santa Fe railroad crosses it at Needles, and again set forth across the formidable desert.

From your Pullman you may follow the next fifteen days of their travel. Dry, hard, hot, completely barren. Even in later years, when the route was marked and known, this was a journey of hardship, of suffering, and of death. For twenty miles at a time, under the power of the desert sun, they plodded across a crust of thin white salt, through the surface of which they broke at every step. They underwent the tortures of a thirst that edged close to delirium. The horses gave out, laid down, died, and their bodies were left to parch dry—the first of many that in later years would mark the trail. But they arrived. Late in November they stood on the summit of a pass just south of Cajon looking out across blue distances to the west. They were alive, and well. They had their long rifles and their traps, and the most valuable of the trade goods, and eighteen horses of the fifty they had started out with and of those they had bought from the Mojaves.

But here were water and strong grass. The blacktailed deer bounced and bounded down the chaparral-clad slopes. Before them slumbered the valleys of California.

The tall mountain men rode down the pass, into the valley, spying curiously about them. They noted the huge herds of cattle and horses, the flocks of sheep. They wondered at the Indians they encountered, mainly because they were so entirely different from the Indians they had known. One of the savages guided the little party to the mission of San Gabriel, where they camped.

Here was a fluttering in the sleepy old dovecotes of the mission! The advent of these buckskin-clad frontiersmen, with their long rifles and their scalping knives and their compact, hard, efficient attitude, caught the good fathers all aflutter. Not knowing what else to do they caused a cow to be killed and cornmeal and wine to be brought for the men, and invited Jedediah Smith himself for supper, where he sat at a well-appointed table and had a variety of things to eat, with wines, and a sup of whiskey, and cigars. Even their simpler fare was sheer mad luxury to the trappers, and it is recorded that *they feasted heartily, as they were pretty hungry, not having had any good meat for some time.*

All of which was most pleasant, but was in reality a temporizing until the padres could find out what to do.

But when their messenger returned from the nearest civil authority at Los Angeles, they were no better off than they were before. That dignitary did not know what to do either. It was bad enough to have to deal with the occasional Boston traders and smugglers along the coast. What could be the sinister purport of this invasion from the east? The old army game of passing the buck is not so modern. Case referred to governor Echeandia at San Diego. Nothing doing. It must probably be referred on to Mexico. Exchange of letters and assurances. Finally Jedediah, losing patience himself, went down to San Diego to see what he could do.

They did not see him again until the middle of January. In the meantime life was not so bad. Lacking a definite policy one way or another, the padres of the mission reconciled themselves to the idea that they must support these uninvited guests. Possibly they rather welcomed this clash of barbaric cymbals across the sweet monotonous flow of their Te Deums. At any rate they gave to the adventurers of their best, and that best was very good indeed. Andy ate and drank things he had almost forgotten existed. He stood by with interest, watching the intricate and varied industries and activities of the mission people. There were about a thousand of the latter, mostly Indians. They raised apples, peaches, oranges, figs. They grew grain and grapes. They made blankets and wine, and distilled whiskey. They herded thousands of cattle and horses.

It was a beautiful country, with much flowing water and green irrigated fields, and beyond them the rolling, low, flower-starred hills where the cattle ranged. And even beyond that the stark, high fastness of the timbered, snow-clad mountains. That is where the eyes of the trappers turned. Mout be beaver thar! But until Jedediah Smith brought permission, they must not move.

Still, not so bad! There was a wedding, and numberless *fandangos* and *bailes*, and parades of the garrison of soldiers. They could ride, and there were plenty of horses available. They had certain necessary matters of their own to attend. The padres presented them with sixty-four yards of shirting which they gladly accepted, for they were nearly naked. In return, and at the request of the priest, they fashioned for him, in the blacksmith shop, a huge bear trap. When it was finished he told them he wanted it to set in his orange garden to catch Indians when they entered there at night. Andy found the priests and the few Spanish residents courteous and interesting. He spent much time in their company, and with his usual facility with languages, soon picked up a fair working knowledge of Spanish. But he was sorry for the Indians. In comparison with the wild Indians to whom he was accustomed, these seemed a crushed and broken race. They were ruled by fear, disciplined severely for the smallest offenses. Andy saw five of them whipped at the stake for not going to work at the proper time. They were all five old men, too. Though the Indians were Christian converts supposed to be held by brotherly love, the latter quality was helped out by a strong military force with no fewer than four field guns. Andy liked to draw a little aside from it all near sunset. From the low rise of a near-by hill, mellowed by evening light, with the joyous liquid notes of the meadow larks and the challenge of quail, the mission and its surrounding buildings seemed to bask in a golden dream. The hordes of Indians eddying slowly from their work toward the common center stirred a dust shot with gold. Gold spread its blankets over the hills where the rich poppies blazed. And golden the vibrating resonance of the mission bells sounding the Angelus.

Jedediah Smith was back. He had used his best diplomacy, but he had not accomplished much. The governor could not understand this invasion, he was suspicious of it.

"We were compelled to enter California because we were out of provisions and water," Smith pleaded. This was stretching it a bit, but in the governor's ignorance, it would do. Nevertheless Echeandia did not like it. The best Smith could obtain was that the party would not be jailed and sent to Mexico. He was privileged to return the way he had come, and he was permitted to buy such horses and such provisions and such equipment as he would need for that purpose.

The men set to with a will on their preparations. They had had about enough of inaction, even in such pleasant circumstances. They bought and packed provisions, they jerked meat, they fashioned pack saddles, they did the best they could in a short time to break the sixty-eight fresh horses. That was a job, for these animals were of the good Spanish stock, well fed and mettlesome. When, finally, they started out, the whole outfit broke away and ran wildly eight or ten miles, packs and all, before they could be headed.

Obeying orders, like good boys, they backtracked their old route until they had passed San Bernardino. Then they turned north. Cut back over all that desert country? Return without a look at the mountains of California? Just because some greaser told them to? Besides, there was the Buenaventura. Had to see where that came out! Maybe, when they found it, they could ascend its course. So they crossed the Tehachapis, and for three hundred miles they proceeded leisurely up the great interior valley.

It was spring. The hills and the plains were paint-new with the incredibly vivid green of the California season. The poppies glowed like little suns. The wild mustard gilded the outlines and the crevices in the folded hills. The spread-wide blankets of lupins mantled the slopes and carpeted the plains. Only the cloudless sky outmatched in vividness their blue. The air was golden with the rich notes of the meadow larks, atwitter with the smaller busy voices of song sparrows in the grass, of orioles and vireos in the trees, exultant with the wild clamor of innumerable wild fowl that from every stream and lake and pond and tule swamp rose before the cavalcade in clouds, with a roar of wings like the falling of waters. Small hawks hovered, poised on rapidly beating wings, falcons darted in pursuit with the speed of arrows, vultures and eagles wheeled in slow spaced soarings across the remote, leisured calm of the upper sky.

The plains swarmed with game. Deer in hundreds, tule elk in thousands, bear everywhere, very tame and scornful, phantomlike antelope wherever one looked, herds of wild horses, heads and tails high, nostrils distended, dashing away, wheeling, circling back in curiosity, the little brothers of the wolf, the coyotes, adding the voice of the diabolic to the great exultant wild fowl chorus of the night, *blacktail rabbits*, as the trappers called them, hopping up and away until at times the whole surface of the ground seemed alive. Fat doings! They looked eagerly for buffalo, but there were none.

The plains spread wide and abundant. To their right rose the high, glittering, and formidable wall of the Sierras, white with snow. Far along the western horizon ran the Coast Range, blue in a distance at which they could only guess. Beyond them must be the California of the Spanish, and the sea. They did not know how far that might be. Jedediah Smith guessed it might be a hundred and fifty miles or so.

They took their time, trapping here and there in the foothills as they moved on. They found a few beaver in favorable places, but many more cuttings in the driftwood on the bars. If only they had time to explore back farther up the canyons! There must be plenty of fur under the high peaks. But if they were to get back for this year's rendezvous they could not linger, and they did not think then they could stay over a season without being reported to the Spanish.

The Buenaventura did not materialize. There were several good-sized streams, but obviously they rose near at hand in the Sierras, whose ramparts continued unbroken. Finally they gave it up and turned east.

It was now well into May, but to their surprise, they discovered the snow so deep in the high altitudes that they could not make way through it. They had to return to the valley, after a loss of five horses.

What next? They talked it over exhaustively. Smith, who did not readily acknowledge that he could not do what he set out to do, was still convinced that he could get through with one or two men. He had agreed to meet Sublette and Jackson and it was up to him to do so. He announced his intention and asked for volunteers. From those who offered he selected Silas Gobel, the blacksmith, and Andy Burnett. Andy was both pleased and disappointed. Pleased that he had been considered worthy of choice, disappointed that he was not to remain longer in this fascinating country. Those who were left behind were to await Smith, who was to return immediately after the rendezvous, with more men and more supplies, after which they would continue on north to see about this Buenaventura business and the possibilities of beaver country, and all the rest of it. In the meantime, they could look about in the vicinity. It was not the prime of the fur at this season, so it was useless to hunt beaver. If the Spanish got wind of them they would have to handle the situation according to circumstances—fight, yield, or flee. Only they'd better not fight if they could help it. Goodbye and good luck!

So Jedediah Smith and Silas Gobel, the blacksmith, and Andy Burnett, furnished out with nine animals, again tackled the Sierras. They were about thirty miles north of the Yosemite. After eight days of terrible struggle they managed to make the summit of the main ridge. Here the snow lay eight or ten feet deep, but so close packed that the horses sank only a foot or so below the surface. Still, that was enough to make progress slow and uncertain. Three of the nine animals had already perished.

To gain the summit was a triumph in itself. But the nature of the topography, which now for the first time became evident, gave them another flicker of cheer. From westward the Sierras rise slowly to their heights, through ridge after ridge of lesser ranges, so that from foothill to summit is often from fifty to eighty miles of difficult mountain travel. To the eastward they drop off precipitously, almost in one jump. So Jedediah Smith and his two companions, struggling at last to the narrow flat of the skyline, found they had only to drop down a few thousand feet—a matter of hours instead of days—to water, warmth, and grass. But before they did so, Jedediah Smith took careful bearings.

The country, viewed map-like from above, did not look inviting. Nor did the event belie its first impression. For three solid weeks, they traveled. There was no game, little water, scanty grass. Occasionally, for as long as two days at a stretch, they found their way over sandy wastes where was nothing. Then they thirsted. If the sandy wastes should continue on beyond a certain and very definite maximum, they must perish. They had no reason to believe that such would not be the case. But always, just short of disaster, they found a *tenaja* of water in the rocky hills, and with it sparse grasses. They were led to these discoveries by small indications—the flight of rare desert birds, minute differences in configurations of the hills, and the like. At such places, generally, a few Indians were encamped. They were the most wretched people Andy had ever seen. They had no clothing, their hair was long, matted, and unkempt. They appeared to subsist solely on grass seed, grasshoppers, desert mice, lizards, and snakes. No information could be had from them. They strayed as little as possible from the miserable safety of their *tenaja*. Pausing only just long enough to draw breath, the white man headed forth once more into the unknown desert.

The horses died one by one. They were gaunt, desiccated, skin and bones. Nevertheless each, as it fell, was carefully cut up and the meat, such as it was, saved. That was all they had to eat. It was curious, Andy remarked, how a horse seemed to die just in the nick of time, when it looked as though they would have to take to grasshoppers or starve, and how the *tenajas* of water in the hills appeared to linger in obstinate concealment until they were so far gone in the tortures of thirst that delirium hovered, lowering its claws to snatch, and then revealed themselves, again just in the nick of time. But it was equally curious that they always did! Of course it was not necessary to wait for a horse to die. They could kill one. But they could not smite a rock, like Moses, to call forth a gushing spring. And anyway, the horse business was getting to be a hairline affair. Horses were needed to eat, but also to carry. Long since the little party had stripped down. Long since they had left their saddles, with all else of their goods but the barest necessities. They walked, but they were in no condition to carry other burdens than their long rifles. Andy had plenty of time to think about these things as he trudged along. There seemed no end to it. The character of the barren and desolate country never changed. A series of last-moment miracles had saved them up to now. Suppose one miracle should lack or should delay too long?

It would have been easy to despair, and despair would most certainly have disintegrated the last of their slender resistance. Dogged tenacity can accomplish wonders, but its power has limits. Here something more was needed, an unwavering faith. Jedediah Smith possessed it, and his complete and implicit confidence communicated itself to his companions.

Jedediah Smith was a remarkable character, an anomaly to the plains and mountains of those days. In addition to being a practiced frontiersman, a man of fierce courage, great enterprise, and untiring energy he was a sincere and practicing Christian. As his companions were fond of saying of him, *"He fit like an Injin and preached like a parson."* His first possession was his rifle, his second, and equally important, was his Bible. Nevertheless so eminent was his leadership, so broad his humanity, so shrewd and efficient his practical qualities, that he gained not only the respect and admiration but the liking of the rough mountain men. Jed Smith had no manner of doubt as to the continuance of the miracles, showed no surprise at them. Andy and Silas could not doubt either.

"'I will lift up mine eyes to the hills from whence cometh my help,'" he read to them. "'The Lord shall preserve thee from evil.'"

"Dang if that ain't right!" the literal blacksmith confided to Andy apart. "The hills, that's whar we find the *tenajas*."

And again, when the desert seemed at last outstaring them with its brazen face, he said, "The Lord is my shepherd, I shall not want. He maketh me to lie down in green pastures, he leadeth me beside the still waters. Yea, though I walk through the valley of the shadow of death, I will fear no evil, for Thou art with me."

That very day, the twentieth since leaving the cold Sierras, they sighted Salt Lake. They led one gaunt horse, and one skeleton mule.

This was the story they had to tell at rendezvous. They brought back no beaver, and no news of beaver near enough to be profitable. They had failed to find the Buenaventura or to get any news of it. The expedition might well be considered a failure. It was a failure as far as its conscious objectives were concerned. But Jedediah Smith was going back immediately after rendezvous. His excuse was that he must pick up the men the Sierra snows had forced him to leave behind. But they were old mountain men and could well have found their own way back without waiting to be led out, like a dog on a string, by Jed. No, it was evident enough that Jed wanted another shot at the lovely land. The journey would not this time be so difficult or uncertain. He considered that now he knew the way.

Andy hurt his foot. It was only a sprain, but it was sufficient to prevent his being one of the eighteen men who elected to try the California adventure. At the time he raged in disgust against his unlucky fate, but he was lucky. Jedediah Smith returned from this second expedition two years later with only three survivors. Ten of the eighteen were massacred by the very Mojaves who had been so helpful before. They had been warned by the Spanish to permit no more white men to pass. Fifteen more were murdered by the Umpquas as Smith, and his party at last headed out of California after vexing imprisonments and difficulties with the Spaniards. The four men who escaped made their difficult way through the forests of Oregon to the Hudson's Bay Post at Fort Vancouver.

Here ruled John McLoughlin, the White Eagle of the Indians. Powerfully made, over six feet tall, with a massive head and a splendid mane of white waving hair, he was a magnificent figure. His mere word was the law of the land for a thousand miles about. In him was vested and personified the mighty power of the ancient company of Gentlemen Adventurers known as the Hudson's Bay, so that he was generally known as the Czar of the West.

To his great establishment then, one by one, the destitute survivors made their way. Arthur Black was the first, brought in at night by friendly Indians. He was utterly broken by hunger and destitution. For some time he was so affected by his escape and rescue that he could not speak. Then he said that he thought himself the only survivor of all the party.

McLoughlin was a man of instant action. He rewarded the Indians liberally. He dispatched runners with tobacco to all the Willamette chiefs, asking them to send their people immediately in search. He then equipped a strong party of forty to set out from the fort but just as they were about to start, Jedediah Smith arrived, and following him two more who had made their way unaided. *To my great joy*, as McLoughlin records his own feeling.

But while the rescued men were being fed and otherwise comforted, White Eagle slipped from the room and called to him Thomas McKay, the partisan in charge of the armed expedition that had already been gathered. To him he gave written instructions.

"Do not look at them, Tom, until you have reached the Umpqua River," said he. "It's safer. Some of the officers might learn of them, and talk among themselves, the men would hear of it, and from them it would get to the Indians through the squaws."

McKay marched his men to the Umpqua. He opened the sealed orders. They instructed him *to invite the Indians to bring their furs to trade, just as if nothing had happened. Count the furs, but as the American trappers mark all their skins, keep these all separate, give them to Mr. Smith and not pay the Indians for them, telling them that they belonged to him, that they got them by murdering Smith's people.*

McKay followed these instructions and successfully. He recovered thus not only most of the beaver of the ill-fated party but also many of their horses and some of their personal belongings. Among the latter was fortunately the detailed diary of Harry Rogers, from which we learn many things. Its last entry rejoiced that in only fifteen miles more of travel their troubles would be over.

These things, all of them, McLoughlin returned to Jedediah Smith intact. He went further. As it would be difficult or impossible to transport the peltries overland, McLoughlin appraised them truly and gave Smith a draft on London for $20,000. From the value of the furs he deducted only the expenses of the expedition that had recovered them. He charged against them the men's time—at the rate of sixty dollars a year apiece— and four dollars apiece for several horses that were lost on the trip.

Jedediah Smith was overwhelmed by White Eagle's magnanimity to a foeman completely at his mercy. For by now, the Rocky Mountain Company and the Hudson's Bay had become formidable competitors. But McLoughlin waved his protests aside.

"I do this from a principle of Christian duty," said he.

Probably both remembered, though neither mentioned, that spring of 1825 when Ashley and Peter Skene Ogden had met in the valley of the Great Salt Lake. In March, with his surviving companions, Jedediah Smith set out on his return journey. In August he ran into Sublette and Jackson, who were anxiously searching for him, and by them was guided to the rendezvous of that year, at Wind River.

But this was not quite all, the episode was not finished. In face of the obstinate resistance of his partners, in face of the horrified opposition of every mountain man of the lot, Jedediah Smith persisted.

"My mind is made up," he repeated over and over again. "No firm of which I am a member shall operate west of the Divide. I will not trespass on territory that McLoughlin considers belongs to him." In the end he won. Reluctantly, almost sullenly, they yielded. Back from the new rich country they trailed, over the mountain country to the east. A knightly gesture! Lowered swords!

So Jedediah Smith's three years ended. What had he accomplished? Nothing, grumbled his associates. Less than nothing. He had acquired no new trapping grounds. Worse, through his quixotic ideas, he had lost that which had been gained. Why did they yield to him? He was only one man among many. However, they did.

But here is a curious thing, his trail into California is almost exactly that of the present-day routes of the Salt Lake and the Santa Fe railroads, his return journey, that of the Union Pacific, his way north, that of the Shasta route of the Southern Pacific. Later, various spectacular pathfinders would discover them. But the way was already open, waiting only the covered wagons and the rails.

Chapter 18
Battle

Nearing the second third of the century the general conditions in the West were becoming more and more unsatisfactory. Three great companies stood in rivalry. Each had its particular advantages, each its weakness, in antiphony of balance and counterbalance. Each possessed roughly its own sphere of influence, its own territory, but none acknowledged the other's exclusive right, and each crowded it wherever it could.

The Hudson's Bay Company operated to the north and to the far west. It had the strength of long establishment, of an almost fanatical loyalty on the part of able men. Its weakness, as far as these present rivalries went, was its remoteness—and its policy of semipeonage, because of which some of its rank and file were discontented and like to prove treacherous. But it was the most firmly established in its own proper territory and met effective opposition only when it attempted to push east toward the Divide.

The Rocky Mountain Fur Company, the company of the mountain men, operated, as its name implies, in the Rockies themselves, and especially in the country just west of the Divide, which the mountain men had themselves discovered. Its strength was in its personnel, and in the fact that it trapped the finest beaver streams, both for quantity and quality, in the West. No men ever lived possessed of greater courage, greater initiative, or greater ability to sustain themselves in a hostile wilderness. Its weakness came from the same root. Its men were individualists. The organization which they served was hardly an organization at all, in the sense of its rivals. It was a loose association, serving a temporary purpose. Until late in its existence it did not even legally operate under the name by which it was popularly known. Its ownership passed rapidly through several sets of hands. Ashley and Henry started it. Henry got discouraged and sold out. Jedediah Smith, Jackson, and Sublette carried on for four years. By that time, they were satisfied with the profits they had made. Sublette came to the rendezvous in 1830 with a magnificent caravan of eighty-odd men mounted on Missouri mules, ten heavy wagons drawn by five mules each, two traveling one mule *dearborns*. And just to complete this magnificent gesture, he drove in a dozen cattle, including one milch cow! Milk in their coffee! Fat doings! Incidentally this was the very first of the tens of thousands of wheeled caravans that later were to plod over the Oregon Trail. He and his partners sold out to five of their associates, among whom were Fitzpatrick and Jim Bridger. Then they packed the ten wagons with furs and headed back for St. Louis. They took the milch cow with them. And thus it went. The Rocky Mountain Fur Company was not an organization. It was men.

The American Fur Company, the third of the rivals, was, on the other hand, first of all an organization. It had the men—Mackenzie, Crooks, Farnham, Kipp, Chouteau, Foutenelle, many others almost equally distinguished, and behind them the mighty figure of Astor himself. But it had also three other potent weapons—politics, a policy, and a long patience. To back these qualities it also commanded the almost inexhaustible wealth that makes for stability. It could weather reverses, it could take a loss in order to eliminate opposition. It was content to wait. Let others break ground. When this was done, move in and occupy. That occupation was the field to which to apply the resources of its tremendous power in the ruthless crushing of all opposition. One great advantage it possessed, its right hand and its left hand were geographically so far apart that there was no reason at all why the one should know what the other was doing. Business could be one thing looking east, quite another looking west.

"It is enough," the East virtuously put itself on record, "that our laws prohibit the introduction of ardent spirits into the Indian country, and it is our bounden duty to conform honestly thereto."

"Liquor we must have or we might as well give up," grumbled the West. So liquor they had. Some of it was smuggled. Some of it was brought in by political influence. Some of it by subterfuge. Thus permission was obtained to import spirits at the rate of one gill a day for each boatman during the period of his absence, *to relieve his necessities.*

Boatmen multiplied overnight. They were even employed on routes over high prairies miles from any navigable waters. And, curiously enough, the period of each one's absence was never less than a full twelve months! Mackenzie had a brainstorm. Bringing liquor into the Indian country was forbidden, but the law said nothing about its manufacture! He imported and set up a still, and was doing very well for a while. But that was a little too raw—when news of it crossed the Mississippi. The virtuous East had to call him off. But there were other methods too.

Fitzpatrick, entering a Crow village to get permission to make his fall hunt in their country, was immediately set upon and robbed of everything he and his men possessed. This was astonishing. The Crows had always been friendly. They gave him no time, as he says, for *form or ceremony of any kind*. He charged the Indians with having been instigated by the American Fur Company. The Crows freely confessed it. The company's agent admitted it—and laughed.

Mackenzie wrote Pierre Chouteau gleefully, *Fitzpatrick was robbed of a hundred horses, all his merchandise, some beaver and traps, his capote, and even his watch. That party can consequently make no hunt this fall.* As a final gesture he blandly informed Fitzpatrick that the latter could have back his goods by paying their value in trade, plus the expense of making the trade with the Crows! *I make this proposal as a favor, not as a matter of right*, said he, *for I consider the Indians entitled to trade any beaver in their possession to me or any other trader.*

It was about this time that Mackenzie ordered sent out from England, of all things, a coat of mail! This was considered a huge joke. It might not have been so much of a joke after all. Fitzpatrick returned to the mountains boiling mad.

Andy Burnett viewed this slow change of condition with troubled mind. He had been now in the wilderness for upward of ten years. He was a seasoned mountain man. He had had his share of hardship and narrow escape. He had made his friends and his enemies. The crack of his long rifle had echoed on the walls of the cliffs and canyons from the Colorado to the Kootenai, and beyond. It is probable that at that time he knew more of the topography of the West than any other one man, for his Indian affiliations opened to him country into which others were as yet unable to penetrate. For weeks and months at a time he and his few companions, if he had any, would travel and trap in what seemed to be a limitless wilderness. They encountered no human being. There was no diminution of the game, nor, except very locally, much diminution of the beaver. General knowledge was yet fifteen years away, general travel, as many more, general pacification, over a half-century, occupation, three generations distant. Yet to the mystic perception that was the basis of Andy's otherwise stolid character was wafted the uneasy breath of change. To his solitary camp, remote in some hidden park in the Rockies, came a whisper of unease.

These were not things seen or experienced. His wanderings and his rare contacts taught him little. The winters he spent with his friends, the Blackfeet. Once he varied this by a few months at one of the white men's winter camps, but he did not especially enjoy that. It brought to him undeniably what he wanted to forget, and that was that gradually a great many rough and brutal characters were drifting into the country. The old mountain men were, many of them, rough, and some of them were, at times, brutal. But these were different. They were composed of a coarse blunt bestiality that the mountains had cleansed from even the worst of the old-timers. When drunk they were very quarrelsome, apt to be dangerous, at any rate trouble makers. At all times they displayed a good streak of the loud-mouthed swaggering bully. Andy could take care of himself, though, as a matter of fact, he had very little trouble. Even those stranger to his reputation stepped around the quiet, steady competence of the tall frontiersman. He was recognized at sight as bad medicine. A great many of them were killed, for they had not the quiet alert plainscraft of the old-timers, and the tally of reprisals was steadily growing between them and the Indians. The *bad* men tended to drift together, to form bands, the beginning of later *gangs*—such as the notorious Deschamps family from Missouri, who constituted a good-sized gang without going out of the family. There were the old man, and ten grown sons, and a nephew or so, and they robbed, whipped, plundered, and murdered the Indians wherever they found them. They all had squaws and swarms of children. They were a tribe in themselves. The worst of the lot was the old woman. At last the country rose against them, white and red, and cornered them in a log house. They dug holes in the earth floor where fire could not reach them and bit back at their assailants like mad dogs. In the height of the storm the old woman, relying on her age and sex, stepped to the door brandishing a peace pipe. She was instantly shot down.

"There's an end to the mother of devils!" cried a white man.

The Deschamps were stamped out to the last living creature. It was the first vigilante movement, the first dime-novel Wild West.

Feeling of all sorts ran high. The rival companies bit and snarled. Men who changed allegiance were often mysteriously shot. In spite of prohibitions liquor flowed into the country.

In the Blackfoot lodges, during the bitter cold winters, Andy and Joe Crane and Mat-o-suki and Kiasax and the grave blanketed warriors talked of these things. There could be no real defense, on the one side or the other. It was a mess, a wild, dangerous, exciting mess. Only the older men were able to consider it soberly, in its consequences, were able to deplore. To the younger it was adventure. And even among the Blackfeet liquor was making way. They had been one of the sober tribes. Even when they began to drink, the privilege was at first confined to the chiefs and upper warriors.

A few years later that convention was to break down, and the Blackfeet were to go to the other extreme until Washington Irving was to say of them, *"They are extremely fond of spirituous liquors and tobacco, for which nuisances they are ready to exchange not merely their guns and horses, but even their wives and daughters."* That had not yet come, but it was on the way. It was in the air. Sensitive instincts felt its shadow.

Those few possessing spiritual antennal—Andy Burnett, the Blackfeet elders—caught its chill. Each reacted in his own way. The Blackfeet became more implacably, uncompromisingly hostile to the whites. Andy, mistakenly, pleaded for a better understanding, urging his friends to come in to rendezvous, to go to council with the men he knew—Sublette, Campbell, Fitzpatrick. He, like the others, thought in terms of individuals.

It was all a matter of individuals. Red against white, the beginning of a bitter struggle. Yet on either side men stood out, men who had the respect, if not the liking, of their antagonists. Sublette was one of them, the Indians called him Fate. Fitzpatrick was another, he was known as Bad Hand. Beckworth, the mulatto, had a curious prestige. Jim Bridger enjoyed an enormous reputation and respect. And, strangely enough, the youngster who had so recently come into the country, the boy who had run away and for whose return had been advertised the munificent reward of one cent, Kit Carson, had in a few years made way to the forefront of renown. There were others on both sides of the fence. Andy knew these men, liked them, and trusted them. He had not thought the thing out—Andy was not a rationalizing creature—but somehow he wanted his friends to get together. Long hours he spent in the Blackfoot lodges arguing his point. He made a scant impression.

"These be great warriors, I-tam-api," they told him, "but they are our enemies. All white men are our enemies."

In vain Andy introduced himself, Joe Crane, Berger, who dealt with the Bloods. They listened, but as far as he could see he made no progress.

When spring came, he set out for the hidden parks, traveling for days until he had reached the solitudes. Under the shadows of the great mountains it sometimes seemed to him he had escaped. They encircled him about. On their summits slept the pure calm of eternal snows. The clear stream of the valley flashed and gleamed among the cottonwoods and willows. Flowers starred the meadows of rich grasses bending before the breeze. The sun shone warm through the nip of the highland air. Game herds grazed on the flats and far up the fling of the foothill slopes. All the littler creatures chirped and rustled and sang. As he waded up the smaller tributaries, setting his traps, or squatted on his heels before his graining block, or pressed the trigger of the old Boone gun, or lay before the waxing gleam of his fire as the evening fell, for a little he was back in the old serenity that here had dwelled for thousands of undisturbed and undisturbing years. But sooner or later, over the ranges, like an invisible, impalpable mist crept the influence of the outside stir, seeking him out. He could not banish thought or recollection.

However little as yet the vastness of the Western solitude had been touched, in his world things had changed.

Kelly had never come back. Joe Crane rarely accompanied him now. Crane seemed to have settled down comfortably to family life, with a growing brood of half-breed children, to be increasingly content.

"Hard doin's and I had jist my rifle and my possibles," he argued comfortably. "Easy doin's and I got 'em jist the same, and a warm lodge and my woman and young 'uns. I've larned, Andy. Wagh!"

Jedediah Smith had been killed by the southwestern Indians down in the Cimarron. Sublette was busy with the demands of the company. The old mountain men were killed, scattered, lost in the rabble, or, like Fitzpatrick, increasingly absorbed by the new wild life of raid and war and adventure. Andy was only about thirty years old, but unknowing, he was running true to his kind, close to the genius of his spiritual kinsmen, the genius that took Boone in his old age out of his beloved Kentucky to the Missouri when the country got crowded, and a neighbor only fifteen miles away.

Joe Crane and Andy Burnett drew rein as they surmounted the rise. They looked down on a beautiful prairie-like valley. Over against them rose the formidable peaks of the Three Tetons. Meandering lines of cottonwood and dense willow thickets marked the course of a main river and numerous tributaries. Elsewhere were no trees, merely lush grasses starred with wildflowers. This was Pierre's Hole and the agreed rendezvous for the year 1832.

"Wagh!" cried Joe in astonishment. "They's a passel of 'em! More'n I ever see afore! Big doin's!"

He clapped his heels to his horse and plunged down the slope. Andy and Plying Woman followed more soberly. Long since had he matured beyond his mentor, Joe was the perpetual boy. He helped Flying Woman select an appropriate place for the lodge, saw to the horses, there, and not until then, walked across to the main encampment to bear the news. As he strode along, he looked about him curiously. The Indians were more numerous than usual. Nez Percés and Flatheads he noted. Both were deadly enemies of the Blackfeet. Among the white men were many strange faces. He nodded to an acquaintance or so, greeted one or two friends, pressed on to where the main concourse was squatted about. Joe was arguing heatedly with someone. Andy saw a shock of red hair recognized with surprise a man he had not seen for many years, one who had been of the Taos party when Andy was new to the plains and who had gone over to the employ of the American Fur Company instantly the latter had established itself. He was now bareheaded and facing Joe with a sneering grin that indicated to Andy that he was having the best of it, for Tilton's temper had always been notoriously short. Andy's arrival broke up the argument, whatever it was, for he had become a personage of importance in the West and men pressed about him for recognition or acquaintance. Even Ben Tilton accorded him a surly greeting.

Andy seated himself and accepted a pipe. Big news! A number talked at once. Finally he straightened it out. The rival companies were coming to grips at last. Heretofore, a rendezvous had been a one-firm affair. This year the American Fur Company had advertised its attendance with a full line of trade to be offered in competition. Ben Tilton and a few companions were the bearers of that news. Tilton was now avowedly an A.F.C. man. He spoke up, swaggering, bragging what his employers were going to do.

"We aim to git the trade," he boasted, "and when we aim to git a thing, we git it!"

Joe bristled again at this, they were old enemies, and anything sufficed as a provocation. But Andy intervened.

"Well," he asked reasonably, "how is the trade going?"

That was just it! That is what made this such a wonderful sporting event! Sublette was on his way from St. Louis with the Rocky Mountain Fur Company's goods, Vanderburgh was coming from the Missouri on behalf of the American Fur Company. Neither had arrived. Whoever got there first would take the bulk of the trade. It was a race.

Nobody knew where either of the partisans were by now, how far they were away. No one, naturally, could guess what difficulties they might have encountered to delay them. There was always the good possibility that a skillful Indian raid might have put one or the other of them afoot. The Sublette party was laboring under one handicap. It knew of no particular occasion for haste, for it was unaware of this new *démarche* on the part of its rival. Fitzpatrick had set out alone, only a few days ago, to find Sublette if he could, and hurry him along. Aside from all party prejudice, here was a grand opportunity for gambling, better than any horse race.

Although, outside Tilton and his men, there were few active sympathizers with the American Fur Company present, the majority were at heart indifferent. Andy looked them over thoughtfully, reflecting on the changes. The old-time mountain men were already in the minority. The type was changing. Most of these were bearded men. In the old days, nearly everyone went shaven because one got along with the Indians if he could, and the Indians looked down on anyone with a hairy face. Now, nobody cared what Indians thought. There was hardly a flint gun in the lot. Joe was about the only one, who could afford something else, who still clung to his prejudice. Strange faces everywhere. Andy inquired about them from his friend Hal Mulford, who reclined at his elbow. They were a picturesque mixed lot. That was Chabonard, a half-breed, with a good-sized band of his like, the generation from the squaw man was grown up to introduce a new element to the West. That white man yonder was Sinclair, from the lower Missouri, he commanded a party of fifteen free trappers, good men all, but hampered by no allegiances. There was even a scattering of Mexicans from Taos way. Plenty who did not give a hoot which trading party won the race, but ready to hail the affair as a grand sporting event on which to lay their bets. Of course the Indians, the Nez Percés and the Flatheads, camped yonder in the bottom, would sell to the first buyer.

"And I'll tell you this, Andy," Mulford informed him, "ef'n Bill Sublette don't top that rise fust, there's goin' to be mouty few of us old-timers gits off with a shirt on our backs or a hoss under our tails!"

They drew apart to talk it over away from the crowd. As has been from the dawn of history, the lament was over the *good old days*.

"Hard doin's sometimes," said Mulford. "Injins was bad sometimes, but not like now. They was more playfurlike, not real mean. They'd mebbe steal yore hoss or lift yore ha'r, ef'n yo' didn't watch out, but they knowed when yo' had yore eyes shinin', and when the joke was on them, they'd laugh too, and mebbe give yo' a woman to keep yore winter lodge warm. Everything was in the sperrit of play, as you mout say. When you traveled, you tied yore hosses in rifle shot durin' daylight, and penned them at night. And, Andy, even the game ain't what it was. I'm tellin' yo. You don't know. Back in yore kentry it's different. But down whar I been—why, in the old days the buffalo bulls were so bold they'd come right up to the hoss pens and paw and snort, so I didn't go fur for meat. What lettle you see now is bull meat. The mountains is pore. The game is all gittin' druv out. No place for a white man, too pore, too pore! In the old days, it was sometimes a leetle more dangersome for a lone man, but more beaver, too, and plenty grease around the buffalo ribs. Them was good times! But a white man has no business yere now!"

He spat thoughtfully into the fire.

"They's good kentry yet, this side the Divide," he acknowledged. "But she's gittin' small. You got a good kentry, Andy. But yore Blackfeet is bad. You don't know it, but you—and Joe—they's a good deal of talk agin you. Not that I hold with it, nor the old-time mountain men. We know how it is. But these new ones—they don't love you, Andy. I ain't blamin' them much, nuther." Mulford was fair. "The Blackfeet is bad. Nearly got my ha'r this year. Stole a lot of traps on me, and yo' kain't make traps out of greasewood. The Nez Percés and Flatheads—the Blackfeet been a-massacreein' them too. Bad medicine, Andy. I wisht you and Joe could call 'em off. I know you kain't. I wisht old Bill Sublette would hurry along."

"So do I," said Andy.

"Or anybody else," continued Mulford frankly. "I'd trade with the devil himself for a slug of likker. I'm low in my mind."

Andy was low in his mind, too, when late that evening, he returned to the lodge. He found that Mulford had spoken truly. Except among his old friends, he found himself looked upon in many quarters, if not with hostility, at least with a veiled resentment. The newer elements, it was evident, identified him with the Blackfeet. In the encampments of the Nez Percés and the Flatheads, men eyed him sullenly, muffling themselves in their robes as he passed. The Blackfeet had that season treated them roughly. The Flatheads, in especial, were a broken people. Andy was relieved to find that Flying Woman had not been molested. He resolved to move the lodge to a safer place on the morrow.

Joe was not low in his mind. He was sizzling. The old smoldering enmity between himself and Ben Tilton had blazed up. The redhead had conducted himself with an arrogance born of his affiliation with the great company whose waxing power was just beginning to make itself felt. Joe had bet everything he owned on Sublette.

He won. Sublette arrived first. But Joe's public triumph was somewhat dimmed by the cause of the delay. Sublette had sustained a night attack by the Blackfeet, and although he had beaten it off, he had lost horses and mules. Still, he had arrived. With him, besides his seasoned veterans of the trail, were a number of green recruits from St. Louis, and a quaint party he had picked up on the road and brought along out of sheer kindness of heart—Nathaniel Wyeth and his New Englanders. He had found them completely stranded. Knowing nothing of the country, nothing of plainscraft, nothing of Indian trade, they had brought goods according to their own ideas of what Indians would want, had outfitted themselves according to their own notions of what wilderness travel required, and had pushed off. Not one of the party had ever seen an Indian, had even handled a rifle! It did not occur to them to provide themselves with a guide and interpreter! Sublette found them completely bogged down, took them in tow, and brought them along. They huddled together and stared wide-eyed at the wild assembly that awaited them.

Sublette had seen nothing of Fitzpatrick. He was much worried. But a few days later, Fitzpatrick came in, escorted by two Iroquois hunters. He was totally destitute, and so emaciated that at first he was not recognized. The Blackfeet had found him. He escaped from them at first, losing only one horse and his outfit. After lurking three days in the mountains, he ventured out. Again the Blackfeet discovered him. Again he escaped, but this time he lost everything except his rifle and the one charge with which it was loaded. For some days, he crawled among the mountain cliffs. Then, having shaken off his enemies, he started back afoot for the rendezvous. He ate berries and roots. He patched his moccasins with his hat. He lost his rifle swimming in a river. The Iroquois found him as he was about to perish. His plight aroused the greatest indignation. Again, the Blackfeet!

Vanderburgh of the A.F.C. came in, but his supplies had been delayed. There were now present several hundred Whites besides the Indians. It was the greatest rendezvous in the history of the mountains. Sublette took advantage of his opportunity. For eight days, he had a free field.

Andy finished his business early and would willingly have left at once for the backcountry. He had no mood for the celebrations and sprees. Little given to the surface imaginations, he nevertheless was keenly sensitive in his deeper psychic faculties. The portent whose impalpable mist had followed him into the remoteness of his solitary mountain fastnesses here thickened to the darkness of a shadow. Andy did not see it, he felt it. All he knew was that he was uneasy, that he had no stomach for the companionship of even his oldest friends, that he wanted to get through and get out as soon as he could. But Joe was having his one big time of the year. It would be unfair to drag him away. So he waited with what patience he could summon, and tried in one way and in others to shake off that growing shadow of portent.

He spent much time alone by the river. One afternoon, returning to camp, he discovered it violently agitated. Men were gathered in a close knot about some center of interest. Others were running toward the group, shouting back fragments of news to others still more distant. A fight, probably, or perhaps merely some gambling game with stakes heavier than the ordinary. Andy was not particularly interested. He was about to pass but found himself impelled to turn aside. He was recognized by a few on the outskirts. They nudged others. Heads turned toward him, a swift silence spread, licking up the hubbub like a flame. Men drew aside to permit him a free passage. Curious!

He found himself in the center of the group, looking down at Joe Crane with a bullet hole in the center of his forehead.

He dropped the butt of the long rifle to earth and slowly surveyed the circle of faces.

"Who did this?" he demanded harshly, after a moment.

For ten seconds, no one spoke, then a dozen spoke at once. "Ben Tilton"..."called him a"..."slapped his face"..."no he didn't!"..."shot it out"...the clamor arose, grew more vehement. There were differences of opinion. Men disputed one another and grew heated over it. Andy took no part, asked no question further, and listened, his elbows on the muzzle of his rifle. Gradually a picture framed in his mind, but whether pieced together from the shouted fragments or from an instinct of the situation, it would be difficult to say. With no one present to restrain it, the old feud had blazed up. The men had fought with rifles. It was a fair fight, several insisted, a regular duel, properly carried out. The men had been placed back to back at four rods' distance, they had turned at the signal. Joe had been much the quicker. But his piece had missed fire.

"It was that old flint gun." They shook their heads. "He was obstinate as a mule, hangin' on to that old thing."

"Then Tilton, taking his time, had shot his man down."

"Joe kep' his nerve," they paid him tribute, "jist stood thar, stiddy as a rock, and took it."

Andy listened, without comment, without change of expression, without a quiver of a muscle, like a bronze fate. Even when the last man had had his say, and the clamor had died, and all looked toward him in expectancy, be continued to stare frowningly before him in silence.

"Were they drunk?" he asked curtly at last.

"Joe was pretty drunk, Tilton was sober." But they hastened to add, "Joe wasn't drunk enough but what he could handle himself all right."

"Where's Tilton?" Andy next demanded.

Nobody knew. He was around somewhere. It was a perfectly fair fight, a number insisted, this time a trifle belligerently. Andy stared at them one by one, but still without comment. These were A.F.C. men, Tilton's friends. They gave him back stare for stare, ready to meet a challenge. But there was none. Andy pondered for a time.

"Take care of him, boys," he said at last, and turned away, thrusting through the crowd. "I'll be back."

"Whar yo' goin'!" someone demanded, "ef'n yore lookin' to make trouble—"

"I must see his woman," said Andy briefly. He looked about him and caught Mulford's eye. "See if you can find Tilton," he told his friend. "Tell him to be looking for me."

They stared after him. Two or three of the A.F.C. men drew together, whispering apart. Mulford thrust himself among them.

"Yo' keep yore hands off'n this," he told them. "This ain't yore business."

They bristled at him, growling in their throats, but subsided as they looked about at the stern faces of the old mountain men surrounding them.

"We just aim to see fair play," one protested.

"Thar'll be fair play," they were promised grimly. "Somebody find Tilton and bring him yere."

———

Andy stooped to the low entrance of the lodge. Flying Woman listened and covered her head. He touched her shoulder and went out.

But as he straightened his tall form, he was arrested by a low whistle from the shelter of the willows near at hand. A man was beckoning him earnestly. Throwing his rifle forward at ready, and glancing keenly to right and left, he obeyed the signal. The man proved to be Chabonard, the half-breed. After a few moments' conversation Andy turned once more toward the gathering place. Chabonard clutched at his hunting jacket. Andy shook him off.

"I'll not betray you," he promised briefly.

Chabonard gazed anxiously at his tall figure as he strode away, then drew back his head and by concealed and devious ways himself returned to the main encampment.

Andy, however, turned aside to the bottomlands, where he caught his horse. At the lodge he saddled the animal, collected certain items of equipment, filled a skin sack with Blackfoot pemmican. Flying Woman looked up at him. He nodded to her. Leading the animal he retraced his steps to where the trappers still waited. Mulford met him.

"Tilton has gone," he told Andy. "Rode off northward an hour ago."

"I thought likely," said Andy.

He dropped the reins of his horse and pushed to the middle of the expectant gathering.

"This was not a fair fight. It was murder," he told them harshly. "Tilton emptied the priming powder out of Joe's pan. He was seen doing it. I'm going after him. It ain't going to be healthy for anyone to follow me. Understand?"

They looked at one another thunderstruck. Andy's straight brows were drawn level. He stared at them slowly one after the other.

"Understand?" he repeated.

"They won't no one foller you," Mulford assured him grimly. "'Less'n yo' want some help."

"This is my business," said Andy.

He turned away and picked up the reins of his horse. But before mounting he spoke to Mulford, at his elbow.

"See to things, Harry," he requested briefly. "Joe—and—better get his woman back to her people."

"Rest yore mind easy, Andy," Mulford promised.

Andy mounted and rode away. They watched his figure until it disappeared. Then an excited buzz of talk broke forth.

By the middle of July business was over and the rendezvous began to break up. A substantial party rode together to the southwest, following the valley of Pierre's Hole, in the upper end of which the gathering had taken place. Fourteen were trappers of the company under the command of Milton, Sublette's brother. Sinclair and his fifteen free trappers, and Wyeth and his Down-Easters completed the body. They camped the first night about eight miles downstream. The following morning, as they were about to start, someone caught sight of a long procession descending the slope of a pass through the mountains. Wyeth possessed a spyglass. They unlimbered it, and Milton Sublette took a look.

"Blackfeet!" he cried.

That word was sufficient to throw all those present into a state of excitement so deeply stirring that clear thought and sound judgment were thenceforth impossible. Across the actuality of this occasion drew the lurid veil of past attack and atrocity. The men huddling hastily together there on the plain saw only what their emotions permitted them. Thus the painted and feathered warriors stood out plainly enough, and the numbers of them, but until after the event few could recollect having noticed the women and children bringing up the rear, nor the animals laden with household goods. A dreaded name obscured such details. It must be admitted that the name had been earned by a consistent hostility. Still it was a great pity that Joe Crane was dead, that Andy Burnett was away on an errand of vengeance. It was a great pity that in Milton Sublette's party were few cool-headed enough to recognize this as a peace party, and that those few had been embittered beyond fairness by Blackfoot attack. For these were Mat-o-suki and his entire village, yielding at last to the often-repeated persuasions of Andy, and for the first time coming in to the white man's rendezvous to trade and make peace!

They defiled out from the mountains and onto the plains, yelling and waving their robes and red blankets exultantly. Mat-o-suki looked from under his shading hand for a response. He had mistaken this encampment for the rendezvous itself, thought that he saw before him all the white men. He was disappointed and a little nonplussed that Joe or Andy did not immediately ride forward. They might be out hunting. Still, Flying Woman must have remained in camp. Mat-o-suki handed a warrior his arms, and rode forward a little, extending before him the peace pipe for a parley.

All might still have gone well had either Milton Sublette or perhaps Sinclair answered the summons. But a half-breed named Antoine Godin mounted his horse and thrust himself forward. Nobody objected to his taking the job. In general opinion Blackfoot and treachery were synonymous terms. If Godin wanted to take a chance he was welcome. He rode out to meet the Blackfoot chief unarmed but accompanied by a Flathead Indian. They met Mat-o-suki halfway. Godin grasped his extended hand firmly and hung on.

"All ready," he said coolly over his shoulder to the Flathead. The latter produced a gun from beneath his blanket, leveled it carefully, and shot down the Blackfoot chief. Godin paused only long enough to snatch Mat-o-suki's heavily ornamented scarlet blanket, and back the two raced, bending low to their ponies' necks, pursued by a hail of ineffective bullets.

It was indubitably an act of treachery. But only the year before Antoine's father had been surprised by the Blackfeet and butchered in cold blood as he stooped to his trap in the little stream that today bears his name, only the year before the power of the once proud Flatheads had crumbled forever beneath the ferocity of the Blackfoot attack. Who are we either to condone or condemn? But we may pity.

The unexpected tragedy threw both parties into confusion. Two of the mounted warriors swooped down to rescue the body of the chief. The others withdrew into the river swamp, a tangle of willow and cottonwood and hanging vines. There the women began at once to dig trenches, to construct a rough breastwork of brush and fallen tree trunks. The men, pausing only long enough to assume their war finery, returned at once to the edge of the woods, ready for either attack or defense. They were, naturally, burning with anger, which was deepened by the consciousness of their own good intentions. They outnumbered the whites and were nearly as well armed. The latter should pay, to the last man, for this outrage! The trappers were not less prompt. A shallow ravine, running nearly parallel with the river, faced the edge of the swamp. In this Milton Sublette's fourteen and Sinclair's fifteen took their stand. Wyeth, for all his inexperience, showed his good sense by picketing his horses in camp, constructing around them a breastwork of packs and saddles, and squatting his Down-Easters behind its protection. They knew nothing of rifles and less of Indians, and that was by far the best place not only for them but for everybody concerned. Then, like the stouthearted New Englander he was, he joined the combatants to do his bit. A long-range skirmish began. The Blackfeet were sure of their victims, but they awaited their chance to finish the job with the least possible damage to themselves.

But in the meantime, a messenger dashed at full speed up the valley to the rendezvous. As he neared the encampment he stood in his stirrups, waved his cap, shouted his message.

"Blackfeet! Blackfeet! A fight in the upper valley! To arms! To arms!"

Men leaped to rifle and to horse. The long-dreaded, long-expected crisis was at hand. From the lodges along the river poured the Nez Percé and Flathead warriors. It was a common cause, hereditary enemies, face to face, at last!

Trapper-fashion the white men left their coats, all their *possibles* in a pile, guarded only by a few of the St. Louis greenhorns, whom Sublette ordered to stay. It was not much of a guard, but in case of victory the things could be reclaimed. In case of defeat they would be powerless and useless. Sublette and Campbell raced up the valley at full speed, in front of a headlong mob of red men and white. As they rode, they made their wills, one to the other. In their minds, and in the minds of all the others for that matter, the situation was very grave. There could be but one explanation of this bold daytime invasion against the gathered rendezvous, The Blackfeet had gathered their full tribal power to settle the issue once and for all.

Mat-o-suki's warriors, peering from the screen of brush, were astounded and dismayed to look forth on the valley swarming with horsemen. They had thought to deal with a few, outnumbering them six to one. Then suddenly, and unexpectedly, found themselves outnumbered. They withdrew to the dark shelter of their impromptu fortification. They blackened their faces and began their death chant.

Sublette took charge. With his usual audacity, he advised an instant attack.

Even the seasoned mountain men for a moment hung back from attempting the tangled thicket. The Nez Percés and Flatheads refused.

"Then I'll go alone," said Sublette.

Robert Campbell stepped forward to accompany him. After a moment's hesitation, Sinclair and several of his men followed. One by one the others, inspired or shamed by this example, wriggled forward into the swamp.

It was impossible to see more than a few yards through the brush and vines. They took turns crawling ahead. After a time the woods opened a bit. They could see the piles of brush, of logs, of blankets, and buffalo robes and lodge covers, of which the Blackfeet had made their stronghold. They took the best shelter they could. The battle began.

Sinclair was shot through the body. Some of his men managed to carry him out, and returned. Sublette caught a glimpse of a Blackfoot through a little opening and planted a rifle ball between the savage's eyes. As he reloaded, he was himself struck. Campbell managed to get him away and out to the care of Wyeth's New Englanders.

"Let the men fight in twos, and only one fire at a time," was his parting instruction to his partner. "And yell. Yelling is very essential to Indian warfare."

Then he fainted.

The battle became a siege, an affair of sharpshooting. The Blackfeet were more and more closely beleaguered. They realized that in time they must be overwhelmed. The death chant never ceased. For hours men, on both sides, lay flat in their concealments, tense and taut, awaiting the chance of an incautious movement. The Nez Percés and the Flatheads were gaining confidence. The legend of the invulnerability of their hereditary enemies was breaking at last. They saw the moment of their supreme triumph approaching. Occasionally some young warrior, carried by excitement beyond the bounds of ordinary good sense, would dash up to the breastworks, fire over them at random, seize a robe or a blanket and dash back, waving it exultantly. Generally he got shot for his pains, but his deed raised the warlike ardor of his companions. So sure now were the Indian allies that they vehemently opposed a proposal to set fire to the fort. Already they looked upon the Blackfoot belongings as certain spoil, and they did not want them destroyed.

There was a continuous din. Beside the crackling of the rifles and the flatter boom of the smooth-bores, the hot close thicket resounded with war whoop, with the fierce yells of the trappers, with the tauntings and braggings of the Indian combatants. And behind it, the unintermitting minor wail of the death chant.

The Blackfeet fought doggedly and bravely. They made no offer to surrender.

"So long as we had plenty of powder and ball, we fought you in the open. Now these are nearly gone and we will die here with our women and children, chanted one in a lull of fighting. You may kill us here, but soon you who are so hungry for fighting will have enough. Near us are four hundred lodges of our brothers. They will soon be here. Their arms are strong. Their hearts are big. They will avenge us."

None of the white men understood the Blackfoot language.

"What is he saying?" Campbell asked of a half-breed.

The breed did not know. He inquired of a Nez Percés, the Nez Percé of a Flathead. By the time the translation had been relayed back to Campbell it would appear that the men of four hundred lodges were at that moment attacking the upper camp.

Campbell consulted Sublette, lying in Wyeth's compound. This was serious. The profits of the entire season, not to speak of the green St. Louis recruits, were imperiled. Hastily, they called in the besiegers. Leaving a small detachment to try to watch the fort, the trappers galloped off up the valley as hastily as they had come.

Returning from this wild goose chase the following morning, they were overtaken by Andy Burnett on a lathered horse. Several shouted at him as he passed, but received no reply. And several hurled curses after him, for the minds of all were sore and heated by battle, and Andy was a Blackfoot man.

Arrived at the scene of the combat, Andy hurled himself from his exhausted animal, and unheeding the shouted warnings of the men lying hidden in the brush, thrust directly through the tangled screen toward the barricade.

"Tarnation fool!" growled one of Sinclair's men. "Does he think he can take the fort alone? Does he want to git himself shot?"

"He's Burnett—the Blackfoot man," explained the mountaineer at his elbow.

"Blackfoot man, huh!" exclaimed the other. "Then I hope he *does* git shot!"

The breastworks held their fire, frowning in the half-light of the thicket. Andy stopped.

"It is I-tam-api!" he called.

There was no reply. He advanced, thrusting aside the screen of cut brush, climbing to the logs of the breastwork. There he stood, looking about him.

No living creature met his eye. In the darkness the Blackfeet had stolen away to the mountains. They had carried away their wounded, perhaps some of the more important dead. Andy's expert eye marked the traces of their going, and the bloody sign where the litters had been borne. But some of the dead remained. One part of Andy's mind automatically began to function with the keen and careful accuracy of the trained mountain man. That part counted the bodies that had been left behind—there were nine. It counted, too, the dead horses—there were thirty-two of these, perhaps thirty-three. It read the signs of departure one by one and made its automatic swift calculations as to the numbers involved and the losses sustained. All these things it laid away neatly for the future, pending its master's interest in them. At the moment Andy had no room for them. The first swift and searing horror, the first vain and discarded regret that his arrival had been too late, seemed to have cut some umbilical cord that had held him. As though released, he ascended into a plane of impersonal perceptions. His soul was lost in the contemplation of tragedy, a meaning for which it must find. The meaning must be found in the pure essence, it could not exist in these details, these dead bodies, these hunted human beings in the mountains. That was all useless, horrible, mistaken. If there was a meaning, it must dwell higher in some plane above the specific instance, in a realm of pure quality, where, if anywhere, dwelled justice and right and the reason for things. It did not seem strange to Andy that he had stepped atop the crude breastwork, that he had dropped the butt of the long rifle, and was standing there immobile in his characteristic attitude, forearms crossed on the muzzle, staring steadily into a misty land of philosophy far remote.

Nor at the long last did he clearly perceive anything in that land. It was as though he came to from a reverie, an especially ill-timed daydream. He brought no clear thought back with him, only the enrichment which accompanies perception of the nobility and sublimity that inheres in catastrophe precipitated not by human fault, but by human imperfection. And in the serenity of this insight was no room for violent grief or blame or anger. There dwelled only pity—and awe.

His eyes slowly focused from his visioning. He found himself looking directly into the eyes of a living woman. Slowly, realization grew in him. It was Nit-o-ké-man. A dead warrior lay stretched across her feet. That was Kiasax.

"Nit-o-ké-man!" cried Andy.

She did not reply. Upright against the tree, she might have been a carved image. Except for her eyes. They looked steadily back at him, eloquent with a great reproach.

Nor did they waver when a Nez Percé warrior, who had drawn near unnoticed by Andy, dashed forward past the young man's very elbow. The thing was over before Andy could move. Nit-o-ké-man sank to her knees and toppled forward across Kiasax's body. The Nez Percé, brandishing the bloody Warhawk, threw back his head and uttered his long shrill whoop of triumph.

The long rifle leaped to position, the sights adjusted themselves steadily, Andy's finger, untrembling, pressed toward the trigger.

And suddenly, he was again in the cold, sad serenity to which rose no human passion, to which came no faint echo of little things happening, in which was only weary understanding—and pity, and awe. Andy relaxed his trigger finger, dropped the muzzle of his rifle, and turned away. Why kill? Just more of the same thing!

He made his way out of the thicket, unheeding the rush of men toward the late battle scene. He was quite calm and collected. At the encampment, he sought out his horse and unsaddled it. The men there looked at him askance and muttered to one another. This was the Blackfoot man. He was oblivious of their hostility. He looked about him and caught Mulford's eye.

"This horse is about tuckered," he said to the latter mildly. "Got a fresh one you can trade me?"

"Sure," agreed Mulford. "Take that pinto there."

Andy deliberately saddled the animal, looking neither to the right nor left. Slowly, the men gathered, watching him in silence. Mulford hovered uneasily on the point of speech but thinking better of it. When the cinch had been tightened, Andy stood for a moment, lost in thought as though trying to recollect something. Then, he untied an object from his saddle horn and cast it on the ground. Then he mounted.

"What yo' doin', Andy?" asked Mulford.

"Pulling out," replied Andy briefly.

Mulford hesitated.

"Well, so long," he said at last.

"So long," said Andy.

He gathered the reins and rode slowly up the valley. They looked after him. One of the men touched the discarded object with the toe of his moccasin.

"Thought Burnett never took scalps," he observed.

"Never knew him to afore," said Mulford.

They stared at the thing for another period of silence.

"This one's got red ha'r," remarked someone gratuitously.

At the upper camp, Andy sought out Hachter, the Little Burgeway.

"Got any money, Hachter?" he asked. "Give me what you can spare, and charge against me in St. Louis."

He refused to answer questions.

"They'll tell you," said he.

He stowed the money in his *possible* sack and remounted.

"What you want money for, Andy?" asked Hachter curiously. "Where you going?"

"Pulling out," replied Andy briefly.

Methodically, he gathered his horses, packed his belongings, rode out of camp toward the west. His face was expressionless. At the top of the hills, he drew rein and for a long time, looked back. Item by item, his eyes passed over the scene before him, registering its details. The encampment, struck small by distance, far below, the prairie-like valley with its meandering strips of cottonwood, the upfling of dark green timber on the mountain slopes, the serene and brooding peaks of the Three Tetons beyond.

Andy felt drained and old. It was as though a reservoir, heretofore full and sparkling, had been suddenly emptied, leaving only the slime of the bottom. A few days ago, life had been brimming, but now it was empty. Kelly gone, Joe Crane gone, Mat-o-suki, Kiasax, Nit-o-ké-man. The whites, sullen with hostility against him as a Blackfoot man—impossible, after this outrage to show himself among the Blackfeet. The beaver going. Bitterness and discord and strife! No good to lose himself in the mountain solitudes he knew so well. They were no longer solitudes. Into every valley and canyon and park of them, no matter how remote, seeped that impalpable, invisible mist of unrest. Andy was tired, tired with a deadly weariness. He shifted his gaze to westward. Before him stretched the wide sweep of the high plateau, with its blue brittle mountains and its castellated buttes and its crystalline clarities of immense space. But Andy was not seeing these things. His eyes were filled with a remembered vision of brooding oaks and warm fields and drowsy, peaceful hills, and in his ears sounded the mellow gold of the San Gabriel mission bells. The lovely land!

He gathered the bridle reins and whistled to the packhorses. He glanced down at the long rifle across his saddlebow, the old Boone gun.

"Reckon you've done your job—such as it is!" he murmured and sighed.

He looked back. His keen frontiersman's eyes sought the great cottonwood at the side of the late rendezvous beneath which slept Joe Crane.

"So long, Mountain Man," he said aloud.

Note

Necessarily in the compilation of this story, I have consulted and used material from a great many volumes dealing with the time, one hundred and twenty-three of them to be exact. The list runs through trappers' journals and memoirs, books of contemporary travelers and chroniclers, and the more careful compilations of later historians. Those familiar with these materials will readily recognize many of the sources, and will be able to detect the fact that I have journeyed at times not only with Andy Burnett, but with Dillin, Ruxton, Nierhardt, Chittenden, Irving, Farnham, Dale, and many others. As this is a work of fiction it seems unnecessarily cumbersome to publish a complete bibliography, as would be seemly were it a historical study. It should be sufficient to express my indebtedness and appreciation and to assure those who may notice similarities that I am fully aware, of having borrowed source materials as the necessities of the tale demand, and am duly grateful. Whenever historical characters or institutions have appeared, I have carefully followed historical fact. Estimates of either are also based on record and can be substantiated.

A Look at Book Four:
The Personal Narrative of James O. Pattie

A first-hand account of a daring and brash adventurer whose exploits shaped the American West.

In 1830, a mysterious traveler, known only as 'a passenger from Vera Cruz,' caught the attention of Cincinnati locals with his cryptic remarks about Mexico. Little did they know, this enigmatic figure was James O. Pattie, whose extraordinary tales would captivate readers for generations.

Renowned author Timothy Flint, intrigued by Pattie's stories, delved into the adventurer's remarkable life, uncovering a treasure trove of daring escapades and remarkable encounters. From traversing the untamed Western plains to navigating the complexities of Native American relations, Pattie's journey was one of resilience, ambition, and boundless curiosity.

In this meticulously crafted memoir, Win Blevins brings to life James O. Pattie's explorations with vivid descriptions and raw authenticity.

AVAILABLE OCTOBER 2024

About the Author

Win Blevins was an award-winning author best known for his fiction and non-fiction books of Western lore and Native American leaders, lifestyle, and spirituality. He was the recipient of a lifetime achievement award from the Western Writers of America, and a member of the Western Writers Hall of Fame; a three-time winner of Wordcraft Circle Native Writers and Storytellers Book of the Year; two-time winner of a Spur Award for Best Novel of the West; and was nominated for a Pulitzer for his novel about Crazy Horse, *Stone Song*.

Blevins, whose own origins were a mix of Cherokee, Welsh-Irish, and African American, published his first novel in 1973. That book, *Give Your Heart to the Hawks, a Tribute to the Mountain Man*, is still in print fifty years later and recently returned to the *New York Times* bestseller list.

Over his long career, Blevins wrote nearly forty books, including the historical fiction Rendezvous series, a dozen screenplays, and numerous magazine articles. His *Dictionary of the American West* is held in 750 libraries.

Born in Little Rock, Arkansas, on October 21, 1938, Blevins was an honors graduate of Columbia University—where he earned a master's degree—and the Music Conservatory of the University of Southern California. He began his writing career as a music and drama critic for the *Los Angeles Times* and became the principal entertainment editor for the *The Los Angeles Herald Examiner*. During that time, he hung out with the likes of Sam Peckinpah and Strother Martin, and began diving into the lives of Mountain Men and Native Americans of the West.

He also served as the Gaylord Family Visiting Professor of Professional Writing at the University of Oklahoma. For fifteen years, he was a book editor for Macmillan Publishing and TOR/Forge Books.

Win loved and felt a deep connection with nature. He climbed mountains on four continents and was a boatman-guide on the Snake River. Once caught in a freak blizzard while climbing, he took shelter inside a tree for more than twenty-four hours. His feet were frozen, but he refused to have them amputated. Almost twenty years after that event, he climbed the Himalayas—despite an awkward gait.

Native Spirituality suited him. He was pierced during a Lakota ceremony and was a pipe carrier. He went on twelve vision quests and felt the pull of the red road.

Win spent the last twenty years of his life, living quietly in the Southwest among the Navajo. His passions grew with time. In the center was his wife Meredith, their children, and many grandchildren. Classical music, baseball, roaming red rock mesas, and rafting were great loves, and he considered himself blessed to create new stories about the West. He was also proud to call himself a member of the world's oldest profession—storytelling.

www.ingramcontent.com/pod-product-compliance
Lightning Source LLC
Chambersburg PA
CBHW010856090426
42737CB00020B/3388